D1570751

THE PROMISE OF RESPONSE TO INTERVENTION

The Promise of Response to Intervention

Evaluating Current Science and Practice

Edited by
TODD A. GLOVER
SHARON VAUGHN

THE GUILFORD PRESS

New York   London

© 2010 The Guilford Press
A Division of Guilford Publications, Inc.
72 Spring Street, New York, NY 10012
www.guilford.com

Printed in the United States of America

This book is printed on acid-free paper.

Last digit is print number: 9 8 7 6 5 4 3 2 1

Library of Congress Cataloging-in-Publication Data

The promise of response to intervention : evaluating current science and practice /
edited by Todd A. Glover, Sharon Vaughn.
    p. cm.
Includes bibliographical references and index.
ISBN 978-1-60623-562-1 (hardcover : alk. paper)
1. Remedial teaching. 2. School failure—Prevention. I. Glover, Todd A.
II. Vaughn, Sharon, 1952–
  LB1029.R4P76 2010
  372.43—dc22

                                                          2009052909

About the Editors

Todd A. Glover, PhD, is Research Assistant Professor at the Nebraska Center for Research on Children, Youth, Families and Schools at the University of Nebraska–Lincoln. His research focuses on response to intervention (RTI), academic and behavioral interventions and assessments for students at risk, and methods for integrating empirical evidence and practice. Dr. Glover is the principal or co-principal investigator of several ongoing grant projects funded by the United States Department of Education's Institute of Education Sciences and the Nebraska Department of Education, including a state RTI consortium, postdoctoral training program, and various research studies investigating service delivery and professional development for RTI.

Sharon Vaughn, PhD, is the H. E. Hartfelder/Southland Corporation Regents Chair in Human Development and Executive Director of the Meadows Center for Preventing Educational Risk at the University of Texas at Austin. She is the principal investigator or co-principal investigator of numerous research grants funded by the National Institute of Child Health and Human Development, the Institute of Education Sciences, and the Texas Education Agency.

Contributors

Lynanne Black, PhD, Department of Educational and School Psychology, Indiana University of Pennsylvania, Indiana, Pennsylvania

Karen Blase, PhD, FPG, Child Development Institute, University of North Carolina at Chapel Hill, Chapel Hill, North Carolina

Christina H. Boice, MA, School Psychology Program, University of Minnesota, Minneapolis, Minnesota

Matthew K. Burns, PhD, School Psychology Program, University of Minnesota, Minneapolis, Minnesota

Theodore J. Christ, PhD, School Psychology Program, University of Minnesota, Minneapolis, Minnesota

Ben Clarke, PhD, Instructional Research Group, Los Alamitos, California, and Pacific Institutes for Research, Eugene, Oregon

Susan De La Paz, PhD, Department of Special Education, University of Maryland, College Park, College Park, Maryland

Carolyn A. Denton, PhD, Children's Learning Institute, University of Texas Health Science Center at Houston, Houston, Texas

Christine Espin, PhD, Department of Education and Child Studies, University of Leiden, Leiden, The Netherlands, and Department of Educational Psychology, University of Minnesota, Minneapolis, Minnesota

Dean Fixsen, PhD, FPG, Child Development Institute, University of North Carolina at Chapel Hill, Chapel Hill, North Carolina

Russell Gersten, PhD, Instructional Research Group, Los Alamitos, California

Todd A. Glover, PhD, Nebraska Center for Research on Children, Youth, Families and Schools, University of Nebraska–Lincoln, Lincoln, Nebraska

John M. Hintze, PhD, Department of Student Development and Pupil Personnel Services, University of Massachusetts Amherst, Amherst, Massachusetts

Robert H. Horner, PhD, Special Education Department, University of Oregon, Eugene, Eugene, Oregon

Tanya Ihlo, PhD, Nebraska Center for Research on Children, Youth, Families and Schools, University of Nebraska–Lincoln, Lincoln, Nebraska

Joseph F. Kovaleski, DEd, Program in School Psychology, Indiana University of Pennsylvania, Indiana, Pennsylvania

Amanda M. Marcotte, PhD, Department of Student Development and Pupil Personnel Services, University of Massachusetts Amherst, Amherst, Massachusetts

Kristen L. McMaster, PhD, Department of Educational Psychology, University of Minnesota, Minneapolis, Minnesota

Melissa Nantais, PhD, School Psychology Department, University of Detroit Mercy, Detroit, Michigan

Rebecca Newman-Gonchar, PhD, Instructional Research Group, Los Alamitos, California

Deborah Reed, PhD, Meadows Center for Preventing Educational Risk, University of Texas at Austin, Austin, Texas

George Sugai, PhD, Educational Psychology Department, Neag School of Education, University of Connecticut, Storrs, Connecticut

Isadora Szadokierski, MA, School Psychology Program, University of Minnesota, Minneapolis, Minnesota

Sharon Vaughn, PhD, Meadows Center for Preventing Educational Risk, University of Texas at Austin, Austin, Texas

Jeanne Wanzek, PhD, School of Teacher Education, Florida Center for Reading Research, Florida State University, Tallahassee, Florida

Preface

Teachers confront considerable challenges in supporting students in their classrooms. Given unique learning and behavioral concerns, competing time demands, and a wide range of political and cultural influences, the provision of equitable educational opportunities for *all* children and adolescents requires skillful attention to the appropriate use of new strategies and resources. Although traditional models for the delivery of instruction support select students, educators have continued to press for novel approaches to meet a wider range of individuals' needs.

Given its potential to impact school outcomes for numerous students, educators have recently focused significant attention on a response-to-intervention (RTI) model for guiding their work in schools. Within an RTI framework, school personnel set strong standards for achievement and work together to use student data to inform the implementation of research-based instruction and intervention to maximize opportunities for students' success. Assessment tools are used to make decisions about the effectiveness of instruction and students' need for and response to scientifically based intervention, and practices are implemented for all students based on clearly identified instructional goals.

Because the impact of RTI is contingent upon the quality of its implementation, critical consideration of which specific RTI processes and practices optimize student success is needed. By continuing to investigate aspects of an RTI model, researchers are better able to identify which components are necessary and vital for promoting student success. By integrating practices identified as optimally effective within classrooms, school stakeholders increase opportunities for positive outcomes.

The purpose of this book is to provide a synopsis of the current state of research pertaining to the implementation of RTI. For school practitioners and administrators, it highlights the implications from extant research on key service delivery components. For researchers, it provides a framework for considering and advancing future investigations.

Each chapter of this book provides a critical account of research pertaining to aspects of service delivery for RTI. The book begins with an introduction to the potential of RTI as a framework for supporting all students. Several key service delivery components of RTI are introduced in Chapter 2, along with considerations for using research to guide implementation. A discussion of the practical implications from research on each of the key RTI service delivery components is described throughout the remainder of the book. Chapter 3 provides a synopsis of research and implementation efforts from multiple states pertaining to a multi-tier prevention/intervention framework for service delivery. Chapter 4 summarizes key considerations for student assessment and data-based decision making. A synopsis of critical considerations from research on instruction and interventions in the areas of reading, mathematics, writing, and behavioral supports is then provided in Chapters 5 through 10. Chapter 11 includes considerations about the interface between service delivery for RTI and special education. The book then concludes with a discussion of the development of systems-level capacity to implement RTI.

ACKNOWLEDGMENTS

We acknowledge those in the academic, practicing, and political communities who have contributed to the advancement of science pertaining to RTI. Sincere gratitude is extended to Jim DiPerna at The Pennsylvania State University and to the Co-Directors of the Nebraska RTI Consortium and Tanya Ihlo for insights pertaining to the components of successful RTI service delivery implementation. Thanks also to Holly Sexton for editorial assistance with the final manuscript. We particularly appreciate those in our families who have provided ongoing inspiration and support, especially Michaela Glover, Anne Glover, Alec Glover, and James Dammann.

Contents

THE PROMISE OF RESPONSE TO INTERVENTION

1

Supporting All Students

The Promise of Response to Intervention

Todd A. Glover

The educational community has reason to be optimistic. Perhaps for the first time, educators are beginning to attend to large-scale, systematic reform driven by principles that link the multidisciplinary communities addressing schooling. School personnel have already begun to reach across divisions once fragmenting student supports in our schools. With a renewed focus on the integration of services that promote the success of students along a continuum of need, school administrators, classroom teachers, school psychologists, content area specialists, special educators, and others have begun to work together toward a collective vision.

Among many educational innovations developed to help meet the needs of all students (some have already come and gone), perhaps no practice has garnered as much recent attention as response to intervention (RTI) for its ability to accommodate students with such varying service demands (e.g., high-performing students, students academically or behaviorally behind their classmates in various content domains, those diagnosed with specific learning disabilities). By making use of systematic student data collection, carefully defined instructional decision-making criteria, and the application of scientifically based core programs and intervention, school personnel operate within an RTI framework via a continuum of services. Through the collective participation of administrators, data collectors, classroom teachers, school psychologists, content specialists, special educators, and others, RTI provides a cohesive schoolwide mechanism for ongoing support for *all* students.

THE POTENTIAL OF RTI: PROFESSIONAL EMPOWERMENT TO SUPPORT ALL STUDENTS

The success of RTI is predicated upon the notion that (a) educational systems have the potential, based on rigorous expectations and standards, to support *all* students and (b) research- and data-based assessment and instructional tools, when applied appropriately, lead to professional empowerment.

Within an RTI framework, strong performance standards are established and instruction and intervention are implemented based on regularly identified needs to help ensure that all students attain their potential. Low-performing and at-risk students are systematically identified and provided appropriate services to bolster achievement, while typical and high-performing students are provided with ongoing opportunities for continued growth and development. By establishing clearly defined expectations and systematically utilizing student progress data and empirical evidence to guide educational decisions, educators create equal opportunities for all students to learn within the classroom.

School personnel involved in the implementation of service delivery for RTI (e.g., teachers, administrators, special educators, school psychologists) are empowered as professionals by the use of research- and data-based assessment and instructional tools that provide the potential to (a) accurately identify students' progress in meeting performance expectations, (b) implement core instruction and intervention supports with demonstrated effectiveness for the students they serve, and (c) continually monitor and refine the education process to ensure that the provision of services promotes the attainment of clearly defined goals and objectives for learning growth and development.

By using information from rigorous research on instructional approaches/practices and data collected within their schools, educational stakeholders have the freedom to make strategic decisions that maximize the opportunities to support their students. School personnel are systematic within an RTI framework in (a) regularly identifying instructional needs through the collection of information on students and school practices and (b) selecting appropriate practices for which research has demonstrated the greatest potential in supporting these needs. Through a process of continuous improvement, they are able to make refinements in services that promote student success.

When implemented appropriately, RTI can provide the basis for an integrated system of student support facilitated by multiple school stakeholders with complementary expertise in a variety of content domains. School personnel participate in clearly defined activities designed to identify student needs and provide supports where needed. Administrators, teachers, specialists, and support personnel regularly assess the effectiveness of their core instructional and behavioral support programs. Periodic screening is administered by school staff and used to collect academic and/or behavior indicators for all students and to guide school personnel in identifying the need for additional instructional alterations and/or intervention. Core programs are modified by administrators, teachers, and specialists based on their effectiveness (as demonstrated locally and via empirical research). Additional progress monitoring assessments are administered by support staff, and interventions with scientific evidence of their effectiveness are provided (often via multiple tiers of service) and modified for students whose needs continue to be unmet by the general curriculum. To ensure equity in the treatment of all students, clearly defined data-based rules are used to make decisions about individuals' eligibility for specific instructional programs and interventions. Throughout a process of systematic reflection and intervention, school stakeholders thus have the potential to address the needs of students within their schools (Brown-Chidsey & Steege, 2005).

RTI AS A FRAMEWORK FOR SCHOOL REFORM: THE IMPORTANCE OF "DOING IT RIGHT"

With such great promise, teachers and administrators have already begun to implement components of RTI within their schools. School personnel have begun to participate in professional development related to student assessment, data-based decision making, and the application of scientifically based interventions. Administrators, teachers, support personnel, and others are beginning to modify and adopt new approaches to assessment and interventions within their schools.

Unfortunately, although the potential of RTI is great, schools confront considerable challenges. As indicated by the 2007 National Assessment of Educational Progress report, less than one-third of students are proficient in math and reading in both fourth and eighth grades (outcomes are slightly better for fourth-grade math students, with 39% of the students scoring "proficient"). Further, the achievement gap between racial/ethnic minority students and their Caucasian classmates is significant, and students diagnosed with a specific learning disability continue to lag behind. Without a doubt, considerable change is needed to address the unmet needs of so many students.

For RTI to achieve its greatest potential, the educational community must not only attend to simply *whether* RTI is in place; but, more importantly, they must also carefully consider *how* it is implemented. This involves critically examining aspects of RTI and whether they are effective to ensure that we are "doing it right." It requires continually conducting and evaluating the rigor of research on key components of RTI models, investigating the adaptation of research-based practices in specific settings, and regularly adhering to process guidelines that are based on strong standards and empirical support.

Critical Consideration of Research

A critical first step to ensuring that we are "doing it right" involves carefully considering ongoing research on RTI. Research on specific RTI components (e.g., program and interventions, multi-tier service delivery, student assessment, and decision making) is important in providing information about which educational processes and practices are most effective. To help ensure that significant school resources are allocated appropriately in ways that support positive student outcomes, critical attention to the use of methods that maximize the validity and replicability of research findings (e.g., controlled experimental trials, psychometrically appropriate validation studies) is required. By attending to the distinction between valid and reliable research findings and potentially inaccurate information from poorly designed studies, we can improve our ability to make informed decisions about how to address students' needs (Albers & Glover, 2007; Glover & DiPerna, 2007). By setting a strong standard for identifying credible research and by using credible research findings to guide educational implementation, we can better promote the use of effective practices within our schools.

Investigation/Adaptation of Practices for Setting Appropriate Learning Needs

"Doing it right" also requires that, as practices supported by rigorous research are adapted within classrooms, educators regularly investigate outcomes to determine whether they are appropriately addressing specific learning needs (e.g., students with specific skill acquisition difficulties, those for whom English is a second language, those with developmental concerns, typically performing students). Additional regular evaluation in schools can help to determine whether processes and practices are effectively serving their intended function. These efforts are vital for establishing when school implementation requires refinement or modification to best support students.

Attention to Process Guidelines

Finally, because the impact of any process or practice is affected greatly by the quality of its implementation, "doing it right" requires attending to whether school practices adhere to research-supported guidelines for implementation. By regularly monitoring the fidelity of implementation of assessment processes, instructional decision making, and intervention provision, educators can determine whether they are maximizing opportunities for student success. Information collected on implementation can then be used formatively to impact future training opportunities for school personnel (Gansle & Noell, 2007).

STRATEGICALLY MAXIMIZING SUPPORT FOR ALL STUDENTS

Educators confront significant challenges in meeting the needs of all students. Given its attention to regularly monitoring student outcomes and providing research-based core program and intervention supports, RTI holds considerable promise as a mechanism of service delivery and school reform. Critical to the success of RTI is the careful use of research to inform practice, the continual evaluation of RTI components in schools, and regular adherence to implementation guidelines. By strategically critiquing research and application on an ongoing basis, rather than simply "adopting and implanting" RTI, educators can systematically maximize opportunities for all students to succeed.

The chapters in this book provide an initial starting point for empowering educational professionals to become critical consumers in evaluating RTI research with practical implications. Within each chapter, a research synopsis is provided along with future research needs to guide educators in determining optimal RTI processes, procedures, and practices. It is hoped that the content in these chapters will promote continued reflection and consideration among educators about the appropriate implementation of services that support all students in schools.

REFERENCES

Albers, C. A., & Glover, T. A. (2007). How can universal screening enhance educational and mental health outcomes? *Journal of School Psychology, 45*, 113–116.

Brown-Chidsey, R., & Steege, M. W. (2005). *Response to intervention: Principles and strategies for effective practice.* New York: Guilford Press.

Gansle, K. A., & Noell, G. H. (2007). The fundamental role of intervention implementation in assessing resistance to intervention. In S. R. Jimerson, M. K. Burns, & A. M. VanDerHeyden (Eds.), *Handbook of response to intervention: The science and practice of assessment and intervention* (pp. 244–251). New York: Springer Science.

Glover, T. A., & DiPerna, J. C. (2007). Service delivery models for response to intervention: Core components and directions for future research. *School Psychology Review, 36*, 526–640.

2

Key RTI Service Delivery Components

Considerations for Research-Informed Practice

Todd A. Glover

Successful educational innovations are not only the product of cutting-edge ideas. They also involve the translation of theories and concepts into clearly operationalized, empirically supported applications. The focus of this book is based on the premise that successful implementation of response to intervention (RTI) requires examination of specific components of service delivery though research and the continual refinement and adjustment of practices in school settings to maximize student success. Several key components required to implement RTI are introduced in this chapter. Throughout the remainder of the book, a critical account of the research with implications for practice is provided for each of these aspects of service delivery. The components and their importance are described first, followed by criteria for evaluating their empirical support. The chapter concludes with a discussion of the importance of collecting and responding to fidelity-monitoring data in the implementation of all processes and practices for RTI.

KEY SERVICE DELIVERY COMPONENTS FOR RTI

By using data on students' performance to identify instructional and intervention needs and then systematically implementing educational supports with fidelity at varying levels of intensity, service delivery within an RTI framework has the potential to maximize learning for all students. RTI implementation involves attending to multiple aspects of service delivery: (a) coordinating the involvement of multiple educational stakeholders, (b) providing support to all students via a multi-tier system, (c) using student data to inform instructional decisions systematically, and (d) delivering instruction and interventions that have been found through research to promote student performance.

Stakeholder Involvement

Because service delivery for RTI takes place schoolwide, multiple stakeholders are required to coordinate implementation efforts. Typically, school teams composed of general and special education teachers, administrators, and various specialists and support personnel (e.g., reading specialists, school psychologists, speech–language pathologists) work together throughout implementation of services for RTI. Through regular meetings and collaborative activities, these teams regularly conduct and participate in ongoing professional development, establish and maintain protocols for student assessment and intervention, systematically review student data, and examine and monitor the appropriateness of core instruction and interventions. Parents are also typically informed about the service delivery framework for RTI and are notified about and involved in team meetings pertaining to decisions affecting their children.

Multi-Tier Implementation

To accommodate students with varying levels of need, services for RTI are provided within a multi-tier framework. Often this framework is composed of three tiers derived from the field of public health (e.g., see Sugai & Horner, 2006; Walker & Shinn, 2002). An illustration of a three-tier model is provided in Figure 2.1. As depicted, core scientifically based programs and assessments are provided to all students at the primary level of the system (Tier 1). This level is designed to support the majority (typically at least 80%) of students (Walker & Shinn, 2002). All students are screened. In addition to receiving core instruction and behavioral supports, students who do not meet performance expectations based on systematic screening are provided with additional, secondary-level (Tier 2) intervention, often within a smaller group setting. These students are then assessed at regular intervals to determine whether they are responding to additional research-based supports. Students who do not respond to secondary intervention are then provided with more intensive, individualized tertiary-level (Tier 3) support. As depicted in Figure 2.1, regular progress monitoring data and

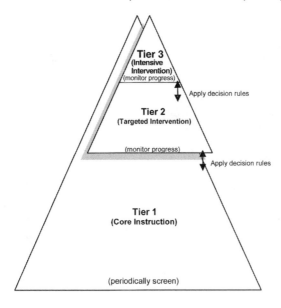

FIGURE 2.1. Three-tier service delivery model for RTI.

systematic decision rules are used to determine intervention differentiation within tiers and the appropriateness of movement between tiers for students who do not meet screening benchmark expectations.

Student Assessment and Data-Based Decision Making

To help ensure that students are provided with opportunities to succeed, data on all students are collected within an RTI service delivery framework and compared with clearly defined benchmark expectations for performance. Screening takes place at regular intervals throughout the school year (typically once in the fall, winter, and spring) by measuring performance on skill-based and behavioral indicators found through research to predict future academic success. The data are analyzed to determine (a) whether the majority of students meet benchmark expectations in response to core instruction and (b) which students may require additional intervention. Diagnostic assessments and interventions are provided to students who do not meet benchmark levels of performance, and comparable forms of skill-based and behavioral progress monitoring assessments are collected at regular intervals (e.g., weekly) to determine whether these students are responding to intervention. These data are also used to guide the differentiation of instruction and/or changes to intervention provision after a set period of time (e.g., 8 weeks). Typically, performance rate (e.g., improvement over time) and level goals are set for each student, and students are monitored to determine whether their performance (e.g., rate of growth and level) is meeting predefined, data-based objectives (e.g., Fuchs, 2003).

Evidence-Based Instruction and Intervention Provision

To maximize opportunities for student success, core instruction, supports, and interventions provided within an RTI service delivery framework are selected and monitored to ensure they are in alignment with practices found through research to be effective in meeting students' needs. Instruction and interventions are chosen and evaluated based on empirical support for their content and instructional method. Before selecting and implementing interventions within an RTI service delivery framework, core programs are regularly evaluated for their content and implementation fidelity and are modified, if necessary, to help ensure that they are meeting the needs of most students. Typically, once the core has been found to support at least 80% of students, interventions are then selected based on their research support and are regularly monitored throughout their implementation with students requiring additional assistance.

Given the importance of empirically supported instruction and intervention, several guides have emerged to support school personnel in the selection process. This is particularly true in the area of reading (e.g., *A Consumer's Guide to Evaluating a Core Reading Program Grades K–3: A Critical Elements Analysis* [Simmons & Kame'enui, 2003] and *Guidelines for Reviewing a Reading Program* [Florida Center for Reading Research, 2007]).

USING RIGOROUS RESEARCH TO GUIDE RTI SERVICE DELIVERY IMPLEMENTATION

Implementation of the aforementioned key service delivery components based on theory and sentiment alone is insufficient for ensuring their success. The impact of RTI is dependent upon the *quality* of component implementation. Accordingly, attention to credible evidence from methodologically rigorous research on specific components (e.g., processes, interventions, and assessments) continues to be critical for informing educators about aspects of the implementation process that promote positive student outcomes.

Although existing research is useful in guiding the implementation of key components (i.e., coordination of multiple stakeholders, multi-tier service delivery, assessment and data-based decision making, and delivery of instruction), additional investigations are needed to determine the utility of specific practices required to implement RTI. To generate valid conclusions from such research, attention to methodological rigor is needed. Further, the educational community must consider (a) whether accumulated evidence is sufficient to make informed judgments and (b) whether research contexts studied pertain to real-world applications of interest (Glover & DiPerna, 2007; Kratochwill, Clements, & Kalymon, 2007).

Consideration of Existing and Needed Research on Key Service Delivery Components

Although research on service delivery for RTI has begun to emerge, there is an ongoing need for the continued investigation of the impact and utility of specific aspects of implementation. Specific research recommendations are described in subsequent chapters in this book; however, at least three general research foci will be important to consider in the ongoing appraisal of the state of research designed to inform practice (Glover & DiPerna, 2007). First, it will be helpful to consider research on the overall impact and utility of process and practices provided within an RTI service framework. It will be important to evaluate existing and needed research on outcomes associated with implementing entire multi-tier models and specific model features. In addition, it will be useful to evaluate the effects and resource demands associated with specific instructional approaches and interventions and the utility of (a) assessment protocols used for screening and monitoring students' progress and (b) approaches for engaging multiple stakeholders in collaborative decision making (Glover & DiPerna, 2007; Kovaleski, 2007).

Second, to determine which approaches are optimal for assessing student performance and promoting student success, it will be important to evaluate the effects of systematically varying specific processes and practices. Multiple investigations examining the impact of intervention alternatives within tiers as well as aspects of these interventions (e.g., composition, intensity, and individualization for specific students) will be useful in determining which interventions are most effective with which students during various stages in the implementation process. Investigations of variations in assessment procedures and protocols will also be helpful in ascertaining which approaches are optimally useful for informing instructional and intervention decisions.

Finally, to determine which supports are useful and necessary for maintaining RTI service delivery within schools, it will be important to evaluate the outcomes of various system-level capacity-building approaches and their specific features. Especially helpful will be the consideration of research on the efficacy of approaches for professional development and ongoing personnel support (and the feasibility and fidelity of these approaches; Glover & DiPerna, 2007).

Methodological Considerations for Research on Processes and Practices

In addition to considering the focus of existing and needed research on key components of RTI, educators must also attend to the rigor with which the research is conducted. Stakeholders who generate educational decisions and allocate resources based on inaccurate research conclusions inadvertently negatively impact (sometimes significantly) the lives of the students they intend to support. The appropriateness and quality of a research approach dictate the confidence with which conclusions can be made. Although various aspects of the research process are important, in considering research on RTI service delivery process and practices (i.e., research evaluating the coordination of multiple stakeholders, multi-tier service delivery, implementation of instruction or intervention), attention to the use of an appropriate research design warrants special consideration (Glover & DiPerna, 2007).

Both the type of research design that is selected and the manner in which the design is implemented are critical for determining whether evidence from a research study is appropriate for generating inferences about impacts in real classrooms. Although a review of research methodology is beyond the scope of this chapter, common approaches used in educational research to evaluate the impact of processes or practices involve the use of pre–post, matched, single-case, or randomized experimental designs. Before describing the gold standard (randomized experiments), it is important to acknowledge practical advantages and disadvantages of alternative designs.

Pre–Post Design

The primary benefit of the pre–post design, in which pre- and postintervention data are compared to investigate an intervention's effectiveness, is its simplicity and ease of use in school settings. Despite its practical appeal, without a control group, it is impossible to rule out other factors such as historical events (e.g., other practice or policy changes occurring during the same time that the intervention takes place), the effects of repeated assessment (e.g., previous assessment exposure or test learning effects), or participant maturation (e.g., natural development-related increases in performance) as equally plausible alternative explanations for any observed study findings. As a result, conclusions from pre–post investigations are often invalid (Myers & Dynarski, 2003; Shadish, Cook, & Campbell, 2002).

A common example illustrating the invalidity of pre–post designs is a highly visible randomized trial of Even Start, a literacy program for disadvantaged families that was found to have no impact on children's school readiness. Had a pre–post design been implemented in this case, investigators would have observed an increase in school readiness for program participants. Without knowledge of a comparable increase in school readiness for control participants (who did not receive the intervention), they would have erroneously concluded from the pre–post study that Even Start (rather than an equally plausible explanation, such as the children's natural development) led to the observed improvement in performance (U.S. Department of Education Institute of Education Sciences, 2003).

Matched Comparison Group Designs

To help alleviate concerns about random assignment of participants to research conditions, matched comparison group designs, in which control participants are selected based on similarity with respect to specified characteristics to those receiving an intervention, have been regarded as a plausible alternative. Unfortunately, despite the convenience in the selection of control participants, an inability to match on vital variables while accounting for other important differences in participant characteristics or experiences prevents investigators from determining whether comparison groups within a matched design are characteristically different. This potential incomparability makes it difficult to rule out other plausible explanations for observed study findings attributed to differences between the intervention and control participants (e.g., differences in experience, local policies/practices, motivational factors; Shadish et al., 2002).

Agodini and Dynarski (2004) provide an example among several from the empirical literature illustrating the potential invalidity of matched comparison group designs. In evaluating the impact of dropout prevention programs, they found that, even when using sophisticated matching techniques, matched designs were unable to replicate findings from well-implemented randomized trials, and that, in some cases, the use of a matched approach actually led to different study findings (i.e., programs found effective through one approach were found ineffective using the other). Unfortunately, in this case, given the importance of dropout prevention, policy decisions based on invalid conclusions from matched designs could have profound consequences impacting many students' lives.

Single-Case Designs

Single-case designs involving the observation of individual-case (e.g., individual participant) data are also commonly used in educational settings and regarded as a practical, efficient alternative to resource-intensive group designs. Unfortunately, simple single-case designs, such as *A-B or A-B-A designs*, which involve repeated observations of case data during a baseline phase before intervention (A), throughout an intervention phase (B), and, in the case of the A-B-A design, during a phase once the intervention has been removed (A), fail to rule out as alternative explanations for observed outcomes some threats to validity such as other historical events that occur during the introduction or removal of intervention. The *concurrent multiple-baseline design*, which typically involves collecting data on multiple cases at the same points in time while delaying the introduction of phases across individual cases to compare not only within but also across cases, provides a significantly improved alternative to simple single-case methods. Unfortunately, despite its strength in reducing alternative explanations for observed findings, data analytic approaches for this design (as with any single-case method) do not permit a high degree of certainly about the likelihood of observed study outcomes (Levin, 1992; Shadish et al., 2002). This presents a significant problem in generating policy or practice recommendations and in considering the allocation of resources based on single-case study findings.

Randomized Experiment: The Gold Standard Research Design

The best possible design in maximizing the confidence with which study conclusions can be attributed to the process or practice of interest (and not alternative explanations for observed outcomes) is a well-implemented randomized experiment (or randomized trial). In randomly assigning intervention recipients (e.g., students, classrooms, teachers) to intervention or control conditions, systematic differences between compared groups other than the intervention itself are minimized, leading to increased confidence in attributions about the impact of the process or practice under investigation. As Levin and O'Donnell (1999) note, a well-implemented randomized design takes into account the potential of systematic variation (other than the intervention provision itself) at the level at which the intervention is provided (e.g., student, classroom, school). Accordingly, the benefits of randomization are optimized when random assignment and intervention provision take place at the same level (e.g., when an intervention is provided individually to students and the students, not classrooms, are randomly assigned; or when an intervention is provided to entire classrooms, and the classrooms, not schools, are randomly assigned). Given their superiority in ensuring that there are no systematic differences between intervention and comparison groups other than the presence or absence of an intervention (or variations of an intervention) under investigation, well-implemented randomized experiments provide the strongest possible evidence for informing policy, practice, and decisions about the allocation of resources.

Methodological Considerations for Research on Assessments and Data-Based Decision Making

As with investigations of processes and practices, attention to methodological rigor is also needed in considering research on assessments and data-based decision making. Within an RTI service delivery framework, assessments and accompanying data-based instructional decision-making criteria are used to periodically screen students to determine their level of performance relative to benchmark expectations and to regularly monitor students' response over time. Although several aspects are important in considering the appropriateness of assessments for each of these functions, attention to the use of appropriate methods for determining measurement reliability and validity is especially critical for helping to ensure that the correct data-based decisions are made to promote student performance. The consequences associated with inadequate attention to methodological rigor in psychometric investigations are great. Poorly tested, unreliable, or invalid measures yield inconsistent or inaccurate indicators of student performance, which can lead to erroneous determinations about student response to instruction or intervention and the need for additional supports. As a result of poor assessment precision, students may not receive and subsequently benefit from much-needed services.

Correlational approaches are useful in investigating the reliability of both screening and progress monitoring assessments. By obtaining correlation coefficients ranging in value between 0 and 1 (with higher values indicating greater reliability), investigators are able to discern the strength with which (a) items or sets of items are related to the total assessment outcome (*internal consistency*), (b) students' levels of performance on multiple administrations of the same assessment are related (*test–retest reliability*), (c) multiple forms of an assessment are related (*alternate form reliability*), and (d) the scoring of an assessment is consistent across scorers (*interscorer reliability*).

Multiple approaches are helpful in investigating the validity of assessments. Correlational methods are useful for determining the degree to which (a) items or subscales within an assessment are measuring the same general construct (*construct validity*), (b) an individual assessment item is effective in discriminating between those at different performance levels (*item discrimination*), or (c) the assessment is concurrently related to other assessments designed to measure the same construct (*concurrent validity*). Descriptive investigations of proportions of students are also beneficial for determining the difficulty of individual assessment items (*item difficulty*). In addition, comparisons between subgroups using nonparametric, contingency table, or item response theory approaches are useful for determining *differential item functioning* for those with specific demographic characteristics (e.g., males vs. females; Glover & Albers, 2007; Salvia & Ysseldyke, 2004).

In evaluating screening assessments, special attention to an instrument's accuracy in distinguishing between students who are and are not at risk for experiencing difficulties (*predictive validity*) in the future is warranted. Predictive validity is especially important within an RTI framework, given the need to identify at-risk students and to provide intervention before pervasive academic difficulties significantly impede students' progress and negatively impact long-term outcomes. Although assessment developers sometimes use correlational approaches to investigate predictive validity, these methods fail to determine an instrument's accuracy in correctly identifying individual students (and caution should be exercised in adopting screening assessments with only correlational evidence of predictive validity; Satz & Fletcher, 1988). A classification approach is a better alternative for determining the proportion of students for whom a screening instrument correctly predicts subsequent performance difficulties. A classification approach yields several important indicators of an instrument's accuracy in predicting subsequent performance difficulties, including the instrument's *sensitivity* (proportion of students correctly identified among those *actually* at risk), *specificity* (proportion of students correctly identified among those *actually* not at risk), *positive predictive value* (proportion of students correctly identified among those *identified* as at risk), and *negative predictive value* (proportion of students correctly identified among those *identified* as not at risk; Glover & Albers, 2007; Satz & Fletcher, 1988).

The Accumulation of Relevant Evidence to Guide Practice

In considering all research on key components of service delivery for RTI, it is crucial to note (a) whether accumulated evidence is sufficient for making informed educational decisions and (b) whether the research contexts studied pertain to the applications of interest. As educators implement practices relevant to service delivery for RTI, it will be important to take into account guidelines from professional organizations and to exercise discretion in the review of evidence supporting various processes and practices. Given concerns about the impact of a research approach on the validity of research conclusions, task force guidelines presented by professional organizations in the social, behavioral, and educational sciences typically recommend that at least one randomized experiment demonstrate positive effects for a process or practice for it to be considered efficacious or effective. These guidelines commonly suggest that educators cautiously regard processes or practices supported solely by single-case or matched designs until evidence of efficacy or effectiveness is demonstrated via randomized experiments. Unfortunately, although there is sufficient support for the efficacy and effectiveness of processes and practices to meet professional guidelines in select domains (e.g., in the content of reading instruction/intervention), research evidence pertaining to several content areas (e.g., mathematics, writing, behavioral supports) has historically been limited with respect to empirical rigor. As a result, educators are forced to make educational decisions without sufficient empirical guidance.

In the absence of a strong research base established via randomized experiments, members of the educational community must take into account the *best available* evidence. In light of the methodological limitations previously described for alternative research designs, Institute of Education Sciences (IES) guidelines established by the Board of Advisors from the Coalition for Evidence-Based Policy recommend that educators regard evidence from *pre–post investigations* as inappropriate for making educational decisions. As previously described, findings from pre–post studies on a wide range of educational processes and practices (e.g., the previously mentioned investigation of Even Start; investigations of various academic curricula, instructional strategies, intervention programs, and technological innovations) are especially problematic in establishing evidence given their vulnerability to confounding influences and potential invalidity. IES guidelines further recommend that findings from *matched comparison group research* be considered as a means of "establishing 'possible' evidence of … effectiveness, and thereby generating hypotheses that merit confirmation in randomized controlled trials" (U.S. Department of Education, IES, 2003, p. 4). Evidence from well-designed *single-case studies* may also be useful in considering practices delivered to individual students; however, as previously indicated, it is important to acknowledge that analytic approaches for this form of research do not permit a high degree of certainly about the likelihood of observed study outcomes. This may present significant limitations in generating policy or practice recommendations that pertain to multiple students in various contexts that may or may not resemble those that were studied.

Contextual relevance is also important in considering support from empirical research. Processes or practices useful in certain settings for specific individuals may not be appropriate in other contexts. For example, in the area of reading, although there may be extensive support for the efficacy of a fluency intervention in assisting students who have acquired basic phonological awareness, the intervention may not benefit those who have not yet mastered phoneme identification, segmentation, or blending. Although attention to all possible student and contextual variables impacting contextual relevance is impossible, consideration of factors for which there is an empirical or theoretical justification for context-specific appropriateness is important.

IMPLEMENTATION FIDELITY

Another final consideration pertaining to the quality of integration of key service delivery components for RTI, *implementation fidelity*, warrants special attention. In transporting research-supported processes and practices into school settings, alignment of local efforts with implementation protocols specified by developers and in empirical studies is critical for ensuring that educators are able to replicate positive outcomes found in research. Unfortunately, as articulated by Gansle and Noell (2007), local implementation efforts without regular attention to fidelity are apt to deteriorate over time, making it difficult to discern whether processes and practices as conducted will effectively meet students' needs. By monitoring fidelity adherence and providing periodic maintenance training as needed, school personnel are able to maximize opportunities for the quality implementation of key components.

Although extensive additional empirical investigations are needed to determine optimal approaches for monitoring and maintaining fidelity, professional guidelines and emerging research suggest that careful consideration of at least three aspects related to the maintenance of implantation fidelity is needed (Gansle & Noell, 2007; Johnson, Mellard, Fuchs, & McKnight, 2006). First, to help facilitate ongoing monitoring and maintenance of fidelity, attention should be given to the involvement of multiple stakeholders in the collection and analysis of fidelity-monitoring data. The participation of administrators, who set and enforce expectations about fidelity adherence, and teachers and well-trained staff members, who collect and analyze fidelity data, can be useful for increasing buy-in and the perceived utility of the fidelity-monitoring process (Kovaleski, Gickling, & Marrow, 1999).

Second, consideration of objectivity in fidelity assessment is needed for determining the accuracy of fidelity judgments. Commonly used methods of fidelity data collection include self-appraisal, direct observations, and permanent products. Although self-appraisal (e.g., use of teacher self-report checklists to identify level of adherence) is perhaps the easiest and most efficient approach, it has often been found to be upwardly biased (e.g., Gansle & Noell, 2007; Noell et al., 2005; Wickstrom, Jones, LaFleur, & Witt, 1998). A more objective alternative involves conducting direct observations and collecting and coding permanent products (e.g., instructional materials, student work samples) at multiple points in time by trained personnel to determine the level of adherence to critical steps/components preidentified for implemented processes and practices (Gansle & Noell, 2007). A hybrid fidelity assessment approach, whereby schools use efficient self-appraisal approaches accompanied by periodic direct assessment validations of fidelity, may be most practically feasible for use in schools. Additional investigations of this approach are warranted to determine its accuracy and utility.

Finally, attention to the quality of protocols for promoting fidelity adherence (e.g., training or feedback protocols) is needed. In addition to assessing the alignment of content foci with needs identified through fidelity assessments, it is also important to consider whether approaches for bolstering fidelity address factors responsible for drift in implementation. As Gresham and his colleagues (e.g., Gresham, MacMillan, Beebe-Frankenberger, & Bocian, 2000; Reschly & Gresham, 2006) posit, several factors may reduce the fidelity of implementation, including (a) the complexity of implementation guidelines, (b) the level of resources required, (c) stakeholder perceptions about effectiveness, and (d) the motivation and expertise of implementation agents. Two promising approaches with demonstrated support for fidelity maintenance include (a) the provision of direct training in process and practice components (i.e., the use of rehearsal or feedback training; e.g., Sterling-Turner, Watson, & Moore, 2002; Watson & Robinson, 1996) and (b) the use of performance feedback in reviewing implementation data (e.g., DiGennaro, Martens, & McIntyre, 2005; Jones, Wickstrom, & Friman, 1997; Noell et al., 2005).

BRIDGING THE RESEARCH–PRACTICE DIVIDE

The success of RTI implementation will likely depend on the quality of the implementation of key service delivery components. By attending to credible evidence from methodologically rigorous research on specific components and by monitoring and maintaining alignment between local efforts and empirically supported protocols for implementation, educational stakeholders will maximize opportunities to promote positive student outcomes. By further continuing to critically evaluate aspects of service delivery for RTI, researchers, practitioners, and other members of the educational community can work together to refine processes and practices to better meet students' needs. School stakeholders (e.g., administrators, school psychologists, special educators, classroom teachers) can collaboratively identify and implement processes and practices supported by existing empirical evidence and inform researchers about the ongoing need for future investigations. Researchers can, in turn, communicate with school personnel to identify and investigate pressing aspects of practical significance. In the absence of empirical research, mutual consultation among educational stakeholders with professional knowledge and experience in schools will be useful for advancing educational decisions pertaining to service delivery for RTI.

Just as RTI data are used to inform ongoing decisions about the need for refinement and adaptation of educational supports to meet students' needs, so too can empirical investigations be used to inform existing efforts and to investigate additional questions about how to best implement components of the larger model of service delivery for RTI. Several considerations are provided both within this chapter and throughout the remainder of this book to guide researchers and practitioners in seeking out evidence to validate the implementation process. It is hoped that these considerations will be useful in advancing research-informed practice that creates an optimal learning environment to support all students.

REFERENCES

Agodini, R., & Dynarski, M. (2004). Are experiments the only option? A look at dropout prevention programs. *Review of Economics and Statistics, 86*(1), 180–194.

DiGennaro, F. D., Martens, B. K., & McIntyre, L. L. (2005). Increasing treatment integrity through negative reinforcement: Effects on teacher and student behavior. *School Psychology Review, 34*, 220–231.

Florida Center for Reading Research. (2007). *Guidelines for reviewing a reading program*. Tallahassee: Author.

Fuchs, L. S. (2003). Assessing intervention responsiveness: Conceptual and technical issues. *Learning Disabilities Research and Practice, 18*, 172–186.

Gansle, K. A., & Noell, G. H. (2007). The fundamental role of intervention implementation is assessing response to intervention. In S. R. Jimerson, M. K. Burns, & A. M. VanDerHeyden (Eds.), *Handbook of response to intervention* (pp. 244–251). New York: Springer.

Glover, T. A., & Albers, C. A. (2007). Considerations for evaluating universal screening assessments. *Journal of School Psychology, 45*, 117–135.

Glover, T. A., & DiPerna, J. C. (2007). Service delivery for response to intervention: Core components and directions for future research. *School Psychology Review, 36*, 526–540.

Gresham, F. M., MacMillan, D. L., Beebe-Frankenberger, M. E., & Bocian, K. M. (2000). Treatment integrity in learning disabilities intervention research: Do we really know how treatments are implemented? *Learning Disabilities Research and Practice, 15*(4), 198–205.

Johnson, E., Mellard, D. F., Fuchs, D., & McKnight, M. A. (2006). *Responsivness to intervention (RTI): How to do it*. Lawrence, KS: National Center on Learning Disabilities.

Jones, K. M., Wickstrom, K. F., & Friman, P. C. (1997). The effects of observational feedback on treatment integrity in school-based behavioral consultation. *School Psychology Quarterly, 12*, 316–326.

Kovaleski, J. F. (2007). Response to intervention: Considerations for research and systems change. *School Psychology Review, 36*, 526–540.

Kovaleski, J. F., Gickling, E. E., & Marrow, H. (1999). High versus low implementation of instructional support teams: A case for maintaining program fidelity. *Remedial and Special Education, 20,* 170–183.

Kratochwill, T. R., Clements, M. A., & Kalymon, K. M. (2007). Response to intervention: Conceptual and methodological issues in implementation. In S. R. Jimerson, M. K. Burns, & A. M. VanDerHeyden (Eds.), *Handbook of response to intervention: The science and practice of assessment and intervention* (pp. 25–52). New York: Springer.

Levin, J. R. (1992). Single-case research design and analysis: Comments and concerns. In T. R. Kratochwill & J. R. Levin (Eds.), *Single-case research design and analysis: New directions for psychology and education* (pp. 213–225). Hillsdale, NJ: Erlbaum.

Levin, J. R., & O'Donnell, A. M. (1999). What to do about educational research's credibility gaps? *Issues in Education, 5,* 177–229.

Myers, D., & Dynarski, M. (2003). *Random assignment in program evaluation and intervention research: Questions and answers.* Washington, DC: U.S. Department of Education Institute of Education Sciences.

Noell, G. H., Witt, J. C., Slider, N. J., Connell, J. E., Gatti, S. L., Williams, K. L., et al. (2005). Treatment implementation following behavioral consultation in schools: A comparison of three follow-up strategies. *School Psychology Review, 34,* 87–106.

Reschly, D. J., & Gresham, F. M. (2006, April). *Implementation fidelity of SLD identification procedures.* Presentation at the National SEA Conference on SLD Determination: Integrating RTI within the SLD Determination Process, Kansas City, Missouri.

Salvia, J., & Ysseldyke, J. E. (2004). *Assessment in special and inclusive education* (9th ed.). Boston: Houghton Mifflin.

Satz, P., & Fletcher, J. M. (1988). Early identification of learning disabled children: An old problem revisited. *Journal of Consulting and Clinical Psychology, 56,* 824–829.

Shadish, W. R., Cook, T. D., & Campbell, D. T. (2002). *Experimental and quasi-experimental designs for generalized causal inference.* New York: Houghton Mifflin.

Simmons, D. C., & Kame'enui, E. J. (2003). *A consumer's guide to evaluating a core reading program grades K–3: A critical elements analysis.* Eugene: University of Oregon, College of Education.

Sterling-Turner, H. E., Watson, T. S., & Moore, J. W. (2002). Effects of training on treatment integrity and treatment outcomes in school-based consultation. *School Psychology Quarterly, 17,* 47–77.

Sugai, G., & Horner, R. (2006). A promising approach for expanding and sustaining school-aide positive behavior support. *School Psychology Review, 35,* 245–259.

U.S. Department of Education, Institute of Education Sciences. (2003). *Identifying and implementing educational practices supported by rigorous evidence: A user friendly guide.* Washington, DC: Author.

Walker, H. M., & Shinn, M. R. (2002). Structuring school-based interventions to achieve integrated primary, secondary, and tertiary prevention goals for safe and effective schools. In M. R. Shinn, H. M. Walker, & G. Stoner (Eds.), *Interventions for academic and behavior problems: II. Preventative and remedial approaches* (pp. 1–25). Bethesda, MD: National Association of School Psychologists.

Watson, T. S., & Robinson, S. L. (1996). Direct behavioral consultation: An alternative to traditional behavioral consultation. *School Psychology Quarterly, 11,* 267–278.

Wickstrom, K. F., Jones, K. M., LaFleur, L. H., & Witt, J. C. (1998). An analysis of treatment integrity in school-based behavioral consultation. *School Psychology Quarterly, 13,* 141–154.

3

Multi-Tier Service Delivery

Current Status and Future Directions

Joseph F. Kovaleski
Lynanne Black

Since its earliest conceptualizations, response to intervention (RTI) has been associated with a multi-tier service delivery (MTSD) format. Indeed, the terms are often used interchangeably. For example, Torgesen (2007) has articulated that RTI has been understood as both an instructional delivery system and an assessment methodology. Consequently, it is perhaps necessary to start this chapter by differentiating RTI and MTSD. RTI has been defined as "the practice of providing high-quality instruction and interventions matched to student needs and using learning rate over time and level of performance to make important educational decisions" (Batsche et al., 2005, p. 5). MTSD is a structure for planning and organizing the provision of increasingly intense interventions delivered in general, remedial, and special education. Typically, assessment of a student's RTI is the vehicle by which decisions are made regarding the provision of services and supports within an MTSD model.

This chapter reviews recent attempts to scale up MTSD in local education agencies (LEAs) or on a statewide level. Although the list is not exhaustive, we have identified a number of the most salient models that are currently in operation. We also look retrospectively at some of the models that were precursors to contemporary MTSD structures. In doing so, we address critical program features that are common to most approaches to MTSD as well as those that are unique to particular projects.

For simplicity, throughout the chapter we describe the basic MTSD structure as a three-tier model. Although various MTSD projects have used different numbers of tiers (typically three or four), we utilize the three-tier format described by the National Association of State Directors of Special Education (NASDSE; Batsche et al., 2005) when discussing the overall approach. In brief, Tier 1 relates to the provision of a comprehensive general education program, including core curricula that are aligned with state or national standards, along with appropriate supplemental supports that aim to help teachers differentiate students in their classrooms. Tier 2 refers to more intensive interventions, programs, and services that are provided over a limited period of time to individuals or small groups of students beyond the regular classroom in an attempt to improve their performance and bring them closer to expected levels of proficiency. Tier 3 corresponds to very intense services that are provided to individual students over longer periods of time. It includes special education as well as other general education programs that are also of high intensity and long duration.

We also, in this chapter, refer to critical program features of both the precursor models and contemporary MTSD systems, often using these "ingredients" to distinguish between the two. First, both historically and currently, teaming is a foundational aspect of all of these efforts. Schools have impaneled groups of teachers, specialists, and administrators to make decisions and orchestrate services. Typically, these teams use the problem-solving process (Tilly, 2008) as their common operating procedure. Second, teams have increasingly used data from student assessments to guide decision making. These data may be derived from general screenings of all students, in-depth assessments of students' academic skills, and progress monitoring of individual students. Third, teams have designed interventions for students who fail to meet desired benchmarks, either on an individual basis or collectively in groups of students who display similar needs.

This chapter also covers various types of outcome data that schools have used to evaluate the effects of these practices, including improvements in overall student achievement, progress of individual students, referrals to special education, and consumer satisfaction. It is not our goal to review the foundational literature on particular program features such as curriculum-based measurement (CBM), progress monitoring, standard protocol interventions, or problem-solving teaming. Rather, we examine the evidence that currently exists regarding the effectiveness of precursor models and current MTSD structures. In doing so, we also address aspects of MTSD that have not as yet been empirically tested or fully supported and make recommendations regarding needed research directions.

PRECURSORS OF MTSD

In this section, we review the history of team-based attempts to provide enhanced supports in general education to struggling students. These initiatives have featured as their central organizing structure a team of teachers and other specialists typically using some variant of the problem-solving process (Tilly, 2008) as its central modus operandi. We particularly highlight those models that have served as precursors to current, more fully articulated MTSD structures. These precursor models have the following aspects in common: (1) They predate the use of the RTI terminology, (2) they are generally based on the implementation of problem-solving teams, and (3) they include aspects of contemporary MTSD models but do not fully address all tiers as currently conceptualized. Although these pioneering efforts have provided a conceptual and procedural basis of the contemporary MTSD format, they are frequently misunderstood as full multi-tier models. Consequently, their inclusion here not only serves a historic function but also will be used to distinguish the critical features of the fully implemented MTSD models.

Overview of Problem-Solving Teams

Over the past 30 years, beginning with teacher assistance teams (TATs) in the late 1970s (Chalfant, Pysh, & Moultrie, 1979), various scholars, state department officials, and local practitioners have developed team-based structures that have attempted to assist teachers in meeting the needs of difficult-to-teach students. Among the labels used over the years are problem-solving teams (Tilly, 2003), mainstream assistance teams (Fuchs, Fuchs, & Bahr, 1990), intervention assistance teams (Graden, 1989), instructional consultation teams (Rosenfield & Gravois, 1996), instructional support teams (Kovaleski, Tucker, & Stevens, 1996), and prereferral intervention teams (Graden, Casey, & Christenson, 1985). There have also been thousands of locally developed teams with an even wider variety of titles. In fact, a recent survey of state officials regarding these practices (Truscott, Cohen, Sams, Sanborn, & Frank, 2005) indicated that 69% of states required prereferral intervention and a full 86% recommended that these interventions be provided using a team format. Further, in a separate survey of 200 randomly selected schools in 50 states, these researchers found that 85% of the schools had prereferral teams. These incidence rates were substantially higher than those cited by Buck, Polloway, Smith-Thomas, and Cook (2003), who found that 43% of the states required prereferral intervention processes and an additional 29% recommended them, data that were similar to those gathered a decade earlier by Carter and Sugai (1989). Another indication of the prevalence of these team approaches is the regular occurrence of summary articles and reviews over the past 30 years, including Nelson, Smith, Taylor, Dodd, and Reavis (1991); Schrag and Henderson (1996); Sindelar, Griffin, Smith, and Watanabe (1992); Safran and Safran (1996); and Bahr, Whitten, Dieker, Kocarek, and Manson (1999).

In spite of their common use of the problem-solving process, these various models have a number of different features (Bahr & Kovaleski, 2006). Tracing the development of different models over the years, increasing sophistication and differentiation can be seen, with different specialists, assessment procedures, and modes of intervention being added to the basic TAT model, in which teachers consulted with peers in a generally qualitative manner. Consequently, it is difficult and perhaps erroneous to draw general conclusions about their overall effectiveness. One attempt to discern overall effects was the meta-analysis conducted by Burns and Symington (2002). Identifying a small number of qualifying studies of prereferral intervention teams, these researchers found significant effect sizes for a number of dependent variables, including teacher ratings and observed behavior. A particularly interesting aspect of this study was the greater effect sizes for university-based initiatives compared with field-based initiatives, a finding that speaks to the importance of treatment fidelity in assessing the impact of these teams. Nonetheless, given the wide diversity in program features as well as the paucity of studies that are analyzable through meta-analysis, it is perhaps more useful to examine some of the most salient of the problem-solving team models. As we review some of these early efforts, it is interesting to note the gradual evolution of personnel and procedures attendant to each approach.

Teacher Assistance Teams

As initially articulated by Chalfant et al. (1979), TATs featured teams of teachers working together to identify problems, set goals, brainstorm solutions, monitor implementation, and evaluate outcomes. Specialists and administrators were specifically not involved in these deliberations, because the TAT was conceptualized as an egalitarian process. Verbal consultation techniques were the predominant mode of problem solving. Chalfant and Pysh (1989) reported the results of these efforts in an analysis of five studies on 96 teams implementing TATs, finding that teachers using TATs rated large percentages of students as meeting their set goals. There was also some evidence reported of decreases in referrals to special education and of teachers' satisfaction with the TAT process.

Instructional Support Teams

Pennsylvania was perhaps the first state to mandate that elementary schools implement prereferral teams. The Instructional Support Team (IST) Project operated from 1990 to 1997 and succeeded in implementing ISTs in more than 1,700 schools (Kovaleski & Glew, 2006). The membership of ISTs included a team of teachers, although specialists (e.g., remedial teachers, school psychologists, counselors) were encouraged to participate. Unlike TATs, the school principal was also included as a critical team member.

Using the problem-solving process as its basic operating procedure, the IST model featured a thorough curriculum-based assessment (CBA; Gickling & Rosenfield, 1995) of the student and the establishment of an intervention in the classroom by a specially designated support teacher.

In an extensive study of Pennsylvania's statewide IST data, Hartman and Fay (1996) found that the typical IST worked with approximately 9% of the school population in a given year. The success rate of ISTs, defined as the percentage of IST-served students who were not referred for further evaluation for special education, averaged 84% each year. Referrals to special education decreased in IST schools compared with schools that had not yet implemented IST. In reviewing these data, Kovaleski and Glew (2006) expressed the opinion that referrals to special education were particularly decreased in IST schools when the process was fully utilized. In perhaps the first study that attempted to directly assess the impact of prereferral team intervention on student performance, Kovaleski, Gickling, Morrow, and Swank (1999) found that students served by ISTs improved on measures of academic learning time compared with students with similar needs in non-IST schools, but only when the IST schools implemented the process with a high degree of fidelity.

Instructional Consultation Teams

Rosenfield and Gravois's (1996) instructional consultation teams (ICTs) predated Pennsylvania's IST model and are still in operation in many schools, predominantly in the Middle Atlantic states. Like ISTs, ICTs utilize an expanded team membership and enhance the problem-solving process with the collection of CBA data and ongoing progress monitoring. The predominant difference between the two models is that ICTs feature a case management approach to teacher support. Students identified for ICT support are reviewed by the team, which assigns one of its members to consult more intensively with the classroom teacher. ISTs, on the other hand, utilize a single support teacher to provide most of this teacher consultation. ICTs also serve as an organizing structure for professional development activities in the school. Gravois and Rosenfield (2006) reported that, in addition to overall decreases in referrals to special education, schools using ICTs also showed a decrease in the disproportionate representation of minorities in special education. It is believed that this study is the first to investigate the effects of prereferral teaming on this important variable.

Creative Problem-Solving Teams

In the last 10 years, the state of Indiana has implemented Creative Problem Solving for General Education Intervention (CPS-GEI) teams in more than 239 schools (Bahr et al., 2006). These teams used a version of the problem-solving process in which brainstormed ideas were funneled through a best-practices perspective to develop interventions. Results indicated positive outcomes on a number of variables based on a satisfaction survey of CPS-GEI team members compared with members of teams that did not receive CPS-GEI training.

MTSD MODELS

The precursor models that have been described were pioneering efforts that generally produced beneficial effects on a number of critical variables. Although each of these models included procedures and structures that are often components of MTSD systems, those features are typically found only at Tier 2 of contemporary models (Kovaleski, 2007). Since these models were initiated in the 1990s, a number of research-based procedures and other promising practices have been articulated as essential aspects of a fully formed MTSD system. The two most salient of these practices are the use of universal screening and its analysis as a method of improving implementation of research-based core curricula in Tier 1 and the use of "standard protocol" interventions as the primary method of intervening with students at Tiers 2 and 3.

The advent of large-scale academic screening measures designed for use at periodic intervals throughout the school year has revolutionized the way in which schools gather information and make decisions about students' responses to the general curriculum and instructional program. Instruments such as the Dynamic Indicators of Basic Early Literacy Skills (DIBELS; Good & Kaminski, 2005), AIMSweb (Shin & Shinn, 2002), 4Sight (Slavin & Madden, 2006), STAR Early Literacy (Renaissance Learning Inc., 2008a), STAR Literacy (Renaissance Learning Inc., 2008b), and STAR Mathematics (Renaissance Learning Inc., 2008c) have allowed schools to collect data on important literacy and numeracy skills for all of their students in an efficient manner. By assessing students approximately three times per year, schools can identify which students are in need of further supports beyond Tier 1. Shapiro and his colleagues (Shapiro, Kellar, Lutz, Santoro, & Hintze, 2006; Shapiro, Solari, & Petscher, 2008) have demonstrated that these types of measures, both individually and in tandem (e.g., DIBELS and 4Sight), are highly predictive of student performance on state basic skills tests.

In addition to their use in identifying students in need of further intervention, Kovaleski and Pedersen (2008) have articulated procedures by which data analysis teams can assist teachers in making improvements to the overall instructional program at Tier 1. The schoolwide application of universal screening, particularly the use of problem-solving teaming to improve instruction at Tier 1, represents a significant advancement beyond the problem-solving team format embodied in the precursor models. In essence, these procedures have operationalized unique features of the first tier of an MTSD system. Historically, problem-solving teams in the precursor models utilized the problem-solving process to customize individualized interventions for students who were experiencing particular performance deficits (cf. Tucker & Sornson, 2007). Although this function has been carried forward in most MTSD systems, a critical difference is that Tier 1 data analysis teams in MTSD systems examine group data to make classwide changes to instructional procedures and to identify interventions for groups of students at Tier 2.

The second critical feature that differentiates the precursor models from many of the current comprehensive MTSD systems is the use of standard protocol interventions at Tiers 2 and 3. As conceptualized by Fuchs, Mock, Morgan, and Young (2003), these interventions feature the "use of the same empirically validated treatment for all children with similar problems in a given domain" (p. 166). In contrast to the individualized student-by-student approach in which interventions are selected or created by a problem-solving team, standard protocol interventions are intended to be implemented with a very high degree of fidelity with groups of students based on similar assessment results. These interventions are typically commercially produced. The rationale behind the use of standardized approaches to intervention was captured well by Reyna (2004), who noted that "despite the intuitive appeal of the familiar slogan 'one size does not fit all,' some educational practices are broadly effective; they can be generalized widely across contexts and populations" (p. 56). How standard protocol interventions are implemented in an MTSD system is discussed as representative projects are reviewed in the following sections.

At this point, we review those projects and initiatives that have put MTSD systems in place at an LEA, regional, or statewide level. We investigate critical program features of each model and examine any available data on outcomes.

Heartland Area Education Agency

The Heartland Area Education Agency (AEA) in Iowa has a long history of utilizing problem-solving teams to address student needs, and their pioneering efforts as a precursor to MTSD have been well documented (Ikeda, Tilly, Stumme, Volmer, & Allison, 1996; Ikeda et al., 2007; Tilly, 2003, 2008). Their efforts are included in this section because, unlike some other precursors, Heartland AEA has continued to evolve their model and presents as a fully articulated MTSD at this time. Heartland's original model was a four-level approach in which teachers expressing a concern about a student had access to consulting specialists (e.g., school psychologists) at Level II before proceeding to extended consultation with a problem-solving team, an approach similar to that described by Graden, Casey, and Christenson (1985). Recently, however, Heartland has moved from a four-level approach to a three-tier model. In describing this transition, Tilly (2003) explained the need to move from an individualized approach to one that addresses the needs of more students. At Level 1, learning problems of groups of students are identified through universal screening using DIBELS, and students' needs are addressed through modification of the core instructional curriculum. At Level 2, supplemental instructional resources are added to core instruction. Level 3 consists of intense services provided to individual students. Throughout these three levels, Heartland has maintained the problem-solving process as its central operating method. They have also incorporated data-based progress monitoring procedures, implemented curriculum-based evaluation (Howell & Nolet, 2000) to inform decision making at later levels, and infused their selection of strategies with research-based practices. Results of these changes have indicated decreases in special education placements over an 8-year period in 36 schools (Tilly, 2003). Significantly, however, in addition to this traditionally used measure of effectiveness, Heartland has also begun to investigate the effects of its MTSD model on overall performance in general education, finding that students in 121 implementing schools increased their overall proficiency rates on three DIBELS measures over a 4-year period.

Florida's Problem-Solving/RTI Model

Florida's Problem-Solving/RTI model (Batsche, Curtis, Dorman, Castillo, & Porter, 2007; Florida Department of Education, 2006) is a good example of a statewide approach to scaling up an MTSD model that features RTI. Three salient aspects characterize Florida's approach (1) the project is embedded in the general education program, (2) the model is based on a series of earlier statewide initiatives, and (3) the project is being initiated in a small number of pilot schools. The Florida model is a three-tier framework: In Tier 1, schools are encouraged to use evidence-based practices based on scientifically supported curricula in the general classroom; in Tier 2, a problem-solving team forms and orchestrates more intensive interventions that are supplemental to core instruction and are implemented over a short period of time in small groups; in Tier 3, more long-term interventions are individualized by the problem-solving team and may lead to or include special education. The suggested amount of time allocated for Tier 2 and 3 interventions ranges from 15 to 30 weeks. Florida has also required that all kindergarten students be screened with DIBELS, and that progress monitoring be conducted using CBM and DIBELS in all Reading

First schools. Like the Heartland model, the central operating procedure is problem solving; however, there is some indication that standard protocol interventions (although not identified by that term) are encouraged in that interventions are intended to be "scripted or very structured ... with a high probability of producing change for most at-risk students" (Florida Department of Education, 2006, p. 4). Significantly, the Florida project also includes screening and intervention in regards to student behavior as well as academics. To date, Florida's pilot project has been implemented in 18 schools in three school districts. Results of the project have yet to be published.

Ohio Integrated Systems Model

Like Heartland AEA, the Ohio Integrated Systems Model (OISM) has evolved from a problem-solving team structure into a full MTSD system (Graden, Stollar, & Poth, 2007). Historically, Ohio utilized an intervention assistance team (IAT) model, which was based on the work of Graden, Casey, and Christenson (1985) and had much in common with the original Heartland model. In developing the OISM, Ohio harvested a number of state initiatives to add to its foundation in IATs, including a large pilot program involving intervention-based assessment in the 1990s. The OISM appears to have a strong basis in general education and links with the state's efforts at schoolwide improvement and accountability. It features a three-tier model that integrates both behavior and academics. Tier 1 of the OISM includes research-based core instruction with the goal of improving overall rates of literacy and appropriate student behavior. All students are screened for both academics (typically with DIBELS) and behavior (using office discipline referrals). In Tier 2, targeted interventions are added for those students displaying difficulty with the core program. These interventions are crafted by a problem-solving team that analyzes needs of groups of students and plans for supplemental small-group instruction. Frequent progress monitoring conducted at Tier 2 provides the team with feedback on the success of the interventions and targets students needing more extensive supports at Tier 3. At this stage, the problem-solving team designs intensive, individualized supports that supplement the student's continued involvement in the core instruction. Both Tiers 2 and 3 are general education programs and lead to consideration for special education only if the student fails to respond to these intensive interventions. In addition to these features, the OISM also incorporates efforts to use culturally responsive practices. Graden et al. (2007) report that OISM is being implemented in more than 300 schools on a voluntary basis, although there are clear indications that a full statewide scaling-up is being planned. At this time, no results of this program have been published.

Pennsylvania's RTI Model

Although the Commonwealth of Pennsylvania pioneered the IST model in the 1990s, their recent effort in developing a comprehensive MTSD has taken a different direction and is only indirectly connected to the IST model. The Pennsylvania model features three tiers, all within general education (Shapiro & Kovaleski, 2008). Tier 1 includes the provision of standards-aligned curricula and universal screening of reading using either DIBELS or AIMSweb at early grades and 4Sight in intermediate and middle grades. (Some schools are also screening for math skills using AIMSweb, 4Sight, or other instruments.) Grade-level data analysis teams are utilized at Tier 1 to analyze universal screening data for the purpose of assisting Tier 1 instruction for all students. In Tiers 2 and 3, standard protocol interventions are implemented, typically during extra periods of supplemental "tier time." Data analysis teams match these interventions to students' needs as indicated by universal screening data as well as progress monitoring, which occurs twice per month at Tier 2 and weekly at Tier 3. Procedures typically associated with the problem-solving approach are utilized at Tier 3 if standard protocol interventions fail to produce the desired outcomes. Eligibility for special education is considered if a student at Tier 3 fails to make acceptable progress. Although Pennsylvania's RTI model has been piloted in seven elementary schools, numerous other schools throughout the state have received local or regional training and are implementing the model according to state guidelines. Preliminary results have indicated increases in the number of students reaching proficiency and more students moving from more intensive to less intensive services compared with less intensive to more intensive services (Shapiro & Kovaleski, 2008).

Illinois Flexible Service Delivery Model

Since 1994, a group of 19 school districts comprising the Northern Suburban Special Education District (NSSED) has implemented the Flexible Service Delivery System (FSDS; Peterson, Prasse, Shinn, & Swerdlik, 2007). Originally based on the Iowa (i.e., Heartland AEA) problem-solving model, the FSDS has evolved into a three-tier model based on the NASDSE framework (Batsche et al., 2005). Similar to other models, Tier 1 in the FSDS model consists of the provision of research-based curricula and instruction in general education, and in Tier 2 selected interventions are provided to students who struggle in the general education program. Tier 3 consists of intensive interventions that are typically provided through special education. Here again, problem solving serves as the organizing principle embedded in a team structure. Universal screening (typically through DIBELS) and progress monitoring using CBM are essential aspects of the model.

The Illinois group has designed an extensive program evaluation component to assess the outcomes of FSDS. Results of a survey of both parents and education staff have indicated that respondents are satisfied with the implementation of FSDS (Peterson et al., 2007). Parents attended 91% of FSDS problem-solving meetings, and a great majority of those parents indicated that they had a better understanding of their children's needs and the process facilitated their children's success in school. Surveyed school personnel also gave the opinion that students served by the FSDS system improved academically and behaviorally. A review of individual case files indicated that 75% of the goals for students served were met, exceeded, or showed some improvement in performance. During the years of the program evaluation, referrals for special education eligibility remained stable, although the authors reported a decreasing trend in initial evaluations. The NSSED group also reported some interesting data about the three-tier process, noting that an average FSDS intervention took approximately 24 days. In addition, almost half (48%) of the interventions were conducted by the classroom teacher, with smaller percentages (6–17%) being conducted by special education teachers, reading improvement teachers, teacher assistants, and related services personnel.

Idaho Results-Based Model

Another statewide MTSD project is the Idaho Results-Based Model (RBM; Callender, 2007). As of 2005, 150 elementary and secondary schools had implemented this model, representing 40% of all districts within the state. RBM is a systems-level, proactive, preventive approach that makes use of standard protocol interventions. Level I/Tier I of this model consists of basic/general education for all students in the school. Level II/Tier II, which consists of standard protocol treatments delivered via small-group intensive instruction by general education, Title I, and special education teachers, is available to all students as needed. Level III/Tier III consists of targeted individual interventions conducted by general education, Title I, and special education teachers. Level IV/Tier IV consists of special education programming and an individual education plan and essentially entails intensive, long-term services.

Idaho's RBM incorporates several key elements, including formative system evaluation, early identification of problems, and evaluation of a problem's context. When schoolwide programs are not effective, problem-solving teams are used to create a student intervention plan (I-plan) for student problems. The RBM utilizes a modified version of Bransford and Stein's (1984) IDEAL model of problem solving. Teams of four to eight people meet weekly, and the student's I-plan and progress are examined over a 9- to 27-week period. Functional assessment is used to enhance problem analysis and to "identify specific skill deficits for instructional purposes/ identifying appropriate programming" (Callender, 2007, p. 334), with the goal of matching students' skills to their prescribed interventions. Teams emphasize outcome-oriented interventions by establishing a list of research-based, standard protocol programs available for each grade level and for specific areas of concern. Progress monitoring data are collected at the benchmark (universal screening assessment, Level I), strategic (assessment every 3–4 weeks, Level II), and intensive levels (assessment two times per month, Level III). Parents are actively involved in the process, participating in team problem solving and home-based interventions. Finally, schools use a dual-discrepancy approach for determining eligibility for special education. Eligibility requirements include discrepancy from peers, multiple indicators, response to intervention, and the need for specially designed instruction.

To evaluate the Idaho RBM, special education information from schools participating and not participating in the model was collected and analyzed. Between fall of the 2002–2003 and fall of the 2004–2005 school years, enrollment in statewide special education increased by 1%. Districts with at least one RBM school (most districts had more than one school) demonstrated a 3% decrease in special education placements, with RBM reportedly accounting for the majority of the decrease. Furthermore, the reading skills of 1,400 students in kindergarten to grade 3 improved, and those students in RBM schools with intervention plans progressed significantly more than those in schools without intervention plans (effect size of 1.10; Callender, 2007). It was also reported that practitioners' knowledge, skills, and perceptions of the problem-solving teams increased from 26 to 90% from pre- to post-assessments. In addition, there was a high degree of satisfaction in first-year schools implementing RBM because of a decrease in students "falling between the cracks" (p. 340). Finally, Callender reported that neither problem-solving teams nor standard protocol interventions alone addressed the needs of all the students in schools.

RTI in Minnesota

Although there have been no published reports of a statewide initiative for RTI, a number of school districts in Minnesota have reported on efforts to implement MTSD systems. Four models from this state are discussed: Minneapolis Public Schools, the St. Croix River Education District, the Chisago Lakes School District, and the East Central School District.

The Minneapolis Public Schools implemented a four-step problem-solving model (PSM), including defining the problem; selecting and implementing an intervention; monitoring the student's progress and response to intervention through the use of CBM, district assessment, and state assessment data; and repeating the sequence if the child is not making progress

(Marston, Lau, & Muyskens, 2007). Teachers in the district developed a manual outlining an introduction to CBM, administration guidelines and probes, as well as district norms and comparisons of these data with state-wide assessment data. These steps were implemented through three stages. Stage 1 of the PSM is classroom interventions, in which classroom teachers are asked to define the difficulties of the student, collect baseline data, choose an intervention, and document the results. In Stage 2, the PSM team puts in place high-quality, research-based interventions and reviews data 6 to 8 weeks after the intervention begins. Teams are typically composed of the regular education teacher, a social worker, a school psychologist, a special education teacher, an administrator, and other specialists as needed. During Stage 3, the focus is on an evaluation of the need for special education services. Students receive intensive interventions, which may be so successful that special education services are not warranted. In this case, a child is identified as a student needing alternative programming (SNAP). If not, Stage 3 involves an evaluation for special education, which includes the progress monitoring data collected during the MTSD process.

Marston et al. (2007) reported that using PSM did not significantly reduce the prevalence of students with high-incidence disabilities, nor did it reduce the number of students identified with learning disabilities or mild mental retardation. However, disability terms were replaced with SNAP categorization. On the other hand, students participating in the PSM showed higher achievement levels than those in the traditional setting. Furthermore, students participating in the PSM were provided with specialized interventions at a younger age than those in the traditional setting.

The St. Croix River Education District (SCRED) in Minnesota developed its MTSD model with a focus on improving reading achievement in kindergarten through eighth grade (Bollman, Silberglitt, & Gibbons, 2007). SCRED administers benchmark assessments three times per year, strategic assessments once a month, and intensive assessments once a week. Benchmark assessments are conducted with all students in general education (Tier I), strategic assessments with students who have needs beyond what can be provided in general education (Tier II), and intensive assessments with students who have needs well beyond what can be provided in general education (Tier III). Instructional changes implemented in this district's program were based on research in the area of reading and reading instruction, including the primary areas of reading skill development and how these reading skills should be taught. SCRED uses a problem-solving organization that includes (1) continued measurement of all students throughout the school year and frequent measurement of students needing strategic and intensive interventions, (2) grade-level team meetings consisting of grade-level teachers who meet to review student achievement at least once per month, (3) grade-level scheduling so that basic skill instruction is commonly scheduled, making small-group instruction more easily planned, (4) flexible grouping in which students are grouped together according to achievement levels, with movement between groups dependent on student progress, and (5) concentrated resources to support reading for specific grade levels at the same time each day. In SCRED schools there is one problem-solving team per building, which meets once a week to assist grade-level teams with student difficulties and intervention design.

Bollman et al. (2007) noted several outcomes of the SCRED program based on CBM data collected by all five districts in SCRED since 1996. First, the percentage of students meeting benchmark scores for CBM in reading increased from 35% (over the past decade) to 68%. Second, in grades 1 through 6, the 10th percentile scores of reading CBMs were raised in each grade level. Third, the percentage of students reaching grade-level standards on the statewide test grew from 51% in 1998 to 80% in 2005. Fourth, the number of students performing at the lowest level on the Minnesota state test declined from greater than 20% in 1998 to 6% in 2005. Fifth, SCRED had fewer students scoring at the lowest achievement level on the Minnesota Comprehensive Assessment-Reading than students in the state of Minnesota as a whole. Sixth, according to the authors, "the [learning disability] rate at SCRED has dropped dramatically over the past decade, by more than 40%" (p. 326). Finally, SCRED had the lowest incidence of students with specific learning disabilities in the state.

Windram, Scierka, and Silberglitt (2007) outlined two model MTSD programs in Minnesota that targeted secondary students. Although these two models are not full MTSD systems, they are included here because they represent a rare report of implementation of MTSDs at the secondary level. Chisago Lakes School District has developed a five-step problem-solving model through its student assistance teams. To fit in the 15- to 30-minute interventions that student assistance teams often recommend, students are assigned an 85-minute study hall through block scheduling. The primary overall strategy suggested was cooperative learning, although no specific interventions were noted. An RTI English class was also created to help improve the basic reading and writing skills of struggling students, based on a review of their assessment data. These interventions are dubbed Tier 2 interventions and include the core ninth-grade curriculum taught at a slower pace to meet the needs of the learners. Each day 30 to 40 minutes of the block period focuses on individual/group reading or writing tasks. Reading assessment data are collected weekly and writing assessment data twice per month.

Results of this model were based on the data of the 18 students who participated in the intervention and were compared with their own previous performance. They indicated that 12 of the 18 students participating in the RTI English class passed the Minnesota Basic Skills Test in reading,

11 students were at or above the eighth-grade reading fluency benchmark, eight students were at or above the eighth-grade writing fluency benchmark, eight students approached or met the Measures of Academic Progress (MAP) benchmark for ninth-grade spring students, and 14 students showed overall improvement in their MAP scores (Windram et al., 2007). In addition, students demonstrated a growth of 1.01 words per minute each week in reading fluency.

The second model described by Windram et al. (2007) was implemented in East Central School District in rural Minnesota. Sixteen students who scored below a cutoff score on the MAP in math opted to attend a math resource class (Tier 2) in lieu of an elective class or physical education. The curriculum was based on the MAP Learning Continuum, which identifies areas where students are struggling. Outcome data, gathered from the 16 students who participated in the intervention, indicated that students in the math RTI program achieved twice as much growth as typically observed in eighth-grade students. Nine of the 16 students made significant gains over the 5-month period, although they did not reach the target score, and four students did not make significant growth.

System to Enhance Educational Performance

Witt and VanDerHeyden and their colleagues have collaborated with a number of school districts in Louisiana, Arizona, and other states in developing their System to Enhance Educational Performance (STEEP) model (VanDer-Heyden, Witt, & Gilbertson, 2007; Witt & VanDerHeyden, 2007). They describe STEEP as a hybrid three-tier model that incorporates standard protocol interventions within a problem-solving process. STEEP utilizes CBM for universal screening to address classwide problems and to identify individual students with academic deficiencies. Based on their previous research concerning the questionable validity of teacher referrals (VanDerHeyden, Witt, & Naquin, 2003), STEEP incorporates a number of procedures to validate students' academic problems. Included in this process is a "can't do–won't do" assessment, which distinguishes between students whose difficulties are skill based or performance based. Specific procedures are incorporated to assess intervention fidelity throughout the process. Progress monitoring is conducted using CBM.

The developers of STEEP have conducted a number of research studies to evaluate the model. VanDerHeyden et al. (2003) found that teachers became more accurate in their referrals for assistance when using STEEP procedures. VanDerHeyden and Burns (2005) observed significant gains in mathematics for at-risk students using STEEP as well as improved large-group test scores. In five STEEP school districts in the southwestern United States, VanDerHeyden et al. (2007) reported decreased referrals for evaluation for special education and higher percentages of students identified as eligible in schools using the STEEP process. In a particularly interesting study involving minority students, VanDerHeyden and Witt (2005) found that although minority students were disproportionately identified as low achievers, almost half significantly improved their academic performance based on individual STEEP interventions.

The Michigan Model

The Michigan statewide program (Ervin, Schaughency, Goodman, McGlinchey, & Matthews, 2007) is a data-driven problem-solving approach for improving reading and behavior through multiple levels of intervention. The levels of intervention include (1) all students in a school (Tier 1), (2) selected groups of students displaying some difficulties (Tier 2), and (3) students experiencing significant difficulties (Tier 3). Prevention is aimed at reducing antisocial behavior and illiteracy. The model includes an explicit focus on student outcomes, the selection and implementation of evidence-based practices, ongoing collection and use of local performance data to guide decision making, and a focus on the development of systems to support and sustain practice. No data were available on the effectiveness of this model.

Common Features of MTSD Models

In summary, across the reviewed MTSD models, the following features appear to be most common: a three-tier system of instructional supports, universal screening, progress monitoring, CBM, research-based core curricula and supplemental interventions, and problem-solving teams. Less often discussed was the utilization of standard protocol interventions, although these types of interventions will likely be implemented more frequently because of an increase in the number of studies demonstrating their effectiveness. Individual features infrequently cited, although important to consider, are the inclusion of behavior interventions and culturally responsive practices. However, more research is needed regarding the effectiveness of these components for any of them to be included among the salient features most widely comprising a MTSD model. Finally, two models indicated that they were specifically designed for at-risk secondary students. At this time, the dearth of research in this area prevents any conclusions about salient features specific to secondary MTSD models.

OUTCOMES OF PRECURSOR AND MTSD MODELS

Throughout the history of both the precursor team-based approaches to providing support to teachers and the contemporary MTSD models, researchers and model developers have endeavored to appraise the effects of these initiatives. These research studies and program evaluations have varied in the outcome variables investigated and in the rigor of their research designs. In this section, we review those outcomes as they have been put forth to this point. It should be noted that this review will not be exhaustive of all variables or published studies. For example, we do not review results of studies that evaluated the effects of various components of MTSD models (e.g., specific standard protocol interventions) in an experimental setting. Rather, we report only on outcomes associated directly with implementation efforts regarding the precursor or MTSD models. As an aid to tracking the extant research efforts, Table 3.1 includes the types of outcome variables that have been studied by the various precursor and current MTSD models. Following this review, we analyze the state of the research in this area, which will lead us to a consideration of future research efforts.

Special Education Referrals and Placements

Arguably the most frequently assessed outcome of both precursor approaches and MTSD approaches has been the numbers of students referred for evaluation for or placed in special education. The popularity of this measure reflects the historic concern with overidentification of specific learning disability (SLD), which has served as a salient rationale for the development of these approaches (Chalfant et al., 1979; Graden, Casey, & Christenson, 1985; Fuchs, Fuchs, & Bahr, 1990; Kovaleski, Tucker, & Stevens, 1996).

As indicated in Table 3.1, studies of the impact of precursor models reported decreases in referrals for evaluation or identification of students eligible for special education for child study teams (Graden, Casey, & Bonstrom, 1985), TATs (Chalfant & Pysh, 1989), ICTs (Gravois & Rosenfield, 2006), and ISTs (Hartman & Fay, 1996; Kovaleski & Glew, 2006). In regard to MTSD models, decreases in special education identification have been reported in Iowa (Tilly, 2003), Idaho (Callender, 2007), and SCRED in Minnesota (Bollman et al., 2007) and by the developers of STEEP in the southwestern United States (VanDerHeyden & Witt, 2005; VanDerHeyden et al., 2007). In Illinois, Peterson et al. (2007) reported that the FSDS had decreased initial evaluations, although the number of students identified as eligible for special education remained essentially the same, whereas the Minneapolis group did not report increases in the number of students identified with high-incidence disabilities after their model was initiated (Marston, Muyskens, Lau, & Canter, 2003; Marston et al., 2007).

A related metric (see Table 3.1) is the percentage of students receiving the support of problem-solving teams who are not referred for evaluation. In this regard, Chalfant et al. (1989) reported a "success rate" of 79% for TATs, and Kovaleski and Glew (2006) reported a figure of 84% for ISTs,

TABLE 3.1. Dependent Outcome Variables Included in Research on Various Precursor and MTSD Models

Precursors	Special education identification	Success rate	Minority overrepresentation	Goals attained	Academic performance (individual)	Academic performance (school)	Teacher satisfaction	Information reprocess
ICTs	X		X					
ISTs	X	X			X			
TATs	X	X		X			X	
MTSD models								
Chisago Lakes					X			
East Central					X			
Heartland	X					X		
Idaho RBM	X			X		X	X	X
Illinois FSDS	X						X	X
Minneapolis	X				X			
Pennsylvania						X		X
SCRED	X					X		
STEEP	X		X	X				

Note. MTSD, multi-tier service delivery; ICTs, instructional consultation teams; ISTs, instructional support teams; TATs, teacher assistance teams; RBM, results-based model; FSDS, flexible service delivery system; SCRED, St. Croix River Education District; STEEP, system to enhance educational performance.

implying that the majority of students served by these models were successful in general education.

A related and important question is the impact of these support models on the overrepresentation of minority students in special education, which has been an intractable problem in many locations for decades, especially in urban areas (Donovan & Cross, 2002; Reschly, 1988). To date, two published studies have addressed disproportionality as a dependent variable (see Table 3.1). As indicated earlier, VanDerHeyden and Witt (2005) found that minority students were disproportionately identified as low achievers on universal screening but were nonetheless able to make significant progress when individualized interventions were developed using STEEP procedures. Gravois and Rosenfield (2006), in their study of ICTs in Maryland, found that disproportionality decreased in schools that implemented ICTs. The ICT results are indeed promising, especially because they were achieved without benefit of the other potentially robust aspects of full MTSD models.

Academic Improvement of Students Served by the Model

Decreases in referrals to special education are a meaningful outcome of the implementation of supportive services only if the students who are not being referred for evaluation are making meaningful progress in the general education program (Vaughn & Fuchs, 2006). Otherwise, these models could be accused of organizationally inhibiting referrals for evaluation even though the students are failing. Consequently, some developers have analyzed the performance of students who receive the support provided by these structures.

As indicated in Table 3.1, a number of models have attempted to track students' performance during the time that they were supported by problem-solving teams or MTSD structures. Chalfant and Pysh (1989) and Peterson et al. (2007) reported that large percentages of students undergoing TAT and FSDS supports met, exceeded, or showed some progress in meeting goals set by their teams. Kovaleski et al. (1999) found that students supported through ISTs had enhanced gains on measures of academic learning time (consisting of time on task, task completion, and task comprehension) compared with similar students in schools that had not implemented ISTs, but only if the level of IST implementation was very high. Marston et al. (2007) reported enhanced achievement on direct measures of academic performance for students in Minneapolis's PSM approach than for students in the traditional setting. Windram et al. (2007) reported academic gains in their two secondary implementation sites, with students displaying progress on measures of reading and writing fluency as well as increased scores on statewide tests.

Performance Gains for All Students on a Schoolwide Basis

RTI and the MTSD structures that support it not only have been conceptualized as providing support for students who are at risk for school failure but also have been premised on the notion that these structures can facilitate the acquisition and maintenance of enhanced academic performance for all students (Batsche et al., 2005). With the advent of No Child Left Behind (NCLB), school reform structures are now expected to produce marked increases in student skills so that schools can meet their adequate yearly progress benchmarks (Kovaleski, 2007; Kovaleski & Glew, 2006). Consequently, metrics such as overall percentages of students scoring in the proficient range on large-scale statewide tests have superseded earlier and more modest targets such as decreases in referrals to special education or improved performance of students provided with essentially Tier 2 or 3 interventions. As indicated in Table 3.1, this level of program evaluation can be found in reference to a number of the contemporary MTSD models (and are noticeably absent in reports of the precursor models).

Heartland's data are particularly encouraging in this regard, as Tilly (2003) reported increases in overall performance on DIBELS measures for all students in 121 schools in Iowa over a 4-year period. Similarly, Callender (2007) reported that students in grades K–3 in Idaho's RBM schools showed significantly greater overall improvement in reading skills than students whose schools had not implemented the model. Shapiro and Kovaleski (2008), working in seven pilot RTI schools in Pennsylvania, reported increases in DIBELS and 4Sight scores in most grade levels on a K–5 basis, especially when implementation rates were high. In individual school districts, SCRED in Minnesota has done an exemplary program evaluation of their efforts, finding that schools using their MTSD model showed overall increases in performance on reading CBM and statewide tests as well as decreases in the number of students scoring at the lowest levels of the state tests (Bollman et al., 2007).

Teacher Satisfaction

A long-standing measure regarding problem-solving teams has been the extent to which teachers approved of the process and found their skills to be enhanced as a result of team-based support. As indicated in Table 3.1, positive appraisals by participants have been recorded for TATs (Chalfant & Pysh, 1989; Kruger, Struzziero, Watts, & Vacca, 1995) and for problem-solving teams (Myles, Simpson, & Ormsbee, 1996). In regard to participants' perceptions of MTSD models, Callender (2007) reported a high degree of satisfaction among members of problem-solving teams in Idaho's

RBM model, and Peterson et al. (2007) obtained similar reports from both staff and parents who were involved with the FSDS in Illinois.

Information about the MTSD Process

In addition to data about student attainments and overall perceptions of the effectiveness of various models, there has long been considerable interest regarding the nature of the MTSD process, especially as it relates to RTI issues. Many specific details about MTSD models have yet to be elucidated and are covered in the next section on future research directions. However, some initial information about the structures is beginning to emerge (see Table 3.1).

Peterson et al. (2007) have reported that a typical FSDS intervention was conducted for 24 days, and approximately half of those were conducted by the classroom teachers. Specialists (e.g., special education teachers, reading teachers, related services personnel, teacher assistants) accounted for smaller percentages of persons identified as interventionists. At least a few reports (Marston et al., 2007; Shapiro & Kovaleski, 2008) have confirmed the expectation that students would be provided with specialized interventions at a younger age than under traditional models, largely because of the emphasis on intervening early in the primary grades. Shapiro and Kovaleski also tracked students moving from tier to tier, finding that more students moved from more intensive to less intensive tiers than vice versa. Although these researchers reported substantial student progress using a standard protocol model, Callender (2007) argued that the experience in Idaho indicated that a combination of standard protocol interventions and individualized strategies crafted by problem-solving teams was more effective in meeting the needs of all students.

Status of the Existing Research

From this review, it is clear that there is a good deal of published evidence regarding the impact of both precursor models and currently implemented MTSD approaches on a number of variables related to the performance of individual students undergoing support as well as to larger systemic outcomes (e.g., overall proficiency levels of students in schools using the process, referrals to special education). Almost all of this evidence is encouraging. Nonetheless, it must be acknowledged that all of this evidence is based on program evaluation rather than research per se. That is, the extant literature on MTSD models can be characterized as post hoc evaluations of applied programs that have been implemented on a local, regional, or statewide basis. None of this evidence conforms to the hallmarks of rigorous scientific research as articulated by the Coalition for Evidence-Based Policy

(CEBP; 2003), which would include such factors as randomized controlled trials, comparisons of closely matched comparison or control groups, double-blind studies, and reports of intervention effect sizes. That is not to say that the models' components are not based on rigorous research. Indeed, common MTSD features such as CBM, progress monitoring, and various standard protocol interventions have been vigorously investigated for more than 30 years and would be indicative of what the CEBP would identify as strong research support. Rather, it is when these components are coalesced into models that the research becomes (perhaps unavoidably) less rigorous. Consequently, these extant evaluations of various MTSD models would be more appropriately characterized as promising or "possible" in CEBP terminology.

The nature of evaluating multifaceted models such as MTSD presents a unique research conundrum. On the one hand, it is difficult to utilize standards of rigorous research such as randomized assignment with treatment and control groups in applied settings, because few schools that have none of the program features of MTSD exist. Consequently, the best that can be expected is for program developers and researchers to organize very robust, scientifically based components into applied models and determine the effects of those models. However, once a multifaceted model has been implemented, it is difficult to determine which aspects of the model are individually or collectively causal in producing the desired effects (e.g., on student achievement). This dilemma is further exacerbated by the fact that the model does not operate in isolation of the existing school milieu, which includes variability in such factors as curriculum, training of teachers, and so on. Some thoughts about how researchers can come to some coherence in the face of these challenges are presented in the next section.

FURTHER RESEARCH DIRECTIONS

In spite of the challenges of doing rigorous research in this area, a number of specific questions can be posed about the MTSD process itself and its outcomes on students and schools. These questions will require extensive research efforts, which can be conceptualized in regard to the overall effects of MTSD models and which aspects of these models are critical in realizing desired outcomes.

Effects of MTSD Models on Student Performance

When considering the need for further research, it is perhaps best to start with questions that pertain to the fundamental rationales that are the basis for the widespread promulgation of RTI. First, it must be asked whether

MTSD models help schools improve the performance of individual students who receive these supports. Shapiro and Clemens (2009) proposed a series of program evaluation procedures that can be used to address these questions, including examining whether students are appropriately placed in tiers as a result of universal screening, the extent of students' movement between tiers, the extent of students' rates of improvement (ROIs), and whether students are appropriately referred for special education services. Generally, if MTSD models are effective, one should see improved accuracy in identifying tiered supports for individual students, greater movement from more intensive to less intensive supports than vice versa, improvements in students' ROIs after the provision of intensive interventions, high percentages of students identified as eligible for special education after undergoing multiple tiers of support, and potentially fewer students identified with high-incidence disabilities. One would also expect to find that the performance of students identified as having SLDs using RTI procedures should conform to the dual-discrepancy parameters in which deficiencies are determined in level of achievement and ROI in response to intensive interventions (Fuchs & Fuchs, 1998). In essence, the research questions here are involved with whether scaled-up MTSD models are effective in realizing the type of outcomes that have been evidenced in clinical and experimental studies.

Closely related to these questions about the effects of MTSD models on the performance of individual students is the impact of these models on schoolwide academic indicators. As discussed previously, MTSD models have been "sold" not only as structures to address the needs of at-risk students but also as vehicles for overall school improvement. Consequently, further studies on the extent to which MTSD models increase overall proficiency levels will need to be conducted. It is encouraging that some program developers have already included these measures as part of their program evaluation efforts. It is important to note here that increases in overall proficiency levels cannot be assumed to be directly related to decreased numbers of students in high-incidence disability categories such as SLD. That is, decreasing numbers of SLD students by creating success for students in Tiers 2 and 3 may not increase the overall proficiency levels of all students. Research regarding the effectiveness of Tier 1 efforts will also be needed to ensure that MTSD models in their entirety are producing the desired outcomes. Further, research regarding the extent to which these models also produce improvements in domains beyond reading (e.g., mathematics, behavior) is also needed. No one study of program outcomes is likely to lead to direct inferences about causality because of the limitations in such research as described previously. However, if MTSD models that share common features produce consistent results in the expected directions, reasonable conclusions about the effectiveness of such models may be reached, assuming that treatment fidelity of the delivery of the models is adequate (see later discussion).

Discerning Critical Aspects of MTSD Models

In the nearly three decades of implementation of precursor models and MTSD, there are no studies pertaining to which components of either problem-solving teams or MTSD models are essential in producing desired outcomes, in spite of the plethora of speculations about the relative importance of these program features (Burns, Wiley, & Viglietta, 2008; Kovaleski, 2002). Local practitioners might well wonder which of the many articulated components must be included in local implementation and in which order of initiation. Conversely, might some features be superfluous? A number of research lines can be conceptualized to address these questions.

Tier 1 Programs

At Tier 1, are there differential outcomes associated with the use of various curricular materials? If schools are to realize the goal of bringing 80% of their students to proficiency on the basis of Tier 1 alone (Batsche et al., 2005), it will be critical to provide teachers with highly robust curricular tools and sufficient training to use these tools at a high degree of fidelity. There are an increasing number of Internet sites by organizations such as the Florida Center for Reading Research and University of Oregon that provide guides to consumers regarding the extent to which various curriculum packages line up with the "big ideas" in reading. However, actual outcomes studies of the use of these materials across multiple school districts have not yet been undertaken. It is also not known whether various curriculum packages work better in different communities depending on different demographics. Studies that investigate the effects of newly implemented curriculum materials (e.g., reading series) as contrasted with outcomes realized with previously used materials could be conducted. If certain curriculum packages reliably produced gains across implementation sites, increased confidence in the effectiveness of these packages can be realized.

Interventions at Tiers 2 and 3

A similar issue pertains to intervention packages used at Tiers 2 and 3. There is a growing body of research that has examined the effectiveness of individual interventions in raising the achievement of low-performing students. The initial studies in this line of research have been conducted in applied settings but not within the context of full MTSD structures (e.g., Vaughn, Linan-Thompson, & Hickman, 2003; Velluntino et al., 1996). Vaughn, Wanzek, Woodruff, and Linan-Thompson (2007) reported on a study of individual interventions that was conducted within a three-tier model. Continued research in both of these formats is needed. First, tightly controlled studies using random assignment of subjects to treatments will continue to be needed as new intervention packages are developed. Second, applied studies of the efficacy of these packages when implemented in actual schools that are using MTSD should also be conducted. Finally, it is also unknown as to whether certain combinations of core curricular resources and particular intervention packages produce better outcomes than other combinations. It seems reasonable to hypothesize that combinations that have better coherence between various interventions (e.g., parallel language, instructional procedures) would be less confusing for teachers and students and lead to superior results. However, this hypothesis has been untested to date.

The Effects of Teaming

As indicated earlier, the problem-solving process has been conceptualized as the central modus operandi of MTSD (Batsche et al., 2005) and in some cases is believed to be synonymous with RTI. However, as Kovaleski and Glew (2006) have noted, problem-solving teaming is likely to look different in full MTSD models than it has previously. Three different uses of problem-solving teaming can be imagined within MTSD: First, data analysis teams, consisting of teams of teachers from the same grade level along with the principal and specialists, analyze universal screening data to plan instruction to raise the proficiency of all students and to identify students needing additional supports at Tiers 2 and 3 (Kovaleski & Pedersen, 2008). Next, traditional problem-solving teams work to customize interventions for students in Tiers 2 and 3 based on data from individual assessments and progress monitoring. A third type of team that can be conceptualized within an MTSD model is a building-level organizing group that analyzes trends in data (universal screening, state testing) to evaluate program efforts and to plan for deployment of school resources. There is little, if any, research on how these teams work, either singly or in combination. Further, which components of their operation (e.g., membership, meeting schedule) are critical to their effectiveness has yet to be investigated. Finally, the extent to which interventions need to be customized by problem-solving teams may be called into question, because many contemporary MTSD models (e.g., Pennsylvania) identify groups of students for standard protocol interventions instead of problem solving for individual students.

Assessment in MTSD

Fuchs and Fuchs (2007) noted that there are three functions of assessment in an MTSD system: screening, progress monitoring, and instructional planning. Although these authors propose that CBM has been validated for these purposes, Christ and Hintze (2007) have addressed a number of issues related to the psychometric integrity of these measures that will likely spawn an extensive line of future research on issues such as the reliability and standard error of estimates of CBM and other measures used in MTSD applications. Other researchers and program developers have begun to incorporate other assessments beyond CBM into their MTSD models. A good example is the Pennsylvania model, in which 4Sight is used as a universal screening tool for reading comprehension at third grade and above, with Shapiro and Kovaleski's (2008) finding that the addition of this measure to typical universal screening approaches improves the prediction to performance on state tests. The National Center on Student Progress Monitoring has identified a number of measures that can be used for progress monitoring (*www.studentprogress.org*), some of which (e.g., Star Reading) are computer administered, which adds increased efficiency to the data collection process (Renaissance Learning Inc., 2008b). The relative merits of these alternatives represent yet another line of research that will likely proceed in the near future.

A final measurement issue is the extent to which universal screening and progress monitoring are sufficient in designing instructional plans for students who respond poorly to core instruction and intensive supplemental interventions. Whether in-depth academic assessment procedures such as curriculum-based evaluation (Howell & Nolet, 2000) or curriculum-based assessment (Gravois & Gickling, 2008) help schools improve the precision of interventions for these students is worthy of continued study.

Treatment Fidelity

The issue of treatment fidelity in regards to MTSD has been correctly identified as the sine qua non of RTI (Kovaleski, 2007). That is, the extent to which MTSD can be evaluated as being effective in realizing its stated goals depends upon whether practitioners implement both the overall model as well as the individual components of the model with precise adherence to the procedural aspects of these features. All implementers of MTSD models will need to plan and execute specific fidelity reviews, ranging from checks on implementation of various components of the overall system to adherence to manualized procedures in regard to assessments, core instruction, and interventions. For example, the term *standard protocol intervention* is based on the notion that practitioners will follow a standard sequence of instructional delivery procedures when implementing the intervention. States, in particular, will need to promulgate guidelines as to what constitutes a sufficient level of implementation of MTSD on the whole. For example, Pennsylvania has developed a Response to Intervention (RTI) Readiness and Implementation: Self-Assessment Tool for school districts to use in monitoring their progress in instituting RTI locally (*www.pattan.k12.pa.us/ Publications.aspx?pageNumber=1&ContentLocation=/teachlead/Responsetolntervention.aspx*).

In regard to individual intervention packages, fidelity checklists are beginning to proliferate. For example, a fidelity checklist for the REWARDS strategy is available from Sopris West (Archer, Gleason, & Vachon, 2005). From a practice perspective, procedures for how treatment fidelity will be appraised will need to be developed. Some options include self-assessments by teachers and teams, peer checks, and observations by administrators. From a research perspective, which factors or procedures are associated with sufficient implementation will need to be addressed. For example, it is well established that feedback to teachers improves treatment fidelity (Noell et al., 2005). How these and other procedures will work within MTSD structures has yet to be empirically studied.

System Issues

There has been extensive speculation about how MTSD and other school improvement efforts should be introduced and carried out in the schools. For example, it is commonly articulated that there should be substantial support among teachers and other practitioners (e.g., 80% buy-in) before a new initiative should be introduced (Horner, Sugai, Todd, & Lewis-Palmer, 2005). However, these pronouncements are essentially not empirically based and might be called into question, especially in view of what is at stake. If NCLB requires all schools to use scientifically based instruction procedures and be responsible for bringing 100% of their students to proficiency by 2013–2014, should a school not implement robust techniques of proven MTSD systems because staff is not supportive? This issue has special pertinence to those schools that continue to display shockingly low levels of student proficiency. In this regard, the teacher satisfaction data described previously seem particularly unsatisfying. Research is needed to determine not whether MTSD models are popular but rather which program features and/or professional development programs need to be put in place to gain the enthusiastic support of the practitioners.

A closely related issue is the role of leadership, including the active involvement of principals in the MTSD process and the strong support of central office administrators in the success of MTSD. Although these factors have almost universally been identified as critical in instituting MTSD systems, the actual body of research in this area is very sparse. Rafoth and Foriska (2006) reviewed this literature and posed a number of suggestions for possible research endeavors.

PRACTICAL APPLICATIONS

Over a 30-year period, the provision of supports for students who fail to perform at appropriate levels of proficiency has evolved from teams of teachers working together to full MTSD models. Currently, there appears to be a headlong rush to implement MTSD as the operating system for RTI. This trend is supported by rigorous research that has been conducted on individual aspects of the model and promising program evaluations of both precursor and current MTSD models. Given the aforementioned need for continued research on MTSD models and their individual components, what can be recommended for practitioners who endeavor to scale up MTSD in their schools? First, it seems reasonable to hypothesize that combining individual research-based components into full MTSD systems will lead to the imagined outcomes of the process as a whole. As implementers attempt to discern which of the many proposed elements of MTSD are critical, a few guidelines may be offered:

1. Those procedures that have clear research support should be implemented first. Schools should select assessments for universal screening, progress monitoring, and individual skills analysis based on published reviews of their psychometric characteristics and on studies that indicate the extent to which they are predictive of desired outcomes (e.g., performance on statewide testing).

2. Similarly, core curricular materials and standard protocol interventions should also be selected based on the extent of their research support. Implementers need to be cautious about vendors' claims that a particular instructional package or program is research based and use objective Internet-based sources and published research to guide the acquisition of instructional materials.

3. While being cautious about moving in new directions that may not have conclusive research support, practitioners should also not hesitate to question and possibly abandon historic and revered structures that are no longer needed. For example, in our state (Pennsylvania), as school districts grapple with converting their IST procedures into full MTSD (RTI) models, teams are examining issues such as the need for role changes by many practitioners (e.g., support teachers, school psychologists) and the transition from individual problem solving to a more group-based focus.

4. The evaluation of local implementation efforts needs to be a standard aspect of all MTSD programs. Because it is currently unknown which aspects of MTSD are critical, the program evaluation needs to be formative as well as summative, so that the effects of individual elements (e.g., data analysis teaming, standard protocol interventions) can be appraised as they are incrementally added to local procedures. Ongoing assessments of the treatment fidelity of all aspects of the program will be essential in this regard.

In the face of a research context that continues to emerge, these recommendations speak to the need for schools to embrace and plan for local accountability. If practitioners design and analyze based on both published research and by conducting local program evaluation, the gains that are anticipated for MTSD may be realized.

REFERENCES

Archer, A., Gleason, M. M., & Vachon, V. (2005). *REWARDS intermediate teacher's guide and poster set.* Frederick, CO: Sopris West.

Bahr, M. W., & Kovaleski, J. F. (2006). The need for problem-solving teams: Introduction to the special issue. *Remedial and Special Education, 27*(1), 2–5.

Bahr, M. W., Walker, K., Hampton, E. M., Buddle, B. S., Freeman, T., Ruschman, N., et al. (2006). Creative problem solving for general education intervention teams. *Remedial and Special Education, 27,* 27–41.

Bahr, M., Whitten, E., Dieker, L., Kocarek, C., & Manson, D. (1999). A comparison of school-based intervention teams: Implications for educational and legal reform. *Exceptional Children, 66,* 67–84.

Batsche, G., Elliott, J., Graden, J., Grimes, J., Kovaleski, J. F., Prasse, D., et al. (2005). *Response to intervention: Policy considerations and implementation.* Alexandria, VA: National Association of State Directors of Special Education.

Batsche, G. M., Curtis, M. J., Dorman, C., Castillo, J. M., & Porter, L. J. (2007). The Florida problem-solving/response to intervention model: Implementing a statewide initiative. In S. R. Jimerson, M. K. Burns, & A. M. VanDerHeyden (Eds.), *Handbook of response to intervention: The science and practice of assessment and intervention* (pp. 380–397). New York: Springer Science.

Bollman, K. A., Silberglitt, B., & Gibbons, K. A. (2007). The St. Croix River Education District model: Incorporating systems-level organization and a multi-tiered problem-solving process for intervention delivery. In S. R. Jimerson, M. K. Burns, & A. M. VanDerHeyden (Eds.), *Handbook of response to intervention: The science and practice of assessment and intervention* (pp. 319–330). New York: Springer Science.

Bransford, J., & Stein, B. (1984). *The ideal problem solver: A guide for improving thinking, learning, and creativity.* San Francisco: Freeman.

Buck, G. H., Polloway, E. A., Smith-Thomas, A., & Cook, K. W. (2003). Prereferral intervention processes: A survey of state practices. *Exceptional Children,* 69(3), 349–360.

Burns, M. K., & Symington, T. (2002). A meta-analysis of prereferral intervention teams: Student and systemic outcomes. *Journal of School Psychology, 40*(5), 437–446.

Burns, M. K., Wiley, H. I., & Viglietta, E. (2008). Best practices in implementing effective problem-solving teams. In A. Thomas & J. Grimes (Eds.), *Best practices in school psychology V* (pp. 1633–1644). Bethesda, MD: National Association of School Psychologists.

Callender, W. A. (2007). The Idaho results-based model: Implementing response to intervention statewide. In S. R. Jimerson, M. K. Burns, & A. M. VanDerHeyden (Eds.), *Handbook of response to intervention: The science and practice of assessment and intervention* (pp. 333–344). New York: Springer Science.

Carter, J., & Sugai, G. (1989). Survey on prereferral practices: Responses from state departments of education. *Exceptional Children, 55*(4), 298–302.

Chalfant, J. C., & Pysh, M. V. (1989). Teacher assistance teams: Five descriptive studies on 96 teams. *Remedial and Special Education, 10*(6), 49–58.

Chalfant, J. C., Pysh, M. V., & Moultrie, R. (1979). Teacher assistance teams: A model for within-building problem solving. *Learning Disability Quarterly,* 2(3), 85–96.

Christ, T. J., & Hintze, J. M. (2007). Psychometric considerations when evaluating response to intervention. In S. R. Jimerson, M. K. Burns, & A. M. VanDerHeyden (Eds.), *Handbook of response to intervention: The science and practice of assessment and intervention* (pp. 93–105). New York: Springer Science.

Coalition for Evidence-Based Policy. (2003, December). *Identifying and implementing educational practices supported by rigorous evidence: A user friendly guide.* Washington, DC: U.S. Department of Education.

Donovan, M., & Cross, C. (2002). *Minority students in special and gifted education.* Washington, DC: National Academy Press.

Ervin, R. A., Schaughency, E., Goodman, S. D., McGlinchey, M. T., & Matthews, A. (2007). Moving from a model demonstration project to a statewide initiative in Michigan: Lessons learned from merging research-practice agendas to address reading and behavior. In S. R. Jimerson, M. K. Burns, & A. M. VanDerHeyden (Eds.), *Handbook of response to intervention: The science and practice of assessment and intervention* (pp. 356–379). New York: Springer Science.

Florida Department of Education. (2006). *Technical assistance paper: The response to intervention (RTI) model.* Retrieved November 17, 2008, from the University of South Florida, Student Support Services website: *www.sss.usf.edu/Resources/taps/2006/2006_8.pdf.*

Fuchs, D., & Fuchs, L. S. (1998). Treatment validity: A unifying concept for reconceptualization the identification of learning disabilities. *Learning Disabilities Research and Practice, 13,* 204–219.

Fuchs, D., Fuchs, L. S., & Bahr, M. W. (1990). Mainstream assistance teams: A scientific basis for the art of consultation. *Exceptional Children, 57*(2), 128–139.

Fuchs, D., Mock, D., Morgan, P. L., & Young, C. L. (2003). Responsiveness-to-intervention: Definitions, evidence, and implications for the learning disabilities construct. *Learning Disabilities Research and Practice, 18*(3), 157–171.

Fuchs, L. S., & Fuchs, D. (2007). The role of assessment in the three-tier approach to reading instruction. In D. Haager, S. Vaughn, & J. Klingner (Eds.), *Evidence-based practices for response to intervention* (pp. 29–44). Baltimore: Brookes.

Gickling, E. E., & Rosenfield, S. (1995). Curriculum-based assessment. In A. Thomas & J. Grimes (Eds.), *Best practices in school psychology III* (pp. 587–595). Washington, DC: National Association of School Psychologists.

Good, R. H., & Kaminski, R. A. (2005). *Dynamic indicators of basic early literacy skills* (6th ed.). Frederick, CO: Sopris West.

Graden, J. L. (1989). Redefining prereferral intervention as intervention assistance: Collaboration between general and special education. *Exceptional Children, 56*, 227–231.

Graden, J. L., Casey, A., & Bonstrom, O. (1985). Implementing a prereferral intervention system: Part II. The data. *Exceptional Children, 51*(6), 487–496.

Graden, J. L., Casey, A., & Christenson, S. L. (1985). Implementing a prereferral intervention system: Part I. The model. *Exceptional Children, 51*, 377–384.

Graden, J. L., Stollar, S. A., & Poth, R. L. (2007). The Ohio integrated systems model: Overview and lessons learned. In S. R. Jimerson, M. K. Burns, & A. M. VanDerHeyden (Eds.), *Handbook of response to intervention: The science and practice of assessment and intervention* (pp. 288–299). New York: Springer Science.

Gravois, T. A., & Gickling, E. E. (2008). Best practices in instructional assessment. In A. Thomas & J. Grimes (Eds.), *Best practices in school psychology V* (pp. 503–518). Bethesda, MD: National Association of School Psychologists.

Gravois, T. A., & Rosenfield, S. A. (2006). Impact of instructional consultation teams on the disproportionate referral and placement of minority students in special education. *Remedial and Special Education, 27*, 42–52.

Hartman, W. T., & Fay, T. A. (1996). Cost-effectiveness of instructional support teams in Pennsylvania. *Journal of Educational Finance, 21*(4), 555–580.

Horner, R. H., Sugai, G., Todd, A. W., & Lewis-Palmer, T. (2005). Schoolwide positive behavior support. In L. M. Bambara & L. Kern (Eds.), *Individualized supports for students with problem behaviors* (pp. 359–390). New York: Guilford Press.

Howell, K. W., & Nolet, V. (2000). *Curriculum-based evaluation: Teaching and decision making* (3rd ed.). Florence, KY: Wadsworth Thomson Learning.

Ikeda, M. J., Rahn-Blakeslee, A., Niebling, B. C., Gustafson, J. K., Allison, R., & Stumme, J. (2007). The Heartland Area Education Agency 11 problem-solving approach: An overview and lessons learned. In S. R. Jimerson, M. K. Burns, & A. M. VanDerHeyden (Eds.), *Handbook of response to intervention: The science and practice of assessment and intervention* (pp. 257–270). New York: Springer Science.

Ikeda, M. J., Tilly, W. D., III, Stumme, J., Volmer, L., & Allison, R. (1996). Agency-wide implementation of problem-solving consultation: Foundations, current implementation, and future directions. *School Psychology Quarterly, 11*, 228–243.

Kovaleski, J. F. (2002). Best practices in operating pre-referral intervention teams. In J. Grimes & A. Thomas (Eds.), *Best practices in school psychology IV* (pp. 645–655). Washington, DC: National Association of School Psychologists.

Kovaleski, J. F. (2007). Response to intervention: Considerations for research and systems change. *School Psychology Review, 36*(4), 638–646.

Kovaleski, J. F., Gickling, E. E., Morrow, H., & Swank, P. R. (1999). High versus low implementation of instructional support teams: A case for maintaining program fidelity. *Remedial and Special Education, 20,* 170–183.

Kovaleski, J. F., & Glew, M. C. (2006). Bringing instructional support teams to scale: Implications of the Pennsylvania experience. *Remedial and Special Education, 27*(1), 16–25.

Kovaleski, J. F., & Pedersen, J. (2008). Best practices in data analysis teaming. In A. Thomas & J. Grimes (Eds.), *Best practices in school psychology V* (Vol. 2, pp. 115–129). Bethesda, MD: National Association of School Psychologists.

Kovaleski, J. F., Tucker, J., & Stevens, L. (1996). Bridging special and regular education: The Pennsylvania initiative. *Educational Leadership, 53*(7), 44–47.

Kruger, L. J., Struzziero, J., Watts, R., & Vacca, D. (1995). The relationship between organizational support and satisfaction with teacher assistance teams. *Remedial and Special Education, 16*(4), 203–211.

Marston, D., Lau, M., & Muyskens, P. (2007). Implementation of the problem-solving model in the Minneapolis public schools In S. R. Jimerson, M. K. Burns, & A. M. VanDerHeyden (Eds.), *Handbook of response to intervention: The science and practice of assessment and intervention* (pp. 279–287). New York: Springer Science.

Marston, D., Muyskens, P., Lau, M., & Canter, A. (2003). Problem-solving model for decision making with high-incidence disabilities: The Minneapolis experience. *Learning Disabilities Research and Practice, 18*(3), 187–200.

Myles, B. S., Simpson, R. L., & Ormsbee, C. K. (1996). Teacher's perceptions of the effectiveness of preassessment for students with behavior and learning problems. *Preventing School Failure, 41*(1), 14–19.

Nelson, J. R., Smith, D. J., Taylor, L., Dodd, J. M., & Reavis, K. (1991). Prereferral intervention: A review of the research. *Education and Treatment of Children, 14,* 243–253.

Noell, G. H., Witt, J. C., Slider, N. J., Connell, J. E., Gatti, S. L., Williams, K. L., et al. (2005). Treatment implementation following behavioral consultation in schools: A comparison of three follow-up strategies. *School Psychology Review, 34*(1), 87–106.

Peterson, D. W., Prasse, D. P., Shinn, M. R., & Swerdlik, M. E. (2007). The Illinois flexible service delivery model: A problem-solving model initiative. In S. R. Jimerson, M. K. Burns, & A. M. VanDerHeyden (Eds.), *Handbook of response to intervention: The science and practice of assessment and intervention* (pp. 3000–3318). New York: Springer Science.

Rafoth, M. A., & Foriska, T. (2006). Administrator participation in promoting effective problem-solving teams. *Remedial and Special Education, 27*(3), 130–135.

Renaissance Learning Inc. (2008a). *Star early literacy: Computer-adaptive diagnostic assessment.* Wisconsin Rapids, WI: Author.

Renaissance Learning Inc. (2008b). *Star math: Computer-adaptive math test.* Wisconsin Rapids, WI: Author.

Renaissance Learning Inc. (2008c). *Star reading: Computer-adaptive reading test.* Wisconsin Rapids, WI: Author.

Reschly, D. J. (1988). Special education reform: School psychology revolution. *School Psychology Review*, 17, 459–475.

Reyna, V. F. (2004). Why scientific research? The importance of evidence in changing educational practice. In P. McCardle & V. Chhabra (Eds.), *The voice of evidence in reading research* (pp. 47–58). Baltimore: Brookes.

Rosenfield, S., & Gravois, T. (1996). *Instructional consultation teams: Collaborating for change*. New York: Guilford Press.

Safran, S. P., & Safran, J. S. (1996). Intervention assistance programs and prereferral teams: Directions for the twenty-first century. *Remedial and Special Education*, 17, 363–369.

Schrag, J. A., & Henderson, K. (1996). *School-based intervention assistance teams and their impact on special education*. Alexandria, VA: National Association of State Directors of Special Education.

Shapiro, E. S., & Clemens, N. H. (2009). A conceptual model for evaluating system effects of RTI. *Assessment for Effective Intervention*, 35, 3–16.

Shapiro, E. S., Keller, M. A., Lutz, J. G., Santoro, L. E., & Hintze, J. M. (2006). Curriculum-based measures and performance on state assessment and standardized tests: Reading and math performance in Pennsylvania. *Journal of Psychoeducational Assessment*, 24(1), 19–35.

Shapiro, E. S., & Kovaleski, J. F. (2008). *Report on the 2007–2008 response-to-intervention pilot districts*. Harrisburg, PA: Pennsylvania Training and Technical Assistance Network.

Shapiro, E. S., Solari, E., & Petscher, Y. (2008). Use of a measure of reading comprehension to enhance prediction on the state high stakes assessment. *Learning and Individual Differences*, 18(3), 316–328.

Shin, M. R., & Shinn, M. M. (2002). *Reading curriculum-based measurement (R-CBM) for use in general outcome measurement*. San Antonio, TX: Pearson.

Sindelar, P. T., Griffin, C. C., Smith, S. W., & Watanabe, A. K. (1992). Prereferral intervention: Encouraging notes on preliminary findings. *Elementary School Journal*, 92, 245–260.

Slavin, M. R., & Madden, N. A. (2006). *4Sight benchmark assessments*. Baltimore: Success for All Foundation.

Tilly, W. D. (2003 December). *How many tiers are needed for successful prevention and early intervention? Heartland Area Education Agency's evolution from four to three tiers*. Paper presented at the National Research Center on Learning Disabilities Responsiveness-to-Intervention Symposium, Kansas City, MO. Retrieved from *http://www.nrcld.org/symposium2003/index.html*.

Tilly, W. D. (2008). The evolution of school psychology to a science-based practice: Problem solving and the three-tiered model. In J. Grimes & A. Thomas (Eds.), *Best practices in school psychology V* (pp. 17–36). Bethesda, MD: National Association of School Psychologists.

Torgesen, J. K. (2007). Using an RTI model to guide early reading instruction: Effects on identification rates for students with learning disabilities (Tech. Rep. No. 7). Retrieved December 10, 2009, from *Florida Center for Reading Research*, Florida State University website: *http://www.fcrr.org/Technical Reports/Response_to_intervention_florida.pdf*.

Truscott, S. D., Cohen, C. E., Sams, D. P., Sanborn, K. J., & Frank, A. J. (2005). The current state of prereferral intervention teams: A report from two national surveys. *Remedial and Special Education, 26*, 130–140.

Tucker, J. A., & Sornson, R. O. (2007). One student at a time; one teacher at a time: Reflections on the use of instructional support. In S. R. Jimerson, M. K. Burns, & A. M. VanDerHeyden (Eds.), *Handbook of response to intervention: The science and practice of assessment and intervention* (pp. 269–278). New York: Springer Science.

VanDerHeyden, A. M., & Burns, M. K. (2005). Using curriculum-based assessment and curriculum-based measurement to guide elementary mathematics instruction: Effect on individual and group accountability scores. *Assessment for Effective Intervention, 30*, 15–31.

VanDerHeyden, A. M., & Witt, J. C. (2005). Quantifying the context of assessment: Capturing the effect of base rates on teacher referral and a problem-solving model of identification. *School Psychology Review, 34*, 161–183.

VanDerHeyden, A. M., Witt, J. C., & Gilbertson, D. (2007). A multi-year evaluation of the effects of a response to intervention (RTI) model on identification of children for special education. *Journal of School Psychology, 45*, 225–256.

VanDerHeyden, A. M., Witt, J. C., & Naquin, G. (2003). Development and validation of a process for screening referrals to special education. *School Psychology Review, 32*, 204–227.

Vaughn, S., & Fuchs, L. (2006). A response to "Competing views: A dialogue on response to intervention": Why response to intervention is necessary but not sufficient for identifying students with learning disabilities. *Assessment for Effective Intervention, 32*(1), 58–61.

Vaughn, S., Linan-Thompson, S., & Hickman, P. (2003). Response to instruction as a means of identifying students with reading/learning disabilities. *Exceptional Children, 69*(4), 391–409.

Vaughn, S., Wanzek, J., Woodruff, A. L., & Linan-Thompson, S. (2007). Prevention and early identification of students with reading disabilities. In D. Haager, J. Klingner, & S. Vaughn (Eds.), *Evidence-based reading practices for response to intervention* (pp. 11–27). Baltimore: Brookes.

Vellutino, F., Scanlon, D., Sipay, E., Small, S., Pratt, A., Chen, R., et al. (1996). Cognitive profiles of difficult to remediate and readily remediated poor readers: Early intervention as a vehicle for distinguishing between cognitive and experimental deficits as basic causes of specific reading disability. *Journal of Educational Psychology, 88*, 601–638.

Windram, H., Scierka, B., & Silberglitt, B. (2007). Response to intervention at the secondary level: Two districts' models of implementation. *Communiqué, 35*(5), 43–45.

Witt, J. C., & VanDerHeyden, A. (2007). The System to Enhance Educational Performance (STEEP): Using science to improve achievement. In S. R. Jimerson, M. K. Burns, & A. M. VanDerHeyden (Eds.), *Handbook of response to intervention: The science and practice of assessment and intervention* (pp. 345–355). New York: Springer Science.

4

Student Assessment and Data-Based Decision Making

John M. Hintze
Amanda M. Marcotte

RESPONSE TO INTERVENTION AS DATA-BASED DECISION MAKING

Beginning with the pioneering work of Stanley Deno in the early 1970s and continuing to today, data-based decision making has provided both general and special education teachers with efficient and accurate ways of assessing the effects of instruction. Building on the accumulating knowledge from contemporary behavioral assessment, data-based decision making has sought to provide teachers with the types of academic measures that could be (1) collected on a frequent basis (e.g., daily, weekly), (2) graphed, and (3) evaluated for evidence of student learning across short periods of time (Shinn & Bamonto, 1998). The validation and ongoing development of assessment techniques that could be used in data-based decision making began in earnest in the late 1970s and continues to the present. Indeed, perhaps more so than any other educational assessment tools, data-based decision-making measures have been vigorously examined with school-age children, with and without disabilities, regarding their technical properties and ease of administration (Shinn & Bamonto, 1998). At present, the use of such simple measures for educational decision making, particularly within the context of response to intervention (RTI), has become a focus of study.

Although from a policy perspective a relatively new phenomenon, the rationale for RTI can be traced back to the 1982 National Research Council report (Heller, Holtzman, & Messick, 1982) questioning the validity of special education classification. In that report, Heller et al. (1982) proposed a tripartite decision-making analysis whereby (1) the quality of the general education program was such that adequate learning could be expected; (2) if adequate learning could be expected, would the instructional techniques available in special education be of sufficient value to improve student outcomes and thereby justify the classification? and (3) were the assessment processes used to determine instructional effectiveness and identification accurate and meaningful? If all three criteria are met, then a special education placement is likely valid. As can be seen, the first two criteria emphasize instructional quality: first, in the setting that the problem develops and, second, under conditions of special education that the classification affords. Moreover, the assessment process serves as a critical linchpin because it is the yardstick by which instructional quality is evaluated. Without psychometrically sound assessment, accurately responding to the first two criteria is extremely difficult, if not impossible.

Building on these seminal notions, Fuchs (1995) operationalized the Heller et al. (1982) process (see also Fuchs & Fuchs, 1998) using a population-based preventive tiered framework that included three assessment phases. In doing so, Fuchs and colleagues extended the reasoning of such an approach to include informed instructional decisions for all students in schools, not just those at risk or being considered for special education. In the first phase (i.e., Tier 1), point estimates for all students are collected and organized. The purpose of this phase of assessment is to determine whether the aggregate rate of responsiveness to the general education instructional environment is sufficiently effectual such that student progress should be expected. If the mean rate of growth across students is low compared with other classes in the same building, in the same district, or in the nation, then the appropriate decision is to intervene at the aggregate level to develop a stronger or more beneficial general education instructional program. Regardless of whether the unit of analysis is the classroom, grade level, school, district, state, or nation, students at the aggregated level should be progressing at an appropriate rate, without greater-than-expected numbers of students falling behind. In doing so, Tier 1 assessment addresses the first criterion as proposed by Heller et al. (1982); that is, the quality of general education is such that adequate learning might be expected.

After the effectiveness of the general education curriculum has been addressed, Tier 2 assessment involves the identification of students whose current levels of performance *and* rate of improvement over time are both below the aggregate mean or what would be expected compared with their peers. Here the purpose of assessment is to identify a subset of students who may be at risk for continued poor academic outcomes and possibly specific learning disabilities, as indicated by the lack of adequate responsiveness to the generally effective general education curriculum. For this subset of students, standard or manualized interventions are provided that have been specifically chosen to supplement the general education curriculum and provide needed remediation in specific areas of skill development. Assessment in Tier 2 consists of both frequent (e.g., weekly) progress monitoring and the periodic assessment activities described in Tier 1. Tier 2 assessment data are graphically presented in a time-series format and are summarized via slope (or rate) of improvement over time. Students who are responsive to Tier 2 intervention (i.e., those whose performance is similar to that of students in the Tier 1 aggregate) exit and return to Tier 1 status.

Students whose response to Tier 2 intervention support is lacking and who fail to demonstrate change in performance level or rate of improvement are transitioned to Tier 3, where an individualized education plan is developed and delivered with a low student-to-teacher ratio. The purpose of Tier 3 intervention and assessment is to determine whether and with what types of intervention supports the general education setting can be transformed into a productive learning environment for students most at risk for significant performance difficulties and/or specific learning disabilities. As in Tier 2, student responsiveness to intervention efforts is monitored on a continuous, frequent basis to evaluate changes in performance level and rate of improvement. Moreover, assessment serves a formative function whereby ongoing data are used to make instructional changes and decisions regarding the effectiveness of the individualized interventions.

RTI'S MULTIPLE MEASUREMENT PERSPECTIVES

With a reliance on a dual-discrepancy approach to determining intervention responsiveness (Fuchs, 1995; Fuchs & Fuchs, 1998), RTI combines two distinct measurement perspectives into decision making (Christ & Hintze, 2007). One form, relative (or *vaganotic*) measurement, yields data that are dependent on same standard or set of references for decision making (Johnston & Pennypacker, 2008). Here the meaning of any relative measurement outcome is made in reference to a normative distribution (e.g., national or local norm) or criterion of reference (e.g., benchmark). Within the context of an RTI approach, relative measurements are used to compare an individual's performance with that of a peer group or criterion value (Christ & Hintze, 2007). For example, in Tier 1 local or aggregated performance data are typically collected in the fall, winter, and spring of the academic year to define typical performance expectations. These data are then summarized using descriptive statistics, which establish what is typical at each of the three seasonal points of the academic year. Subsequently, the performance of each child is interpreted relative to the performance of their same-grade peers, and decisions are made with respect to each child's development at that point of time relative to some peer standard. Importantly, decisions regarding individual student performance are tied to the context, content, and normative sample that was used to devise the psychometric characteristics of the measurement instrument (Christ & Hintze, 2007). If violated, just as with any other norm- or criterion-referenced assessments, the decision-making accuracy is in question because the normative data used for guiding instructional decisions are not aligned with the measurement system. Such "mixing and matching" of measurement systems and normative data leads to increased errors in decision making, with the greatest problem being that one never knows quite when an error has been made. For this reason, RTI profits from measurement systems or approaches that allow for the measurement of general outcomes that can be generalized across a wide range of academic contexts and contents (Fuchs & Deno, 1991).

Absolute (or *idemnotic*) measurement, the second form, produces scores that have meaning independent of the measurement context (Johnston & Pennypacker, 2008). Such values are distinct from relative measurements as described previously and share features with those scales of measurement that are more commonly seen in the natural sciences and established in space and time. For example, pounds, gallons, and inches all have absolute values that may be interpreted independent of a comparison group. A person is 72 inches tall regardless of the ruler that is used for measurement. The measurement value retains its absolute value regardless of the height among those in the comparison group. The raw score in inches has an absolute quality inherent in the outcome that is distinct from a score on a relative or normative scale. The practical distinction is that absolute measurements are interpretable in and of themselves, whereas relative measurements are interpretable only in reference to an external criterion. A raw score of 50% on norm-referenced tests is meaningless unless one has peer/age norms, criteria for expected performance, or additional measures of the individual's response.

As can be seen, measurement outcomes have the property of either relative or absolute values, and interpretations can be made in a relative or absolute sense as well. As such, although a person's height can be measured in inches (in the absolute sense), the actual interpretation of that measurement outcome may depend, in part, on the age and gender of the individual. For example, the mean height $\pm$ 1 SD of an adult male is 70 ($\pm$ 2.5) inches and that an adult female is 64 ($\pm$ 2.5) inches. Sixty-six inches is within the average range for a typical adult female, but below the average range for a typical adult male. The 66-inch-tall adult female approximates the 79th percentile, whereas the 66-inch adult male approximates the 5th percentile. In this case, an intervention decision (e.g., the possibility of human growth hormone) depends not simply on the absolute measurement or outcome but also on developmental expectations expressed in normative physical development. Here absolute measurement is interpreted both absolutely and in the context of relative development.

Using both measurement approaches extends to RTI, where both absolute and relative measurements are used to determine risk status and responsiveness to intervention over time (Hintze, Christ, & Methe, 2006). Currently, curriculum-based measurement (CBM) is the most common set of assessment procedures used within RTI. As a variant of curriculum-based assessment, CBM yields direct measures of academic performance in the basic skill areas of early literacy and reading, early numeracy and mathematics, spelling, and written expression (Deno, 1985; Deno, Mirkin, & Chiang, 1982; Shinn, 1989). Unlike most other assessments of academic skill performance, CBM direct measurement procedures yield an absolute measurement outcome (as opposed to a raw score that is subsequently transformed into some type of standard scores). For example, in reading CBM a student who reads 32 words correct in 1 minute reads half as many words as a student who reads 64 words correct in a minute. There is an absolute quality to reading CBM outcomes, so that a student who progresses from 30 to 45 words correct/minute over 3 weeks has indeed improved his or her oral reading fluency by 15 words correct/minute.

In addition to absolute qualities, CBM is sensitive to relative qualities brought about by the context of observation or individual differences across students. For example, varying difficulty of reading material as a function of within- and across-grade materials, changes in performance as a function of the passage of time or instruction, and sensitivity to differences in reading ability, to name a few, represent relative measurement aspects that CBM has been demonstrated to be sensitive to both across general and special education curricula and samples (Fuchs & Deno, 1992; Hintze & Christ, 2004; Hintze, Daly, & Shapiro, 1998; Hintze, Owen, Shapiro, & Daly, 2000: Shinn, Gleason, & Tindal, 1989). For these reasons, CBM is particularly well suited for decision making within an RTI model; however, it represents just one approach. Nevertheless, because of its reliance on two forms of measurement (i.e., both absolute and relative), in order to fully implement a dual-discrepancy approach to RTI assessment, systems that provide for both absolute and relative forms of measurement are highly recommended.

EVALUATING AND USING RTI STUDENT ASSESSMENT MATERIALS FOR DATA-BASED DECISION MAKING

Because student assessment within an RTI approach requires measuring student performance at one point in time and rate of growth across time, assessment measures must satisfy the psychometric requirements of both relative (vaganotic) and absolute (idemnotic) measurement. Until recently, the specific psychometric points of reference used to satisfy these requirements have been largely left to the individual researcher or evaluator. However, in 2008 the National Center on Response to Intervention (NCRTI; *www. rti4success.org*) put forth an organizational heuristic by which RTI student assessment measures could be evaluated with respect to their psychometric properties and used in screening students for relative decision making and progress monitoring for evaluating student absolute growth across time in response to instruction and intervention. Here screening refers to the type of periodic assessment of a large number of students with the goal of identifying those students at risk for academic difficulties. Progress monitoring, on the other hand, refers to the frequent assessment of select students in order to evaluate their growth over time. This unique approach to evaluating the psychometric merit of student assessment materials forces RTI practitioners to focus on both relative and absolute forms of educational measurement as opposed to solely norm-referenced evaluation approaches, on which educational assessment has historically relied heavily.

Evaluation of Relative RTI Student Screening Assessment Approaches

In considering RTI student assessment, the NCRTI defines relative assessment as "screening that involves brief assessments that are valid, reliable, and evidence based [that] are conducted with all students or targeted groups of students to identify students who are at risk of academic failure and, therefore, likely to need additional or alternative forms of instruction to supplement the conventional general education approach." The evaluation of such student assessment tools is made along four core considerations: (1) reliability, (2) validity, (3) classification accuracy, and (4) generalizability.

Reliability refers to the consistency of a set of measurements or measuring instrument, often used to describe student assessment performance. As with any other measurement system, reliability is a necessity because it ensures, to some extent, that the data gathered are reflective of the measurement system's intent and not systematic or random error. Reliability is inversely related to random error such that minimizing error improves reliability. From a decision-making perspective, higher reliability is a necessary but not sufficient condition for adequate data-based decision making. Reliability may be estimated through a variety of methods that fall into two general types: multiple administration and single administration (Crocker & Algina, 2006). Multiple-administration methods require that a minimum of two assessments are administered. *Test–retest* reliability refers to situations in which the same assessment measure is administered twice over some period of time (Allen & Yen, 2001). Here reliability is estimated through the Pearson product–moment correlation coefficient between the two administrations of the same measure. *Alternate-form* reliability refers to situations in which different or multiple forms of an assessment measure are administered, usually together (Allen & Yen, 2001). Again, reliability is estimated using the Pearson product–moment correlation coefficient of the multiple forms of the measure. Multiple-administration approaches to reliability estimation are particularly relevant to relative/screening RTI student assessment because typically multiple similar forms of student academic performance are collected concurrently and summarized descriptively using a measure of central tendency. As such, test–retest and/or alternate-form reliability is a highly desired property of RTI student screening assessment. Single-administration methods of estimating reliability include *split-half* and *internal consistency*. The split-half method treats the two halves of a measure as alternate forms. Reliability is again estimated using the Pearson product–moment correlation and then adjusted to the full test length using the Spearman–Brown prediction formula (Allen & Yen, 2001). The most common form of internal consistency measure is Cronbach's alpha, which is usually interpreted as the mean of all possible split-half coefficients (Allen & Yen, 2001). Although single-administration methods to estimate reliability are desirable, they may be less applicable to RTI student screening assessment when the tests are designed and administered in a speeded nature. In evaluating reliability, generally correlation coefficients in the magnitude of .80 and greater are desirable (Salvia, Ysseldyke, & Bolt, 2006). Coefficients in the range of .60 to .80 may be appropriate under specific circumstances, and coefficients less than .60 generally insufficient for demonstrating reliability.

Validity refers to the extent to which an assessment measure correlates with criterion measures that are known to be valid. As with any other assessment measure, validity is a necessity because it allows the evaluator to make inferences from the data regarding the intended measurement domains of interest. Like reliability, validity can be established using a variety of methods. *Concurrent validity* refers to situations in which scores on a new experimental measure are correlated with those on a criterion measure that are collected at the same time as the new experimental measure. *Predicted validity* refers to situations in which the criterion measure is collected at some later point in time than the new experimental measure. Last, *content validity* refers to the extent to which the new experimental measure is related to other measures as dictated by theory. As with reliability, each of these forms of validity is generally established using the Pearson product–moment correlation and often adjusted using a correction of attenuation formula, which considers the less-than-perfect reliability under which each assessment is measured (Allen & Yen, 2001). Generally, validity correlation coefficients of .70 or greater are desirable for RTI student screening assessment.

Classification, or diagnostic, accuracy is extremely relevant for RTI relative measures because of their use in making screening decisions. When used as part of a tiered approach to data-based decision making, the initial assessment question of "who is currently at risk for continued academic performance difficulty" is most often determined through the use of universal screening measures. If the measures have not demonstrated adequate classification accuracy, inordinately high levels of false-positive and false-negative results will occur. When this happens, students who are truly at risk will not be identified and will be in danger of further deteriorating academic skill development, or students who are truly not at risk will be provided supplemental academic supportive interventions when none are required, thus wasting valuable resources that could otherwise be used for those in true need. With its reliance on population-based preventive approaches to service provision, RTI has been demonstrated to be a forerunner in the careful examination of classification and diagnostic accuracy of the measures that it uses for screening purposes.

Classification, or diagnostic, accuracy refers to the extent to which a screening measure is able to accurately classify students into "at risk for academic difficulties" or "not at risk for academic difficulties" categories. Investigations of diagnostic accuracy assume that the true diagnostic status of a sample is known. In a typical study, the diagnoses derived through the experimental measure are compared with the diagnostic classifications for known criterion groups (i.e., those for which the characteristics of interest have been established as being either present or absent). By cross-classifying the known criterion status with the outcomes of the experimental procedure, the accuracy of decisions may be summarized fourfold (Macmann & Barnett, 1999). True positives and negatives indicate agreement with criterion status; false positives and negatives represent diagnostic errors. Two basic measures of diagnostic accuracy are sensitivity and specificity. These measures estimate the conditional probability of selected diagnostic outcomes (i.e., the likelihood of A given B). Sensitivity refers to the probability that an individual whose known diagnostic status is present will be correctly classified by the experimental measure; and specificity is the probability that an individual whose diagnostic status is absent on the criterion will be correctly identified by the experimental measure. These estimates are affected by the base rate and selection rate for the diagnostic procedure. The base rate is established by the proportion of the sample identified by the criterion, whereas the selection rate refers to the proportion of the sample correctly identified through the experimental measure. For example, in a sample of 100 adult men, if it is known from some incontrovertible measure that 20 of them have high blood pressure, the base rate would be 20%. Selection rate would then refer to the ability of some second measure in corroborating the same percentage of men. The cut scores on the experimental measures are typically determined using receiver operating characteristic (ROC) curves (Hintze, Ryan, & Stoner, 2003; Hintze & Silberglitt, 2005; Silberglitt & Hintze, 2005). Here cut scores refer to some criterion standard that separates the population into groups (e.g., those who have high blood pressure and those who do not). ROC curves are a generalization of the set of potential combinations of sensitivity and specificity possible for the experimental measure. The area under the curve (AUC) statistic represents an overall indication of the diagnostic accuracy of the ROC curve. AUC values closer to 1 indicate that the screening measure reliably distinguishes among students with satisfactory and unsatisfactory academic performance, whereas values of .50 indicate that the experimental measure is not better than chance. Generally speaking, AUCs of .90 and higher are considered very good and AUCs greater than .80 acceptable (Swets, 1986, 1988, 1992; Swets, Dawes, & Monahan, 2000).

Last, *generalizability* refers to the extent to which results generated from one sample can be applied to another sample. RTI relative screening measures are considered to be more generalizable if replication studies have been conducted on large representative samples with cross-validation observed. Generally, large representative national samples or multiple regional/state samples with cross-validation are preferred over a sample of convenience.

Data-Based Decision Making Using Relative RTI Student Screening Assessment Approaches

Once adequate reliability, validity, and classification/diagnostic accuracy conditions are satisfied, RTI screening measures can be used to (1) evaluate the overall quality of the general education program and (2) determine those students for whom the general education program is insufficient for ensuring adequate academic development, thus placing them at risk for further academic difficulty and worsening (Fuchs, 1995; Heller et al., 1982). In doing so, one of two general approaches is commonly used to determine the effectiveness of the general education program and identifying students who are at risk for academic difficulties. In one approach, a single cut score is used to determine risk status. Table 4.1 presents reading CBM (R-CBM) data for a large national sample of third-grade students based on this single cut score. To determine risk status, the 25th percentile may be used as a benchmark to identify those students who are at risk for current and continued academic difficulties. As such, any student whose R-CBM score was equal to or lower than the R-CBM score noted for the particular time of the school year would be identified as at risk. Students whose R-CBM

TABLE 4.1. Third Grade R-CBM Data: Risk Status Based on Cut Scores

	R-CBM score		
Rank	Fall	Winter	Spring
90th	137	156	171
75th	110	133	146
50th	82	104	118
25th	53	76	89
10th	33	47	60

Note. R-CBM, reading curriculum-based measurement.

scores were higher than those associated with the 25th percentile would not be considered at risk. The second approach separates the continuum of R-CBM scores into gradients of risk status. Table 4.2 presents R-CBM data for a large national sample of third-grade students based on this approach. As noted previously, it is important to recall that the data used for decision making are tied closely to the context, content, and normative sample that were used to devise the psychometric characteristics of the measurement instrument used to collect the data. In this approach students would be categorized according to risk status.

Once students are appropriately categorized using either approach, questions regarding risk status and the effectiveness of the general education program can be addressed. In response to the latter, the percentage of students who are considered to be either not at risk or at low risk (using either of the two approaches noted previously) is noted and compared with accepted performance expectations. Generally, schools may expect that approximately 80% of their school population should meet benchmark standards in response to the general education curriculum. Furthermore, it may be expected that approximately 15% of the school population may require both the general education curriculum plus supplemental support in order to successfully meet benchmark target. Finally, schools may antici-

TABLE 4.2. Third Grade R-CBM Data: Risk Status Based on Score Gradient

Variable	Low risk	Moderate risk	High risk
Fall R-CBM score	≥ 82	81-48	≤ 47
Winter R-CBM score	≥ 104	103-61	≤ 60
Spring R-CBM score	≥ 118	117-79	≤ 78

Note. R-CBM, reading curriculum-based measurement.

pate that approximately 5% of the school population can require long-term intensive support (possibly supported through special education) to profit from the general education curriculum (Hintze, 2009).

Once the school's percentages are calculated, they can be compared with these benchmark expectations. Analyzing the effect of the general education curriculum involves a number of comparisons of the observed data to the expected data. First, if 80% or more of the school population are meeting benchmark expectations, it is reasonable to conclude that the general education is having its desired effect. If less than 80% of the school population is meeting benchmark expectations, with increased numbers of students at moderate levels of risk, the school should explore supplementing or modifying the general education curriculum with targeted areas of focus, with the goal of increasing the number of students who meet benchmark expectations. Last, if significant numbers of students are at moderate to high levels of risk, the school may consider an overhaul of the general education curriculum under the presumption that what is currently in place is not meeting the needs of the majority of the school's students.

In addition, a second major data-based decision-making function of relative screening assessment is to identify those individual students who likely require supplemental instructional support in addition to the general education curriculum. Here students whose level of performance falls below benchmark expectations in comparison to one of the two approaches noted previously are identified, and supplemental instructional assistance is provided (Hintze, 2009). For these students ongoing progress monitoring will be conducted (discussed next) in addition to periodic universal screening. Continued need for supplemental instructional support will be made based on a dual-discrepancy analysis, which was explained briefly previously and is elaborated on later.

Evaluation of Absolute RTI Student Progress Monitoring Approaches

As with screening measures, the NCRTI defines absolute progress monitoring as "repeated measurement of academic performance to inform instruction of individual students in general and special education [which] is conducted at least monthly to (a) estimate rates of improvement, (b) identify students who are not demonstrating adequate progress, and/or (c) compare the efficacy of different forms of instruction to design more effective, individualized instruction." Absolute student progress monitoring tools are evaluated based on six core considerations distinct from those considered for screening instruments: (1) alternate forms, (2) specified rates of improvement, (3) end-of-the-year benchmarks, (4) sensitivity to student improvement, (5) reliability of slope, and (6) predictive validity of slope of improvement.

For progress monitoring purposes, *alternate forms* refers to the provision of multiple forms of relatively equal difficulty that can be administered repeatedly weekly or minimally monthly (as opposed to multiple forms given in one administration, as with screening instruments). Alternate-form reliability is again estimated using the Pearson product–moment correlation coefficient, with coefficients ranging from .60 (minimally) to greater than .80 (preferred) considered sufficient.

Specified rates of improvement refers to minimal acceptable growth standards presented as either slope of improvement or average weekly increase in score. Generally calculated using ordinary least squares regression, slope or rate of improvement indicates the average increase in academic performance scores that can be expected from one week to the next. When factors such as standardized scoring and administration and alternate forms are tightly controlled, slope of improvement provides an accurate prediction of expected rate of academic growth over time under typical instructional conditions (Fuchs, Fuchs, Hamlett, Walz, & Germann, 1993; Hintze & Christ, 2004; Hintze et al., 2000; Hintze & Shapiro, 1997; Hintze, Shapiro, & Lutz, 1994). Relatedly, *sensitivity to student improvement* refers to differing rates of improvement that are observed as a function of validated interventions (Fuchs & Fuchs, 1986a, 1986b; Hintze & Pelle Petitte, 2001; Silberglitt & Hintze, 2007). Interpreted similarly to specified rates of improvement, sensitivity to student improvement addresses the differential rates of growth or rate of academic growth that should be observed in response to validated interventions.

End-of-the-year benchmarks refer to the same benchmark expectations noted in data-based decision making using screening measures noted previously; however, in the case of progress monitoring, such benchmarks are used to develop long-term end-of-the-year goals for students whose progress is being monitored on a frequent basis (Fuchs, 1989). Here end-of-the-year benchmarks are used to construct a goal line against which student performance is compared in response to validated instruction. Without such standards, formative data-based decision making is all but impossible because growth data cannot be summarized using conventional descriptive statistics (e.g., mean), and visual analysis has been demonstrated as unreliable and subject to autocorrelation (DeProspero & Cohen, 1979; Ottenbacher, 1990).

Reliability of slope refers to the ratio of true slope variance to total slope variance or, more simply, the extent to which the data accurately represent student performance. Reliability of slope is affected by uncertainty in the individual data points that might arise from some of the conditions noted previously (e.g., problems with unstandardized scoring and administration of measures, poor alternate-form reliability). Reliability of slope is critically important to data-based decision making because formative evaluation assumes that the data are representative of student academic performance as opposed to systematic or random error (Christ, 2006). When reliability of slope is low, data-based formative decision making is affected, and practitioners may make incorrect instructional decisions on the basis of measurement error. When this occurs, practitioners may erroneously modify or jettison an otherwise effective intervention prematurely or unknowingly continue with an ineffective intervention that appears to be successful (Hintze, Wells, & Marcotte, 2009). Relatedly, *predictive validity for slope of improvement* refers to the correlation between slope and some achievement outcome. As with other forms of validity, predictive validity of slope assumes that growth on general outcome measures should be related to overall levels of academic achievement. Lack of such validity calls into question the soundness of the RTI measure used for progress monitoring.

Data-Based Decision Making Using Absolute RTI Student Progress Monitoring Approaches

Once the technical and psychometric properties associated with progress monitoring have been addressed, practitioners may use a number of data-based decision-making rules to evaluate the effects of instructional intervention on individual student performance. Evaluating progress monitoring time-series data follows a three-step process. First, a sufficient number of data points need to be collected before data-based decision making. As a rule, it is recommended that a minimum of eight to 10 weekly data points be collected before formative decision making. Collecting at least this amount of data provides some level of assurance that the data trend is reliable and that data-based decision making will not be unduly influenced by measurement (Good & Shinn, 1990; Hintze et al., 2000; Shinn, Good, & Stein, 1989). Fewer than eight to 10 data points increases the likelihood that the times-series data trend will be unreliable and the accuracy of formative decision making will be sacrificed (Hintze et al., 2000).

Next, once a sufficient amount of data has been collected, the first of two decision-making heuristics is implemented. The first uses the five most recent data points for making a formative decision (Hintze et al., 2009). For example, if eight data points have been collected, the five most recent data points would be used. If 13 data points have been collected, again the five most recent data points would be used. Once identified, if the five most recent data points are all above the goal line that has been established for the student, the data-based decision is to keep the intervention, increase the long-term goal, and continue progress monitoring (see Figure 4.1 for an example). Conversely, if the five most recent data points are all below the goal line, the data-based decision is to modify the instructional intervention, keep the long-term goal, and continue progressing monitor (Figure 4.2).

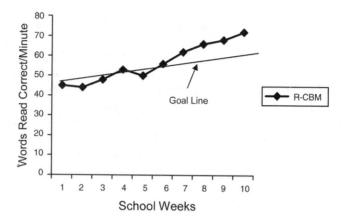

FIGURE 4.1. Example of the "5-point rule" in which the five most recent data points are all above the goal line (R-CBM, reading curriculum-based measurement).

Finally, if the five most recent data points are neither consistently above nor below the goal line, then the second data-based decision-making heuristic is used.

This second decision-making heuristic involves comparing the student's trend line with the established goal line (Fuchs, 1989). The trend line summarizes the student's performance over the time of intervention and is usually calculated using ordinary least squares regression, as noted previously.

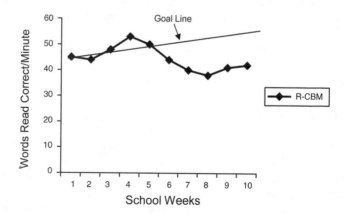

FIGURE 4.2. Example of the "5-point rule" in which the five most recent data points are all below the goal line (R-CBM, reading curriculum-based measurement).

If the student's trend line is steeper than the established goal line, the data-based decision is to keep the intervention, increase the long-term goal, and continue progress monitoring (Figure 4.3). If the student's trend line is shallower than the established goal line, the data-based decision is to modify the instructional intervention, keep the long-term goal, and continue progress monitoring (Figure 4.4). Finally, if the student's trend line is roughly parallel to and at the same level of the established goal line, the data-based decision is to keep the instructional intervention, keep the long-term goal, and continue progress monitoring.

Combining Relative Screening and Absolute Progress Monitoring Data-Based Decision Making into a Dual-Discrepancy Approach of Data-Based Decision Making

When both screening and progress monitoring forms of student assessment are in place, a dual-discrepancy approach to data-based decision making can be used to judge the effectiveness of instructional intervention (Fuchs & Fuchs, 1998, 2005; Fuchs, Mock, Morgan, & Young, 2003). Again, the decision-making heuristic is relatively straightforward once the necessary data have been collected and organized and the student has had sufficient exposure to a validated instructional intervention.

As a first step in the decision-making process, a validated instructional

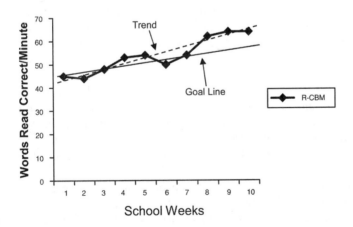

FIGURE 4.3. Graph depicts a situation in which a student's trend line is steeper than the established long-term goal line (R-CBM, reading curriculum-based measurement).

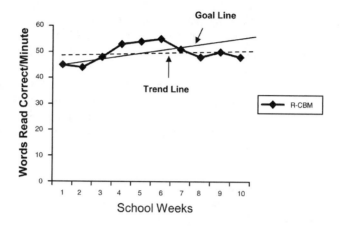

FIGURE 4.4. Graph depicting a situation in which a student's trend line is shallower than the established long-term goal line (R-CBM, reading curriculum-based measurement).

intervention should be provided with high levels of integrity and of sufficient duration to have beneficial effect for typical students. Typically, such interventions are provided for a 10- to 12-week period to ensure ample opportunities to respond and for responsiveness to be measured. At the point of formal intervention evaluation, the progress monitoring data are summarized via slope or rate of growth. As previously noted, the resultant slope statistic represents the average growth or responsiveness to the intervention from one week to the next. In addition, the students' most recent universal benchmark screening assessment information is gathered. If the intervention has been in place for the 10- to 12-week recommended time frame, this benchmark screening assessment will be the one that has occurred since the students' original entry into instructional intervention (assuming that most benchmark assessments are spaced approximately 9 weeks apart). If no new benchmark screening assessment has occurred during this time frame, this assessment information should be updated to a current benchmark assessment.

Once these two pieces of assessment information are gathered, evaluation via a dual-discrepancy approach proceeds as follows. First, if students' current benchmark performance levels place them as not at risk using either of the two data-based screening evaluation methods noted previously, they are returned to Tier 1 and the supplemental intervention is discontinued. The students' responsiveness to the instructional intervention has been of sufficient magnitude that their rate of progress has resulted in their ability to be able to meet benchmark-level performance expectations successfully.

Second, if students' current benchmark performance levels continue to be below benchmark expectations (continuing to place them at risk) but their rate of growth or slope is equal to or exceeds expectations, as determined by the progress monitoring data-based decision-making heuristics noted previously or in comparison to peer growth expectations, they may be maintained in the Tier 2 instructional intervention. The assumption is that the students' responsiveness to the instructional intervention has been positive but needs to be continued in order for them to meet benchmark-level performance expectations in the future. During this time, formative data-based decision making will continue using either the 5-point rule or comparison of trend line to goal line approach, with instructional modifications made as required.

Finally, if after sufficient or repeated validated instructional intervention (e.g., 10–12 weeks) students continue to perform at levels that are below benchmark expectations and their responsiveness as measured over time continues to be low, they may be considered for comprehensive evaluations and possible special educational services.

SUMMARY

This chapter has attempted to summarize many of the salient measurement and psychometric features associated with data-based decision making and RTI dual-discrepancy approaches in particular. Although somewhat new to most educators, data-based measurement systems have a long history, with much of the work associated with academic assessment occurring over the better part of the last 30 years. Indeed, very few educational assessment technologies have been scrutinized as intensely as data-based decision-making measurement.

The balance of this research has demonstrated data-based decision-making systems to be highly reliable and valid forms of educational assessment. In comparison to more typical approaches to assessment, which rely on point estimates of student performance gathered at one or perhaps two points in time maximally, data-based assessment has been highly successful in its ability to provide multiple alternate assessment forms, which allows for the evaluation of student growth over time in a manner that is sensitive to both instructional effects and development changes. In providing such assessment technology, the field now has a strong and ever-improving understanding of typical growth rates for student development in basic academic areas and criterion standards by which sound educational and instructional decisions can be made.

Nonetheless, with the increased call for data-based decision making, particularly within an RTI approach, further research of such measures appears needed. First, although much has been learned with respect to classification accuracy, continued research in this area is warranted. Further examination of the cut scores used to determine risk, variations of risk status, and comparison to multiple external criteria represent just a few of the areas that require future consideration. Moreover, with enhanced statistical technology, the continued evaluation of reliability of slope is of paramount importance. Until very recently, the reliability of the trend data that are used for data-based decision making has been all but ignored. If the data that represent student trends are of dubious quality, it stands to reason that the instructional decisions made on such data will be of dubious quality as well. Increasing the reliability of slope and reducing measurement error will help ensure that accurate data-based instructional decisions are being made. Last, in an increasingly pluralistic society, the generalizability of data-based decision-making measurement technology needs further development. Studies involving large samples with resampling can help improve the generalizability of data-based decision making, and focused studies with disaggregated diverse populations will enhance the validity of instructional decisions for those from diverse backgrounds.

REFERENCES

Allen, M. J., & Yen, W. M. (2001). *Introduction to measurement theory*. New York: Waveland Press.

Christ, T. J. (2006). Short term estimates of growth using curriculum-based measurement of oral reading fluency: Estimates of standard error of slope to construct confidence intervals. *School Psychology Review, 35,* 128-133.

Christ, T. J., & Hintze, J. M. (2007). Psychometric considerations when evaluating response to intervention. In S. R. Jimerson, M. K. Burns, & A. M. VanDerHeyden (Eds.), *Handbook of response to intervention: The science and practice of assessment and intervention* (pp. 99–105). New York: Springer Science.

Crocker, L. M., & Algina, J. (2006). *Introduction to classical and modern test theory*. New York: Cengage Learning.

Deno, S. L. (1985). Curriculum-based measurement: The emerging alternative. *Exceptional Children, 52,* 219-232.

Deno, S. L., Mirkin, P., & Chiang, B. (1982). Identifying valid measures of reading. *Exceptional Children, 49,* 36-45.

DeProspero, A., & Cohen, S. (1979). Inconsistent visual analysis of intrasubject data. *Journal of Applied Behavior Analysis, 12,* 573-579.

Fuchs, D., Mock, D., Morgan, P. L., & Young, C. L. (2003). Responsiveness-to-intervention: Definitions, evidence, and implications for the learning disabilities construct. *Learning Disabilities Research and Practice, 18,* 157-171.

Fuchs, L. S. (1989). Evaluating solutions, monitoring progress, and revising intervention plans. In M. R. Shinn (Ed.), *Curriculum-based measurement: Assessing special children* (pp. 153–181). New York: Guilford Press.

Fuchs, L. S. (1995, May). *Curriculum-based measurement and eligibility decision making: An emphasis on treatment validity and growth.* Paper presented at the Workshop on Alternatives to IQ Testing, Washington, DC.

Fuchs, L. S., & Deno, S. L. (1991). Paradigmatic distinctions between instructionally relevant measurement models. *Exceptional Children, 57,* 488–500.

Fuchs, L. S., & Deno, S. L. (1992). Effects of curriculum within curriculum-based measurement. *Exceptional Children, 58,* 232–243.

Fuchs, L. S., & Fuchs, D. (1986a). Curriculum-based assessment of progress toward long- and short-term goals. *Journal of Special Education, 20,* 69–82.

Fuchs, L. S., & Fuchs, D. (1986b). Effects of systematic formative evaluation on student achievement: A meta-analysis. *Exceptional Children, 53,* 199–208.

Fuchs, L. S., & Fuchs, D. (1998). Treatment validity: A unifying concept for reconceptualizing identification of learning disabilities. *Learning Disabilities: Research and Practice, 14,* 204–219.

Fuchs, L. S., & Fuchs, D. (2005). Responsiveness-to-intervention: A blueprint for practitioners, policymakers, and parents. *Teaching Exceptional Children, 38,* 57–61.

Fuchs, L. S., Fuchs, D., Hamlett, C. L., Walz, L., & Germann, G. (1993). Formative evaluation of academic progress: How much growth can we expect? *School Psychology Review, 22,* 27–48.

Good, R. H., & Shinn, M. R. (1990). Forecasting accuracy of slope estimates for reading curriculum-based measurement: Empirical evidence. *Behavioral Assessment, 12,* 179–193.

Heller, K. A., Holtzman, W. H., & Messick, S. (Eds.). (1982). *Placing children in special education: A strategy for equity.* Washington, DC: National Academy Press.

Hintze, J. M. (2009). Conceptual and empirical issues related to developing a response-to-intervention framework. *Journal of Evidence-Based Practices for Schools, 9,* 128–147.

Hintze, J. M., & Christ, T. J. (2004). An examination of variability as a function of passage variance in CBM progress monitoring. *School Psychology Review, 33,* 204–217.

Hintze, J. M., Christ, T. J., & Methe, S. A. (2006). Curriculum-based assessment. *Psychology in the Schools, 43,* 45–56.

Hintze, J. M., Daly, E. J., & Shapiro, E. S. (1998). An investigation of the effects of passage difficulty level on oral reading fluency for progress monitoring. *School Psychology Review, 27,* 433–445.

Hintze, J. M., Owen, S. V., Shapiro, E. S., & Daly, E. J. (2000). Generalizability of oral reading fluency measures: Application of G theory to curriculum-based measurement. *School Psychology Quarterly, 15,* 52–68.

Hintze, J. M., & Pelle Petitte, H. A. (2001). The generalizability of CBM oral reading fluency measures across general and special education. *Journal of Psychoeducational Assessment, 19,* 158–170.

Hintze, J. M., Ryan, A. L., & Stoner, G. (2003). Concurrent validity and diagnostic accuracy of the Dynamic Indicators of Basic Early Literacy Skills and the Comprehensive Test of Phonological Processing. *School Psychology Review*, 33, 258–270.

Hintze, J. M., & Shapiro, E. S. (1997). Curriculum-based measurement and literature-based reading: Is curriculum-based measurement meeting the needs of changing reading curricula? *Journal of School Psychology*, 35, 351–375.

Hintze, J. M., Shapiro, E. S., & Lutz, J. G. (1994). The effects of curriculum on the sensitivity of curriculum-based measurement in reading. *Journal of Special Education*, 28, 188–202.

Hintze, J. M., & Silberglitt, B. (2005). A longitudinal examination of the diagnostic accuracy and predictive validity of R-CBM and high-stakes testing. *School Psychology Review*, 34, 454–474.

Hintze, J. M., Wells, C. S., & Marcotte, A. M. (2009). *Decision making accuracy of CBM progress monitoring time series data*. Manuscript submitted for publication.

Johnston, J. M., & Pennypacker, H. S. (2008). *Strategies and tactics of behavioral research* (3rd ed.). Hillsdale, NJ: Erlbaum.

Macmann, G. M., & Barnett, D. W. (1999). Diagnostic decision making in school psychology: Understanding and coping with uncertainty. In C. R. Reynolds & T. B. Gutkin (Eds.), *The handbook of school psychology* (pp. 519–548). New York: Wiley.

National Center on Response to Intervention. (2008). *Tools/interventions: Screening reading tools chart*. Retrieved April 21, 2009, from *httpp://www.rti4success. org/index.php?option=com_content&task=view&id=1091&Itemid=139*.

Ottenbacher, K. J. (1990). Visual inspection of single-subject data: An empirical analysis. *Mental Retardation*, 28, 283–290.

Salvia, J., Ysseldyke, J. E., & Bolt, S. E. (2006). *Assessment: In special and inclusive education* (10th ed.). New York: Cengage Learning.

Shinn, M. R. (Ed.). (1989). *Curriculum-based measurement: Assessing special children*. New York: Guilford Press.

Shinn, M. R., & Bamonto, S. (1998). Advanced applications of curriculum-based measurement: "Big ideas" and avoiding confusing. In M. R. Shinn (Ed.), *Advanced applications of curriculum-based measurement* (pp. 1–31). New York: Guilford Press.

Shinn, M. R., Gleason, M. M., & Tindal, G. (1989). Varying the difficulty of testing materials: Implications for curriculum-based measurement. *Journal of Special Education*, 23, 223–233.

Shinn, M. R., Good, R. H., & Stein, S. (1989). Summarizing trend in student achievement: A comparison of methods. *School Psychology Review*, 18, 356–370.

Silberglitt, B., & Hintze, J. M. (2005). Formative assessment using CBM-R cut scores to track progress toward success on state-mandated achievement tests: A comparison of methods. *Journal of Psychoeducational Assessment*, 23, 304–325.

Silberglitt, B., & Hintze, J. M. (2007). How much growth can we expect? A conditional analysis of R-CBM growth rates by level of performance. *Exceptional Children*, 74, 71–84.

Swets, J. A. (1986). Form of empirical ROCs in discrimination and diagnostic tasks: Implications for theory and measurement of performance. *Psychological Bulletin, 99*, 181–198.

Swets, J. A. (1988). Measuring the accuracy of diagnostic systems. *Science, 240*(4857), 1285–1293.

Swets, J. A. (1992). The science of choosing the right decision threshold in high-stakes diagnostics. *American Psychologist, 47*, 522–532.

Swets, J. A., Dawes, R. M., & Monahan, J. (2000). Psychological science can improve diagnostic decisions. *Psychological Science in the Public Interest, 1*, 1–26.

5

Preventing and Remediating Reading Difficulties

Perspectives from Research

Carolyn A. Denton
Sharon Vaughn

INTRODUCTION

Large numbers of students in U.S. schools have reading difficulties of varying severity. Although the 2007 results of the National Assessment of Educational Progress reflected small but significant gains in fourth- and eighth-grade reading achievement, about 33% of fourth-grade students and 26% of eighth-grade students still failed to demonstrate even "partial mastery of prerequisite knowledge and skills that are fundamental for proficient work at a given grade" (Lee, Grigg, & Donahue, 2007, p. 6).

For students from poverty-level backgrounds and members of ethnic and linguistic minority groups, these percentages are appreciably higher. Moreover, about 80 to 90% of students identified as having specific learning disabilities (SLDs) have significant reading difficulties (Kavale & Reese, 1992; Lerner, 1989). This situation has significant consequences for individual students, for schools, and for the country. The purpose of this chapter is to provide school psychologists and other practitioners with up-to-date information about evidence-based practices in the prevention and remediation of reading difficulties.

PREVENTION OF READING DIFFICULTIES

Although interventions designed to reduce risk may be provided at any age, the word *prevention* in reading education is commonly used to describe interventions that are provided to young children, usually in the primary grades. Because students are just beginning to read at this age, intervention is delivered with the goal of preventing eventual reading difficulties. In this chapter, we refer to reading intervention provided to children in the primary grades as *prevention*, and intervention for older students who have already experienced some degree of reading failure as *remediation*.

Recent educational initiatives have emphasized the critical role of early reading instruction in the prevention of reading difficulties, recognizing that students who do not learn to read adequately in the primary grades typically have persistent reading difficulties throughout their school years (Francis, Shaywitz, Stuebing, Shaywitz, & Fletcher, 1996; Juel, 1988; Torgesen & Burgess, 1998). Over the past 20 to 30 years, a considerable research base has produced converging findings about critical elements of reading instruction associated with improved outcomes for students. These findings have been synthesized and summarized in several high-profile reports, including the report of the National Research Council in 1998 (Snow, Burns, & Griffin, 1998), the report published 2 years later by the National Reading Panel (2000), and the RAND Reading Study Group report (2001). Since the publication of these documents, several meta-analyses and systematic research syntheses have been published, confirming the knowledge base about the prevention of reading difficulties. Both classroom and tutorial studies have shown that early intervention reduces the number of students at risk for reading difficulties, including those who might eventually be identified as having learning disabilities (Mathes & Denton, 2002; Torgesen, 2000).

This growing research base provides guidelines about factors that need to be in place for preventing reading difficulties in young students. In this section, we describe these factors, addressing both the content that should be addressed and characteristics of effective instruction for these students. We organize this description within the context of multitiered reading intervention models commonly associated with the implementation of response-to-intervention (RTI) approaches. We begin with a brief overview of RTI models in reading, followed by a description of evidence-based practices in classwide reading instruction and in small-group reading interventions.

RTI in Preventive Reading Models

Based on the large body of research related to effective instruction for the prevention of reading difficulties, preventive RTI models for early reading have emerged. In large part, these models were also derived from research on "prereferral intervention," in which teachers provide intervention and adaptations to reduce the overidentification of students with learning and behavioral disabilities when their problems could be addressed within general education.

One widely adopted preventive RTI reading model consists of multiple tiers of intervention of increasing intensity that are delivered as students demonstrate insufficient response to less intensive intervention. These tiered prevention models are delivered using methods of empirically validated reading instruction. Assessment is a cornerstone of RTI models, including assessment for the purposes of screening to identify students at risk for reading difficulties, planning instruction that targets the needs of struggling readers (i.e., diagnostic assessment), monitoring student progress, and measuring outcomes.

Preventive RTI reading models often consist of three tiers of intervention (see, e.g., Batsche et al., 2006; Denton, Fletcher, Simos, Papanicolaou, & Anthony, 2007; Denton & Mathes, 2003; Fletcher, Denton, Fuchs, & Vaughn, 2005; Vaughn, Wanzek, Woodruff, & Linan-Thompson, 2007). The first tier consists of high-quality classroom-level reading instruction delivered to all students. This typically includes differentiation of instruction to better address the unique needs of all students, particularly those at risk for reading difficulties. Students with inadequate RTI in Tier 1 receive Tier 2 intervention in addition to quality classroom instruction, provided by either their classroom teachers or other interventionists. However, even when these two levels of intervention are highly effective, there is a small population of students who receive supplemental intervention but continue to struggle. Under a three-tier model, these students would receive Tier 3 intensive intervention.

Exactly how these Tier 3 interventions are provided differs in implementation. For some schools, this tertiary intervention is provided in "special education" (e.g., Denton & Mathes, 2003). That is, to receive a Tier 3 intervention, the student must be declared eligible for special education services. In other intervention approaches, Tier 3 is considered a general education intervention and is provided to all students who need it. In some school implementation models, only students who require this level of intensive intervention *over an extended period of time* would be candidates for special education (e.g., Batsche et al., 2006). In other models, Tier 3 intervention is provided by special education teachers even if all Tier 3 students do not have IEPs; in this case entitlement to special education is not a requirement for receiving Tier 3 intervention.

Students who are identified as inadequate responders under a tiered intervention model have been found to differ from students with other forms of low achievement in cognitive characteristics and preintervention achievement scores (Stage, Abbott, Jenkins, & Berninger, 2003; Vaughn, Linan-Thompson, & Hickman, 2003; Vellutino, Scanlon, & Jaccard, 2003), as well as in their neurological processing when engaged in reading tasks (Simos et al., 2007a, 2007b). Tiered intervention models hold considerable promise for implementing RTI as a component in the identification of SLDs, while also serving as a vehicle for providing intervention to all young children who are at risk for reading difficulties, regardless of eligibility for special education services.

Effective Classwide Reading Instruction

The first, and arguably the most important, component of effective early reading intervention is the provision of evidence-based high-quality classroom reading instruction to all students in the primary grades. Quality classroom reading instruction can have a large impact. For example, Foorman, Francis, Fletcher, Schatschneider, and Mehta (1998) demonstrated that first-grade classroom reading instruction that included explicit, systematic instruction in the alphabetic principle within a print-rich environment brought 75% of at-risk readers to average word-reading levels.

Snow and her colleagues (1998) in the National Research Council early reading group, concluded that "Adequate progress in learning to read English beyond the initial level depends on having established a working understanding of how sounds are represented alphabetically, sufficient practice in reading to achieve fluency with different kinds of texts written for different purposes, instruction focused on concept and vocabulary growth, and control over procedures for monitoring comprehension and repairing misunderstandings" (Snow et al., 1998, p. 223). They emphasized the importance of providing (1) explicit instruction in phonemic awareness and phonics, (2) instruction in making meaning from text, and (3) many opportunities to read and write connected text within a literature-rich environment, both with teacher support and feedback and independently. Finally, they identified the need to adapt instruction (including grouping practices and the level of explicitness) to meet the needs of each student.

These recommendations have been echoed in subsequent research syntheses and meta-analyses. The National Reading Panel (2000) described the critical content that should be the focus of reading instruction in the primary grades: phonemic awareness, phonics, fluency, vocabulary, and comprehension. Converging research evidence has demonstrated that effective classroom instruction for most students in kindergarten through third grade includes explicitly and directly teaching phonics or word study and providing opportunities to apply skills while reading and writing connected text (e.g., Ehri, 2003; National Reading Panel, 2000; Rayner, Foorman, Perfetti, Pesetsky, & Seidenberg, 2001; Snow et al., 1998). Effective K–3 instruction also includes integrated instruction in fluency, vocabulary, and comprehension (e.g., Chard, Vaughn, & Tyler, 2002; Jitendra, Edwards, Sacks, & Jacobson, 2004).

Implementation and Adaptation of an Evidence-Based Core Reading Program

Teachers should not be expected to reinvent the wheel in designing classroom reading instruction. A quality, evidence-based published program is the foundation of Tier 1 instruction. To ensure the provision of quality classroom reading instruction, administrators and teachers (1) adopt a published curriculum that has evidence of effectiveness from the converging research base in reading instruction, (2) ensure that teachers have adequate training (and ongoing coaching, if possible) to implement the program with confidence and fidelity, and (3) monitor the effective implementation of the curriculum.

Adaptation of Classroom Instruction for At-Risk Readers

Effectively teaching reading to each child in a primary-grade classroom presents substantial challenges, because a typical classroom may include students who are unable to read even at basic levels, along with students who are already proficient readers and need instruction in advanced comprehension and vocabulary strategies. It is common that some students in a primary classroom will have identified disabilities, whereas others may have severe learning and behavioral difficulties that have not yet been identified as disabilities. Still others may be identified as having gifts and talents and require specialized instruction. Increasing numbers of students do not speak English as their primary language but receive their reading instruction in an English-only classroom. Meeting the needs of each individual student is a tall order for one teacher, a task that should not be underestimated.

DIFFERENTIATING INSTRUCTION

A key characteristic of quality Tier 1 class-wide intervention is *differentiation of instruction*. Differentiation means providing groups of students within the classroom with instruction that is purposefully planned to address their needs. Typically, it involves teachers implementing reading instruction in small groups, in addition to whole-class and peer-partner formats. Differentiated instruction for young students at risk for reading difficulties usually includes the use of diagnostic- and progress-monitoring assessment (e.g., program placement or mastery tests, inventories of sight word or letter–

sound knowledge, repeated measures of reading and reading-related skills) that can provide information to teachers about student strengths and needs. The results of these assessments can be used to form small, flexible groups of students with similar needs and to plan their instruction. Some teachers may need support in designing effective differentiated instruction, managing small-group instruction, and establishing classroom routines that enable students with whom the teacher is not working to engage in independent practice of concepts and skills they have already been taught without direct teacher monitoring.

Although a quality reading curriculum will provide the foundation for effective classwide instruction, it is typically necessary for teachers to *adapt instruction* for at-risk readers. For example, programs typically introduce skills at a rapid rate and often do not provide enough practice opportunities for struggling readers. Quality core reading instruction can be adapted for at-risk readers by making it more explicit and systematic and by increasing opportunities for practice with and without teacher feedback and scaffolding. These approaches are described in the following sections.

INCREASING EXPLICITNESS OF INSTRUCTION

A teacher who provides *explicit instruction* (1) plans lessons purposefully with clear objectives in mind, (2) clearly models or demonstrates skills and provides clear descriptions of new concepts (including both examples and nonexamples), (3) provides guided practice, (4) checks for understanding, (5) provides timely feedback as well as deliberate scaffolding, (6) monitors independent practice, (7) provides opportunities for cumulative practice of previously learned skills and concepts, and (8) monitors student progress, providing reteaching as necessary. When at-risk learners receive clear, explicit instruction, they are not left to infer information. Students who are easily confused are more likely to be successful when teachers demonstrate and clearly explain what they need to learn. On the other hand, if points of confusion are not addressed and foundational skills are not mastered, students will likely fall farther and farther behind their peers.

For example, imagine that Teacher 1 is reading a book aloud to kindergarten students. She comes to the word *pebble* in the book and asks, "Who knows what a pebble is?" Several students answer at once. One calls out, "Part of a flower"; another says, "A rock." The teacher says, "Yes. See the pebbles in the picture?" pointing to the pebbles in the book's illustration, then continues to read the story. Now imagine Teacher 2 reading the same book to her kindergarten class. She has identified in advance three or four words that may be unfamiliar to the students and that are appropriate to teach, and she has written simple, easy-to-understand definitions, as well as more elaborate descriptions, for each word. She selects the word *pebble* because it is important to the understanding of the book she is reading and it appears in traditional stories but is not commonly used in oral conversations. When she comes to the word *pebble*, she says clearly, "A pebble is a little rock. Look at the picture of a pebble here in the book. This big rock is not a pebble [pointing to the illustration], but this little rock is a pebble. Say *pebble*. [Students repeat the word.] Sometimes children like to pick up little pebbles and throw them out into the water." After reading the book, she returns to the word and asks students about times they may have picked up pebbles. She makes sure that students actually use the word *pebble*. She provides feedback or support if students have problems using the word correctly. She will return to the word in future days and use it again to give students multiple exposures to it. Teacher 1 requires students to infer what a pebble is from the picture, and many students may be left confused. Teacher 2 is providing explicit vocabulary instruction.

PROVIDING SYSTEMATIC INSTRUCTION

Systematic instruction is carefully sequenced, so that easier skills are presented and mastered before more complex skills are introduced, and confusions are minimized. For example, a systematic beginning reading program would introduce new letter–sound correspondences in a sequence designed so that letters are separated from each other if they are potentially visually confusing (e.g., *b* and *d*; *p* and *q*; *v* and *w*) or have similar sounds (e.g., "short" *e* and *i*). Skills and strategies are taught in a predetermined order according to a clear scope and sequence so that "holes" are not left in students' learning. Students' accumulation of concepts, skills, and strategies is monitored so that reteaching can occur when needed.

Students with reading difficulties tend to benefit when instruction progresses systematically from simple skills, words, and text to more complex words, higher-level vocabulary, and more challenging comprehension strategies. In most effective reading intervention programs, the pace of introduction of new material is reasonable to ensure mastery by at-risk readers, and the amount of new information introduced at any one lesson is kept to a minimum. Much of the lesson consists of practice of previously introduced skills, strategies, and concepts and the integration of these with the newly taught material. The most important way schools can ensure that teachers provide systematic instruction to students with reading difficulties is by adopting and using curricula developed in this way.

INCREASING OPPORTUNITIES FOR PRACTICE

Published core reading programs rarely include enough *practice activities* for at-risk readers to master skills. Students with learning difficulties typically need extended guided, independent, and cumulative practice. During *guided practice*, students practice reading skills in isolation, as well as the application of skills in reading and writing, *with teacher feedback*. Students need both positive and corrective feedback. Specific positive feedback calls attention to behaviors and processes they are implementing well and also reinforces partially correct responses and attempts, even when they do not result in correct answers. Students also need to know when they have made mistakes. If clear, corrective feedback is not provided, students are likely to continue making the same errors, in effect "practicing their mistakes" (Denton & Hocker, 2006, p. 17), forming habits that are difficult to break. Students also need *independent practice*, during which they implement skills and strategies without teacher support (but with close teacher monitoring and reteaching when necessary).

Finally, students at risk for reading difficulties need large amounts of *cumulative practice* to learn skills and strategies to the point at which they can apply them automatically, as proficient readers do. In cumulative practice, students practice items they have previously learned and integrate them with newly learned items, supporting retention of previously learned material. Cumulative practice also provides at-risk readers with the opportunity to *discriminate* between previously and newly learned items such as letter–sound correspondences and high-frequency irregular words. For example, imagine that a student has previously learned to recognize the words *was* and *what*. In a new lesson, the student learns the word *who*. It will be important to provide opportunities to practice quickly and accurately discriminating between these words and other words the student knows in order to integrate new and prior learning.

Two Tier 1 Adaptations

Two broad categories of research-supported, classroom-based Tier 1 adaptations have potential for affecting reading performance without requiring major restructuring of the reading program: classwide peer tutoring and computer-assisted instruction. These are *not* substitutes for the high-fidelity implementation of an evidence-based core reading program or for differentiated instruction for at-risk readers, as described previously. However, both can be effective in providing additional reinforcement and practice in previously taught concepts, skills, and strategies.

CLASSWIDE PEER TUTORING

Solid research evidence supports the effectiveness of classwide peer-tutoring models implemented in the early grades to aid in reading development (Fuchs & Fuchs, 2005; Mathes, Torgesen, & Allor, 2001; McMaster, Fuchs,

& Fuchs, 2006; Saenz, Fuchs, & Fuchs, 2005). In a typical implementation described by Mathes, Grek, and Howard (1999), low-performing readers are paired with more skilled readers. In these pairs, students engage in highly standardized practice of previously learned elements such as letter–sound correspondences and high-frequency words followed by paired reading that includes a simple prereading and postreading comprehension routine. It is critical that students are carefully and explicitly taught *routines* to follow when engaging in peer tutoring so that they can implement this format independently with little off-task time.

COMPUTER-ASSISTED INSTRUCTION

Hall, Hughes, and Filbert (2000) conducted a systematic synthesis of the research on computer-assisted instruction (CAI) for students with learning disabilities, locating experimental, quasi-experimental, and single-case studies involving students in kindergarten through high school. They found that most computer applications studied for this population are designed to provide *extra* drill and practice in basic skills. The intensity of CAI provided varied greatly from study to study, with students receiving from 1 to 50 sessions lasting from 10 to 40 minutes each. Hall et al. found evidence of effectiveness of CAI in supporting reading growth for students with learning disabilities, particularly in providing additional opportunities for practice in skills that had been previously taught. It is important to note that *in no case was a computer application suggested as a replacement for teacher-delivered instruction.*

The Hall et al. (2000) review revealed that in 13 of the 17 studies that met their criteria for inclusion in the synthesis, computer programs were designed to incorporate teaching strategies that have been found effective for students with learning difficulties, and that all of these studies resulted in significant effects favoring the CAI application. Specifically, effective programs included (1) those in which skills and strategies were introduced in a systematic order; (2) those that provided elaborated error correction (i.e., correction that included instruction) rather than simply informing students that they had made an error or simply provided the correct response; and (3) those that cycled back through previously missed items, providing additional rehearsal of correct responses (i.e., cumulative practice). Hall and colleagues suggested that educators evaluate computer applications for these and other characteristics associated with effective instruction.

When Classwide Instruction Is Not Enough— Tier 2 Intervention

In multitier prevention models, students with an unsatisfactory response to quality classwide instruction in the primary grades are provided with Tier 2 intervention in addition to their regular classroom reading instruction. This is sometimes referred to as secondary prevention or secondary intervention. The primary goal of Tier 2 intervention is to reduce the performance gap between at-risk readers and their typically developing peers. Given that closing this gap—like catching up in a race—necessitates that at-risk readers learn at a faster rate than their average-performing peers, secondary intervention for these at-risk readers must be both *highly effective* and *efficient*. Unlike traditional "remedial reading" classes, Tier 2 interventions are delivered with a level of intensity that will accelerate the progress of students who have previously demonstrated slow growth on repeated measures of reading skills. Both McMaster, Fuchs, Fuchs, and Compton (2005) and Mathes et al. (2005) found that potentially less than 5% of first-grade students would remain at risk for reading difficulties if high-quality Tier 2 interventions supplemented Tier 1 instruction in first grade.

Characteristics of Effective Intervention

Converging research evidence supports the efficacy of intervening with young students at risk for reading difficulties, both for monolingual English readers and more recently, for English language learners. (For monolingual, see Blachman et al., 2004; Denton, Fletcher, Anthony, & Francis, 2006; Felton, 1993; Jenkins & O'Connor, 2002; Kamps & Greenwood, 2005; Lovett, Steinbach, & Frijters, 2000; Mathes et al., 2005; Torgesen et al., 1999; Torgesen, Alexander, et al., 2001; Vellutino et al., 1996. For English language learners, see Vaughn, Cirino, et al., 2006; Vaughn, Linan-Thompson, et al., 2006.) A recent systematic research synthesis examined implications of studies of long-term, "extensive" early reading interventions, defined as those in which small-group interventions were provided as supplements to regular classroom reading instruction for at least 100 sessions (e.g., daily for about 20 weeks; Wanzek & Vaughn, 2007). Wanzek and Vaughn included studies published in peer-reviewed journals between 1995 and 2005 in which participants in kindergarten through third grade were described as having reading difficulties, being at risk for reading difficulties, having learning disabilities, and/or having speech–language disorders. They concluded that providing small-group intervention for at least 20 weeks was feasible for schools, that such interventions have resulted in positive outcomes for students, and that interventions with the strongest effects included *both* phonics instruction and text reading. These findings are congruent with those of Snow et al. (1998), discussed previously.

In additional exploratory analyses, Wanzek and Vaughn (2007) found that regardless of intervention duration, interventions provided in one-on-one formats tended to have higher effects than those provided in small groups of two to eight students. However, they cautioned against overinterpreting these findings; causal inference is not possible because none of the synthesized studies experimentally manipulated intervention duration or group size. Furthermore, based on the synthesized studies, it was impossible to contrast small-group interventions (i.e., two to four students) with intervention provided in larger group sizes.

Wanzek and Vaughn (2007) also contrasted effects of scripted interventions with those of less prescriptive interventions, finding no difference in effects associated with these approaches. This conclusion was based on a relatively small group of studies, but was strengthened by a randomized field trial by Mathes et al. (2005), who compared the effects of two approaches on the reading outcomes of at-risk first-grade readers: one was a fully scripted intervention with a Direct Instruction approach (the Proactive intervention); the other was an intervention in which teachers were provided with a systematic instructional sequence and a menu of fully described activities, from which they designed individualized lessons based on continuous diagnostic assessment (the Responsive intervention). Random assignment to one of the two intervention conditions or to a comparison typical school practice condition was done within schools. Both the Proactive and Responsive interventions were provided in groups of three to four students by highly trained teachers over 30 weeks, and students in both conditions received explicit instruction in phonemic awareness and phonics, integrated with instruction in fluency and comprehension.

The two interventions differed in that students in the Proactive intervention spent comparably more time practicing skills in isolation and applied them in fully decodable text, whereas those in the Responsive intervention spent more time engaged in reading and writing, with teacher feedback and scaffolding, and read text leveled for difficulty but not designed to be decodable. Students in both intervention groups had significantly higher outcomes than those in the typical practice comparison group on multiple reading measures, but the effects of the two interventions differed significantly on only one measure—the Woodcock–Johnson III Tests of Achievement Word Attack subtest (a test of pseudoword reading), in which the Proactive approach had stronger effects. It is important to note that both interventions had characteristics associated with positive outcomes for students with reading difficulties, including explicit instruction, engaged reading practice with feedback, multiple opportunities for practice, and continuous monitoring of student progress. Differences in the level of standardization versus individualization of the two interventions and the use of decodable text did not result in overall significant differences in outcomes.

As shown by these and other studies, outcomes for children at risk for reading difficulties can be significantly affected by intervention that

- is provided in addition to regular classroom reading instruction;
- is provided in small-group or one-on-one formats;

- includes explicit, well-organized (systematic) instruction as well as opportunities to read connected text;
- is provided for 20–40 minutes at least three to five times per week;
- provides extended opportunities for practice, including guided, independent, and cumulative practice with teacher feedback;
- includes continuous progress monitoring assessment.

What is considered appropriate Tier 2 intervention differs across models of tiered reading intervention being implemented in various locations. In some, the approaches that we have described as Tier 1 adaptations would be considered Tier 2 interventions. In other implementations, students receive a few weeks of Tier 2 tutoring 3 or 4 times per week, while students in some schools receive Tier 2 intervention daily for 20 to 30 weeks. When making decisions regarding the duration of Tier 2 and Tier 3 intervention, it is critical to remember that, in a relatively brief amount of time, we hope to have at-risk readers catch up with their peers. At the same time it is important to think about the implications of providing intervention for long periods of time without evaluation for special education services.

As educators select or develop instructional programs and curricular materials to implement during Tier 2 or Tier 3 intervention, they should consider whether a program (1) has research-backed evidence of effectiveness with at-risk readers at the grade level and level of severity of the students in their schools, (2) addresses the specific needs of the students, and (3) is designed to give students many opportunities to actively participate in hands-on activities that provide practice in key skills and engaged reading practice with teacher feedback.

Implementation of Reading Intervention

Providing quality reading intervention to all students who respond inadequately to Tier 1 classroom instruction can be challenging, given the realities associated with limited time, personnel, and funding in schools. The extent of the resources needed to provide Tier 2 and Tier 3 intervention will be determined by the number of students at risk for reading problems. If a large percentage of students in a school need Tier 2 intervention, it is advisable to examine Tier 1 classroom reading instruction to determine whether (1) an evidence-based core reading program has been adopted and is being *implemented with fidelity* by teachers; (2) teachers have been provided with adequate professional development to implement the core reading program competently and confidently; (3) teachers are providing differentiated instruction to meet the needs of diverse learners; and (4) teachers are adapting instruction for at-risk readers by making it more explicit and systematic, increasing opportunities for practice, and providing instruction using appropriate materials, including instructional-level text (text that can be read accurately with teacher support). As a rule of thumb, the more students in a school who require Tier 2 intervention, the more critical it is that Tier 1 classroom teachers adapt their instruction as described.

Supplemental intervention can be provided within various formats. Students may receive "push in" intervention, in which the interventionist provides tutoring in the student's regular classroom, or "pull-out" intervention, in which tutoring is provided outside the regular classroom setting. In some schools, intervention is provided before or after school. In others, students in the primary grades leave their classrooms for a few minutes for each intervention lesson. In any case, Tier 2 intervention should be provided *in addition to* Tier 1 rather than replacing it. Students who struggle to learn to read need *more* instruction and practice, and, even if their decoding is impaired, they can benefit from grade-level instruction in comprehension and vocabulary.

INTERVENTIONISTS

Tier 2 intervention can be provided by (1) general education classroom teachers who work cooperatively to organize their daily schedules to provide interventions; (2) reading specialists or other certified teachers, including special educators; or (3) carefully selected, highly trained paraprofessionals who receive sustained coaching and supervision from a skilled and experienced teacher. Although having certified teachers provide reading intervention may be ideal, research evidence indicates that Tier 2 intervention provided by well-trained paraprofessionals or tutors who are provided ongoing feedback and support is associated with improved outcomes for students (Elbaum, Vaughn, Hughes, & Moody, 2000; Grek, Mathes, & Torgesen, 2003). If paraprofessionals provide Tier 2 intervention, the following are important considerations: (1) the paraprofessionals should be carefully selected (e.g., able to pass a test of phonemic awareness, possess experience in working positively with children); (2) group sizes should be kept very small (i.e., ratios from 1:1 to 1:3) to provide effective instruction, feedback, and behavior management; (3) published, highly structured reading intervention programs should be implemented, supporting inexperienced tutors; and (4) an experienced full-time teacher should coach the paraprofessionals, spending extended amounts of time observing the tutoring, modeling effective instruction, problem-solving when students fail to make adequate progress, and providing follow-up training sessions. By contrast, Tier 3 intervention should be provided by experienced reading teachers or special educators. Students in Tier 3 are the most challenging to teach, and they need (and deserve) instruction from the most knowledgeable and experienced teachers.

GROUP SIZE AND DURATION

Although providing one-on-one instruction to at-risk readers has been associated with positive outcomes (e.g., Simos et al., 2002; Torgesen et al., 2001; Velutino et al., 1996), this is often not feasible in school settings. In several studies, a large percentage of students have responded positively to Tier 2 intervention delivered in small groups of three to five students (e.g., Mathes et al., 2005; Vaughn & Linan-Thompson, 2003). In general, intervention provided in groups of about three students with one teacher can have comparable effects at Tier 2 to one-on-one interventions (Elbaum, Vaughn, Hughes, & Moody, 2000; Vaughn et al., 2003). Conversely, there is evidence that students benefit significantly less from intervention provided in groups of about 10 students (Vaughn et al., 2003).

Increasing intervention intensity at Tier 3 implies smaller instructional group sizes, longer daily sessions, and intervention over a longer term. A landmark study illustrates what highly intensive intervention can achieve: Torgesen, Alexander, and colleagues (2001) provided students with severe reading needs in grades 3–5 (all of whom had identified learning disabilities) with intervention for 2 hours per day over an 8-week period in a clinical setting. The intervention was associated with substantial standard score gains in decoding and comprehension, which were maintained for 2 years following intervention. Denton et al. (2006) evaluated the effectiveness of Tier 3 intervention provided in school, rather than in clinical settings. In that study, students who previously had inadequate RTI in a less intensive intervention, along with a group of teacher-identified students with severe reading difficulties and disabilities, were provided with daily intervention in groups of two students with one teacher over a 16-week period. For the first 8 weeks, intervention was provided for 2 hours per day using a published program that emphasized phonemic awareness and phonemic decoding. Following this phase, students received intervention targeting oral reading fluency for 1 hour per day for an additional 8-week period. Although the results of this study were not as robust as those reported by Torgesen et al. (2001), students made significant pre–post growth over the initial decoding-focused phase in basic reading skills (word recognition and phonemic decoding) and in reading comprehension. During the second, fluency-oriented phase, students made significant growth in oral reading fluency. Despite this significant growth in mean standard scores, there was considerable variation in individual students' RTI (Denton, Fletcher, et al., 2007). Some students clearly required either a different type of intervention or intervention provided for a longer duration than the 16 weeks provided in this study.

Although providing intervention for 2 hours per day may not appear feasible in school settings, only a very small percentage of students should require this level of intervention intensity if Tiers 1 and 2 are of high quality. In the implementation of this model in school settings by Denton and her colleagues (2006), the 2-hour intervention block replaced a portion of the Tier 3 students' regular reading instruction (which many received in resource room settings). If Tier 3 intervention is delivered in addition to students' regular classroom reading instruction, somewhat shorter intervention periods may be sufficient. For example, Vaughn, Wanzek, Linan-Thompson, and Murray (2007) described a program of research in which Tier 3 intervention was provided for 50 minutes every day.

Prevention Models and Special Education

For some students who continue to demonstrate inadequate response to intervention of increasing intensity, a full comprehensive evaluation for special education eligibility is indicated. Measures of students' RTI when provided with quality intervention (such as repeated assessments used for monitoring student progress) become a key element of that comprehensive evaluation. For a discussion of the relationship between Tier 3 intervention and special education, and of the nature of the comprehensive evaluation in an RTI model, see Batsche et al. (2006).

REMEDIAL INTERVENTIONS FOR OLDER READERS WITH READING DIFFICULTIES AND DISABILITIES

Considerably more is known about teaching younger students with reading difficulties and disabilities than teaching older students. Early interventions for reading difficulties are typically provided before age 8 and are considered preventive—with instructional goals expressly designed to prevent further reading difficulties and to ensure that students are reading on grade level or above. Interventions for older students typically are remedial, with the goal of enhancing reading performance so students can read for pleasure and learning.

Three syntheses of studies have recently been conducted examining the effects of reading interventions for older students (Edmonds et al., 2009; Reutebuch, Vaughn, & Scammacca, 2009; Scammacca et al., 2007). Each of these syntheses reviewed relevant research on intervention for older students with reading difficulties but employed different criteria to select the synthesized studies. For example, the synthesis provided by Edmonds et al. summarized interventions for 4th through 12th graders with reading difficulties, with an expressed focus on how the interventions influenced comprehension outcomes, whereas the Scammacca et al. (2007) synthesis looked at broader outcomes (e.g., fluency and vocabulary) and that by Reutebuch et al. (2009) focused specifically on students with disabilities.

These syntheses provided the foundation for our analysis and interpretation of effective interventions with older readers. Although the goals of each of these syntheses have a somewhat different focus, many of the outcomes are converging. We have organized the findings from these interventions based on the primary instructional focus of the intervention study: word study, reading fluency, vocabulary, and reading comprehension. We first briefly describe each of these instructional foci, with special consideration for what it means for instructing older students with reading difficulties, and then summarize the relevant research findings.

Word Study

Many educators wonder whether word study is still a relevant instructional focus for older students. We define word study for older students as explicit instruction in word analysis that allows students to be more proficient word-level readers. For older students this may be a review of some of the phonics rules and skills that were either not acquired or incorrectly applied (e.g., vowel rules, reading digraphs). Word study for older students also frequently involves reading multisyllable words. Older students who read words accurately and fluently, and within two grade levels of their current grade, may not require further word study instruction. However, many students are reaching the upper grades deficient in the skills necessary for them to become competent readers, including the ability to read words accurately.

Fletcher (2007) reported that as many as 60% of older students who have reading difficulties have impaired word reading. An additional percentage can recognize words accurately but read slowly, essentially because of slow and nonautomatic word recognition. Thus, many older students with reading difficulties or disabilities will require additional word study instruction to become proficient word readers so that they can learn effortlessly from the text. These students may have learned ways to compensate for their poor decoding by using listening comprehension to avoid reading. Many of these students have listening comprehension abilities that exceed their reading comprehension, with slow and inaccurate decoding as the likely reason (Shankweiler et al., 1999).

There is evidence that older students who fall behind may benefit considerably from specialized, intensive instruction aimed at improving word reading (e.g., Torgesen, Alexander, et al., 2001). Although decoding instruction is typically associated with reading instruction for younger students, age should not be the factor in determining the focus of reading instruction (Moats, 2001) but rather the critical skills students need for success. Some older students with reading difficulties are proficient decoders and need instruction in comprehension and vocabulary, but many have reading difficulties that are more comprehensive and require an integrated approach that addresses all aspects of reading, including quick and accurate word reading. For a discussion of the use of assessments to identify students' instructional needs, see Denton, Bryan, et al. (2007).

Word Study Instruction for Older Students

Curtis (2004) indicated that word study interventions with older readers might address one or both of the following: word recognition instruction or word analysis instruction. Word study intervention with older students does not typically include instruction in phonemic awareness, although this domain may be addressed for students with severe word-reading difficulties, particularly those with dyslexia.

Word recognition instruction is focused on the phonic elements, syllabication or chunking strategies, and irregular word-reading practice needed by many older readers with reading difficulties. This instruction typically occurs through a diagnostic teaching process that involves identifying those phonic elements students know well and can apply consistently and proficiently and those phonic elements that are either unknown or applied inconsistently. Word study instruction for older students differs from that provided to younger students in that the goal is to move as quickly as possible, teaching the critical and missing phonic elements and applying them to many word types, including multisyllable words and both frequently and infrequently encountered words, spending little or no time reteaching elements the students have mastered. This procedure is necessary because older students have considerably less time to accelerate their reading performance and considerably more complex words to read. As students' reading improves, word study becomes more advanced, addressing application to increasingly complex, novel, and multisyllable words.

Word study instruction for older students normally includes instruction in morphology, including affixes, root words, and derivations. The focus is on teaching students practices for gaining access to word reading and meaning by purposely breaking words into meaningful parts such as prefixes, suffixes, root words, and syllables. Students are usually taught to "chunk" words into parts that allow them to quickly read and understand the meaning of the word.

Research on Word Study Interventions

Edmonds et al. (2009) identified three studies of word-level interventions with older students with reading difficulties that had reading comprehension as an outcome, yielding a mean weighted effect size of about 0.33 SD. They concluded that word study interventions significantly influenced comprehension. These findings are important because they build a stronger case for the value of teaching word study to older students with reading difficulties, and benefits are evident for comprehension as well as for word reading.

Although there is not an abundance of experimental studies with older readers that specifically focus on word recognition instruction, a study by Bhattacharya and Ehri (2004) provides evidence supporting the use of graphosyllabic analysis to help students read and spell. Bhattacharya and Ehri designed and implemented an intervention that capitalized on the words students knew automatically and accurately (sight words) to teach word parts and components for decoding unknown words to increase word reading accuracy. Students were taught to break words into syllables orally and count their "beats," then map these oral beats or syllables to the words' corresponding graphemic components, and then blend the components into words. Following the intervention, participants performed about 1 *SD* higher than a similar group of nonparticipants on tasks that required decoding novel words and about 0.75 *SD* better on word reading and spelling.

Intervention research on the benefits of morphological instruction, Curtis's (2004) second word study domain, is in the beginning stages and suggests promise rather than proven practice (Ebbers & Denton, 2008). Although morphology does not contribute to word reading at the same level as cognitive ability, vocabulary, and phonology (Deacon & Kirby, 2004; Singson, Mahony, & Mann, 2000), morphological awareness does contribute about 4 to 5% of the variance in decoding (Deacon & Kirby, 2004; Mahony, Singson, & Mann, 2000), with a shift in emphasis from phonology to morphology as students encounter more difficult words and text (at about 4th grade; Carlisle, 2000; Green et al., 2003).

An experimental study by Abbott and Berninger (1999) provided a rigorous test of the effectiveness of morphology instruction with older students with reading difficulties. Students were randomly assigned to an intervention that focused on structural (morphemic) analysis with training in the alphabetic principle or to an intervention consisting of alphabetic principle training alone. Because both treatment groups received instruction in word recognition using graphophonemic relationships, whatever effects resulted could be attributed to instruction on structural analysis (i.e., morphology). Controlling for instructional time, the students who received the structural analysis intervention with alphabetic principle intervention outperformed the students who received alphabetic principle intervention alone.

Word study is likely to be an important part of reading instruction for older readers with reading difficulties. Although instruction in multisyllable words, complex word types, affixes, prefixes, and root words are all essential elements of word study, providing students with extensive practice reading words in connected text is also necessary to support the development of automatic word recognition.

Reading Fluency

Reading fluency is another important element of reading instruction for older students. Fluency can be described as the ability to read text with appropriate speed, accuracy, and expression (i.e., inflection and phrasing). Fluency can be affected by several factors, particularly the ability to recognize words automatically. For typically developing readers, vocabulary knowledge also appears to influence fluency beyond the contribution of word recognition (Torgesen, Rashotte, & Alexander, 2001). Fluency can also be affected by older students' awareness of the purpose of reading and by their metacognitive monitoring of comprehension. That is, skilled readers slow their reading rate when reading challenging material when the intent is to learn from text, and they slow down or reread sections of text when comprehension breaks down.

For older students with reading difficulties, fluency is primarily affected by the ability to recognize words automatically at sight. Torgesen, Rashotte, Alexander, Alexander, and MacPhee (2003) described the situation faced by older students with word-level reading difficulties: "When they are asked to read material that is close to their grade level in difficulty, these children recognize far fewer words in the passage at a single glance than do children who read in the average range. It is the necessity of slowing down to phonemically decode or guess at words that is the most critical factor in limiting the reading fluency of children with severe reading difficulties" (p. 293). Word reading with accuracy and appropriate speed, also known as reading with automaticity, is considered an important element of reading instruction for older students because poor readers typically demonstrate low levels of fluency, and the ability to read words correctly, with appropriate speed and inflection, is predictive of reading comprehension (Kuhn & Stahl, 2000; Meyer, & Felton, 1999; Shinn & Good, 1992).

Chall (1983) was one of the first to recognize the role of fluency in skilled reading and included it in her six-stage model of reading. She described fluency as "ungluing from print" by using automaticity to make use of the features in text, such as stress and intonation, while reading. Chall saw fluency as a transition stage promoting comprehension. Support for Chall's interpretation of the relationship between fluency and comprehension can be drawn from evidence that students' scores on brief measures of oral reading fluency are highly predictive of scores on standardized tests of reading comprehension (Fuchs, Fuchs, Hosp, & Jenkins, 2001), although it appears that relationships between measures of fluency and comprehension are weaker for middle school students than for younger students (Denton et al., 2009).

Older students who read effortlessly and successfully typically read between 120 to 170 words correctly per minute, adjusting their reading rate for text difficulty and purpose of their reading (Tindal, Hasbrouck, & Jones, 2005). Students with reading difficulties typically read fewer than 100 words correctly per minute and with little expression. There seems to be general consensus that students with reading difficulties read slowly and less accurately than proficient readers. There is considerably less consensus about how to effectively promote automatic word reading among older readers with reading difficulties. Little evidence suggests that focusing specifically on those reading fluency activities that are beneficial to younger readers will be associated with the type of reading improvement needed by older readers. More likely, these students will require extensive interventions that also address word study and comprehension.

Fluency Instruction for Older Students

Fluency instruction for younger students typically consists of some variation of repeated reading. There are many ways repeated reading is achieved with elementary-grade children, including partner reading, rereading while listening to a model reader on audiotape, and rereading through "readers' theater." Considerably less is known about effective fluency intervention for students at the secondary level. Research has yet to identify the types of fluency activities that are most appropriate for secondary-level readers, particularly whether instructional time with these students is better used by addressing word-reading accuracy, fluency, and comprehension through reading of a wide range of different texts rather than rereading the same text multiple times.

What researchers do know is that older readers need many opportunities to read text at their instructional and independent reading levels, whether these opportunities are provided through rereading or continuous reading of text. Closing the gap between the lower reading level of students with reading difficulties and the expected reading level is unlikely to occur without organized opportunities for extensive reading, both with and without teacher feedback.

Research on Fluency Interventions for Older Students

A recent synthesis by Scammacca et al. (2007) reported on the limited available research, showing that fluency interventions with older readers with reading difficulties had a very small effect on students' improved reading rate and accuracy ($g = 0.26$, $n = 4$, 95% confidence interval = –0.08, 0.61) and no effect on standardized measures of reading comprehension ($g = -0.07$, $n = 2$, 95% confidence interval = –0.54, 0.39). This synthesis reflects data from the few available studies that met inclusion criteria for the review ($n = 4$). In all studies the intervention was provided for a limited time, suggesting low intensity. These studies were largely variations of repeated reading. Repeated reading with older students appears to help students' sight-word reading, and therefore, gains are generalized to unpracticed passages only when those passages share a large number of the same words as the passages students practiced repeatedly (Rashotte & Torgesen, 1985). This contrasts with the National Reading Panel's (2000) report, which found support for repeated oral reading with younger children. More experimental research is needed to validate effective practices for supporting fluency development for older students with reading difficulties. It may require a combination of focusing more on word study plus increasing considerably the amount of time allotted for students reading texts.

Vocabulary

Although vocabulary development is normally considered to be necessary with younger readers, it is often neglected as part of an effective intervention for older students with reading difficulties. This is unfortunate because many older readers have underdeveloped vocabularies and concept knowledge, which interferes with their understanding and learning from text. The influence of vocabulary on learning and understanding extends beyond reading in English and language arts classes; it also influences learning in social studies, science, and math. It is precisely because of this prevailing influence of vocabulary on learning and comprehension that *all* teachers—not just reading teachers—can aid learning by spending several minutes every day highlighting and explicitly teaching the key vocabulary needed to understand and learn from oral presentations and text reading. Improving reading outcomes requires ongoing support for vocabulary development because text understanding is significantly influenced by word meaning (Graves, 1989; Graves, Brunetti, & Slater, 1982). However, as in other domains, more experimental research on effective vocabulary instruction for older students is warranted. Although research has documented that vocabulary instruction is related to comprehension, there is minimal research with older readers demonstrating that vocabulary instruction leads to improved comprehension (Kamil, 2003; Stanovich, 2000).

Although vocabulary instruction is highly valuable and likely necessary for the majority of students with reading difficulties, some students' underdeveloped vocabulary knowledge may be related to their limited reading and the low background knowledge they have acquired. This suggests that, as in the case of word-reading instruction, a combination of direct instruction and engaged reading practice in text of appropriate difficulty may be necessary for the remediation of vocabulary difficulties in older students.

Vocabulary Instruction for Older Students

Much like Curtis's (2004) description of word study instruction, vocabulary instruction has two goals: to teach the meanings of specific words and to teach word-learning strategies, that is, strategies students can implement independently to infer meanings of unfamiliar words while reading.

The first step in planning instruction in the meanings of specific words is word selection. In this step, teachers consider the words students need to know in order to communicate effectively and understand what they hear and read. Particular focus is placed on academic vocabulary, words that students may not know but are likely to encounter frequently in academic settings. Several of these occur frequently in written directions. Some examples are *summarize, initial, represent, survey, conclusion, resolution, bias, similarly,* and *sequence.* In addition, students need to know and understand the academic vocabulary specific to various content areas (e.g., *amoeba, hypotenuse*) as well as words that have different meanings in different content areas (e.g., chemical *solutions* and *suspensions* contrasted with *solutions* to problems and *suspension* of reality, a *sine wave* and an *ocean wave*).

The second step in planning instruction considers the depth of knowledge students need to have for specific words. There is a big difference between *knowing* a word on a superficial level (e.g., enough to match it with a memorized definition on a weekly quiz) and being able to *use* a word effectively in communication. More than 40 years ago vocabulary learning was described by Dale (1965) based on four stages of "knowing" a word:

- Stage 1: No knowledge of the word—never saw it or heard it before.
- Stage 2: Heard or read the word before but doesn't know the meaning.
- Stage 3: Knows something about the word when it is seen or heard in context.
- Stage 4: Knows and understands the meaning(s) of the word and can use it in speaking and writing.

Ideally, students should have as many words in Stage 4 as possible and will increase considerably their number of words in Stage 3.

There is evidence from research that we can effectively teach students the meanings of specific words, but because of the sheer number of words students encounter, the goal is to also teach students word-learning strategies that enable them to infer word meanings independently. Two word-learning strategies, *morphemic analysis* and *contextual analysis,* are typically thought to be highly valuable practices for improving vocabulary acquisition. Two studies of vocabulary instruction conducted with fifth graders provide evidence that instruction in morphemic and contextual analysis, either in combination or alone, can improve vocabulary but not necessarily comprehension (Baumann et al., 2002; Baumann, Edwards, Boland, Olejnik, & Kame'enui, 2003).

Researchers have also explored the benefits of fostering *word consciousness* (Graves & Watts-Taffe, 2002; Nagy & Scott, 2000), but the relationship of this construct to improved comprehension has not been established. Word consciousness is a kind of metalinguistic awareness, or awareness of language (Nagy, 2007; Nagy & Scott, 2000). Students with high levels of word consciousness are responsive to words they see and hear. For example, they notice the similarities between words that share common roots (e.g., import, portable). Another promising area in vocabulary learning is the learning of new words and their meanings incidentally through reading of content (e.g., history, science) (Carlisle, Fleming, & Gudbrandsen, 2000).

Research on Vocabulary Interventions for Older Students

Several reviews and syntheses identify practices that are associated with improved vocabulary knowledge (Bryant, Goodwin, Bryant, & Higgins, 2003; Ebbers & Denton, 2008; Jitendra et al., 2004). The following are some of the research-supported practices:

- Using key words and mnemonic devices to build associations between words and meanings.
- Providing understandable, clear definitions and descriptions of what words mean and do not mean, including examples and nonexamples of words and allowing students sufficient practice with feedback to learn and use new words accurately.
- Illustrating what words mean and how they are related through semantic mapping, graphic organizers, and other concept-enhancement procedures.

The meta-analysis by Scammacca et al. (2007) examined the effectiveness of vocabulary interventions for older students with reading difficulties. The researchers identified six vocabulary intervention studies that met their criteria for inclusion. Vocabulary interventions were associated with the overall highest effect sizes, compared with word study, fluency, and comprehension. However, this finding is mitigated by the fact that none of the six intervention studies used standardized outcome measures, and researcher-developed outcome measures typically lead to higher effects. The report indicated that the overall effect size for these researcher-developed measures was 1.62 (very large effect) that differed significantly from

0 (95% confidence interval = 1.13, 2.10). Largely, these studies measured whether students learned the words that were taught. Whether these interventions had an impact on reading comprehension could not be determined.

Reading Comprehension

Word study, fluency, and vocabulary are promoted as a means of improving the reading comprehension of students. Many older readers are not given instructional opportunities designed specifically to improve their understanding and processing of text in later grades. There are several possible explanations (RAND, 2002) for this, including the following:

- Teaching students how to read is frequently not considered the role of secondary teachers.
- Teachers may assume if students can read the words, they can understand the text.
- Teachers may not have the knowledge and skills to promote reading comprehension.

For example, the RAND report highlighted that most upper-grade teachers lack adequate preparation for teaching the components of reading. Thus, if effective reading comprehension instruction for older students with reading difficulties is to occur, additional professional development for teachers will be required.

Comprehension Instruction for Older Students

Many students with reading difficulties have significant challenges understanding and learning from text even when they are able to decode adequately. Reading comprehension is a process of determining an author's intent and constructing meaning by coordinating a number of complex processes (Jenkins, Larson, & Fleischer, 1983; O'Shea, Sindelar, & O'Shea, 1987). Reading for understanding and learning requires the ability to successfully apply complex inferential and analytical skills (Duke & Pearson, 2002; Pressley, 2000). It can be hindered by inaccurate word reading, inadequate knowledge of word meanings, insufficient understanding or background knowledge related to the topic, failure to actively monitor understanding while reading, failure to effectively apply comprehension strategies, and undeveloped verbal reasoning (Biancarosa & Snow, 2004; Carlisle & Rice, 2002; Kamil, 2003; RAND, 2002).

Perhaps one of the most complete models of comprehension is provided by Kintsch (1998), in which he differentiates between garnering text-based information through word-level reading and *learning* from text by actively constructing meaning during reading and connecting new information with prior knowledge (Kintsch & Kintsch, 2004). Applying this complex level of processing and connecting within and across text and ideas is challenging for many older readers.

Research on Comprehension Interventions for Older Students

The National Reading Panel report (2000) evaluated empirical comprehension research conducted with students in grades 1 to 11, with most studies including students in grades 3 to 8. The panel highlighted effective comprehension instructional practices, including the following:

- Teaching students to monitor their understanding while reading and to adjust reading practices for different text types.
- Participating in cooperative learning practices that provide interaction with peers about text understanding in the context of reading.
- Developing and interacting with graphic and semantic organizers to help students make meaningful connections within and across texts.
- Engaging students in developing and answering questions about text and about the author's intent, interacting and obtaining feedback from students, and developing and responding to questions about text types.
- Modeling and providing practice with feedback to teach students to write summaries of text.
- Providing students with adequate information prior to reading to understand the text.
- Teaching students to integrate and apply selected and purposively taught comprehension strategies.

Perhaps one of the most consistent findings from syntheses of intervention research on older students with reading difficulties is the effectiveness of *directly teaching comprehension strategies*, or plans of action that students can learn to apply independently to help them make sense of text, monitor their own reading for sense making, organize information, extract key ideas, and remember key information. When students are taught to use cognitive and metacognitive strategies within an instructional framework that provides explicit and systematic instruction with modeling, feedback, and practice, older readers demonstrate improved reading comprehension (Edmonds et al., 2009; Gersten, Fuchs, Williams, & Baker, 2001; Scammacca et al., 2007; Swanson, 1999).

Scammacca et al. (2007) conducted a meta-analysis of 23 intervention studies with older students with reading difficulties or disabilities that included one or more measures of reading comprehension. Because studies that used a standardized measure of reading represented 8 of those 23 studies, these studies were considered separately, as they typically reflect a more rigorous test of the efficacy of an intervention. Overall, effect sizes from these interventions were quite high, and Scammacca et al. reported an effect size of 0.97 across all 23 intervention studies for comprehension. This is an improvement of almost a full standard deviation in favor of the treatment group over the comparison group. However, the overall estimate of effect sizes for the eight studies that used a norm-referenced measure of comprehension was 0.35. This estimate of improvement based on standardized measures is considerably lower than the overall effect for all comprehension outcomes. There was enough variation between effects from various studies to warrant further examination of possible explanations for this difference.

Considering the type of each intervention and its effects on comprehension resulted in the following findings: (1) outcomes were largest for interventions that implemented comprehension strategy instruction, with an overall effect size of 1.35 and an effect size of 0.54 for those studies that used standardized measures; and (2) multicomponent interventions that included instruction in two or more reading domains (e.g., word reading and comprehension) also demonstrated high outcomes in comprehension, with an overall effect size of 0.80 and for interventions using standardized measures, 0.59.

Intervention for Secondary Students with Severe and Persistent Reading Difficulties

As illustrated in the previous discussion, there is an emerging, but still limited, research base on effective reading intervention for older students. There is an even greater need for intervention research that specifically evaluates intervention for students in secondary schools with severe and persistent reading difficulties (i.e., Tier 3 students).

In one such study, Denton, Wexler, Vaughn, and Bryan (2008) provided a multicomponent reading intervention to middle school students with severe reading difficulties. Most of these students were Spanish-speaking English language learners, and nearly all had severe vocabulary deficits. Most bilingual students displayed these vocabulary problems in both languages. Students were randomly assigned to receive either the researcher-developed intervention, consisting of daily explicit and systematic small-group intervention for 40 minutes over 13 weeks, provided in groups of two to four students, or their regularly assigned special education or remedial reading classes. Despite the provision of explicit small-group instruction in the research intervention, there were no significant differences in reading outcomes between the treatment and comparison groups, and neither group made significant standard-score growth over the course of the study. Denton et al. hypothesized that students needed intervention over a longer period of time, or intervention with a different approach or focus. This is an area that merits further study.

CONCLUSION

It has become increasingly clear that if students do not learn to read adequately in the primary grades, it is likely that they will continue to struggle with reading unless they are provided with intensive intervention (Francis et al., 1996; Juel, 1988; Torgesen & Burgess, 1998). As illustrated in the research we have described, remediation of reading difficulties for older students is possible, but remediating severe reading problems in secondary-level students is highly challenging. A prevention model is designed to "catch them before they fall" (Torgesen, 1998, p. 1).

At the same time, the need to provide reading intervention to older students is not likely to disappear. Unless high-quality prevention models are universally employed, there will be students in grades 4 and above who have reading difficulties of different types and levels of severity. Moreover, some students will need continued support throughout their school careers. In particular, some students with attention and behavior difficulties will need consistent, classroom-based, and often more intensive, intervention.

As illustrated in our description of the current research base, much more needs to be learned about reading intervention for students beyond the primary grades, particularly those with severe reading challenges. The best researched domain is comprehension strategy instruction, and evidence supports the effectiveness of this kind of instruction. However, recent research has indicated that many middle school students who fail high-stakes tests of reading comprehension have problems with decoding or fluency or both (Fletcher, 2007). Much less is known about how to address these deficits. Finally, more effective tools are needed to instruct older students who have poorly developed oral vocabularies as well as impairments in decoding, fluency, and comprehension.

Multitiered intervention models are designed to provide all students with the instruction they need to learn to read adequately. Although schools will always face the challenges associated with inadequate funding, time, and personnel, implementation of tiered intervention is feasible. It is a matter of setting priorities in the use of existing resources—and sometimes thinking creatively about obtaining additional resources. Implementing a tiered intervention model within an RTI framework has the potential to address the needs of all students, regardless of the reasons underlying their reading difficulties, and it can provide important data to inform decisions related to the presence of a learning disability and special education eligibility. We suggest that educators should feel a sense of urgency with respect to providing effective preventive and remedial reading interventions. For individual students, time is short. Without effective intervention, weak readers tend to fall farther and farther behind until they exhibit generalized deficit patterns (Stanovich, 1986). If students' reading difficulties are addressed, they will be better able to learn from content-area textbooks, supporting achievement across subject areas and the ability to think and reason about text, certainly an important goal of our educational system.

ACKNOWLEDGMENTS

This chapter is adapted from Denton, C. A., & Vaughn, S. (in press). Preventing and remediating reading difficulties. In M. R. Shinn, H. M. Walker, & G. Stoner (Eds.), *Interventions for achievement and behavior problems III: Preventive and remedial approaches*. Bethesda, MD: National Association of School Psychologists. Copyright by the National Association of School Psychologists. Adapted by permission.

REFERENCES

Abbott, S. P., & Berninger, V. W. (1999). It's never too late to remediate: Teaching word recognition to students with reading disabilities in grades 4–7. *Annals of Dyslexia, 49*, 223–250.

Batsche, G., Elliott, J., Graden, J. L., Grimes, J., Kovaleski, J. F., Prasse, D., et al. (2006). *Response to intervention: Policy considerations and implementation*. Alexandria, VA: National Association of State Directors of Special Education.

Baumann, J. F., Edwards, E. C., Boland, E., Olejnik, S., & Kame'enui, E. J. (2003). Vocabulary tricks: Effects of instruction in morphology and context on fifth-grade students ability to derive and infer word meaning. *American Educational Research Journal, 40*, 447–494.

Baumann, J. F., Edwards, E. C., Font, G., Tereshinski, C. A., Kame'enui, E. J., & Olejnik, S. (2002). Teaching morphemic and contextual analysis to fifth grade students. *Reading Research Quarterly, 37*, 150–176.

Bhattacharya, A., & Ehri, L. C. (2004). Graphosyllabic analysis helps adolescent struggling readers read and spell words. *Journal of Learning Disabilities, 37*, 331–348.

Biancarosa, G., & Snow, C. E. (2004). *Reading next—A vision for action and research in middle and high school literacy: A report from Carnegie of New York*. Washington, DC: Alliance for Excellence in Education.

Blachman, B. A., Schatschneider, C., Fletcher, J. M., Francis, D. J., Clonan, S., Shaywitz, B., et al. (2004). Effects of intensive reading remediation for second and third graders. *Journal of Educational Psychology, 96*, 444–461.

Bryant, D. P., Goodwin, M., Bryant, B. R., & Higgins, K. (2003). Vocabulary instruction for students with learning disabilities: A review of the research. *Learning Disability Quarterly, 26*(2), 117–128.

Carlisle, J. F. (2000). Awareness of the structure and meaning of morphologically complex words: Impact on reading. *Reading and Writing, 12,* 169–190.

Carlisle, J. F., Fleming, J. E., & Gudbrandsen, B. (2000). Incidental word learning in science classes. *Contemporary Educational Psychology, 25,* 184–211.

Carlisle, J. F., & Rice, M. S. (2002). *Improving reading comprehension: Research-based principles and practices.* Baltimore: York Press.

Chall, J. S. (1983). *Stages of reading development.* New York: McGraw-Hill.

Chard, D. J., Vaughn, S., & Tyler, B. (2002). A synthesis of research on effective interventions for building reading fluency with elementary students with learning disabilities. *Journal of Learning Disabilities, 35,* 386–406.

Curtis, M. (2004). Adolescents who are struggling with word identification: Research and practice. In T. L. Jetton & J. A. Dole (Eds.), *Adolescent literacy research and practice* (pp. 119–134). New York: Guilford Press.

Dale, E. (1965). Vocabulary measurement: Technique and major findings. *Elementary English, 42,* 82–88.

Deacon, S. H., & Kirby, J. R. (2004). Morphological awareness: Just "more phonological"? The roles of morphological and phonological awareness in reading development. *Applied Psycholinguistics, 25*(2), 223–228.

Denton, C. A., Barth, A., Fletcher, J. W. M., Wexler, J., Vaughn, S., Cirino, P. T., et al. (2009). *The relations among oral and silent reading fluency and comprehension in middle school: Implications for identification and instruction of students with reading difficulties.* Manuscript submitted for publication.

Denton, C. A., Fletcher, J. M., Anthony, J. L., & Francis, D. J. (2006). An evaluation of intensive intervention for students with persistent reading difficulties. *Journal of Learning Disabilities, 39,* 447–466.

Denton, C. A., Fletcher, J. M., Simos, P. C., Papanicolaou, A. C., & Anthony, J. L. (2007). An implementation of a tiered intervention model: Reading outcomes and neural correlates. In D. Haager, J., Klingner, & S. Vaughn (Eds.), *Evidence-based reading practices for response to intervention* (pp. 107–137). Baltimore: Brookes.

Denton, C. A., & Hocker, J. L. (2006). *Responsive reading instruction: Flexible intervention for struggling readers in the early grades.* Longmont, CO: Sopris West.

Denton, C. A., & Mathes, P. G. (2003). Intervention for struggling readers: Possibilities and challenges. In B. R. Foorman (Ed.), *Preventing and remediating reading difficulties: Bringing science to scale* (pp. 229–251). Timonium, MD: York Press.

Denton, C. A., Wexler, J., Vaughn, S., & Bryan, D. (2008). Intervention provided to middle school students with severe reading difficulties. *Learning Disabilities Research and Practice, 23,* 79–89.

Donovan, M. S., & Cross, C. T. (2002). *Minority students in special and gifted education.* Washington, DC: National Academy Press.

Duke, N. K., & Pearson, P. D. (2002). Effective practices for developing reading comprehension. In A. E. Farstrup & S. J. Samuels (Eds.), *What research has to say about reading instruction* (3rd ed., pp. 205–242). Newark, DE: International Reading Association.

Ebbers, S., & Denton, C. A. (2008). A Root awakening: Effective vocabulary instruction for older students with reading difficulties. *Learning Disabilities Research and Practice, 23*, 90–102.

Edmonds, M. S., Vaughn, S., Wexler, J., Reutebuch, C., Cable, A., Tackett, K., et al. (2009). A synthesis of reading interventions and effects on reading outcomes for older struggling readers. *Review of Educational Research, 79*, 262–300.

Ehri, L. C. (2003, March). *Systematic phonics instruction: Findings of the National Reading Panel.* Paper presented to the Standards and Effectiveness Unit, Department for Education and Skills, British Government, London.

Elbaum, B., Vaughn, S., Hughes, M. T., & Moody, S. W. (2000). How effective are one-to-one tutoring programs in reading for elementary students at risk for reading failure? *Journal of Educational Psychology, 92*, 605–619.

Felton, R. (1993). Effects of instruction on the decoding skills of children with phonological-processing problems. *Journal of Learning Disabilities, 26*, 583–589.

Fletcher, J. M. (2007, February). *Overview of the Texas Center for Learning Disabilities.* Paper presented at the Pacific Coast Research Conference, San Diego, CA.

Fletcher, J. M., Denton, C. A., Fuchs, L., & Vaughn, S. R. (2005). Multi-tiered reading instruction: Linking general education and special education. In International Reading Association, S. O. Richardson, & J. W. Gilger (Eds.), *Research-based education and intervention: What we need to know* (pp. 21–43). Baltimore: International Reading Association.

Foorman, B. R., Francis, D. J., Fletcher, J. M., Schatschneider, C., & Mehta, P. (1998). The role of instruction in learning to read: Preventing reading disabilities in at-risk children. *Journal of Educational Psychology, 90*, 37–55.

Francis, D. J., Shaywitz, S. E., Stuebing, K. K., Shaywitz, B. A., & Fletcher, J. M. (1996). Developmental lag versus deficit models of reading disability: A longitudinal, individual growth curves analysis. *Journal of Educational Psychology, 88*, 3–17.

Fuchs, D., & Fuchs, L. (2005). Peer-assisted learning strategies: Promoting word recognition, fluency, and reading comprehension in young children. *Journal of Special Education, 39*, 34–44.

Fuchs, L. S., Fuchs, D., Hosp, M. K., & Jenkins, J. R. (2001). Oral reading fluency as an indicator of reading competence: A theoretical, empirical, and historical analysis. *Scientific Studies of Reading, 5*, 239–256.

Gersten, R., Fuchs, L., Williams, J., & Baker, S. (2001). Teaching reading comprehension strategies to students with learning disabilities: A review of research. *Review of Educational Research, 71*, 279–320.

Graves, M. F. (1989). A quantitative and qualitative study of elementary school children's vocabularies. *Journal of Educational Research, 82*(4), 203–209.

Graves, M. F., Brunetti, G. J., & Slater, W. H. (1982). The reading vocabularies of primary grade children of varying geographic and social backgrounds. In J. A. Harris & L. A. Harris (Eds.), *New inquiries in reading research and instruction* (pp. 99–104). Rochester, NY: National Reading Conference.

Graves, M. F., & Watts-Taffe, S. M. (2002). The place of word consciousness in a research-based vocabulary program. In A. E. Farstrup & S. J. Samuels (Eds.), *What research has to say about reading instruction* (3rd ed., pp. 140–165). Newark, DE: International Reading Association.

Green, L., McCutchen, D., Schwiebert, C., Quinlan, T., Eva-Wood, A., & Juelis, J. (2003). Morphological development in children's writing. *Journal of Educational Psychology, 95*, 752–761.

Grek, M. L., Mathes, P. G., & Torgesen, J. K. (2003). Similarities and differences between experienced teachers and trained paraprofessionals. In S. Vaughn & K. L. Briggs (Eds.), *Reading in the classroom: Systems for the observation of teaching and learning* (pp. 267–296). Baltimore: Brookes.

Hall, T. E., Hughes, C. A., & Filbert, M. (2000). Computer assisted instruction in reading for students with learning disabilities: A research synthesis. *Education and Treatment of Children, 23*, 173–193.

Jenkins, J. R., Larson, K., & Fleischer, L. (1983). Effects of error correction on word recognition and reading comprehension. *Learning Disability Quarterly, 6*(2), 139–145.

Jenkins, J. R., & O'Connor, R. E. (2002). Early identification and intervention for young children with reading/learning disabilities. In R. Bradley, L. Danielson, & D. P. Hallahan (Eds.), *Identification of learning disabilities: Research to practice* (pp. 99–149). Mahwah, NJ: Erlbaum.

Jitendra, A., Edwards, L., Sacks, G., & Jacobson, L. (2004). What research says about vocabulary instruction for students with learning disabilities. *Exceptional Children, 70*, 299–311.

Juel, C. (1988). Learning to read and write: A longitudinal study of 54 children from first through fourth grades. *Journal of Educational Psychology, 80*, 437–447.

Kamil, M. L. (2003). *Adolescents and literacy: Reading for the 21st century.* Washington, DC: Alliance for Excellent Education.

Kamps, D. M., & Greenwood, C. R. (2005). Formulating secondary-level reading interventions. *Journal of Learning Disabilities, 38*, 500–509.

Kavale, K. A., & Reese, J. H. (1992). The character of learning disabilities: An Iowa profile. *Learning Disability Quarterly, 15*, 74–94.

Kintsch, W. (1998). *Comprehension: A paradigm for cognition.* New York: Cambridge University Press.

Kintsch, W., & Kintsch, E. (2004). Comprehension. In S. G. Paris & S. A. Stahl (Eds.), *Children's reading comprehension and assessment* (pp. 71–92). Mahwah, NJ: Erlbaum.

Kuhn, M. R., & Stahl, S. A. (2000). *Fluency: A review of developmental and remedial practices* (Rep. No. 2-008). Ann Arbor, MI: Center for the Improvement of Early Reading Achievement.

Lee, J., Grigg, W. S., & Donahue, P. L. (2007). *The nation's report card: Reading 2007: National assessment of educational progress at grades 4 and 8* (NCES No. 2007-496). Washington, DC: National Center for Education Statistics. Retrieved November 5, 2007, from *http://nationsreportcard.gov/reading_2007.*

Lerner, J. W. (1989). Educational interventions in learning disabilities. *Journal of the American Academy of Child and Adolescent Psychiatry, 28*, 326–331.

Lovett, M. W., Steinbach, K. A., & Frijters, J. C. (2000). Remediating the core deficits of developmental reading disability: A double-deficit perspective. *Journal of Learning Disabilities, 33*, 334–358.

Mahony, D., Singson, M., & Mann, V. (2000). Reading ability and sensitivity to morphological relations. *Reading and Writing: An Interdisciplinary Journal, 12*, 191–218.

Mathes, P. G., & Denton, C. A. (2002). The prevention and identification of reading disability. *Seminars in Pediatric Neurology, 9*(3), 185–191.

Mathes, P. G., Denton, C. A., Fletcher, J. M., Anthony, J. L., Francis, D. J., & Schatschneider, C. (2005). The effects of theoretically different instruction and student characteristics on the skills of struggling readers. *Reading Research Quarterly, 40*, 148–182.

Mathes, P. G., Grek, M. L., & Howard, J. K. (1999). Peer-assisted learning strategies for first-grade readers: A tool for preventing early reading failure. *Learning Disabilities Research and Practice, 14*, 50–60.

Mathes, P. G., Torgesen, J. K., & Allor, J. H. (2001). The effects of peer-assisted literacy strategies for first-grade readers with and without additional computer-assisted instruction in phonological awareness. *American Educational Research Journal, 38*, 371–410.

McMaster, K. L., Fuchs, D., & Fuchs, L. S. (2006). Research on peer-assisted learning strategies: The promise and limitations of peer-mediated instruction. *Reading and Writing Quarterly, 22*, 5–25.

McMaster, K. L., Fuchs, D., Fuchs, L. S., & Compton, D. L. (2005). Responding to nonresponders: An experimental field trial of identification and intervention methods. *Exceptional Children, 71*, 445–463.

Meyer, M. S., & Felton, R. H. (1999). Repeated reading to enhance fluency: Old approaches and new directions. *Annals of Dyslexia, 49*, 283–306.

Moats, L. C. (2001). When older students can't read. *Educational Leadership, 58*(6), 36–40.

Nagy, W. E., & Scott, R. S. (2000). Vocabulary processes. In M. L. Kamil, P. B. Mosenthal, P. D. Pearson, & R. Barr (Eds.), *Handbook of reading research* (Vol. 3, pp. 269–284). Mahwah, NJ: Erlbaum.

National Reading Panel. (2000). *Teaching children to read: An evidence-based assessment of the scientific research literature on reading and its implications for reading instruction.* Washington, DC: U.S. Government Printing Office.

O'Shea, L. J., Sindelar, P., & O'Shea, D. J. (1987). Effects of repeated readings and attentional cues on the reading fluency and comprehension of learning disabled readers. *Learning Disabilities Research, 2*, 103–109.

Pressley, M. (2000). What should comprehension instruction be the instruction of? In M. L. Kamil, P. B. Mosenthal, P. D. Pearson, & R. Barr (Eds.), *Handbook of reading research* (Vol. 3, pp. 545–562). Mahwah, NJ: Erlbaum.

RAND Reading Study Group. (2002). *Reading for understanding: Toward an R&D program in reading comprehension.* Santa Monica, CA: Author.

Rashotte, C. A., & Torgesen, J. K. (1985). Repeated reading and reading fluency in learning disabled children. *Reading Research Quarterly, 20*, 180–188.

Rayner, K., Foorman, B. R., Perfetti, C. A., Pesetsky, D., & Seidenberg, M. S. (2001).

How psychological science informs the teaching of reading. *Psychological Science in the Public Interest*, 2, 31–74.

Reutebuch, C. K., Vaughn, S., & Scammacca, N. (2009). *Reading intervention research for secondary students with learning disabilities: An effect size and multivocal synthesis.* Manuscript submitted for publication.

Saenz, L. M., Fuchs, L. S., & Fuchs, D. (2005). Peer-assisted learning strategies for English language learners with learning disabilities. *Exceptional Children, 71*, 231–247.

Scammacca, N., Roberts, G., Vaughn, S., Edmonds, M., Wexler, J., Reutebuch, C. K., et al. (2007). *Interventions for adolescent struggling readers: A meta-analysis with implications for practice.* Portsmouth, NH: RMC Research Corporation, Center on Instruction. Available from *http://www.centeroninstruction. org/index.cfm.*

Shankweiler, D., Lundquist, E., Katz, L., Stuebing, K. K., Fletcher, J. M., Brady, S. M., et al. (1999). Comprehension and decoding: Patterns of association in children with reading difficulties. *Scientific Studies of Reading, 3*, 69–94.

Shinn, M. R., & Good, R. H. (1992). Curriculum-based measurement of oral reading fluency: A confirmatory analysis of its relation to reading. *School Psychology Review, 21*, 459–479.

Simos, P. G., Fletcher, J. M., Bergman, E., Breier, J. I., Foorman, B. R., Castillo, E. M., et al. (2002). Dyslexia-specific brain activation profile becomes normal following successful remedial training. *Neurology, 58*, 1203–1213.

Simos, P. G., Fletcher, J. M., Sarkari, S., Billingsley, R. L., Denton, C., & Papanicolaou, A. C. (2007a). Altering the brain circuits for reading through intervention: A magnetic source imaging study. *NeuroPsychology, 21*, 485–496.

Simos, P. G., Fletcher, J. M., Sarkari, S., Billingsley-Marshall, R., Denton, C., & Papanicolaou, A. C. (2007b). Intensive instruction affects brain magnetic activity associated with reading fluency in children with persistent reading disabilities. *Journal of Learning Disabilities, 40*, 37–48.

Singson, M., Mahony, D., & Mann, V. (2000). The relation between reading ability and morphological skills: Evidence from derivational suffixes. *Reading and Writing, 12*, 219–252.

Snow, C. E., Burns, M. S., & Griffin, P. (Eds.). (1998). *Preventing reading difficulties in young children.* Washington, DC: National Academy Press.

Stage, S. A., Abbott, R. D., Jenkins, J. R., & Berninger, V. W. (2003). Predicting response to early reading intervention from verbal IQ, reading-related language abilities, attention ratings, and verbal IQ-word reading discrepancy: Failure to validate discrepancy method. *Journal of Learning Disabilities, 36*, 24–33.

Stanovich, K. E. (1986). Matthew effects in reading: Some consequences of individual differences in the acquisition of literacy. *Reading Research Quarterly, 21*, 360–407.

Stanovich, K. (2000). *Progress in understanding reading: Scientific foundations and new frontiers.* New York: Guilford Press.

Swanson, H. L. (1999). Instructional components that predict treatment outcomes for students with learning disabilities: Support for a combined strategy and direct instruction model. *Learning Disabilities Research and Practice, 14*(3), 129–140.

Tindal, G., Hasbrouck, J., & Jones, C. (2005). *Oral reading fluency: 90 years of measurement* (Tech. Rep. No. 33, Behavioral Research and Teaching). Eugene, OR: University of Oregon.

Torgesen, J. K. (1998). Catch them before they fall: Identification and assessment to prevent reading failure in young children. *American Educator, 22,* 1–8. Retrieved November 7, 2007, from *http://www.aft.org/pubs-reports/american_educator/spring_sum98/torgesen.pdf.*

Torgesen, J. K. (2000). Individual differences in response to early interventions in reading: The lingering problem of treatment resisters. *Learning Disabilities Research and Practice, 15,* 55–64.

Torgesen, J. K., Alexander, A. W., Wagner, R. K., Rashotte, C. A., Voeller, K., Conway, T., et al. (2001). Intensive remedial instruction for children with severe reading disabilities: Immediate and long-term outcomes from two instructional approaches. *Journal of Learning Disabilities, 34,* 33–58.

Torgesen, J. K., & Burgess, S. R. (1998). Consistency of reading-related phonological processes throughout early childhood: Evidence from longitudinal-correlational and instructional studies. In J. Metsala & L. Ehri (Eds.), *Word recognition in beginning literacy* (pp. 161–188). Hillsdale, NJ: Erlbaum.

Torgesen, J. K., Rashotte, C. A., & Alexander, A. W. (2001). Principles of fluency instruction in reading: Relationships with established empirical outcomes. In M. Wolf (Ed.), *Dyslexia, fluency, and the brain* (pp. 333–355). Timonium, MD: York Press.

Torgesen, J. K., Rashotte, C. A., Alexander, A., Alexander, J., & MacPhee, K. (2003). Progress toward understanding the instructional conditions necessary for remediating reading difficulties in older children. In B. R. Foorman (Ed.), *Preventing and remediating reading difficulties: Bringing science to scale* (pp. 275–297). Timonium, MD: York Press.

Torgesen, J. K., Wagner, R. K., Rashotte, C. A., Rose, E., Lindamood, P., Conway, T., et al. (1999). Preventing reading failure in your children with phonological processing disabilities: Group and individual responses to instruction. *Journal of Educational Psychology, 91,* 579–593.

Vaughn, S., Cirino, P. T., Linan-Thompson, S., Mathes, P. G., Carlson, C. D., Cardenas-Hagan, E., et al. (2006). Effectiveness of a Spanish intervention and an English intervention for English language learners at risk for reading problems. *American Educational Research Journal, 43*(3), 449–487.

Vaughn, S., & Linan-Thompson, S. (2003). Group size and time allotted to intervention: Effects for students with reading difficulties. In B. Foorman (Ed.), *Preventing and remediating reading difficulties: Bringing science to scale* (pp. 275–298). Baltimore: York Press.

Vaughn, S., Linan-Thompson, S., & Hickman, P. (2003). Response to instruction as a means of identifying students with reading/learning disabilities. *Exceptional Children, 69,* 391–409.

Vaughn, S., Linan-Thompson, S., Mathes, P. G., Cirino, P. T., Carlson, C. D., Pollard-Durodola, S. D., et al. (2006). Effectiveness of Spanish intervention for first-grade English language learners at risk for reading difficulties. *Journal of Learning Disabilities, 39,* 56–73.

Vaughn, S., Wanzek, J., Linan-Thompson, S., & Murray, C. S. (2007). Monitoring response to supplemental services for students at risk for reading difficulties: High and low responders. In S. R. Jimerson, M. K. Burns, & A. M. VanDer-Heyden (Eds.), *Handbook of response to intervention: The science and practice of assessment and intervention* (pp. 234–243). New York: Springer Science.

Vaughn, S., Wanzek, J., Woodruff, A. L., & Linan-Thompson, S. (2007). A three-tier model for preventing reading difficulties and early identification of students with reading disabilities. In D. Haager, J. Klingner, & S. Vaughn (Eds.), *Evidence-based reading practices for response to intervention* (pp. 11–28). Baltimore: Brookes.

Vellutino, F. R., Scanlon, D. M., & Jaccard, J. (2003). Toward distinguishing between cognitive and experiential deficits as primary sources of difficulty in learning to read: A two year follow-up of difficult to remediate and readily remediated poor readers. In B. R. Foorman (Ed.), *Preventing and remediating reading difficulties: Bringing science to scale* (pp. 73–120). Baltimore: York Press.

Vellutino, F. R., Scanlon, D. M., Sipay, E. R., Small, S. G., Pratt, A., Chen, R., et al. (1996). Cognitive profiles of difficult-to-remediate and readily remediated poor readers: Early intervention as a vehicle for distinguishing between cognitive and experiential deficits as basic causes of specific reading disability. *Journal of Educational Psychology, 88*, 601–638.

Wanzek, J., & Vaughn, S. (2007). Research-based implications from extensive early reading interventions. *School Psychology Review, 36*, 541–561.

6

Research-Based Implications from Extensive Early Reading Interventions

Jeanne Wanzek
Sharon Vaughn

Response to intervention (RTI) provides a framework for accomplishing several highly valued goals: (1) early identification of students at risk for academic difficulties through universal screening practices, (2) early and targeted intervention for students at risk, (3) ongoing progress monitoring—more frequently for students most at risk and less frequently for typical achieving students, (4) use of increasingly more intensive tiers of research-based instruction to meet students' needs, and (5) improved confidence that students who are referred for special education but who participated in evidence-based RTI models are less likely to be academic casualties of inadequate or inappropriate instruction (Fletcher, Coulter, Reschly, & Vaughn, 2004). Although school psychologists embrace these goals conceptually, decisions related to effective implementation of procedures to achieve these goals are often more problematic.

Perhaps the most challenging aspects of RTI model implementation are the decisions about what types of interventions should be implemented, the duration of time interventions, who should provide the interventions, and whether a uniform, more standardized approach or a less standardized, or more individualized, approach to instruction should be implemented (Burns, Appleton, & Stehouwer, 2005; Fuchs, Mock, Morgan, & Young, 2003;

Reschly, 2005; Vaughn & Fuchs, 2003). Fundamentally, an evidence-based approach to addressing these questions would be aligned with the National Association of School Psychologist guidelines as well as recommended practice (for a review, see Kratochwill & Stoiber, 2002).

PURPOSE AND RATIONALE FOR SYNTHESIS

This chapter provides a synthesis of research aimed at exploring some of the fundamental questions related to effective implementation of RTI. We synthesized the extant research on extensive early reading interventions to examine several issues related to RTI implementation: (1) outcomes for students with reading difficulties or disabilities after participation in extensive early reading interventions and (2) features of interventions associated with large effect sizes, including instructional group size, duration, and level of standardization.

We recognized that in order to adequately address these questions we would require a relatively large population of studies that addressed a common academic problem. For this reason, we selected studies that represented early reading interventions (kindergarten through grade 3). Reading interventions were selected because (1) most students are referred for learning disabilities (LDs) because of difficulties with reading (Lyon, 1995), (2) most students diagnosed with LDs have reading as an individualized education program goal (Lerner, 2000), (3) there is a substantial data base of studies on early reading interventions (e.g., McCardle & Chhabra, 2004; Rayner, Foorman, Perfetti, Pesetsky, & Seidenberg, 2001), and (4) many of the recent initiatives at the state level (e.g., Alabama Reading Initiative, Florida Reading Initiative, Texas Reading Initiative) and policies at the federal level (Reading First and Early Reading First programs within the No Child Left Behind Act, 2001) were based on findings from these early reading studies.

EXTENSIVE INTERVENTIONS

For the purpose of this synthesis, we were interested in reading interventions that would be considered more extensive and it provided for a significant enough period of time that students' response to intervention and overall intervention effectiveness could be determined. We defined extensive interventions as occurring for 100 sessions or longer, which is the equivalent of 20 weeks of daily intervention.

Interventions differ from typical reading instruction in that they are designed to address the instructional needs of students who are experiencing difficulties in learning to read or who have reading disabilities. There are several reasons for selecting extensive interventions for this synthesis. First, as Vellutino, Scanlon, and Jaccard (2003) have specified, we can understand whether students have true reading difficulties only if we can control for inadequacies in instruction, best accomplished by providing extensive interventions to students at risk to determine relative progress. Second, previous syntheses of the reading intervention research have not specifically addressed the effectiveness of extensive interventions (Foorman, 2003; McCardle & Chhabra, 2004; Pressley, 2006). Third, within an RTI model, understanding the efficacy of interventions provided to students after classroom instruction and less extensive interventions (depending on criteria used by the district) is essential and less well understood (Vaughn, Wanzek, Linan-Thompson, & Murray, 2007).

TYPES OF EXTENSIVE INTERVENTIONS

A simple view of conceptualizing interventions might be to consider that they could be implemented in two primary ways: standardized or individualized. Standardized interventions specify a priori the elements of reading instruction that will be implemented. The elements selected are (1) associated with improved outcomes in previous studies, (2) well defined in a curriculum, and (3) implemented by personnel who are trained specifically in the implementation of the curricula. Although adjustments may be made to address students' levels, fundamental to applying a standardized approach is using a research-based standard curriculum and ensuring fidelity of implementation.

A second type of intervention is a more individualized approach. In school psychology, this may also be referred to as a problem-solving approach (Bergen & Kratochwill, 1990). Typically, these methods are directed at defining the student's problem in behavioral terms, measuring performance in the natural setting, determining the specific goals to address the problem, designing and/or selecting an intervention to meet those goals, monitoring the student's progress toward those goals to determine the effectiveness of the intervention, adjusting the intervention if needed, and then making decisions about future interventions (Ikeda et al., 2002; National Association of State Directors of Special Education [NASDSE], 2005). In our review of the literature on extensive interventions, we were unable to locate any interventions implemented with an individualized approach. Thus, although it would be valuable to contrast more standardized and individualized interventions, the lack of research in this area prevented us from addressing this question directly.

For the purpose of this synthesis, we examined student outcomes after participation in extensive interventions implemented with varying levels of standardization. The studies reviewed provided a range of descriptions of their standardization of implementation, from high (well-specified curricula provided to all participants with few or no modifications) to low (curricula and instructional practices are less well specified and more responsive to individual students' needs) standardization levels.

In addition to documenting the effects of interventions that were high and low on standardization, we were interested in describing the components of interventions (e.g., instructional elements, personnel) associated with large effect sizes. This is the type of evidence-based information frequently requested by school psychologists and special educators (NASDSE, 2005).

METHOD

Studies were identified through a two-step process. First, we conducted a computer search of ERIC and PsycINFO databases to locate studies published between 1995 and 2005. We selected the decade between 1995 and 2005 because a large number of early intervention studies were reported in the research literature during this period and the studies during this period were the ones that greatly influenced policy related to RTI. Key disability descriptors or root forms of descriptors (reading diff*, learning disab*, delay, disorder*, at-risk, high risk, disab*, dyslex*) were used in combination with key reading descriptors or root forms of descriptors (reading, interven*, instruction, reading intervention, reading strategies, supplemental instruction, special educ*, inclus*, integrat*, phonological awareness, phonemic awareness, phon*, fluency, vocab*, comp*) to identify possible articles. The initial electronic search yielded 26,062 articles. Second, we calculated a hand search of seven major journals for the years 2003 to 2005 (*Exceptional Children, Journal of Educational Psychology, Journal of Learning Disabilities, The Journal of Special Education, Learning Disabilities Research and Practice, Reading Research Quarterly,* and *School Psychology Review*). We selected the years 2003 to 2005 because they were the most recent, and studies during that time would not be located through citation searching and other syntheses.

Studies were selected for inclusion if they met the following criteria: (1) The study was reported in a peer-reviewed journal and printed in English; (2) the participants included students with learning disabilities or students identified as at risk for reading difficulties (e.g., those with low ability, low phonemic awareness, low income, language disorders). Studies with additional participants were included if disaggregated data were provided for the students with LDs or those identified as at risk; (3) the participants were enrolled in grade levels between kindergarten and third grade inclusive; (4) interventions targeted early literacy in an alphabetic language, were provided for 100 sessions or more, and were not part of the general education curriculum provided to all students; (5) interventions were provided as part of the school programming (and not home, clinic, or camp programs); and (6) dependent variables addressed reading outcomes.

Data Analysis

Only studies that met the criteria just listed were coded. The vast majority of studies were eliminated based on information in their abstracts that provided information that assured us the study would not meet criteria. When abstracts were ambiguous or led us to believe that the study met our criteria, we located and reviewed the study to ensure that it did.

Coding Procedures

An extensive code sheet was developed to organize pertinent information about each of the studies. The code sheet was based on others used in previous research (Vaughn, Kim, et al., 2003; Wanzek et al., 2006) as well as the elements specified in the What Works Clearinghouse Design and Implementation Assessment Device (Institute of Education Sciences, 2003). Data were collected on (1) participants' characteristics (e.g., age, gender, exceptionality), (2) methodology (e.g., research design, assignment), (3) intervention and comparison descriptions, (4) measures, and (5) findings. There were three coders for the articles. Interrater agreement was calculated separately for each code sheet category (e.g., participants, design) and reached 91% or greater for all categories. Interrater agreement was calculated as the number of agreements divided by the number of agreements plus the number of disagreements. All code sheets were reviewed by Jeanne Wanzek for comprehensiveness and accuracy.

Effect Size Calculation

Standardized mean difference effect sizes (ESs) and standard errors were calculated using the data reported in each study. For all studies, the procedure for calculating unbiased effect size estimates for Cohen's d provided by Hedges (1981) was used (this statistic is also known as Hedges's g). Effect size estimates and standard errors were computed for all dependent measures and all relevant pairs of groups in instances where the study involved more than two groups that were of interest. In cases where means, standard deviations, and sample sizes were provided for two or more independent groups, these data were used to compute effect sizes. For Mathes et al. (2005), mean differences, sample size, and independent t statistics were used to compute effect sizes and standard errors.

RESULTS

A total of 18 studies, reported in 20 journal articles, met criteria for inclusion in the synthesis. Fourteen studies used a treatment/comparison group design, with five of these studies randomly assigning students to conditions (Gunn, Biglan, Smolkowski, & Ary, 2000; Jenkins, Peyton, Sanders, & Vadasy, 2004; Mathes et al., 2005; Torgesen, Wagner, & Rashotte, 1997; Vadasy, Jenkins, Antil, Wayne, & O'Connor, 1997). Two of the studies with random assignment of students also provided additional data in journal articles published at a later date (Gunn, Smolkowski, Biglan, & Black, 2002; Torgesen et al., 1999). Random assignment is the most critical element of an experimental design, providing the greatest evidence of causal effects. These studies, then, may provide the most reliable evidence of intervention effects. All of these studies also measured intervention effects on standardized, norm-referenced measures, increasing confidence that student gains are generalizable to the broad skills measured (e.g., comprehension, word recognition) and not specific to the intervention skills taught.

Three studies examined student response over time in a single-treatment group (Dev, Doyle, & Valente, 2002; Englert, Mariage, Garmon, & Tarrant, 1998; Vaughn, Linan-Thompson, & Hickman, 2003) and one implemented a single-subject design (Snider, 1997). These studies are not designed to provide causal information, but do offer key information for researchers and educators related to interventions and instruction with potential for affecting student outcomes. Replication of findings and future studies testing these interventions with treatment/comparison designs are needed to confirm the findings and generalize outcomes. A description of the key features for each study is provided in Table 6.1.

Sufficient data for computing effect sizes were included for 13 of the studies. We summarize these study results by examining effects of (1) duration of intervention, (2) instructional group size, (3) grade level of intervention, and (4) degree of standardization. It should be noted that the studies synthesized were not designed to specifically answer questions related to duration, group size, or grade level, and only one study held the degree of intervention standardization constant to examine related effects (Mathes et al., 2005). As a result, these factors and the reported findings may not be causally related. Without the experimental manipulation of these factors of interest, no causal inferences should be made about the factors' individual contributions. Rather, we examine the effects of the individual studies in these areas in order to describe the extant literature available to school psychologists and to identify areas for additional research.

Descriptive information is provided for the five studies in which effect sizes could not be computed (Dev et al., 2002; Englert et al., 1998; Schneider, Roth, & Ennemoser, 2000; Snider, 1997; Vellutino, Scanlon, &

TABLE 6.1. Features of Intervention Studies

Study	n	Grade	Intervention frequency	Duration	Group size	Implementer	High or low standardization
Dev et al. (2002)	11 at risk	1	25–30 min; 2–3×/wk	2 yr	1	Teachers; SLPs	Low
Englert et al. (1998, Study 1)	17–18 LD	1–3	1–2 hr; 5×/wk	2 yr	4–5	Teachers	Low
Foorman et al. (1997)	114 LD	2–3	1 hr; 5×/wk	1 yr	~8	Teachers	High
Gunn et al. (2000, 2002)	198 at risk	1–3	25–30 min; 5×/wk	15–16 mo	2–3	Researchers	High
Jenkins et al. (2004)	99 at risk	1	30 min; 4×/wk	25 wk	1	Paraprofessionals	High
Mathes et al. (2005)	252 at risk/LD	1	40 min; 5×/wk	8 mo	3	Researchers	1 treatment high
1 treatment low							
Miller (2003)	174 at risk	1	40 min; 4×/wk	1 yr	1	Paraprofessionals	Low
Morris et al. (2000)	86 at risk	1	30 min; 5×/wk	8 mo	1	Teachers	Low
O'Connor et al. (1996)	31 with disabilities	K	5–15 min; 5×/wk	6 mo	3–6	Teachers	Low
Santa and Hoien (1999)	49 at risk	1	30 min; 5×/wk	8 mo	1	Teachers; administrators	Low
Schneider et al. (2000)	102 at risk	K	10–15 min; 5×/wk	20 wk	5–8	Teachers	High
Snider (1997)	7 LD	2–3	30–45 min; 5×/wk	9 mo	3–4	Teachers	High

(continued)

TABLE 6.1. (continued)

Study	n	Grade	Intervention frequency	Duration	Group size	Implementer	High or low standardization
Torgesen et al. (1997, 1999)	138 at risk	K	80 min/wk	2.5 yr	1	Researchers; paraprofessionals	1 treatment high, 2 low
Vadasy et al. (1997)	35 at risk	1	30 min; 4×/wk	27 wk	1	Community tutors	High
Vadasy et al. (2005)	57 at risk	1	30 min; 4×/wk	8 mo	1	Paraprofessionals	High
Vadasy et al. (2002)	65 at risk	1–2	30 min; 4×/wk	35–70 wk	1	Paraprofessionals	High
Vaughn, Linan-Thompson, and Hickman (2003)	35 at risk	2	35 min; 5×/wk	20–30 wk	3	Researchers	Low
Vellutino and Scanlon (2002)	37 at risk	1–2	30 min; 5×/wk	2 semesters	1	Researchers	Low

Note. LD, learning disability; SLPs, speech–language pathologists.

Jaccard, 2003). A summary of study findings and the dependent measures included in the effect sizes is provided in Table 6.2.

Effects by Duration of Intervention

Intervention Implemented for 5–7 Months

Two studies implemented a first-grade, phonics-based intervention (Sound Partners) with reading of text (Jenkins et al., 2004; Vadasy et al., 1997). Jenkins and colleagues reported similar effects on measures of prereading and reading, whether students read more decodable (ES range = 0.35–0.99) or less decodable (ES range = 0.41–1.11) text during the intervention. Mean effects for Vadasy et al. were 0.50 (range = 0.31–0.78) when comparing the intervention students with a group of students receiving no additional intervention.

Alternatively, smaller effects were calculated for two studies investigating a phonological awareness (PA) intervention for kindergarten students over a period of 5 to 6 months (O'Connor, Notari-Syverson, & Vadasy, 1996; Schneider et al., 2000). A no-treatment comparison group was not available in the O'Connor et al. study, but students with disabilities in self-contained classrooms were compared with students with disabilities in integrated classrooms who also received the same intervention. The mean effect for students receiving the intervention in the self-contained classrooms was 0.18 (mean ES range = –0.43 to 0.75). However, when compared with students without disabilities receiving the same intervention, the students with disabilities instructed in the self-contained classrooms lagged behind on a number of prereading skills. Schneider et al. also compared students receiving the intervention with students not at risk receiving instruction in typical classrooms. Students receiving a PA intervention over the 5-month period significantly outperformed those not at risk at posttest on measures of PA. However, 1–2 years later, at the end of first and second grade, the comparison group of not-at-risk students maintained significantly higher outcomes on decoding and comprehension. A second group of students in the Schneider et al. study received the PA intervention along with intervention in letter sounds and achieved outcomes equivalent to the not-at-risk students on measures of decoding and comprehension at the end of first and second grade. Student IQ was used as a covariate in the analyses. The students in the typical classrooms participated in social events and games and did not receive any formal reading instruction.

Vaughn, Linan-Thompson, and Hickman (2003) implemented intervention over 30 weeks but allowed students who obtained predetermined fluency levels to exit intervention after 20 weeks. Pre- to posttest standardized mean change effect sizes ranged from 0.53 to 6.06 on measures of word

TABLE 6.2. Effect Sizes by Intervention and Dependent Measure for Studies with Sufficient Data for Calculating Effect Sizes

Study	Intervention	Dependent measures	Effect sizes		
			T1 vs. C	T2 vs. C	T3 vs. C
Foorman et al. (1997)	T1: synthetic phonics T2: analytic phonics C: sight word	Pseudohomophone spelling test Torgesen–Wagner Phonemic Awareness Battery Word reading test	0.05 0.59 0.17	0.23 0.27 0.19	— — —
Gunn et al. (2000, 2002)	T: reading mastery/corrective reading C: no treatment	Oral reading fluency WJ–R Comprehension WJ–R Letter–Word Identification WJ–R Vocabulary WJ–R Word Attack	0.27 0.28 0.34 0.31 0.73	— — — — —	— — — — —
Jenkins et al. (2004)	T1: more decodable text T2: less decodable text C: no treatment	Diagnostic Test of Basic Decoding Skills Text word list Oral reading accuracy controlled text Oral reading fluency controlled text Oral reading accuracy uncontrolled text Oral reading fluency uncontrolled text	0.99 0.93 0.81 0.56 0.44 0.46 0.35 0.55 0.74 0.68 0.86 0.83 0.50	1.11 0.49 0.51 0.48 0.41 0.51 0.79 0.48 0.69 0.69 0.76 0.65 0.48	— — — — — — — — — — — — —
Mathes et al. (2005)	T1: proactive reading T2: responsive reading C: enhanced classroom	CRAB–R Fluency CRAB–R Comprehension WJ–III Comprehension WJ–III Fluency WJ–III Spelling WJ–III Word Attack WJ–III Word Identification	0.26 0.13 0.21 0.00 0.53 0.63 0.52	0.28 0.26 0.30 0.22 0.53 0.24 0.37	— — — — — — —

Study	Condition	Measure		
Miller (2003)	T: partners-in-reading C1: Reading Recovery C2: no treatment	Cohort 1		
		HSTM Developmental Spelling	-0.18^a	0.71^b
		HSTM Word Recognition	-0.18^a	0.74^b
		Cohort 2		
		HSTM Developmental Spelling	-0.14^a	0.81^b
		HSTM Word Recognition	-0.03^a	1.09^b
Morris et al. (2000)	T: Early Steps C: Typical school services	Developmental spelling	0.83	—
		Passage reading	0.79	—
		Word recognition list	0.68	—
		WRMT–R Comprehension	0.74	—
		WRMT–R Word Attack	0.76	—
O'Connor et al. (1996)	T: Activity-based phonological instruction C: T provided in integrated general education classroom	Syllable deletion	-0.43	—
		Blending	-0.28	—
		First sound	0.15	—
		Segmenting	0.37	—
		Rhyme	-0.13	—
		PPVT–R	0.23	—
		Rapid letter naming	0.75	—
		Sound repetition	-0.07	—
		WJ Letter–Word Identification	0.71	—
		WJ Dictation	0.51	—
Santa and Hoien (1999)	T: Early Steps C: Small-group reading	Developmental Spelling	0.59	—
		Passage Reading	0.73	—
		Word recognition list	0.91	—

(continued)

TABLE 6.2. (continued)

Study	Intervention	Dependent measures	Effect sizes		
			T1 vs. C	T2 vs. C	T3 vs. C
Torgesen et al. (1997, 1999)	T1: Phonological awareness plus synthetic phonics	Developmental spelling	0.72	0.00	−0.02
		WRAT–R Spelling	0.53	0.20	0.07
	T2: Embedded phonics	Blend phonemes	0.33	0.24	0.09
	T3: Regular classroom support C: No treatment	Phoneme elision	0.52	−0.23	−0.20
		Phoneme segmentation	0.59	0.07	0.06
		GORT–III Comprehension	0.30	0.30	−0.12
		TOWRE Phonemic Decoding	0.89	0.18	0.11
		TOWRE Sight Word	1.21	0.91	0.79
		WRMT–R Word Attack	1.04	0.33	0.27
		WRMT–R Word Identification	0.36	0.35	0.66
		WRMT–R Comprehension	0.14	0.08	0.43
		Word reading list	0.71	0.26	0.11
		Nonword-reading list	0.93	0.14	0.00
Vadasy et al. (1997)	T: After-school early reading C: No treatment	Analytical Reading Inventory	0.42	—	—
		Dolch Word Recognition	0.31	—	—
		WJ–R Word Attack	0.35	—	—
		WRAT–R Reading	0.59	—	—
		WRAT–R Spelling	0.78	—	—
		Yopp-Singer Segmentation	0.74	—	—
		Writing sample words written	0.42	—	—
		Writing sample words correctly spelled	0.37	—	—

Study	Conditions	Measure			
Vadasy et al. (2005)	T1: Reading practice T2: Word study C: Typical school services	TOWRE Phonemic Decoding	0.51	0.61	—
		TOWRE Sight Word	0.61	0.56	—
		Oral reading fluency	0.50	0.15	—
		Passage reading accuracy	0.41	0.28	—
		WRAT–R Reading	0.93	1.12	—
		WRAT–R Spelling	0.17	0.13	—
		WRMT–R Word Attack	0.99	1.33	—
		WRMT–R Word Identification	0.84	1.04	—
		WRMT–R Comprehension	0.81	0.63	—
Vadasy et al. (2002)	T1: Sound Partners T2: Sound Partners + Thinking Partners T3: Thinking Partners C: Typical school services	TOWRE Phonemic Decoding	—	0.73	-0.09
		TOWRE Sight Word	—	0.71	0.20
		Comprehension questions	—	-0.05	0.10
		Informal Reading Inventory	—	0.56	0.05
		WRAT–R Reading	—	0.92	0.38
		WRAT–R Spelling	—	0.88	0.37
		WRMT–R Word Identification	—	0.76	0.36
		WRMT–R Word Attack	—	0.63	0.29

Note. T, treatment; WRAT-III, Wide Range Achievement Test, Third Edition; C, comparison; WJ-R, Woodcock–Johnson Tests of Achievement—Revised; TOWRE, Test of Word Reading Efficiency; WRAT-R, Wide Range Achievement Test—Revised; WRMT-R, Woodcock Reading Mastery Test—Revised; CRAB-R, Comprehensive Assessment of Reading Battery—Revised; WJ-III, Woodcock–Johnson Tests of Achievement, Third Edition; HSTM, Howard Street Training Manual; PPVT-R, Peabody Picture Vocabulary Test—Revised; WJ, Woodcock–Johnson Tests of Achievement; GORT-III, Gray Oral Reading Test, Third Edition.

[a]T vs. C1; [b]T vs. C2.

125

attack, passage comprehension, fluency, and PA. However, effect sizes calculated for pre- to posttest gains are generally higher than those calculated with a treatment group and a comparison group. The pre- to posttest effects provide an indication of the findings in the Vaughn et al. study but cannot be accurately compared with the treatment and comparison group effects in the other studies.

Interventions Implemented over 8–9 Months

A full range of effects were demonstrated for interventions implemented over approximately 1 school year. No effects were found for students with reading disabilities receiving an intervention of analytic phonics (onset-rime word patterns) incorporated with writing and reading phonetic readers compared with students receiving whole-word instruction on measures of word reading, spelling, and phonemic awareness (mean ES = –0.05, mean ES range = –0.23 to 0.27; Foorman et al., 1997). However, a mean effect of 0.27 (mean ES range = 0.05–0.59) was demonstrated for a synthetic phonics intervention in comparison to whole-word instruction on these same measures. Mathes et al. (2005) reported on two interventions provided for approximately 8 months in addition to enhanced classroom instruction. One intervention provided a standardized protocol, including explicit phonics instruction with decodable text and comprehension strategies (proactive), whereas the other intervention provided word work and reading in leveled books based on individual student needs (responsive). When compared with the outcomes of students receiving only the enhanced classroom instruction, both interventions yielded similar mean effects (mean ES = 0.33, mean ES range = 0.00–0.63, for proactive; mean ES = 0.31, mean ES range = 0.22–0.53, for responsive). Effects specifically for comprehension (Woodcock–Johnson III) were 0.21 and 0.30 for the proactive and responsive interventions, respectively.

Higher mean effects were revealed for two intervention studies implementing Sound Partners with and without text reading for 8 months (Vadasy, Sanders, & Peyton, 2005). In comparison to students receiving typical school instruction, the mean effect size for students in the intervention with text was 0.64 (mean ES range = 0.17–0.99) and for students in the intervention without text reading 0.65 (mean ES range = 0.13–1.33). The same intervention with decodable text reading was implemented over 35 weeks in a previous study (Vadasy, Sanders, Peyton, & Jenkins, 2002). In this study, students increased standard scores into the average range on measures of reading, spelling, and word identification by the end of the intervention. The 2002 study also examined a second intervention (Thinking Partners) for second graders that was implemented for 35 weeks. The Thinking Partners intervention incorporated grade-level trade books and comprehension strategy instruction and yielded a mean effect of 0.23 (mean ES range = 0.09–0.38) over students in typical school instruction (Vadasy et al., 2002).

Three studies yielded larger effects following intervention for 8 to 9 months. Two of the studies examined the same intervention (Early Steps) with first-grade students. The students were provided with supported reading and rereading of leveled books as well as phonics instruction with a focus on word patterns. These interventions were compared with a small-group, pullout intervention provided by the school. On measures of word recognition, word attack, spelling, and comprehension, the mean effect sizes were 0.76 (mean ES range = 0.68–0.83; Morris, Tyner, & Perney, 2000) and 0.74 (mean ES range = 0.59–0.91; Santa & Hoien, 1999). A similar intervention reported by Miller (2003) also yielded high effects on informal measures of word recognition and spelling in comparison to no intervention (mean ES = 0.84, mean ES range = 0.71–1.09). In addition, a single-subject study examining seven students with LDs demonstrated gains in fluency, with all but one student reading at least 70 to 105 words per minute after 9 months of intervention. Vellutino and Scanlon (2002) provided intensive intervention (two semesters) to first and second graders demonstrating either low growth or very low growth (based on Woodcock Reading Mastery Test—Revised Basic Skills Cluster) and reported that 75% of low-growth and 67% of very-low-growth students obtained standard scores of at least 90 on passage comprehension at the end of the third grade. Students were provided with intervention that was based on their individual needs and included daily instruction in phonological skills, irregular word reading, writing, and reading connected text.

Interventions Implemented for More Than 1 School Year

Interventions implemented for more than 1 school year yielded a similar range of effect sizes as the shorter intervention periods. Torgesen et al. (1997, 1999) implemented three interventions in comparison to a no-treatment control. Each of the interventions was implemented over 2½ years, with students starting in the middle of kindergarten and continuing through the end of second grade. A phonics intervention embedded with word-level games, basal stories, and writing activities yielded a mean effect of 0.22 (mean ES range = –0.23–0.91). Similarly, an intervention reinforcing skills and activities taught in the regular classroom reading program yielded a mean effect of 0.17 (mean ES range = –0.20–0.79). In contrast, a phonics intervention with PA, letter sounds, decoding, and encoding taught in isolation along with reading of controlled text (later trade books) and fluency instruction yielded a mean effect size of 0.64 (mean ES range = 0.14–1.21). Effects sizes on two measures of reading comprehension for the students participating in the phonics intervention were 0.30 (Gray Oral Reading Test III) and 0.14 (Woodcock Reading Mastery Test—Revised).

Gunn et al. (2000) reported a mean effect of 0.39 (mean ES range = 0.27–0.73) on measures of fluency, word reading, word attack, vocabulary, and comprehension for a 2-year explicit phonics intervention (reading mastery and corrective reading). The smallest gains were seen on fluency and comprehension measures.

Dev et al. (2002) reported that 10 of 11 students achieved grade-level performance or higher in spelling and demonstrated improvement in reading after 2 years of intervention. Specific data on student performance levels were not provided. Similarly, Englert et al. (1998) reported 13 of 18 students at or above grade-level performance on oral reading accuracy, as measured by the passage level a student could read at 90% accuracy after 2 years of intervention.

Effects by Instructional Group Size

Ten studies implemented interventions for students in a 1:1 format, with one teacher instructing one student (Dev et al., 2002; Jenkins et al., 2004; Miller, 2003; Morris et al., 2000; Santa & Hoien, 1999; Torgesen et al., 1997, 1999; Vadasy et al., 1997, 2002, 2005; Vellutino & Scanlon, 2002). Eight studies implemented interventions with instructional groups ranging in size from two to eight students (Englert et al., 1998; Foorman et al., 1997; Gunn et al., 2000; Mathes et al., 2005; O'Connor et al., 1996; Schneider et al., 2000; Snider, 1997; Vaughn, Linan-Thompson, & Hickman, 2003).

One-to-One Instruction

Jenkins et al. (2004) and Torgesen et al. (1997, 1999) reported similar intervention effects on student outcomes after providing instruction in a 1:1 format. Mean effect sizes of 0.67 (mean ES range = 0.35–0.99) and 0.62 (mean ES range = 0.41–1.11) were found for treatment groups in the Jenkins et al. study. One intervention with explicit phonics instruction in the Torgesen et al. study yielded a mean effect size of 0.64 (mean ES range = 0.14–1.21). However, smaller effects were seen for the embedded phonics intervention (mean ES = 0.22, mean ES range = –0.23–0.91) and for the intervention reinforcing the classroom reading program (mean ES = 0.17, mean ES range = –0.20–0.79).

Three studies by the same research team (Vadasy et al., 1997, 2002, 2005) examined the Sound Partners intervention, a first-grade, phonics-based intervention using decodable books for reading. Mean effects were 0.50 (range = 0.31–0.78; Vadasy et al., 1997) and 0.64 (range = 0.17–0.99; Vadasy et al., 2005). Vadasy et al. (2005) also examined the intervention without the text-reading component with similar results (mean ES = 0.65, mean ES range = 0.13–1.33). Vadasy et al. (2002) combined the first-grade intervention with a second-grade intervention, incorporating comprehension strategy instruction and grade-level trade books. Mean effects for students participating in both the phonics and strategy interventions were 0.64 (mean ES range = –0.05–0.92) and for students completing only the strategy intervention 0.23 (mean ES range = 0.09–0.38) compared with students receiving typical school services.

Two studies yielding larger effects implemented the same intervention incorporating reading/rereading leveled text with phonics instruction in word patterns (mean ES = 0.76, mean ES range = 0.68–0.83 [Morris et al., 2000]; mean ES = 0.74, mean ES range = 0.59–0.91 [Santa & Hoien, 1999]). A similar intervention reported by Miller (2003) produced effects comparable to Morris et al. and Santa and Hoien for intervention participants compared with students not receiving intervention (mean ES = 0.84, mean ES range = 0.71–1.09), although effects on fluency and comprehension were not measured. Students in the intervention were also compared with students receiving school-implemented Reading Recovery. A smaller mean effect in favor of the school-implemented Reading Recovery was realized (mean ES = –0.13, mean ES range = –0.03—0.18; Miller, 2003).

Vellutino and Scanlon (2002) provided 1:1 instruction to first- and second-grade students at risk for reading difficulties for two semesters. Thirty minutes of daily instruction, including 15 minutes of reading connected text and skill instruction, was provided. Students demonstrating low growth and very low growth in basic skills after one semester of intervention were provided a second semester of intervention and monitored. Approximately three-quarters of the students requiring two semesters of intervention reached average levels on measures of comprehension as measured more than a year after the research intervention concluded. However, many students still demonstrated below-average levels on basic skills such as word identification and word attack at posttest.

Group Instruction

When examining group size, we are only able to provide a range of effects rather than direct comparisons between approaches (e.g., 1:1 and small group) because experimental manipulation of these group sizes was not built into the intervention studies we examined. A description of these studies reveals that providing instruction to students in small groups appears to be associated with smaller effects than 1:1 instruction. However, it is important to note that group size was not directly compared in any of these studies and that causal inference cannot be made.

Gunn et al. (2000) and Mathes et al. (2005) implemented interventions in instructional groups of two to three students, yielding similar results; the mean effect size for the students participating in the reading mastery/corrective reading interventions was 0.39 (mean ES range = 0.27–0.73; Gunn et al.) and for students in the proactive and responsive reading interventions 0.33 (mean ES range = 0.00–0.63) and 0.31 (mean ES range = 0.22–0.53), respectively (Mathes et al.). It should be noted that 1:1 instruction was provided to students in the Gunn et al. study if the group instruction was not feasible. Also, the comparison group in the Mathes et al. study comprised students receiving enhanced classroom instruction; thus, smaller effects could be associated with the comparison students' enhanced performance.

Smaller mean effects were seen for one study implementing a PA intervention to kindergarteners in groups of three to six students (mean ES = 0.18, mean ES range = –0.43–0.75; O'Connor et al., 1996). In the O'Connor et al. study, students with disabilities were compared with peers integrated in general education classrooms who also received the same intervention but in a larger group. This comparison of two groups receiving the same intervention may deflate the effect size relative to the other studies reported in this synthesis, where effect sizes were calculated by comparing intervention students with nonintervention students (Swanson, Hoskyn, & Lee, 1999). A second study implementing a PA intervention for at-risk kindergarteners compared their outcomes with those of students not at risk (Schneider et al., 2000). On measures of PA, students in the interventions outperformed not-at-risk students. However, follow-up measures conducted 1 and 2 years after intervention indicated the not-at-risk students outperformed at-risk students who received the PA intervention on measures of decoding and comprehension.

Foorman et al. (1997) reported outcomes for students receiving intervention in groups of about eight students. They found a mean effect of 0.27 (mean ES range = 0.05–0.59) for a synthetic phonics intervention and no effects for an analytic phonics intervention (mean ES = –0.05, mean ES range = –0.23–0.27) compared intervention involving instruction in sight words delivered at teacher-directed centers.

Three additional studies without a comparison group delivered intervention to participants in groups (Englert et al., 1998; Snider, 1997; Vaughn, Linan-Thompson, & Hickman, 2003). All studies noted overall student gains from pretest to posttest, with Vaughn, Linan-Thompson, and Hickman reporting standardized mean difference effects ranging from 0.53 to 6.06 for students receiving intervention in instructional groups of three.

Effects by Grade Level

We would like to remind the reader that we are only able to describe the findings by grade groups and not provide analysis of studies that directly manipulated grade-level variables to determine findings. Thirteen studies provided intervention to students beginning in kindergarten or first grade and five provided intervention beginning in second or third grade. Englert et al. (1998) also included two students who began the intervention in first grade. Gunn et al. (2000) provided intervention to students in first to third grades. Data were not disaggregated by grade level.

Interventions for Kindergarten and First Grade

Two studies implemented interventions in kindergarten. O'Connor et al. (1996) reported mean effect sizes of 0.18 (mean ES range = −0.43–0.75). Schneider et al. reported on two interventions—PA and PA plus letter–sound—for at-risk kindergarten students. Students in both interventions outperformed a comparison group of not-at-risk students on measures of PA at posttest. The not-at-risk students participated in typical German classrooms consisting of social events and games. By the end of first grade and second grade, students receiving the PA-only intervention fell behind their not-at-risk peers on measures of decoding and comprehension; however, those who had received the PA plus letter–sound intervention obtained outcomes equivalent to the not-at-risk group on these same measures (with IQ used as a covariate in the analyses).

Several studies implemented interventions for first-grade students. Mean effects of 0.33 (mean ES range = 0.00–0.63) and 0.31 (mean ES range = 0.22–0.53) were reported for proactive and responsive interventions, respectively (Mathes et al., 2005). Three studies with similar interventions incorporating instruction in word patterns along with teacher-supported reading and rereading of leveled books found higher mean effects (mean ES range = 0.74–0.84; Miller, 2003; Morris et al., 2000; Santa & Hoien, 1999). Three additional studies of first graders implementing variations of the Sound Partners intervention yielded a mean ES range of 0.50 to 0.67 (Jenkins et al., 2004; Vadasy et al., 1997, 2005). The smaller effects reported for proactive and responsive interventions (Mathes et al., 2005) may be partially explained by the overall enhanced reading instruction provided to all students, including those in the comparison group.

Four additional studies began intervention with K–1 students and continued intervention through second grade. Vadasy et al. (2002) provided 2 years of intervention for students beginning in first grade and continuing through second grade. Sound Partners was implemented in first grade and Thinking Partners, an intervention incorporating grade-level trade books with comprehension strategy instruction, was implemented in second grade. The mean effect size for measures of word reading, word attack, spelling, fluency, and comprehension was 0.64 (mean ES range = −0.05–0.92). Similar effects were seen for students participating in a multisensory explicit phonics intervention from kindergarten through second grade (mean ES = 0.64, mean ES range = 0.14–1.21; Torgesen et al., 1997, 1999). However, smaller effects were seen for two alternative interventions also implemented from kindergarten through second grade (embedded phonics [mean ES = 0.22, mean ES range = –0.23–0.91] and regular classroom support [mean ES = 0.17, mean ES range = –0.20–0.79]; Torgesen et al.). Dev et al. (2002) reported student increases in spelling to levels at or above grade level for 10 of 11 students over 2 years (first to second grade). Similarly, Vellutino and Scanlon (2002) reported that 75% of low-growth and 67% of very-low-growth students achieved standard scores of 90 or higher in passage comprehension in third grade, more than a year after intervention concluded. Two years after intervention, in fourth grade, 60% of the low-growth students and 42% of the very-low-growth students scored at or above grade level on silent reading comprehension.

Interventions for Second and Third Grade

Vadasy et al. (2002) compared the Thinking Partners intervention provided to students in second grade with typical school services and found a mean effect of 0.23 (mean ES range = 0.09–0.38) after 35 weeks of intervention. This is in contrast to the higher effects seen for the Sound Partners plus Thinking Partners intervention begun in first grade described in the previous section. Similarly, Foorman et al. (1997) found a mean effect of 0.27 (mean ES range = 0.05–0.59) for a synthetic phonics intervention compared with a sight word intervention provided to second- and third-grade students. No effects were found for students participating in the analytic phonics intervention (mean ES = –0.05, mean ES range = –0.23–0.27; Foorman et al.).

Vaughn, Linan-Thompson, and Hickman (2003) reported pre- to post-test gains for second-grade students participating in an intervention incorporating PA, fluency, word analysis, comprehension, and spelling. Of the 35 students participating in the intervention for 100 or more sessions, 24 met exit criteria for the intervention. Englert et al. (1998) and Snider (1997) also reported high numbers of students on grade level in reading after receiving intervention. No comparison groups were available for these studies.

Effects by Intervention Protocol: High and Low Standardization

To examine effects related to intervention protocol, we first attempted to classify studies into standardized and problem-solving interventions. We defined standardized interventions as those with well-defined daily lessons (many are scripted) and material selection. We defined problem-solving protocols as interventions implemented with daily lessons (components, materials, skills, and strategies) planned based on determination of student needs through a problem-solving process (defining the problem, analyzing reasons for the problem, developing an intervention plan, evaluating the plan; NASDSE, 2005). However, we were unable to locate any studies of extensive interventions implementing a problem-solving approach. Instead, we found that the intervention descriptions provided a range in the degree of standardization. Thus, we classified studies as either high or low on standardization of the intervention implemented.

Studies were classified as "high standardization" if the authors described interventions as having well-defined lessons and materials and the same lessons were provided to all students, with possible adjustments made to accommodate student levels. Studies were classified as "low standardization" if the authors described interventions as having less well-defined lessons and providing opportunities for the teacher to respond to students' needs in the skills/strategies taught and the materials used. In this section, we contrast high-standardization interventions, where instruction is prescribed in advance and provided to students with similar reading difficulties, with low-standardization interventions, which often provide many of the same elements of instruction but are largely organized by the teacher in response to students' needs. It should be noted that high or low standardization does not refer to the extent to which the interventions were based on previous research. Furthermore, it is important to note that we provided the coding for high and low standardization based on specified criteria and that high and low standardization were compared directly only in one study (Mathes et al., 2005).

High Standardization

Four of the interventions we classified as high standardization yielded mean effects ranging from 0.23 to 0.39 (Foorman et al., 1997; Gunn et al., 2000; Mathes et al., 2005 [proactive]; Vadasy et al., 2002 [Thinking Partners]). All other high standardized interventions yielded mean effects ranging from 0.50 to 0.67 (Jenkins et al., 2004; Torgesen et al., 1997, 1999 [PA plus synthetic phonics]; Vadasy et al., 1997, 2002, 2005 [Sound Partners plus Thinking Partners]).

Low Standardization

Similarly, four of the interventions we classified as low standardization yielded mean effects ranging from 0.17 to 0.31 (Mathes et al., 2005 [responsive]; O'Connor et al., 1996; Torgesen et al., 1997, 1999 [embedded phonics and regular classroom support]). Three interventions yielded larger mean effects ranging from 0.74 to 0.84 (Miller, 2003; Morris et al., 2000; Santa &

Hoien, 1999). In addition, Vaughn, Linan-Thompson, and Hickman (2003) reported large pre- to posttest effects for students whose response allowed them to exit intervention as well as students who did not exit interventions after 30 weeks. Vellutino and Scanlon (2002) reported that the majority of students receiving intervention who initially demonstrated low levels of response to intervention achieved average to above-average performance levels on measures of comprehension. Dev et al. (2002) and Englert et al. (1998) reported that the large majority of students were on grade level in reading or spelling.

DISCUSSION

This synthesis reports the research on extensive early reading interventions so that educators will have research-based information to facilitate decision making within RTI frameworks. For the purpose of this synthesis, extensive interventions were defined as those that conducted 100 or more sessions. Instructional features, including duration of intervention, grouping procedures for implementing the intervention, and more or less standardized intervention approaches, were described.

The findings suggest generally positive outcomes for students with reading difficulties and disabilities participating in extensive interventions. These interventions suggest high feasibility of implementation, as demonstrated by 14 of the 18 studies utilizing school personnel for all or part of the implementation. However, practitioners interested in implementing extensive interventions need to realize that the personnel in all studies were provided specific intervention training that included feedback on implementation quality.

The studies with the highest effects emphasized both phonics instruction and text reading. In some of these studies the students used decodable text during reading instruction, whereas in others the text was at students' reading level but was not necessarily strictly decodable. The reported phonics component included in the interventions incorporated instruction in either letter–sound correspondence with word blending or word patterns such as rimes. A few studies also integrated encoding or spelling within the phonics instruction.

Implementing RTI includes the use of interventions that increase in intensity based on student need. In 2000, Torgesen called for further examination of the intensity of instruction required to eliminate reading failure in children. Intensity can be increased in a number of ways, including decreasing group size, increasing time in intervention, and providing more explicit instruction (Torgesen, 2000). In this synthesis, we defined extensive interventions based on number of intervention sessions (100 sessions) and examined the relative intensity in two ways: duration of intervention and instructional group size. Although the interventions synthesized reported ranges from 5 months to 2½ years of instruction, few differences were seen in the magnitude of the effect sizes based on the duration of instruction. This does not mean that students who spent more time in intervention did not make greater gains or progress toward closing the gap with the comparison students, just that the relative impact as measured by effect sizes was not significantly larger. Further examination of the total number of hours of intervention provided to students may extend our understanding of the relative impact based on duration of the intervention. Unfortunately, we were unable to estimate the total hours of intervention provided to students in the large majority of the studies based on the information provided in the article and, thus, could not accurately analyze student outcomes in relation to hours of intervention.

A second way to increase intervention intensity may be to decrease instructional group size. We examined student outcomes in the studies implementing interventions in a 1:1 format (one teacher with one student) as well as studies that implemented interventions in groups (ranging from two to eight students). Studies implementing extensive interventions in 1:1 formats appear to be associated with overall higher effects than those implementing interventions in groups. However, this finding has several caveats. Because of the low number of studies examining small-group instruction (two to four students), we were unable to directly compare the effects of small-group instruction with the effects of 1:1 instruction in this synthesis. Furthermore, at least one of the studies (Mathes et al., 2005) had a robust comparison group that was provided enhanced classroom instruction, mitigating the overall intervention effects. The three studies with the largest group sizes reported the lowest effects among the studies implementing group instruction (Foorman et al., 1997; O'Connor et al., 1996; Schneider et al., 2000).

Early intervention has been heralded as a promising avenue for reducing reading difficulties in recognition of the persistent difficulties students face when they do not learn to read in the primary grades (Francis, Shaywitz, Stuebing, Shaywitz, & Fletcher, 1996; Jenkins & O'Connor, 2002; Juel, 1988). The results of this synthesis further suggest that interventions provided early, beginning in first grade, are associated with higher effects than interventions beginning in second or third grade. The difficulties students face in reading as they enter second or third grade are more complex than in first grade, making significant gains more difficult to achieve. Certainly, the number of skills students must obtain to read successfully increases as they progress through the grades. Another factor to consider may be the severity of the reading difficulties experienced by students in the second- and third-grade samples. For example, three studies examined only students with identified LDs, and each of these studies occurred in the second and third grades. Thus, students with the most severe reading difficulties were represented in the studies conducted in older grades, likely influencing outcomes.

Screening and measurement error is another reason why students receiving intervention in kindergarten and first grade may have less severe reading difficulties than students in second and third grades. Measures for identifying students at risk for reading difficulties/disabilities in the early grades purposefully "overidentify" to ensure that all students who possibly have problems will be provided early support. As a result, there are likely more false positives with less severe difficulties in kindergarten and first-grade samples than in the higher grades, and this could explain the higher effects observed with the interventions beginning in first grade.

As RTI implementation has increased over the past few years, questions related to the relative effectiveness of standardized and problem-solving protocols for intervention have arisen (Fuchs et al., 2003; NASDSE, 2005). We were interested in examining the research evidence on problem-solving and standardized interventions. Unfortunately, we were unable to locate a study examining intensive interventions using a problem-solving approach. As a result, we could not report effects of this protocol implementation. It may be that problem-solving protocols have more typically been implemented in less intensive interventions.

To provide some preliminary information on the effects related to varying intervention protocols, we compared studies implementing more standardized protocols (well-defined previously developed lessons) with those that implemented less standardized protocols (lessons largely organized by the teacher based on student need). There were no differences in overall outcomes between studies implementing these two types of protocols. This finding should be considered while keeping in mind the low number of studies available. However, the finding does align with Mathes et al.'s (2005) study directly comparing more and less standardized interventions. Mathes et al. reported statistically significant differences in favor of students in the more standardized intervention on only one outcome measure: word attack. Effect sizes were moderate for students in both conditions.

Implications and Limitations

School psychologists and special educators play an integral part in the decision making of any RTI implementation. Expert knowledge of the efficacy of interventions in relation to varying student needs is pertinent to effective decision making. When RTI is implemented, the most intensive interventions are typically reserved for students with the most significant difficulties, usually provided after students demonstrate insufficient response to generally effective general education instruction and perhaps less intensive intervention. In this synthesis, we examined interventions implemented for 100 sessions or more. However, only one study synthesized here examined the quality of instruction students received in general education (Mathes et al., 2005) and only two examined intervention for students who had demonstrated previous insufficient response (Vadasy et al., 2002; Vaughn, Linan-Thompson, & Hickman, 2003). As a result, the samples in the majority of the studies synthesized may have included students who had not yet received effective reading instruction or intervention before the study. Many of the participants in these studies were at-risk readers and may not represent students with the most significant reading difficulties/disabilities.

In implementing RTI, the decision making of school psychologists will be improved with data related to students' responses in general education (without intervention and relative to others in the class) as well as data after students are provided supplemental intervention. Adequate access and use of this information assists in referring and identifying students with reading disabilities and planning for more intensive interventions to meet student needs. Future research examining intensive interventions specifically for students with insufficient response to previous intervention will be a high priority for the field to inform best practice for meeting the needs of students with severe reading difficulties/disabilities.

Currently, we know considerably less about students whose response to typically effective interventions is low and who require not just extensive but highly intensive interventions. From our own research and experience, we have learned that students who have not responded to extensive and intensive interventions often demonstrate special needs in many areas (e.g., autism, attention deficit, low language) and require special education interventions that are highly individualized to address their multiple learning needs (Vaughn et al., 2007). Our experience is that highly specialized personnel will be required to provide these interventions.

Future Research

We synthesized studies examining intensive interventions for students with reading difficulties and disabilities in order to explore characteristics of interventions associated with high effects. Although this information identifies several areas for future research and examination, this synthesis cannot provide causal evidence related to the effects of instructional group size, duration, grade level of intervention, or level of standardization on outcomes for students (with the exception of one study, Mathes et al., 2005). Across the studies synthesized here, many intervention components varied and it is not possible to isolate the specific effects of duration, group size, grade level, and level of standardization. Thus, we report a range of effects for each of these factors of interest rather than having adequate studies to make direct comparisons between intervention approaches (recognizing that the latter approach would require experimental manipulation). For this reason, we believe future research directly addressing these factors of interest through experimental studies would be highly valuable and would further our confidence in recommending features of intensive intervention approaches and their outcomes.

Additional information on the use of problem-solving approaches is also needed. Although individualized instruction is generally seen as the hallmark of special education, there is a lack of empirical evidence examining the effects of a problem-solving approach for intensive interventions. Further examination of the effects of problem-solving interventions that are designed to provide differentiated instruction will yield valuable information regarding effective instruction for students with significant reading difficulties and disabilities.

In defining an extensive intervention for this synthesis, we selected the duration of student participation in the intervention of 100 or more sessions. As mentioned previously, the number of hours of student participation could also define the intensity of an intervention; however, we were unable to obtain reliable data (number of days and length of session) in order to select studies based on this definition. The use of duration only as a definition for extensive interventions means that there may be studies that provided more hours of intervention in reading that did not meet our criteria.

Positive outcomes for students participating in extensive interventions have been demonstrated in numerous studies. Further research is needed to address many critical questions, including whether adjusting and changing interventions for students most at risk is associated with greater acceleration in student learning. Further examination of intervention protocols for implementation is warranted to assist in decision making related to the most effective interventions to meet the needs of students with severe reading difficulties and disabilities.

ACKNOWLEDGMENTS

Special thanks to Kim Kayser for her assistance with the selection of articles for the synthesis. We also thank Nancy Scammacca and Kathryn Tackett for their competent assistance in organizing data from the studies.

This chapter is adapted from Wanzek, J., & Vaughn, S. (2007). Research-based implications from extensive early reading interventions. *School Psychology Review*, 36, 541–562. Copyright 2007 by the National Association of School Psychologists. Adapted by permission.

REFERENCES

Bergen, J. R., & Kratochwill, T. R. (1990). *Behavioral consultation and therapy.* New York: Plenum Press.

Burns, M. K., Appleton, J. J., & Stehouwer, J. D. (2005). Meta-analytic review of response-to-intervention research: Examining field-based and research-implemented models. *Journal of Psychoeducational Assessment, 23,* 281–394.

Dev, P. C., Doyle, B. A., & Valente, B. (2002). Labels needn't stick: "At-risk" first graders rescued with appropriate intervention. *Journal of Education for Students Placed At Risk, 7,* 327–332.

Englert, C. S., Mariage, T. V., Garmon, M. A., & Tarrant, K. L. (1998). Accelerating reading progress in early literacy project classrooms. *Remedial and Special Education, 19*(3), 142–159.

Fletcher, J. M., Coulter, W. A., Reschly, D. J., & Vaughn, S. (2004). Alternative approaches to the definition and identification of learning disabilities: Some questions and answers. *Annals of Dyslexia, 54,* 304–331.

Foorman, B. R. (2003). *Preventing and remediating reading difficulties: Bringing science to scale.* Baltimore: York Press.

Foorman, B. R., Francis, D. J., Winikates, D., Mehta, P., Schatschneider, C., & Fletcher, J. M. (1997). Early interventions for children with reading disabilities. *Scientific Studies of Reading, 1,* 255–276.

Francis, D. J., Shaywitz, S. E., Stuebing, K. K., Shaywitz, B. A., & Fletcher, J. M. (1996). Developmental lag versus deficit models of reading disability: A longitudinal, individual growth curves analysis. *Journal of Educational Psychology, 88,* 3–17.

Fuchs, D., Mock, D., Morgan, P. L., & Young, C. L. (2003). Responsiveness-to-intervention: Definitions, evidence, and implications for the learning disabilities construct. *Learning Disabilities Research and Practice, 18,* 157–171.

Gunn, B., Biglan, A., Smolkowski, K., & Ary, D. (2000). The efficacy of supplemental instruction in decoding skills for Hispanic and non-Hispanic students in early elementary school. *Journal of Special Education, 34,* 90–103.

Gunn, B., Smolkowski, K., Biglan, A., & Black, C. (2002). Supplemental instruction in decoding skills for Hispanic and non-Hispanic students in early elementary school: A follow-up. *Journal of Special Education, 36,* 69–79.

Hedges, L. V. (1981). Distribution theory for Glass's estimator of effect size and related estimators. *Journal of Education Statistics, 6,* 107–128.

Ikeda, M. J., Grimes, J., Tilly, W. D., Allison, R., Kurns, S., & Stumme, J. (2002). Implementing an intervention-based approach to service delivery: A case example. In M. R. Shinn, H. M. Walker, & G. Stoner (Eds.), *Intervention for academic and behavior problems: II. Preventative and remedial approaches* (pp. 53–69). Washington, DC: National Association of School Psychologists.

Institute of Education Sciences. (2003). *What Works Clearinghouse study review standards.* Retrieved January 10, 2005, from What Works Clearinghouse website: *www.whatworks.ed.gov/reviewprocess/study_standards_final.pdf.*

Jenkins, J. R., & O'Connor, R. E. (2002). Early identification and intervention for young children with reading/learning disabilities. In R. Bradley, L. Danielson,

& D. P. Hallahan (Eds.), *Identification of learning disabilities: Research to practice* (pp. 99–149). Mahwah, NJ: Erlbaum.

Jenkins, J. R., Peyton, J. A., Sanders, E. A., & Vadasy, P. F. (2004). Effects of reading decodable texts in supplemental first-grade tutoring. *Scientific Studies of Reading, 8,* 53–85.

Juel, C. (1988). Learning to read and write: A longitudinal study of fifty-four children from first through fourth grade. *Journal of Educational Psychology, 80,* 437–447.

Kratochwill, T. R., & Stoiber, K. C. (2002). Evidence-based intervention in school psychology: Conceptual foundations of the procedural Coding Manual of Division 16 and the Society for the Study of School Psychology Task Force. *School Psychology Quarterly, 17*(4), 341–389.

Lerner, J. W. (2000). *Learning disabilities: Theories, diagnosis, and teaching strategies* (8th ed.). Boston: Houghton Mifflin.

Lyon, G. R. (1995). Research initiatives in learning disabilities: Contributions from scientists supported by the National Institute of Child Health and Human Development. *Journal of Child Neurology, 10,* S120–S126.

Mathes, P. G., Denton, C. A., Fletcher, J. M., Anthony, J. L., Francis, D. J., & Schatschneider, C. (2005). The effects of theoretically different instruction and student characteristics on the skills of struggling readers. *Reading Research Quarterly, 40,* 148–182.

McCardle, P., & Chhabra, V. (2004). *The voice of evidence in reading research.* Baltimore: Brookes.

Miller, S. D. (2003). Partners-in-reading: Using classroom assistants to provide tutorial assistance to struggling first-grade readers. *Journal of Education for Students Placed at Risk, 8,* 333–349.

Morris, D., Tyner, B., & Perney, J. (2000). Early steps: Replicating the effect of a first-grade reading intervention program. *Journal of Educational Psychology, 92,* 681–693.

National Association of State Directors of Special Education. (2005). *Response to intervention: Policy considerations and implementation.* Alexandria, VA: Author.

No Child Left Behind Act of 2001. Public Law No. 101-110 (2001).

O'Connor, R. E., Notari-Syverson, A., & Vadasy, P. F. (1996). Ladders to literacy: The effects of teacher-led phonological activities for kindergarten children with and without disabilities. *Exceptional Children, 63,* 117–130.

Pressley, M. (2006). *Reading instruction that works: The case for balanced teaching* (3rd ed.). New York: Guilford Press.

Rayner, K., Foorman B. R., Perfetti, C. A., Pesetsky, D., & Seidenberg, M. S. (2001). How psychological science informs the teaching of reading. *Psychological Science in the Public Interest, 2,* 31–73.

Reschly, D. J. (2005). Learning disabilities identification: Primary intervention, secondary intervention, and then what? *Journal of Learning Disabilities, 38,* 510–515.

Santa, C. M., & Hoien, T. (1999). An assessment of early steps: A program for early intervention of reading problems. *Reading Research Quarterly, 34*, 54–79.

Schneider, W., Roth, E., & Ennemoser, M. (2000). Training phonological skills and letter knowledge in children at risk for dyslexia: A comparison of three kindergarten intervention programs. *Journal of Educational Psychology, 92*, 284–295.

Snider, V. E. (1997). Transfer of decoding skills to a literature basal. *Learning Disabilities Research and Practice, 12*, 54–62.

Swanson, H. L., Hoskyn, M., & Lee, C. (1999). *Interventions for students with learning disabilities.* New York: Guilford Press.

Torgesen, J. K. (2000). Individual differences in response to early interventions in reading: The lingering problem of treatment resisters. *Learning Disabilities Research and Practice, 15*, 55–64.

Torgesen, J. K., Wagner, R. K., & Rashotte, C. A. (1997). Prevention and remediation of severe reading disabilities: Keeping the end in mind. *Scientific Studies of Reading, 1*, 217–234.

Torgesen, J. K., Wagner, R. K., Rashotte, C. A., Rose, E., Lindamood, P., & Conway, T. (1999). Preventing reading failure in young children with phonological processing disabilities: Group and individual responses to instruction. *Journal of Educational Psychology, 91*, 579–593.

Vadasy, P. F., Jenkins, J. R., Antil, L. R., Wayne, S. K., & O'Connor, R. E. (1997). Community-based early reading intervention for at-risk first graders. *Learning Disabilities Research and Practice, 12*, 29–39.

Vadasy, P. F., Sanders, E. A., & Peyton, J. A. (2005). Relative effectiveness of reading practice or word-level instruction in supplemental tutoring: How text matters. *Journal of Learning Disabilities, 38*, 364–380.

Vadasy, P. F., Sanders, E. A., Peyton, J. A., & Jenkins, J. R. (2002). Timing and intensity of tutoring: A closer look at the conditions for effective early literacy tutoring. *Learning Disabilities Research and Practice, 17*, 227–241.

Vaughn, S., & Fuchs, L. S. (2003). Redefining learning disabilities as inadequate response to instruction: The promise and potential problems. *Learning Disabilities Research and Practice, 18*, 137–146.

Vaughn, S., Kim, A., Sloan, C. V. M., Hughes, M. T., Elbaum, B., & Sridhar, D. (2003). Social skills interventions for young children with disabilities: A synthesis of group design studies. *Remedial and Special Education, 24*, 2–15.

Vaughn, S., Linan-Thompson, S., & Hickman, P. (2003). Response to instruction as a means of identifying students with reading/learning disabilities. *Exceptional Children, 69*, 391–409.

Vaughn, S., Wanzek, J., Linan-Thompson, S., & Murray, C. S. (2007). Monitoring response to supplemental services for students at risk for reading difficulties: High and low responders. In S. R. Jimerson, M. K. Burns, & A. M. VanDer-Heyden (Eds.), *Handbook of response to intervention: The science and practice of assessment and intervention* (pp. 234–243). New York: Springer Science.

Vellutino, F. R., Scanlon, D. M., & Jaccard, J. (2003). Toward distinguishing between cognitive and experiential deficits as primary sources of difficult to remediate and remediated poor readers. In B. R. Foorman (Ed.), *Preventing and remediating reading difficulties* (pp. 73–120). Baltimore: York Press.

Vellutino, F. R., Scanlon, D. M., Sipay, E. R., Small, S. G., Pratt, A., Chen, R., et al. (1996). Cognitive profiles of difficult-to-remediate and readily remediated poor readers: Early intervention as a vehicle for distinguishing between cognitive and experiential deficits as basic causes of specific reading disability. *Journal of Educational Psychology, 88,* 601–638.

Wanzek, J., Vaughn, S., Wexler, J., Swanson, E., Edmonds, M. E., & Kim, A. (2006). A synthesis of spelling and reading interventions and their effects on the spelling outcomes of students with LD. *Journal of Learning Disabilities, 39*(6), 528–543.

7

Reading Interventions
for Older Students

Deborah Reed
Sharon Vaughn

Our knowledge and confidence about instructing young children with reading difficulties has grown considerably in the last two decades. Numerous reviews and syntheses have provided summative guidance on improving instructional practices within the classroom as well as for supplemental interventions (e.g., Ehri, Nunes, Stahl, & Willows, 2001; McCardle & Chhabra, 2004; National Institute of Child Health and Human Development, 2000; Snow, Burns, & Griffin, 1998; Wanzek & Vaughn, 2007). Unfortunately, our knowledge about teaching older readers with reading difficulties has received less attention. Because many other sources have compiled information on effective reading interventions for younger students, the review we provide in this chapter addresses the research on reading instruction for older readers (grades 4 and higher) with guidelines for instructional practice.

The majority of students in grades 4 through 12 still need instructional support to read and learn from complex texts (Biancarosa & Snow, 2004; Kamil, 2003; National Joint Committee on Learning Disabilities, 2008; RAND Reading Study Group, 2002; Torgesen et al., 2007). Vocabulary and comprehension instruction are often identified as critical within content area lessons to facilitate learning for many students. Although there is considerable support for enhancing students' knowledge of words and understanding of text, this will be insufficient to ensure that older students with significant reading difficulties can be successful with the literate demands they face in and out of school (Catts, Hogan, & Adlof, 2005; Leach, Scarborough, & Rescorla, 2003).

Contrary to notions that fourth grade signifies an end to "learning to read" and shifts instead to "reading to learn," many students in the intermediate grades and beyond exhibit persistent difficulties with acquiring the more basic components of reading that allow them to access texts necessary for growing their conceptual knowledge. Thus, for many older readers, learning to read is still an integral part of their reading to learn. In a recent study of adolescents who failed a state assessment of reading comprehension, 81% of the sixth-, seventh-, and eighth-grade participants needed interventions in word identification and/or fluency (Texas Education Agency, University of Houston, and the University of Texas System, 2008). There are many possible explanations for this finding, including that some students have never been provided adequate word study instruction in the early grades or have participated in word study instruction but have not adequately acquired and applied word study practices. Other evidence suggests that some students' reading difficulties may not emerge until after third grade, when their comprehension or word-level processing skills suddenly decline precipitously (Leach et al., 2003).

Interventions for older readers do not represent discrete points along a linear continuum of literacy supports. Rather, they are better conceptualized as a layering of instructional options, with the needs of each student determining how many layers of instructional supports are required.

Figure 7.1 provides a model for teaching older students with reading difficulties in which critical elements of instruction are addressed concurrently. One of the fundamental principles of intervention for older readers is that instruction must simultaneously improve their reading levels while also providing them ongoing access to a range of genres of print (e.g., information text) so that their conceptual and domain knowledge grow along with their reading abilities. The rationale is that older students cannot wait to meet the curricular demands of their content area classes while focusing solely on the development of their reading. Therefore, interventions from the inner layers depicted in Figure 7.1 take place throughout the curricula (e.g., social studies, science, math); at the same time, highly trained personnel deliver more intensive interventions through a special reading class. This structure is particularly important for the word-level components in the outer layers of intervention, which most seriously constrain students' ability to attend to meaning in processing text (Perfetti, 1985).

When diagnostic and progress monitoring data indicate that students are demonstrating high need or low functioning in one or more of the

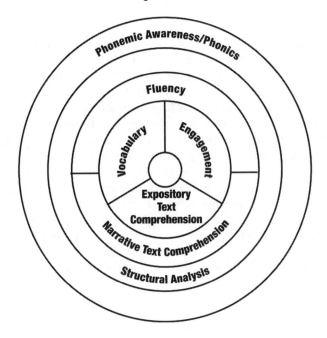

FIGURE 7.1. Layers of reading intervention for older students.

instructional areas represented by the layers in Figure 7.1, effective teachers design instructional practices to support students' acquisition of these skills and processes. Again, because diagnostic testing and ongoing progress monitoring continue at regular intervals, students' success is measured and tracked. When students demonstrate mastery of any of the reading components or layers represented in Figure 7.1, their instructional program is adjusted. Thus, instruction is tailored to address areas of high need. For example, once a student has developed knowledge of short vowels, long vowels, consonant blends, consonant digraphs, diphthongs, and more complex phonics such as -*igh* and -*ock*, it may be no longer necessary to directly teach these foundation skills. That outermost layer can be removed from the instructional menu, although the skills will continue to be reinforced through instruction in structural analysis and fluency practice.

A small but growing number of syntheses and meta-analyses provide guidance on implementing effective practices to address the reading difficulties of older students, and we have relied on these to identify studies for this chapter (e.g., Edmonds et al., 2009; Scammacca et al., 2007; Wexler, Vaughn, Edmonds, & Reutebuch, 2008). Although the group referred to as "older students" is typically considered to encompass students in grades

4 through 12, the majority of extant research has targeted students in the middle grades, 6 through 9. It should be noted that only a handful of studies have included participants from grades 4, 5, 10, 11, or 12. In the following sections, we review findings pertinent to each layer of intervention and provide summary tables with each category's relevant research.

The sections are ordered to correspond with the layers depicted in Figure 7.1, moving from the outside of the figure to the center. When considered within a response-to-intervention (RTI) framework, the outer layers represent more intensive intervention needs that would take place in smaller groups and require more direct instruction time, such as would be provided in Tiers 2 and 3 of a three-tier RTI model. Layers closest to the center in Figure 7.1 could more feasibly occur across classrooms and content areas, consistent with Tier 1, or the schoolwide effective instructional practices implemented in RTI. The summary tables for each section provide descriptions of the group size and setting used in the research. Additional information on incorporating the layers of intervention within an RTI framework is provided at the end of the chapter.

PHONEMIC AWARENESS/PHONICS INTERVENTION STUDIES

Perhaps the smallest percentage of students demonstrating difficulty with reading beyond grade 3 still struggles with phonemic awareness and the alphabetic principle (Roberts, Torgesen, Boardman, & Scammacca, 2008). Nonetheless, poor phonological processing abilities are evident through late adolescence (Catts, Adlof, & Weisner, 2006; Curtis & Longo, 1999; Fawcett & Nicolson, 1995; Shaywitz, 2003) and can preclude the benefits of more advanced word study with syllabic and morphemic analysis, discussed in the next section. Older readers who are significantly behind their grade-level peers (more than three or four grade levels) will require large blocks of time devoted to intervention if they are to accelerate their growth (Fielding, Kerr, & Rosier, 2007; Fletcher, Lyon, Fuchs, & Barnes, 2007).

Often, instruction for these students is systematically sequenced and assists them in understanding and applying phonics rules. Frequency counts indicate which phonemes and graphemes occur most often in written and spoken language so that they can be taught by order of importance. Figure 7.2, based on the work of Fry (2004), lists the major vowel sounds and consonant graphemes, from most frequently occurring to most rare.

Instruction in the phonemes and graphemes on these lists can be supplemented with high-frequency sight words and irregular words, in which

Order of Vowel Sounds	Order of Consonant Graphemes
Short *i*	*r*
Short *a*	*t* and *n*
Short *e*	*s*, *l*, and *c*
Schwa *r*	*d*, *p*, and *m*
Long *o*	*b*
Long *e*	*f* and *v*
Short *u*	*g*
Short *o*	*h*
Long *a*	*k* and *w*
Long *u*	*th*, *sh*, and *ng*
Long *i*	*ch*
r-controlled *a* and *o*	*x*
Vowel pairs *au*, *aw*, *ou*, *ow*, *oo*	*z* and *j*
Vowel pairs *oi*, *oy*, and *ai*	*qu*, *wh*, and *y*

FIGURE 7.2. Vowel sounds and consonant graphemes in order of frequency.

the vowels or consonants do not make their usual or expected sounds. Most importantly, students will need many practice opportunities that incorporate specific instructional feedback, and possibly a self-correction strategy, as they develop their abilities to classify, blend, segment, reverse, substitute, encode (write), and decode (read) the sounds.

Two intervention studies conducted with students in the middle grades and high school (Bhat, Griffin, & Sindelar, 2003; Kennedy & Backman, 1993) support the notion that adolescence is not too late to intervene, even when students are severely impaired. Both treatments used one-on-one instruction, which is common in the extant literature (Swanson & Hoskyn, 2001) but often difficult for schools to feasibly implement. Results indicated that students can make and maintain significant progress in phonological awareness after interventions of shorter duration (18 sessions; Bhat et al., 2003) but likely need more time and comprehensive instruction in order to improve their word recognition, spelling, and paragraph-reading skills (90 sessions; Kennedy & Backman, 1993).

Table 7.1 summarizes participant data, research designs, procedures, and findings from two studies relevant to phonemic awareness and/or phonics intervention. Additional research might address the optimal group size, dosage, and duration of interventions targeting foundational reading skills for adolescents.

TABLE 7.1. Phonological Awareness/Phonics Interventions

Study[a]	Grade/age	Student type[b]	Research design	Total minutes of intervention[c]	Findings
Bhat, Griffin, and Sindelar (2003) • T *(phonological awareness)*: Students received one-on-one direct instruction using a commercial program that followed the sequence: rhyming, identifying words with the same beginning/final sound, blending words/syllables/phonemes, phoneme deletion, phoneme reversal, and phoneme substitution. This was supplemented with additional instruction in blending, segmenting, reversal, and substitution. (*n* = 20) • C *(typical instruction)*: Students did not receive the one-on-one instruction described in T1 until after the midtest, when intervention in the treatment group ended. (*n* = 20)	Grades 6–8	All LD	Treatment/comparison; within groups, repeated measures	NR	Students' phonological awareness skills, as assessed by a standardized measure, significantly improved and were maintained 4 weeks after the conclusion of the treatment. Students' word identification skills did not achieve statistical significance, however.
Kennedy and Backman (1993) • T *(Auditory discrimination in depth)*: Students received individualized tutorials in a multisensory program of phonological awareness and phonics. Students progressed through levels (identifying and classifying speech sounds, matching sounds to orthographic symbols, color encoding sounds, manipulating sounds in a sequence, using articulatory feedback to correct errors, encoding sounds into letters, decoding sequences of syllable patterns) and learned a strategy for self-correction. After 6 weeks of intervention, students returned to the school's typical tutorials in spelling for the remainder of the year. (n = 9) • C *(typical practice)*: Students received the usual individualized tutorials in spelling that emphasized phonetic patterns, word families, tactile cues, auditory analysis, syllabic segmentation, affixes, and irregular patterns. (n = 9)	11–17 years	All LD	Treatment/comparison; matched students; repeated measures	4,500	Both groups significantly improved performance on standardized measures of word recognition, spelling, and paragraph reading. The auditory discrimination group made significantly more progress than the control group in identifying sounds and sound sequences, and phonetic accuracy in spelling real and pseudowords. Growth was maintained through the end of the school year.

[a]T, treatment; C, comparison.
[b]LD, learning disability.
[c]NR, not reported.

STRUCTURAL ANALYSIS INTERVENTION STUDIES

The majority of older students with reading difficulties demonstrate adequate phonological processing skills and decoding of single-syllable words, but they often are not able to read multisyllable words quickly and accurately (Archer, Gleason, & Vachon, 2003; Curtis, 2004). These students lack a process for decomposing a longer word into its constituent parts so it can be pronounced and understood. This process is referred to as structural analysis (Abbott & Berninger, 1999) and can take two forms: identifying the syllable types (i.e., closed, open, silent *e*, *r* controlled, vowel pair, and final stable *-le*) or identifying the morphemes (i.e., prefixes, suffixes, and roots) that make up the word.

In syllabic analysis, emphasis is placed on breaking words into their pronounceable parts, each containing one vowel sound. Students review many of the preskills (e.g., short vowels, long vowels, consonant blends, consonant digraphs, diphthongs) as they are explicitly taught the salient features of the most common syllable types. Activities can include spelling and word analogies that capitalize on recurrent letter-sequence patterns (Penney, 2002). However, perhaps, the most important aspect of instruction is providing ample opportunities for students to apply their knowledge of syllable structures and generalize their understanding as they encounter unfamiliar words in context (Curtis, 2004).

Because English is an orthographically deep language, meaning there are many phonetic irregularities between the written and spoken forms of words, it is believed that knowledge of morphemes becomes increasingly important to students' reading ability through the middle grades and high school (Carlisle & Stone, 2005; Deacon & Kirby, 2004; Nagy, Berninger, & Abbott, 2006). Students taught morphemic analysis learn to decompose words by units of meaning as opposed to the units of sound used in syllabic analysis. Preliminary evidence from a synthesis of morphology interventions suggests that instruction is most effective when it includes root words, as opposed to focusing on only prefixes and suffixes, and follows a sequence appropriate to students' reading development (Reed, 2008). The order in which students tend to acquire knowledge of morphemes is fairly consistent (Cazden, 1968; Rubin, Patterson, & Kantor, 1991; Vogel, 2001):

- Monomorphemic roots (also called base words; e.g., *sand*, *box*).
- Compound words (e.g., *sandbox*) and high-frequency prefixes (e.g., *un-*, *re-*).
- Inflectional suffixes (e.g., *-ing*, *-s*, *-'s*, *-ed*).
- Neutral derivational suffixes (e.g., *-ness*, *-ly*, *-er*, *-ary*, *-en*).
- Nonneutral derivational suffixes (e.g., *-tion*, *-ure*, *-ity*) and low-frequency prefixes (e.g., *fore-*, *ambi-*, *hex-*, *ad-*).

- Multimorphemic words (e.g., *transcendental, hypothesis, synchronize*).

As with syllabic analysis, students learning to identify morphemes can engage in spelling and word analogy activities that help them to generalize their knowledge to unfamiliar words. Learning morphemic analysis serves as a strategic way to process words and be a more efficacious reader.

The ultimate goal of structural analysis instruction is to better equip students to understand word meanings and thus improve comprehension. Indeed, research findings indicate that interventions focusing on identifying the constituent parts of words not only improve students' word attack skills (Bhattacharya & Ehri, 2004; Hasselbring & Goin, 2004) but can also significantly improve passage comprehension (Abbott & Berninger, 1999; Penney, 2002).

Table 7.2 summarizes participant data, research designs, procedures, and findings from four studies relevant to structural analysis intervention. Additional research might address the appropriate mix of syllabic and morphemic analysis for adolescents of varying ability levels as well as whether standardized protocols or problem-solving approaches are more effective.

FLUENCY INTERVENTION STUDIES

Phonemic awareness, phonics, and structural analysis are important elements in developing students' ability to quickly and accurately recognize words. However, evidence suggests that word identification, although related to fluency, is not the same cognitive skill as the ability to read quickly, accurately, and with expression (Fletcher et al., 2007). Moreover, instruction targeting word recognition alone has not proven effective at improving fluency (Morgan & Sideridis, 2006). Unfortunately, very little research on fluency has been conducted with high school students, but findings from studies with students in grades 4 through 8 provide guidance on the elements of intervention for older students.

A common practice involves having students read repeatedly the same text at an independent or instructional level either with the assistance of a tape recording by an expert reader (Conte & Humphreys, 1989) or a peer partner of a slightly different ability level (Homan, Klesius, & Hite, 1993). Although a meta-analysis found some indication that repeated readings are effective for older students, particularly when they are involved in setting goals for their reading rate and accuracy (Morgan & Sideridis, 2006), other researchers maintain that repetitive approaches are not superior to alternative methods (Kuhn & Stahl, 2003). Students provided repeated reading

TABLE 7.2. Structural Analysis Interventions

Study[a]	Grade/age	Student type[b]	Research design	Total minutes of intervention[c]	Findings
Abbott and Berninger (1999) • T1 (*structural analysis*): Students received individualized tutorials on phonological and orthographic skills, alphabetic principle training, phonological decoding, structural analysis (common affixes and roots based on word origins), and oral reading of connected text. (*n* = 10) • T2 (*study skills*): Students received instruction in phonological and orthographic skills, the alphabetic principle, phonological decoding, study skills workbook lessons (e.g., outlining, writing paragraphs, note-taking, using an index), and oral reading of connected text. (*n* = 10)	Grades 4–7	NR (identified as low achieving in reading and from multigenerational LD families)	Multiple treatments; random assignment	960	Both groups significantly improved on standardized measures of orthographic letter clusters, phoneme segmentation, syllable segmentation, and passage comprehension. There were no significant differences between the groups, but there were more individual treatment responders in the structural analysis condition on standardized measures of word identification, word attack, spelling, word-reading efficiency, and orthographic choice.
Bhattacharya and Ehri (2004) • T1 (*graphosyllabic analysis*): Students were taught through whole-group instruction to read a multisyllabic word aloud, explain its meaning, orally divide the word into syllables/beats by raising a finger at each beat, state the number of syllables, match each syllable to its spelling, and blend the syllables to say the word. (*n* = 20)	Grades 6–10	None LD (enrolled in remedial reading classes)	Treatment/comparison; experimental with stratified random sampling	120	On an intervention-specific measure, students trained in graphosyllabic analysis demonstrated better decoding, memory of spellings, and identification and segmentation of syllables than students in either the whole-word or comparison groups. Moreover, (*continued*)

151

TABLE 7.2. (continued)

Study[a]	Grade/age	Student type[b]	Research design	Total minutes of intervention[c]	Findings
• T2 (*whole-word reading*): Students were taught through whole-group instruction to read a multisyllabic word aloud, explain its meaning, and read the word again. (*n* = 20) C (*typical instruction*): A class of 20 students received the school's regular curriculum focused on reading comprehension. (*n* = 20)					a standardized test of students' word attack skills revealed that syllable-trained students were better able to decode unfamiliar words and pseudowords as well as detect subtle misspellings of words. Students in the lowest reading ability group improved the most.
Hasselbring & Goin (2004) • T (*self-paced literacy lab*): Students were pulled out for 30 minutes each day for individualized instruction delivered via computer programs for reading (series of video clips followed by reading a passage on the topic and completion of comprehension activities), word recognition (speed and accuracy of pronunciation), and spelling (speed and accuracy of orthographic knowledge). Instruction lasted all year. (*n* = 63) • C (*typical practice*): Students received the school's typical curriculum in regular education classes. (*n* = 62)	Grades 6–8	NR (school identified as "most disabled readers")	Quasi-experimental (assignment not described)	NR	Students participating in the literacy lab made significant improvements and performed significantly better than students in the comparison on standardized measures of auditory vocabulary, literal and inferential comprehension, and total reading comprehension. No significant differences were found between the groups on standardized measures of phonetic analysis or structural analysis.

152

Penney (2002)	Grades 9–11	None LD (identified as having reading difficulty)	Treatment/ comparison; teacher selection	840–1,008	Students receiving tutoring performed significantly better than the comparison group on standardized measures of word identification, word attack, and passage comprehension. When performance on the pretest was statistically controlled, the effect of tutoring was significant.
• T (word identification drills): Students received one-on-one tutoring focused on word analysis by pronounceable parts and rehearsal with similar letter patterns. Words used in the decoding drills were those on which the student made errors in orally reading a passage. Tutors added three or more words with the same spelling pattern for rehearsal and repetition. Students then reread the passage. (n = 9)					
• C (typical practice): A class of nine students received the school's curriculum developed for a remedial course in reading comprehension. (n = 9)					

[a]T, treatment; C, comparison; T1, treatment 1 (used with multiple treatment designs); T2, treatment 2 (used with multiple treatment designs).

[b]LD, learning disability.

[c]NR, not reported.

interventions performed no better than those who engaged in echo reading (emulating the teacher's reading), cloze reading (filling in words on which the teacher randomly pauses while reading orally), and unison reading (reading with the teacher) on a retell comprehension measure (Homan et al., 1993). Furthermore, students in neither treatment group made significant improvements in their reading rate or accuracy, which any fluency intervention is predicated on achieving. In a recent study of adolescents with severe reading difficulties, Wexler, Vaughn, and Roberts (in press) examined outcomes among students receiving a repeated reading or a continuous reading fluency intervention and a typical instruction as a comparison. Students in the treatment conditions did not outperform comparison students on word reading, fluency, or comprehension.

Students instructed in other aspects of fluency have not fared much better. When provided individualized tutoring in prosodic elements (e.g., inflection, pausing at punctuation, phrasing, pacing) and monitoring for accuracy, students significantly outperformed their counterparts in more typical classroom instruction on a silent reading measure requiring them to select the correct word to complete a sentence from a multiple-choice set. However, both groups had comparable improvement on standardized measures of word identification and comprehension (Allinder, Dunse, Brunken, & Obermiller-Krolikowski, 2001). Better results might be possible for approaches that combine instruction in prosodic features of language with repeated reading (Mercer, Campbell, Miller, Mercer, & Lane, 2000). In addition, fluency instruction is likely more profitable when repetitions are limited to three and when emphasis is placed on reading for meaning rather than speed (O'Shea, Sindelar, & O'Shea, 1987).

Despite the limitations of the extant research, the normative data on fluency suggest that students in middle and high school who are reading fewer than 150 words correctly in a minute are slower readers and may benefit from additional instructional support (Hasbrouck & Tindal, 2006; Yovanoff, Duesbery, Alonzo, & Tindal, 2005). Extremely slow and laborious reading can lead older students to avoid reading altogether (Rasinski et al., 2005), further confounding their lack of skill attainment and reducing their exposure to important conceptual knowledge. Until better empirical evidence is available, instruction should include the prosodic features of language, expert modeling of fluent reading, opportunities for students to apply skills to authentic texts through assisted and repeated readings (not to exceed three repetitions), and immediate instructional feedback related to students' individual goals for rate, accuracy, and expression.

Table 7.3 summarizes the participants, research designs, procedures, and findings from four studies relevant to fluency intervention.

TABLE 7.3. Fluency Interventions

Study[a]	Grade/age	Student type[b]	Research design	Total minutes of intervention[c]	Findings
Allinder, Dunse, Brunken, and Obermiller-Krolikowski (2001) • T *(specific oral reading fluency strategy)*: Students, in classes of 12–21, students were taught a need-based strategy (inflection, not adding words, pausing at punctuation, self-monitoring for accuracy, pacing, attending to word endings, tracking) in individualized conferences with the teacher. Students then alternated reading aloud during whole-class or small-group instruction. (*n* = 33)	Grade 7	Some LD (*n* = 15)	Treatment/comparison; quasi-experimental with random assignment from within intact classes	1,500	Students taught a specific oral reading fluency strategy performed significantly better on a curriculum-based maze assessment involving silent reading. Both the treatment and comparison groups improved on standardized measures of word identification and comprehension.
• C *(typical practice)*: Students were told in individual conferences to do their best while reading aloud in the whole-class or small-group portion of the lesson. (*n* = 16)					
Conte and Humphreys (1989) • T *(repeated reading with tape-recorded material)*: Teachers led students in regular (12–28 pupils) or reduced-size (two to six pupils) resource classes in a picture walk-through of narrative picture books of a slightly more challenging level. Then the children listened to one section of the book on tape repeatedly. Gradually, the students were to add tracking while listening and then reading along with the tape before reading without the tape at a comparable pace. Teachers concluded the session by returning to inferential discussion of the content. (*n* = 13)	9–13 years	Some LD (identified as having difficulty with reading and more than half enrolled in resource classes)	Treatment/comparison; quasi-experimental with random assignment from within intact classes (split-plot)	Average: 600	Students in the repeated-reading group significantly improved performance on an informal oral reading measure from pretest to posttest. However, this did not generalize to silent reading. There were no significant differences between the treatment and comparison groups on the informal tests of oral and silent reading, a standardized measure of reading comprehension, or an informal test of reading and spelling patterns. The comparison group performed significantly better than the repeated-reading group on a standardized measure of word attack skills.
• C *(typical practice)*: Students in regular (12–28 pupils) or reduced-sized (two to six pupils) resource classes received the regular curriculum of instruction in phonics, vocabulary, spelling, and creative writing and then read stories from their leveled basals. (*n* = 13)					

(continued)

155

TABLE 7.3. (continued)

Study[a]	Grade/age	Student type[b]	Research design	Total minutes of intervention[c]	Findings
Homan, Klesius, and Hite (1993) • T1 *(repeated reading)*: Pairs of students alternated reading the same narrative or poetry selection from their basal four times each. They did not assist each other with pronouncing unfamiliar words but were supervised by the teacher. (*n* = 13) • T2 *(assisted nonrepetitive oral reading)*: A teacher led groups of four to five students in reading narrative and poetry selections from the basal by echo reading (emulating the teacher's reading) one day, cloze reading (filling in words on which the teacher randomly pauses) another day, and unison reading (reading along with the teacher) on a third day. Students did not reread or repeat a selection previously read. (*n* = 13)	Grade 6	None LD (enrolled in Chapter 1 reading)	Multiple treatments; random assignment within intact classes	420	All students significantly improved their comprehension, as measured by a retell procedure. There were no significant differences between the treatment conditions. Neither group significantly improved reading rate or accuracy, as determined by individually scoring an audio recording of the students' reading.
O'Shea, Sindelar, and O'Shea (1987) • T1 *(fluency cue)*: Individual students were told to read as quickly and accurately as possible. They were randomly given different passages to read one, three, and seven times. After the final reading of each passage, they were asked to retell the passage. (*n* = 15) • T2 *(comprehension cue)*: Individual students were told to remember as much of a passage as possible. They were randomly given different passages to read one, three, and seven times. After the final reading of each passage, they were asked to retell the passage. (*n* = 16)	Grades 5–8	All LD	Multiple treatments; random assignment	NR	Students cued to read for comprehension retold significantly more story propositions than students cued to read for fluency. Story proposition scores for both groups significantly increased from reading a story one time to reading a story three times but did not improve between reading a story three times versus five times. Reading rates for both groups significantly increased across the number of repeated readings. However, there were no significant differences in reading rates between the two cuing conditions.

[a]T, treatment; C, comparison; T1, treatment 1 (used with multiple treatment designs); T2, treatment 2 (used with multiple treatment designs).
[b]LD, learning disability.
[c]NR, not reported.

NARRATIVE TEXT COMPREHENSION INTERVENTION STUDIES

Because instruction in narrative and expository (informational) texts is critical to successfully reading and understanding materials encountered in and out of school settings, we review the research in each of these areas separately for older students with reading difficulties. Whether in print, on television, or in oral discourse, narrative stories tend to contain similar episodic content (Rumelhart, 1975; Thorndyke, 1977). The consistency of this story grammar (i.e., exposition, rising action, climax, falling action, resolution) can foster the development of mental models or schema that help students more easily understand narratives compared with expository texts (Britton, van Dusen, Glynn, & Hemphill, 1990). Despite the predictability of narrative stories and their dominance in early elementary classrooms (Duke, 2000), not all students acquire an awareness of narrative stories' structural pattern and hence experience difficulty with what is usually considered less challenging text (Kamil, 2003; Saenz & Fuchs, 2002).

At a basic level, older students may struggle to organize the episodic content of stories, to distinguish the main ideas from the supporting details, and to bring sufficient background knowledge or vocabulary to bear on the information. Instruction in identifying story grammar has been effective at improving the narrative text comprehension of students with learning disabilities (Boulineau, Fore, Hagan-Burke, & Burke, 2004; Taylor, Alber, & Walker, 2002) and behavioral disorders (Babyak, Koorland, & Mathes, 2000). Similarly, students have responded well to interventions in identifying main ideas (Jitendra, Hoppes, & Xin, 2000), identifying themes (Williams, Brown, Silverstein, & deCani, 1994), and working collaboratively with peers to read and summarize narrative text (Mastropieri et al., 2001). Students in those studies performed significantly better than those receiving typical reading instruction when assessed with measures closely related to the materials of their interventions.

However, asking students to transfer their comprehension skills to unfamiliar narrative and expository passages has yielded less consistent results. Students receiving special instruction seem to do better when asked to *select* or *identify* main ideas and themes than when asked to *produce* them for stories and passages on which they have not been instructed. They also fail to generalize comprehension strategies to novel situations without being prompted to do so (Wilder & Williams, 2001), and they exhibit difficulty with making inferences, even after having been explicitly taught requisite background knowledge and vocabulary (Snider, 1989).

When interpreting the findings from the studies in the extant literature that we summarize, it is important to consider that most interventions were relatively short in duration: 11 to 15 sessions of 40 to 50 minutes each. For students who have entered adolescence lacking an understanding of narrative text or self-monitoring skills, it is unlikely that 2 or 3 weeks of instruction is sufficient to achieve executive control over comprehension strategies (Brown, Campione, & Day, 1981; Paris, Lipson, & Wixson, 1983). That any improvements were realized within a short duration might be testament to the effectiveness of direct instruction combined with guided practice in how and when to use strategies (Swanson, Hoskyn, & Lee, 1999).

Table 7.4 summarizes participant data, research designs, procedures, and findings from six studies relevant to narrative text comprehension intervention. Additional research addressing the amount of intervention necessary to sustain improvements and promote generalization across narrative texts would improve our understanding.

EXPOSITORY TEXT COMPREHENSION INTERVENTION STUDIES

Reading comprehension is a cognitive skill distinct from decoding and fluency (Fletcher et al., 2007). Comprehension difficulties, although apparent across genres, appear to be more pronounced with expository text than narrative stories. Older readers manifest problems with informational materials by tending to read this text more slowly, less accurately, and with less understanding than narrative text (Saenz & Fuchs, 2002). This is influenced, in part, by a lack of word knowledge (Best, Floyd, & McNamara, 2008) and world or prior knowledge about the text (Wolfe & Mienko, 2007). Both word and world/prior knowledge are crucial to understanding information-based materials. Students with learning disabilities also seem to be hampered by an insensitivity to the text structures (e.g., cause–effect, chronological order, problem–solution, compare–contrast, description) that aid in distinguishing between essential and nonessential information, recognizing the interrelatedness of ideas, and detecting when comprehension has broken down (Englert & Thomas, 1987).

In the intermediate- and secondary-grade levels, textbooks contain an increasing percentage of these more complex and conceptually dense expository passages to which students have had little exposure in the lower elementary grades (Duke, 2000). Therefore, it is suggested that the changing nature of school texts contributes to the slump in reading achievement experienced by some students (Chall, Jacobs, & Baldwin, 1990). Fortunately, instruction in expository text comprehension has proven fruitful in ameliorating these difficulties.

A synthesis of interventions for students with learning disabilities found that significant improvements could be realized in fewer than 4 hours of treatment (Gajria, Jitendra, Sood, & Sacks, 2007). As with the results

TABLE 7.4. Narrative Comprehension Interventions

Study[a]	Grade/age	Student type[b]	Research design	Total minutes of intervention	Findings
Fuchs, Fuchs, and Kazdan (1999) • T (peer-assisted learning strategies [PALS]): Students in remedial reading classes were explicitly taught how to work in assigned pairs to complete partner reading with corrective feedback, a summarizing strategy, and a prediction–(dis)confirmation activity with narrative text. (n = 52; LD = 35) • C (typical practice): Students received reading instruction using a typical curriculum with no peer-mediated reading strategies. (n = 50; LD = 39)	Grades 9–10	Some LD	Treatment/comparison; quasi-experimental using intact classes	1,200–2,400	Students in the PALS condition improved their performance on a standardized measure of narrative reading comprehension significantly more than students in the comparison condition. PALS did not, however, produce significant differences in a standardized measure of fluency. PALS participants reported working harder to improve their reading than did comparison students but did not significantly improve their attitudes about reading.
Jitendra, Hoppes, and Xin (2000) • T1 (main idea and self-monitoring): Small groups of six to eight students from a resource class were provided direct instruction and guided practice in using a prompt card to generate or identify the main idea of narrative passages. Students also learned a four-step self-monitoring procedure to check their use of the strategy. (n = 18) • C (typical practice): Small groups of six to eight students received instruction on the regular curriculum in resource classes. (n = 15)	Grades 6–8	All LD	Treatment/comparison; experimental with stratified random sampling	450–600	Students taught the main idea strategy performed significantly better than the comparison group on researcher-developed measures requiring the selection and production of main idea responses for the training passages. Improvements were maintained in a delayed test administered 6 weeks after the end of the intervention. The main idea group also performed significantly better than the comparison group on researcher-developed measures requiring the selection of main ideas for similar narrative passages and for expository passages. These improvements were maintained in the delayed test for the narrative only. All students' scores on the production of main ideas decreased for both similar narrative passages and expository passages.

(continued)

TABLE 7.4. (continued)

Study[a]	Grade/ age	Student type[b]	Research design	Total minutes of intervention	Findings
Mastropieri et al. (2001) • T (peer tutoring): Students in a special education class were assigned partners of slightly different ability levels and instructed by co-teachers to complete partner reading with error correction, story retell prompting, and summarization paragraphs. (n = 12) • C (typical practice): Co-teachers taught the whole special education class using suggestions from the teacher's edition of the basal (teacher questioning, oral reading, silent reading, and work sheet activities for comprehension and vocabulary). (n = 12)	Grade 7	Some LD (some EMR; all in special education classes)	Treatment/ comparison; random assignment of pairs	1,250	Students in the peer-tutoring condition performed significantly better on open-ended comprehension questions. All students in the tutoring condition reported the purpose of tutoring was to improve their reading ability, and all felt they spent more time reading in the dyads than in the typical instruction.
Snider (1989)[c] • T (direct instruction in background information): Co-teachers explicitly introduced the factual information and/or vocabulary to a resource class of 13 students before having students read passages and complete written exercises to practice the information. Narrative and expository passages were included. Every eighth lesson was a cumulative review. (n = 13) • C (typical practice): A class of 13 students received the school's usual basal curriculum and supplemental vocabulary instruction in their resource classes. (n = 13)	M, 14 years	All LD	Treatment/ comparison; quasi-experimental (assignment based on school in which enrolled)	650	Students receiving direct instruction in background information correctly answered significantly more of the researcher-developed comprehension questions on passages related to the topics covered in the curriculum. All students performed better when the question was based on explicitly stated facts versus when the information needed to answer the question was only implicit. *(continued)*

160

Wilder and Williams (2001)	Grades 6–8	All LD	Multiple treatments; random assignment of intact classes	540	Theme-instructed students significantly improved their knowledge of the concept of theme and outperformed story comprehension-instructed students on this researcher-developed measure as well as a measure of the themes taught in the intervention. Theme-instructed students significantly outperformed story comprehension-instructed students on researcher-developed measures of near transfer (identifying the taught themes in unfamiliar stories and generating their own story incorporating the instructed themes) and far transfer (identifying an uninstructed theme in an unfamiliar story after being prompted to use the steps of the strategy). There was no significant difference between the groups when asked to identify an uninstructed theme in an unfamiliar story without being prompted to use the steps of the strategy. Theme-instructed students scored comparably to story comprehension-instructed students on measures of vocabulary and comprehension specific to the stories in the intervention.

- T1 *(theme identification)*: Groups of seven to eleven students received instruction and guided practice in identifying themes in stories. Teachers conducted a discussion of the topic and purpose before reading each story aloud to students. During the reading, the teacher interposed comprehension questions. After the reading, the class discussed the main points, and the teacher read a summary. Then the teacher used a series of six questions to help students organize story components, state the theme in a standard format, and generalize the theme to other relevant situations. Students then engaged in role-play, art, music, and discussion activities. (*n* = 47)

- T2 *(story comprehension)*: Groups of seven to ten students received more traditional comprehension instruction based on the basal. The teacher began with a prereading discussion and vocabulary development before reading the story aloud to students. During and after the reading, the teacher asked comprehension questions. Students then engaged in art, music, role-playing, and discussion activities. (*n* = 44)

(*continued*)

TABLE 7.4. (continued)

Study[a]	Grade/age	Student type[b]	Research design	Total minutes of intervention	Findings
Williams, Brown, Silverstein, and deCani (1994) • T1 *(theme identification)*: Groups of six students in special education classes received instruction and guided practice in identifying themes in stories. Teachers conducted a discussion of the topic and purpose before reading each story aloud to students. During the reading, the teacher interposed comprehension questions. After the reading, the class discussed the main points, and the teacher read a summary. Then the teacher used five questions to help students organize story components, state the theme in a standard format, and generalize the theme to real-life situations (e.g., role-playing, art, music). (*n* = 53) • T2 *(basal comprehension)*: Groups of six students in special education classes received traditional comprehension instruction based on the basal. The teacher began with a prereading discussion and vocabulary development before reading the story aloud to students. During and after the reading, the teacher asked comprehension questions. (*n* = 40)	Grades 7–8	All LD	Multiple treatments; random assignment of intact classes	480	Theme-instructed students significantly outperformed basal comprehension students on researcher-developed measures of their knowledge of the concept of theme, knowledge of the themes taught in the intervention, ability to identify the taught theme in an unfamiliar story, and comprehension of the taught story. There was no difference between the groups when asked to generate their own story incorporating the instructed theme. Almost no students in either group were able to identify an uninstructed theme in an unfamiliar story or generate their own story incorporating the uninstructed theme. Only the theme-instructed students significantly improved their knowledge of the concept of theme.

[a]T, treatment; C, comparison; T1, treatment 1 (used with multiple treatment designs); T2, treatment 2 (used with multiple treatment designs).

[b]LD, learning disability; EMR, educable mental retardation.

[c]Snider (1989) utilized both narrative and expository passages in the intervention; therefore, it is included in both Tables 7.4 and 7.5.

of research on narrative comprehension, however, transfer of expository text comprehension skills to unfamiliar passages has been more difficult (Boyle, 1996; Moore & Scevak, 1995). In order to independently monitor their comprehension and reason strategically when it breaks down, students need to know how, when, and why to use various strategies across academic settings. Hence, it is recommended that teachers not merely provide comprehension tools, such as graphic organizers, to help students immediately grasp course content (Darch & Gersten, 1986; DiCecco & Gleason, 2002) but also instruct students on how the tools can be used to engage with informational text and self-regulate their learning (Gajria et al., 2007; RAND Reading Study Group, 2002). Students taught to gradually assume responsibility for using comprehension strategies to identify main ideas (Chan, 1991) and summarize content (Gajria & Salvia, 1992) maintained their abilities 1 and 4 weeks, respectively, after the interventions ended, and these students generalized the strategies to new situations.

In addition, students taught to implement reciprocal teaching in either cross-age tutoring or cooperative groups improved their performance on standardized measures of reading comprehension (Klingner & Vaughn, 1996). This is considered a more stringent test of the effects of the intervention because the assessment is not specific to the passages or content of the instruction. Nonetheless, reciprocal teaching methods have been inconsistent at improving students' comprehension of implied main ideas on standardized instruments (Alfassi, 1998). Inferential comprehension of expository text is a much more elusive goal. Even when provided direct instruction in requisite background information and vocabulary, students have not been as successful with questions based on implicit information as opposed to explicitly stated facts (Snider, 1989).

Despite the more intractable problems with transfer of skills and inferential comprehension, much can be done to support students' ability to read and learn from expository texts, which are the prevailing medium in grades 4 through 12. Recent guidance documents indicate that worthwhile components of intervention include semantic mapping, visual displays, mnemonic illustrations, text structure identification, cognitive mapping, identifying main ideas, summarizing, paraphrasing, self-questioning, reciprocal teaching, strategy generalization, building background knowledge, and self-monitoring (Boardman et al., 2008; Kamil, 2003; Torgesen et al., 2007).

Table 7.5 summarizes participant data, research designs, procedures, and findings from nine studies relevant to expository text comprehension intervention. As previously noted, further work is needed to determine how best to improve students' advanced reading skills. Additional research might also confirm the effectiveness of these interventions in grades 10 to 12 and with electronic or digital texts.

TABLE 7.5. Expository Comprehension Interventions

Study[a]	Grade/age	Student type[b]	Research design	Total minutes of intervention	Findings
Alfassi (1998) • T *(reciprocal teaching)*: Students, in classes of eight to 15, alternated reading aloud a segment of text, asking teacher-type questions, summarizing for group members, discussing/clarifying as needed, and making a prediction. (*n* = 53) • C *(typical practice)*: Students received the regular curriculum focused on skill acquisition, such as identifying main idea, summarizing, making inferences, organizing sequential details, and working on vocabulary skill sheets. (*n* = 22)	Grade 9	None LD (all enrolled in Chapter 1 reading)	Treatment/ comparison; quasi-experimental using intact classes	900	Students in the experimental group performed significantly better on a researcher-developed measure of comprehension that utilized all expository passages led with a stated topic sentence. This improvement was maintained in a delayed test administered 8 weeks after the intervention concluded. Students did not, however, perform significantly better than comparison students on a standardized measure of comprehension using 64% narrative passages with implied main ideas.
Boyle (1996) • T *(cognitive mapping strategy)*: After learning a strategy for determining the main ideas and details of each paragraph, students applied the strategy by creating a cognitive map of the main ideas and details while reading a short expository passage. (*n* = 15) • C *(no strategy instruction)*: Students read the short expository passages and were permitted to either take notes or create outlines. (*n* = 15)	Grades 6–8	LD or EMR	Treatment/ comparison; randomly assigned matched pairs of students	550	Students in the cognitive mapping strategy group performed significantly better on curriculum-based literal and inferential comprehension test items. They did not transfer the skill to a timed standardized comprehension measure, nor did they significantly improve their metacognitive and strategy awareness.

164

Study / Treatment	Grade	Sample	Design	N	Findings
Chan (1991) • *T1 (generalization of strategy):* Small groups of five to six students were taught with a gradual-release model how, why, and when to use a self-questioning strategy to identify the main ideas of expository passages. (*n* = 30) • *T2 (standard introduction to strategy):* Small groups of five to six students were provided a demonstration of the self-questioning strategy and then told to practice it on their own while reading expository passages. (*n* = 30) randomly assigned matched students; repeated measures	Grades 5–6	Some LD (matched by age and reading ability to typically achieving students)	Multiple treatments;	200	All students performed better on researcher-developed tests of identifying the main idea, ranking the importance of sentences from the passage, and responding to multichoice comprehension questions when provided the generalization instruction. Students with reading disabilities performed similarly to reading ability-matched students when prompted to use the self-questioning strategy on a delayed test, regardless of the treatment condition. However, only those who received the generalization instruction were able to outperform the reading ability matches when not cued to use the strategy.
Darch and Gersten (1986) • *T1 (advanced organizer):* The teacher pretaught students in a resource class important facts and concepts using an overview organizer depicting relationships among ideas. Students used the organizers to answer questions orally and took turns reading aloud from an expository text about the topic. After reading, the students were allowed to study independently. (*n* = 12) • *T2 (motivational discussion):* The teacher introduced the topic to students in a resource class and attempted to increase their interest and motivation by having students share prior experiences. Students then took turns reading the text aloud, offered other reactions, and studied independently. (*n* = 12)	Grades 9–11	All LD	Multiple treatments; random assignment	450	Students in the advanced organizer condition performed significantly better than students in the motivational discussion on researcher-developed measures of content knowledge.

(continued)

165

TABLE 7.5. (continued)

Study[a]	Grade/ age	Student type[b]	Research design	Total minutes of intervention	Findings
DiCecco and Gleason (2002) • T (graphic organizer): Groups of four students from a resource classroom were pretaught vocabulary, helped to decode the words, and led through a structured preview of an expository passage. Students then took turns reading orally and were periodically asked comprehension questions. After the reading, the teacher provided direct instruction on the content using a graphic organizer that depicted the relationship between the main and subordinate ideas. (n = 12) • C (no graphic organizer): Students in groups of four received instruction identical to the treatment condition, except they were not provided graphic organizers. Instead, they discussed the content after reading and completed a note sheet that did not graphically organize information. (n = 12)	Grades 6–8	All LD	Treatment/ comparison; random assignment within intact classes	800	Students in both the treatment and comparison conditions improved on researcher-developed measures of factual knowledge. On a researcher-developed written measure, students in the graphic organizer group made significantly more relational knowledge statements than students who received only explicit instruction.
Gajria and Salvia (1992) • T (summarization strategy): Groups of three to four students in resource classes received direct instruction and guided practice in a five-step summarization strategy. After mastering each rule in isolation, students were taught to use all five rules together to summarize the content of expository passages. Instruction in and production of summaries were done orally. (n = 15)	Grades 6–9	Some LD	Treatment/ comparison; stratified random sampling by reading level	390–660	Students in the summarization strategy condition performed significantly better than students in both comparison conditions on a researcher-developed measure of comprehension. They performed significantly better than the comparison students in resource classes and comparable to the comparison students in general education on a researcher-developed measure of factual recall. The performance of the summarization condition students was maintained 4 weeks

- C1 *(typical practice, resource)*: Small groups of three to four students in resource classes received the typical program of instruction with no training in the summarization strategy. (*n* = 15) C2 *(typical practice, normally achieving)*: Students who were reported to be reading at grade level or above received the school's typical instruction in general education settings. (*n* = 15)

after the intervention, and their performance on a standardized measure of comprehension also significantly improved.

Klingner and Vaughn (1996)

Grades 7–8

All ESL-LD

Multiple treatments; random assignment

945–1,080

- T1 *(reciprocal teaching with cross-age tutoring)*: Small groups of six to seven students received instruction and guided practice in reciprocal teaching using expository passages for 15 days. Students then tutored sixth graders in the comprehension strategies for 12 days. (*n* = 13)

- T2 *(reciprocal teaching with cooperative grouping)*: Groups of six to seven received instruction and guided practice in reciprocal teaching using expository passages for 15 days. Students then implemented the comprehension strategies in cooperative groups of three to five for 12 days. (*n* = 13)

Both groups improved their performance on standardized measures of reading comprehension. Growth was greatest during the phase when students were instructed in reciprocal teaching and peaked during the tutoring/cooperate grouping phase. Variability of scores was high. Students with initially higher decoding skills, greater oral language proficiency, and lower comprehension skills made the most gains.

(continued)

167

TABLE 7.5. (continued)

Study[a]	Grade/age	Student type[b]	Research design	Total minutes of intervention	Findings
Moore and Scevak (1995) • T *(summarize, link, image, check [SLIC])*: Groups of 10–12 students were taught to summarize graphs and draw lines linking the graph elements to related information in the text. Then they were to "image" their graphs, draw them from memory, and check their understanding. The teacher and students took turns leading the application of SLIC. (*n* = 20) • C *(typical practice)*: Groups of 10–12 students were taught the school's typical curriculum, which included the use of visual aids for expository text. (*n* = 21)	14–15 years	None LD (some identified as below-average readers)	Treatment/ comparison; stratified random sampling	420	Students of average ability in the SLIC condition recalled significantly more details than average-ability students in the comparison condition. No significant effects were found for recall of main ideas, however. SLIC-trained students of average and below-average ability produced significantly more accurate graphs and recalled more details from graphs than students in the comparison group. There was no evidence that SLIC-trained students transferred use of the strategy to an unfamiliar text.
Snider (1989)[c] • T *(direct instruction in background information)*: Co-teachers explicitly introduced the factual information and/or vocabulary to resource class of 13 students before having students read passages and complete written exercises to practice the information. Narrative and expository passages were included. Every eighth lesson was a cumulative review. (*n* = 13) • C *(typical practice)*: Students received the school's usual basal curriculum and supplemental vocabulary instruction in their resource classes. (*n* = 13)	M, 14 years	All LD	Treatment/ comparison; quasi-experimental (assignment based on school in which enrolled)	650	Students receiving direct instruction in background information correctly answered significantly more of the researcher-developed comprehension questions on passages related to the topics covered in the curriculum. All students performed better when the question was based on explicitly stated facts than when the information needed to answer the question was only implicit.

[a]T, treatment; C, comparison; T1, treatment 1 (used with multiple treatment designs); T2, treatment 2 (used with multiple treatment designs); C1, comparison condition 1 (used with multiple forms of typical practice); C2, comparison condition 2 (used with multiple forms of typical practice).
[b]LD, learning disability; EMR, educable mental retardation; ESL, English as a second language.
[c]Snider (1989) utilized both narrative and expository passages in the intervention; therefore, it is included in both Tables 7.4 and 7.5.

VOCABULARY INTERVENTION STUDIES

Vocabulary knowledge and reading comprehension are highly correlated (Joshi & Aaron, 2000), particularly when it comes to expository texts that contain many unfamiliar, domain-specific words (Harmon, Hedrick, & Wood, 2005). The vocabulary of content area material is considered low frequency, in that it does not occur often enough in everyday speech or in general printed English to make the meaning highly accessible to many students, especially those who are poor readers and, thus, low readers. However, rare vocabulary words carry the bulk of the meaning in content area texts (Cunningham, 1998) and occur with more frequency in advanced schooling and on standardized tests of academic achievement (Manzo, Manzo, & Thomas, 2006). In order for older students to adequately comprehend textbooks and other academic material, they must know at least 90% of the words they encounter (Nagy & Scott, 2000). When students are unfamiliar with too many words in the passage, they are unable to infer the meanings of surrounding words or to profit from the incidental exposure to new vocabulary (Swanborn & de Glopper, 2002).

Unfortunately, researchers have found that as little as 1.4% of instructional time in core academic subjects is devoted to vocabulary instruction (Scott, Jamieson-Noel, & Asselin, 2003). Yet it is recommended that students regularly be provided instruction with repeated exposures to words in multiple, meaningful contexts (Blachowicz & Fisher, 2000; Stahl & Fairbanks, 1986). This need not consume large blocks of instructional time, because students' learning will happen incrementally. Moreover, the lessons can incorporate engaging manipulatives such as semantic maps, semantic feature analyses, computer exercises, and mnemonic imagery (Bryant, Goodwin, Bryant, & Higgins, 2003).

Studies have found that vocabulary instruction using semantic maps and semantic feature analyses is more effective in improving students' vocabulary and comprehension performance than traditional methods relying on dictionary definitions and oral recitation (Anders, Bos, & Filip, 1984; Bos & Anders, 1990; Bos, Anders, Filip, & Jaffe, 1989). Although the results were obtained on researcher-developed measures limited to instructed material, students maintained their superior performance in follow-up testing conducted as much as 6 months after the end of the intervention (Bos et al., 1989). This sustained learning has not been achieved through the use of computer practice exercises that do not visually depict the relationship among words and concepts, even when the targeted vocabulary was individually selected based on students' performance on a pretest (Johnson, Gersten, & Carnine, 1987).

Fostering relational connections seems to be more influential in building students' vocabulary knowledge than simply providing repetitions or rehearsal with words and their meanings. Students taught with the aid of cards containing word associations and mnemonic pictures tying together the word clue and meanings demonstrated better recall of instructed words (Mastropieri, Scruggs, Levin, Gaffney, & McLoone, 1985), transfer words (McLoone, Scruggs, Mastropieri, & Zucker, 1986), and conceptual information (Veit, Scruggs, & Mastropieri, 1986) than students provided greater doses of direct instruction. These results are consistent with those obtained by students taught to generate their own mnemonic images (Mastropieri et al., 1985). Of the studies reviewed here, only this latter one explored this process of guiding students to become self-directed in their vocabulary strategy use, but the findings offer encouragement that vocabulary development is not entirely dependent upon the teacher's instruction of each word.

Table 7.6 summarizes participant data, research designs, procedures, and findings from eight studies relevant to vocabulary intervention. Additional research might address how to improve students' generalized vocabulary knowledge, as measured by standardized assessments.

ACADEMIC ENGAGEMENT

Ensuring that students have the word identification, fluency, comprehension, and vocabulary skills necessary to be able to read and learn from school texts is only a part of the instructional milieu that promotes achievement. Perhaps the most challenging aspect of teaching older students is fostering their engagement. The construct of engagement can be defined as students' interest in learning, their internal motivation to work hard and do their best, and their ability to effortlessly enact strategies to support their learning. Engagement has been linked to reading achievement (Gottfried, Cook, & Gottfried, 2005; Guthrie, Schafer, & Huang, 2001), overall academic performance (Fredricks, Blumenfeld, & Paris, 2004), and educational resilience, or decreased risk of dropping out of school (Finn & Rock, 1997; Linnenbrink & Pintrich, 2002). The reading skills of early adolescents seem particularly sensitive to affective factors. Students' perceptions of their reading competence and overall attitudes about reading were found in one study to uniquely contribute 8% of the variance in their word identification abilities, 11% of the variance in their spelling abilities, and 6% of the variance in their reading comprehension (Conlon, Zimmer-Gembeck, Creed, & Tucker, 2006).

The ways in which lessons are structured can influence students' attitudes about the reading tasks and their motivation to be actively involved in them. Students report being more engaged when teachers do more listening than talking, make the material personally relevant, allow some choice in texts or strategies, genuinely respond to student questions or opinions, set

TABLE 7.6. Vocabulary Interventions

Study[a]	Grade/age	Student type[b]	Research design	Total minutes of intervention[c]	Findings
Anders, Bos, and Filip (1984) • T *(semantic feature analysis):* As a class, students and teacher discussed concepts while completing a chart to show whether each concept had a positive, negative, or undetermined relationship with the vocabulary words. Students then read an expository passage to verify their ratings. (*n* = 31) • C *(typical practice):* As a class, students were asked to transpose dictionary definitions for assigned words and use the words in a sentence. Students then read an expository passage to prepare for a comprehension test. (*n* = 31)	Grades 9–11	All LD	Treatment/comparison; quasi-experimental with random assignment of intact classes	200	The students completing the semantic feature analysis scored significantly higher on the commercial text's comprehension test.
Bos and Anders (1990) • T1 *(semantic mapping):* In groups of six to 12, students and researcher completed a map showing the hierarchical relationship among the vocabulary words. Students then read an expository science passage to confirm the relationships before taking a recall test. (*n* = 19) • T2 *(semantic feature analysis):* In groups of six to 12, students and researcher collaboratively completed a matrix to predict relationships among concepts. Students then read the passage to confirm the relationships before taking a recall test. (*n* = 17) • T3 *(semantic/syntactic feature analysis):* In groups of six to 12, students and researcher collaboratively completed a matrix to predict relationships among concepts and used the matrix to answer cloze sentences. Students then read the passage to confirm the relationships before taking a recall test. (*n* = 14)	M, 13.8 years	All LD	Multiple treatments; random assignment	400	Students in the three interactive treatment conditions scored significantly higher than those in the comparison condition on researcher-developed measures of vocabulary and comprehension. These differences were maintained at follow-up testing 4 weeks later. There were no significant differences among the three treatment groups. Analysis of the written responses revealed that differences between the treatment groups' and the comparison's generative vocabulary, conceptual units, and scriptal knowledge were not evident until follow-up testing, when all three treatment conditions demonstrated better productive knowledge and received significantly higher holistic ratings. There were no significant differences among the three treatment groups.

(continued)

171

TABLE 7.6. (continued)

Study[a]	Grade/age	Student type[b]	Research design	Total minutes of intervention[c]	Findings
• C (*definition instruction*): In groups of five, students were directly taught the definitions of words with oral recitation, correct pronunciation, and memorization of the definition within a context. Students then read a passage containing the words and took a written recall test. (*n* = 11)					
Bos, Anders, Filip, and Jaffe (1989)	M, 16.2 years	All LD	Treatment/ comparison; random assignment of intact classes	200	Students in the semantic feature analysis condition scored significantly higher on a researcher-developed measure of vocabulary and conceptual information. These differences were maintained in a delayed test administered 6 months later.
• T (*semantic feature analysis*): Small classes of five to six students and researcher collaboratively defined terms with connections to prior knowledge, predicted the relationship between the vocabulary and key concepts (positive, negative, unknown) on the chart, and orally justified predictions. Students then read an expository social studies passage to clarify relationships. (*n* = 25)					
• C (*dictionary method/typical practice*): After discussing the topic of a passage, teachers provided a list of vocabulary and had the class of five to six students repeat the words orally. Students then copied dictionary definitions and used the words in sentences related to the topic before reading the passage. (*n* = 25)					

172

Johnson, Gersten and Carnine (1987) • T1 *(small teaching set)*: Students in a resource class individually completed vocabulary exercises (teaching frame followed by multiple-choice practice items) on a computer. Words were selected based on student performance on a pretest taken at the start of the lesson. (*n* = 12) • T2 *(large teaching set)*: Students in a resource class individually completed vocabulary exercises (teaching frames, multiple-choice practice items, spelling words to complete sentences, matching games) on a computer. Students received a predetermined set of 25 words at a time. (*n* = 12)	Grades 9–12	All LD	Multiple treatments; randomly assigned matched students	Maximum of 220	Students in the small teaching set condition needed significantly fewer sessions than the large teaching set group to achieve mastery with the words. Both groups performed significantly better on a multiple-choice posttest administered after students achieved mastery on the words, but their performance decreased on a delayed test administered 2 weeks later. Both groups had similarly low performance on an open-ended oral test of word meanings and a written comprehension test.
Mastropieri, Scruggs, Levin, Gaffney, and McLoone (1985) • T1 *(experimenter-provided mnemonic imagery)*: Students were individually taught vocabulary through the use of cards containing the word, word clue, meaning, and an interactive picture. The researcher first introduced all the words and their word clues orally and then presented the cards for 20-second intervals while explaining how to associate the word clue and the picture with the word and its meaning. Students then practiced the mnemonic-retrieval strategy. (*n* = 16) • T2 *(direct instruction)*: Students were individually taught vocabulary words through direct instruction. Words were explicitly introduced in sets of four or five with a card containing the word, its meaning, and a nonmnemonic picture depicting only its meaning. Students were provided 43% more instructional time than students in the mnemonic condition. (*n* = 16)	Grades 7–9	All LD	Multiple treatments; stratified random sampling	NR	Students in the experimenter-provided mnemonic condition recalled the meanings of significantly more words than students who received direct instruction.

(continued)

TABLE 7.6. (continued)

Study[a]	Grade/age	Student type[b]	Research design	Total minutes of intervention[c]	Findings
Mastropieri, Scruggs, Levin, Gaffney, and McLoone (1985) • *T1 (self-generated mnemonic imagery):* Students were individually taught vocabulary through the use of cards containing the word, word clue, and meaning. The researchers first introduced all the words and their word clues orally. Then they presented the cards for 20-second intervals, explained how to associate the word clue with the word, and asked the students to generate their own drawing that would tie together the word clue and meaning. Students then practiced the mnemonic-retrieval strategy. (*n* = 15) • *T2 (direct instruction):* Students were individually taught vocabulary words through direct instruction. Words were explicitly introduced in sets of four or five with a card containing the word, its meaning, and a nonmnemonic picture depicting only its meaning. (*n* = 15)	Grades 7–9	All LD	Multiple treatments; stratified random sampling	NR	Students in the self-generated mnemonic condition recalled the meanings of significantly more words than students who received direct instruction.
McLoone, Scruggs, Mastropieri, and Zucker (1986) • *T1 (mnemonic imagery):* In the training task, students were individually taught vocabulary through the use of cards containing the word, word clue, meaning, and an interactive picture. The researcher first introduced all the words and their word clues orally and then presented the cards for 20-second intervals while explaining how to associate the word clue and the picture with the word and its meaning. Students then practiced the mnemonic-retrieval strategy. In the transfer task, students were taught to independently provide a word clue and interactive picture. (*n* = 30 for training; *n* = 28 for transfer)	Grades 7–8	All LD	Multiple treatments; stratified random sampling	25	Students in the mnemonic condition recalled the meanings of significantly more training and transfer words than students who received direct instruction.

• T2 (direct instruction): In the training task, students were individually taught vocabulary words through direct instruction. Words were explicitly introduced in sets of two or three with a card containing the word and its meaning. Students were prompted to repeat/rehearse the word meanings. In the transfer task, students were taught to independently state each word and definition and then review/rehearse in sets of three. ($n = 30$ for training; $n = 24$ for transfer)					
Veit, Scruggs, and Mastropieri (1986) • T1 (mnemonic imagery): Small groups of two to four students were provided three lessons on a related concept. In each lesson, students were presented the words or concepts on mnemonic cards that also contained a word clue, the definition or factual information, and an interactive picture. The cards were presented for 15-second intervals while the tutor explained the mnemonic connections among the items. (n was not reported; 12 groups) • T2 (direct questioning): Small groups of two to four students were provided three lessons on a related concept. In each lesson, students were presented the words or concepts on a card that also contained a nonmnemonic line drawing or a visuospatial display of the information. The tutor explicitly stated the information on the cards and then had students repeat/rehearse it. (n was not reported; 12 groups)	Grades 6–8	All LD	Multiple treatments; random assignment of small groups (based on schedules)	NR	Groups provided the mnemonic imagery instruction demonstrated significantly better recall of information from all the lessons, except the vocabulary, under strict scoring procedures.

[a]T, treatment; C, comparison; T1, treatment 1 (used with multiple treatment designs); T2, treatment 2 (used with multiple treatment designs); T3, treatment 3 (used with multiple treatment designs).

[b]LD, learning disability.

[c]NR, not reported.

an appropriate level of challenge, and explain the purpose for the activities as well as the knowledge goal for the lesson (Assor, Kaplan, & Roth, 2002; Guthrie & Cox, 2001; Reeve & Jang, 2006). However, in examining 4,295 learning experiences, Yair (2000) found that elements of high-quality lessons, including demanding high-level skills, were infrequently present.

Few reading intervention studies reviewed here included a measure of engagement, so it is not possible to determine whether instruction shown to be effective at improving cognitive reading skills also improves engagement. Available evidence indicates that instructional tools, such as graphic organizers, may be beneficial in improving students' comprehension or vocabulary but are less effective at altering students' reading attitudes or strategy awareness (Boyle, 1996). Although it has been reported that higher academic performance and improved behavior are associated with classrooms that meet students' social needs of belonging and provide opportunities for students to relate to each other (Assor, Kaplan, & Kanat-Maymon, 2005; Furrer & Skinner, 2003), participants in a peer-assisted learning strategies intervention did not significantly improve their attitudes about reading (Fuchs, Fuchs, & Kazdan, 1999). They did, however, report working harder to improve their comprehension and enjoying working with other students (other characteristics of engagement and social belonging, respectively) more often than students who experienced typical classroom practices that did not incorporate peer-mediated reading strategies.

Peer-tutoring practices can increase the amount of time students spend reading in class, but these practices can be tempered by frustrations with partners who do not want to actively participate or who read too quickly (Mastropieri et al., 2001). Similarly, students report liking computer-assisted learning activities more when the content is tailored to their individual skills or needs (Johnson et al., 1987). Recommendations for developing engaging instructional practices must be carefully structured to capitalize on their benefits (Assor et al., 2005; Furrer & Skinner, 2003).

Table 7.7 summarizes the participants, research designs, procedures, and findings from four studies that included measures relevant to academic engagement. Future research in reading interventions should include measures of academic engagement to determine whether improvements in reading skill have concomitant benefits for engagement. Additional research might also determine whether particular practices are more effective at certain grade levels or with particular ability levels.

SUMMARY

This chapter summarizes the extant literature on reading instruction in older students with reading difficulties, highlighting the evidence available for

TABLE 7.7. Academic Engagement

Study[a]	Grade/age	Student type[b]	Research design	Total minutes of intervention	Findings
Boyle (1996) • T (cognitive mapping strategy): After learning a strategy for determining the main ideas and details of each paragraph, students applied the strategy by creating a cognitive map of the main ideas and details while reading a short expository passage. (n = 15) • C (no strategy instruction): Students read the short expository passages and were permitted to either take notes or create outlines. (n = 15)	Grades 6–8	LD or EMR	Treatment/comparison; randomly assigned matched pairs of students	550	Students in the cognitive mapping strategy group did not significantly improve their metacognitive and strategy awareness, as measured by the Rhody Reading Attitude Assessment.
Fuchs, Fuchs, and Kazdan (1999) • T (peer-assisted learning strategies [PALS]): Students in remedial reading classes were explicitly taught how to work in assigned pairs to complete partner reading with corrective feedback, a summarizing strategy, and a prediction–(dis)confirmation activity. (n = 52; LD = 35) • C (typical practice): Reading instruction using typical curriculum with no peer-mediated reading strategies was implemented. (n = 50; LD = 39)	Grades 9–10	Some LD	Treatment/comparison; quasi-experimental using intact classes	1,200–2,400	PALS participants reported working harder to improve their reading than did comparison students but did not significantly improve their attitudes about reading. PALS participants agreed that they liked helping other students and working with other students on reading significantly more often than did comparison students.

(continued)

177

TABLE 7.7. (continued)

Study[a]	Grade/age	Student type[b]	Research design	Total minutes of intervention	Findings
Johnson, Gersten, and Carnine (1987) • T1 (*small teaching set*): Students in a resource class individually completed vocabulary exercises (teaching frame followed by multiple-choice practice items) on a computer. Words were selected based on student performance on a pretest taken at the start of the lesson. (*n* = 12) • T2 (*large teaching set*): Students in a resource class individually completed vocabulary exercises (teaching frames, multiple-choice practice items, spelling words to complete sentences, matching games) on a computer. Students received a predetermined set of 25 words at a time. (*n* = 12)	Grades 9–12	All LD	Multiple treatments; randomly assigned matched students	Maximum of 220	The overwhelming majority of students in both groups reported that they believed the computer helped them learn new words and that they would like to learn more on the computer. Attitudes among the students in the small teaching set were more positive, with a mean rating of 3.4 on a 4-point Likert scale for strength of enjoying working on the computer versus 2.8 in the large teaching set group. Similarly, the only two students who said they would not want to learn more on the computer were in the large teaching set group.
Mastropieri et al. (2001) • T (*peer tutoring*): Students in a special education class were assigned partners of slightly different ability levels and instructed by co-teachers to complete partner reading with error correction, story retell prompting, and summarization paragraphs. (*n* = 12) • C (*typical practice*): Co-teachers taught the whole special education class using suggestions from the teacher's edition of the basal (teacher questioning, oral reading, silent reading, and work sheet activities for comprehension and vocabulary). (*n* = 12)	Grade 7	Some LD (some EMR; all in special education classes)	Treatment/comparison; random assignment of pairs	1,250	Most students (83%) in the peer-tutoring condition reported liking the peer-tutoring condition. All students in the tutoring condition reported the purpose of tutoring was to improve their reading ability, and all felt they spent more time reading in the dyads than in the typical instruction. Some students reported having difficulty correcting their partners' oral reading errors when the partner read substantially faster. Others reported frustration with peers who did not want to actively participate or with figuring out the big words and answering the summarization questions with the time allotment. Many students, however, reported enjoying the opportunity to work with a partner or to "be a boss ... like a teacher."

[a]T, treatment; C, comparison; T1, treatment 1 (used with multiple treatment designs); T2, treatment 2 (used with multiple treatment designs).
[b]LD, learning disability; EMR, educable mental retardation.

178

the critical elements of phonological/phonics, structural analysis, fluency, vocabulary, comprehension for narrative and expository texts, and reading engagement. Several previous syntheses and meta-analyses influenced and guided our identification of key studies (Edmonds et al., 2009; Scammacca et al., 2007; Wexler et al., 2008). Overall, few studies address reading difficulties with older learners, and shockingly few address 10th- through 12th-grade readers. The vast majority of our knowledge about older readers is based on studies conducted with sixth through eighth graders. In these studies, the intervention time was quite brief, and these studies typically addressed a specific intervention. Relatively few studies provided integrated approaches to solving reading difficulties with older readers.

Despite the many caveats about the extant research literature on older students with reading difficulties, the studies identified can be used to provide practical guidelines for meeting the instructional needs of these students. Additional tools and information can be obtained from the following sources:

Boardman, A. G., Roberts, G., Vaughn, S., Wexler, J., Murray, C. S., & Kosanovich, M. (2008). *Effective instruction for adolescent struggling readers: A practice brief.* Portsmouth, NH: RMC Research Corporation, Center on Instruction. Retrieved August 10, 2008, from *www.centeroninstruction.org/files/Adol%20 Struggling%20Readers%20Practice%80Brief.pdf.*
Center on Instruction. (2009). *Adolescent literacy resources: An annotated bibliography* (2nd ed.). Portsmouth, NH: RMC Research Corporation.
McPeak, L., & Trygg, L. (2007). *The secondary literacy and intervention guide: Helping high school districts transform into systems that produce life-changing results for all children.* Mill Valley, CA: Stupski Foundation. Retrieved August 10, 2008, from *www.stupski.org/publications.htm.*
National Center on Response to Intervention(*www.rti4success.org*).
RTI Action Network (*rtinetwork.org*).

REFERENCES

The asterisk (*) indicates references included in the tables.

Abbott, S. P., & Berninger, V. W. (1999). It's never too late to remediate: Teaching word recognition to students with reading disabilities in grades 4–7. *Annals of Dyslexia, 49,* 223–250. (*)
Alfassi, M. (1998). Reading for meaning: The efficacy of reciprocal teaching in fostering reading comprehension in high school students in remedial reading classes. *American Educational Research Journal, 35,* 309–331. (*)
Allinder, R. M., Dunse, L., Brunken, C. D., & Obermiller-Krolikowski, H. J. (2001). Improving fluency in at-risk readers and students with learning disabilities. *Remedial and Special Education, 22,* 48–45. (*)

Anders, P. L., Bos, C. S., & Filip, D. (1984). The effect of semantic feature analysis on the reading comprehension of learning-disabled students. In J. Niles & L. Harris (Eds.), *Changing perspectives on reading/language processing and instruction* (pp. 162–166). Rochester, NY: National Reading Conference. (*)

Archer, A. L., Gleason, M. M., & Vachon, V. L. (2003). Decoding and fluency: Foundation skills for struggling older readers. *Learning Disability Quarterly, 26*, 89–101.

Assor, A., Kaplan, H., & Kanat-Maymon, Y. (2005). Directly controlling teacher behaviors as predictors of poor motivation and engagement in girls and boys: The role of anger and anxiety. *Learning and Instruction, 15*, 397–413.

Assor, A., Kaplan, H., & Roth, G. (2002). Choice is good, but relevance is excellent: Autonomy-enhancing and suppressing teacher behaviors predicting students' engagement in schoolwork. *British Journal of Educational Psychology, 72*, 261–278.

Babyak, A. E., Koorland, M., & Mathes, P. G. (2000). The effects of story mapping instruction on the reading comprehension of students with behavioral disorders. *Behavioral Disorders, 25*(3), 239–258.

Best, R. M., Floyd, R. G., & McNamara, D. S. (2008). Differential competencies contributing to children's comprehension of narrative and expository texts. *Reading Psychology, 29*(2), 137–164.

Bhat, P., Griffin, C. C., & Sindelar, P. T. (2003). Phonological awareness instruction for middle school students with learning disabilities. *Learning Disability Quarterly, 26*, 73–87. (*)

Bhattacharya, A., & Ehri, L. C. (2004). Graphosyllabic analysis helps adolescent struggling readers read and spell words. *Journal of Learning Disabilities, 37*, 331–348. (*)

Biancarosa, G., & Snow, C. E. (2004). *Reading next—A vision for action and research in middle and high school literacy: A report to Carnegie Corporation of New York.* Washington, DC: Alliance for Excellent Education.

Blachowicz, C. L. Z., & Fisher, P. (2000). Vocabulary instruction. In M. L. Kamil, P. B Mosenthal, P. D. Pearson, & R. Barr (Eds.), *Handbook of reading research* (Vol. III, pp. 503–523). Mahwah, NJ: Erlbaum.

Boardman, A. G., Roberts, G., Vaughn, S., Wexler, J., Murray, C. S., & Kosanovich, M. (2008). *Effective instruction for adolescent struggling readers: A practice brief.* Portsmouth, NH: RMC Research Corporation, Center on Instruction.

Bos, C. S., & Anders, P. L. (1990). Effects of interactive vocabulary instruction on the vocabulary learning and reading comprehension of junior-high learning disabled students. *Learning Disability Quarterly, 13*, 31–42. (*)

Bos, C. S., Anders, P. L., Filip, D., & Jaffe, L. E. (1989). The effects of an interactive instructional strategy for enhancing reading comprehension and content area learning for students with learning disabilities. *Journal of Learning Disabilities, 22*(6), 384–390. (*)

Boulineau, T., Fore, C., Hagan-Burke, S., & Burke, M. D. (2004). Use of story-mapping to increase the story-grammar text comprehension of elementary students with learning disabilities. *Learning Disability Quarterly, 27*(2), 105–121.

Boyle, J. R. (1996). The effects of a cognitive mapping strategy on the literal and inferential comprehension of students with mild disabilities. *Learning Disabilities Quarterly, 19*, 86–98. (*)

Britton, B. K., van Dusen, L., Glynn, S. M., & Hemphill, D. (1990). The impact of inferences on instructional text. *Psychology of Learning and Motivation, 25*, 53–70.

Brown, A. L., Campione, J. C., & Day, J. D. (1981). Learning to learn: On training students to learn from text. *Educational Researcher, 10*, 14–21.

Bryant, D. P., Goodwin, M., Bryant, B. R., & Higgins, K. (2003). Vocabulary instruction for students with learning disabilities: A review of the research. *Learning Disability Quarterly, 26*(2), 117–128.

Carlisle, J. F., & Stone, C. A. (2005). Exploring the role of morphemes in word reading. *Reading Research Quarterly, 40*(4), 428–449.

Catts, H. W., Adlof, S. M., & Weisner, S. E. (2006). Language deficits in poor comprehenders: A case for the simple view of reading. *Journal of Speech, Language, and Hearing Research, 49*(2), 278–294.

Catts, H. W., Hogan, T. P., & Adlof, S. M. (2005). Developmental changes in reading and reading disabilities. In H. Catts & A. Kamhi (Eds.), *The connections between language and reading disabilities* (pp. 25–40). Mahwah, NJ: Erlbaum.

Cazden, C. B. (1968). The acquisition of noun and verb inflections. *Child Development, 39*, 433–448.

Chall, J. S., Jacobs, V. A., & Baldwin, L. E. (1990). *The reading crisis: Why poor children fall behind.* Cambridge, MA: Harvard University Press.

Chan, K. S. (1991). Promoting strategy generalization through self-instructional training in students with reading disabilities. *Journal of Learning Disabilities, 24*(7), 427–290. (*)

Conlon, E. G., Zimmer-Gembeck, M. J., Creed, P. A., & Tucker, M. (2006). Family history, self-perceptions, attitudes and cognitive abilities are associated with early adolescent reading skills. *Journal of Research in Reading, 29*(1), 11–32.

Conte, R., & Humphreys, R. (1989). Repeated readings using audiotaped material enhances oral reading in children with reading difficulties. *Journal of Communication Disorders, 22*, 65–79. (*)

Cunningham, P. (1998). The multisyllabic word dilemma: Helping students build meaning, spell, and read "big" words. *Reading and Writing Quarterly: Overcoming Learning Difficulties, 14*(2), 189–218.

Curtis, M. E. (2004). Adolescents who struggle with word identification: Research and practice. In T. Jetton & J. Dol (Eds.), *Adolescent literacy research and practice* (pp. 119–134). New York: Guilford Press.

Curtis, M. E., & Longo, A. M. (1999). *When adolescents can't read: Methods and materials that work.* Cambridge, MA: Brookline Books.

Darch, C., & Gersten, R. (1986). Direct setting activities in reading comprehension. A comparison of two approaches. *Learning Disability Quarterly, 9*, 235–243. (*)

Deacon, S. H., & Kirby, J. R. (2004). Morphological awareness: Just "more phonological"? The roles of morphological and phonological awareness in reading development. *Applied Psycholinguistics, 25*, 223–238.

DiCecco, V. M., & Gleason, M. M. (2002). Using graphic organizers to attain relational knowledge from expository texts. *Journal of Learning Disabilities, 35,* 306–310. (*)

Duke, N. K. (2000). 3.6 minutes per day: The scarcity of informational texts in first grade. *Reading Research Quarterly, 35,* 202–224.

Edmonds, M. S., Vaughn, S., Wexler, J., Reutebuch, C. K., Cable, A., Tackett, K. K., et al. (2009). A synthesis of reading interventions and effects on reading outcomes for older struggling readers. *Review of Educational Research, 79,* 262–300.

Ehri, L., Nunes, S., Stahl, S., & Willows, D. (2001). Systematic phonics instruction helps students learn to read: Evidence from the National Reading Panel's meta-analysis. *Review of Educational Research, 71,* 393–447.

Englert, C. S., & Thomas, C. C. (1987). Sensitivity to text structure in reading and writing: A comparison between learning disabled and non-learning disabled students. *Disability Quarterly, 10,* 93–105.

Fawcett, A. J., & Nicolson, R. N. (1995). Persistence of phonological awareness deficits in older children with dyslexia. *Reading and Writing, 7,* 361–376.

Fielding, L., Kerr, N., & Rosier, P. (2007). *Annual growth for all students, catch-up growth for those who are behind.* Kennewick, WA: New Foundation.

Finn, J. D., & Rock, D. A. (1997). Academic success among students at risk for school failure. *Journal of Applied Psychology, 82*(2), 221–234.

Fletcher, J. M., Lyon, G. R., Fuchs, L. S., & Barnes, M. A. (2007). *Learning disabilities: From identification to intervention.* New York: Guilford Press.

Fredricks, J., Blumenfeld, P., & Paris, A. (2004). School engagement: Potential of the concept, state of the evidence. *Review of Educational Research, 74*(1), 59–109.

Fry, E. (2004). Phonics: A large phoneme-grapheme frequency count revised. *Journal of Literacy Research, 36*(1), 85–98.

Fuchs, L. S., Fuchs, D., & Kazdan, S. (1999). Effects of peer-assisted learning strategies on high school students with serious reading problems. *Remedial and Special Education, 20,* 309–319. (*)

Furrer, C., & Skinner, E. (2003). Sense of relatedness as a factor in children's academic engagement and performance. *Journal of Educational Psychology, 95*(1), 148–162.

Gajria, M., Jitendra, A., Sood, S., & Sacks, G. (2007). Improving comprehension of expository text in students with LD: A research synthesis. *Journal of Learning Disabilities, 40,* 210–225.

Gajria, M., & Salvia, J. (1992). The effects of summarization instruction on text comprehension of students with learning disabilities. *Exceptional Children, 58*(6), 508–516. (*)

Gottfried, A. W., Cook, C. R., & Gottfried, A. E. (2005). Educational characteristics of adolescents with gifted academic intrinsic motivation: A longitudinal investigation from school entry through early adulthood. *Gifted Child Quarterly, 49,* 172–186.

Guthrie, J. T., & Cox, K. E. (2001). Classroom conditions for motivation and engagement in reading. *Educational Psychology Review, 13*(3), 283–302.

Guthrie, J. T., Schafer, W. D., & Huang, C.-W. (2001). Benefits of opportunity to read and balanced instruction on the NAEP. *Journal of Educational Research, 94*(3), 145–162.

Harmon, J. M., Hedrick, W. B., & Wood, K. D. (2005). Research on vocabulary instruction in the content areas: Implications for struggling readers. *Reading and Writing Quarterly, 21*, 261–280.

Hasbrouck, J., & Tindal, G. A. (2006). Oral reading fluency norms: A valuable assessment tool for reading teachers. *Reading Teacher, 59*(7), 636–644.

Hasselbring, T. S., & Goin, L. I. (2004). Reading instruction for older struggling readers: What is the role of technology? *Reading and Writing Quarterly, 20*, 113–144. (*)

Homan, S. P., Klesius, J. P., & Hite, C. (1993). Effects of repeated readings and nonrepetitive strategies on students' fluency and comprehension. *Journal of Educational Research, 87*, 94–99. (*)

Jitendra, A. K., Hoppes, M. K., & Xin, Y. P. (2000). Enhancing main idea comprehension for students with learning problems: The role of a summarization strategy and self-monitoring instruction. *Journal of Special Education, 34*, 117–139. (*)

Johnson, G., Gersten, R., & Carnine, D. (1987). Effects of instructional design variables on vocabulary acquisition of LD students: A study of computer-assisted instruction. *Journal of Learning Disabilities, 20*(4), 206–213. (*)

Joshi, R. M., & Aaron, P. G. (2000). The component model of reading: Simple view of reading made a little more complex. *Reading Psychology, 21*, 85–97.

Kamil, M. L. (2003). *Adolescents and literacy: Reading for the 21st century.* Washington, DC: Alliance for Excellent Education.

Kennedy, K. M., & Backman, J. (1993). Effectiveness of the Lindamood Auditory in Depth Program with students with learning disabilities. *Learning Disabilities Research and Practice, 8*(4), 253–259. (*)

Klingner, J. K., & Vaughn, S. (1996). Reciprocal teaching of reading comprehension strategies for students with learning disabilities who use English as a second language. *Elementary School Journal, 96*, 275–293. (*)

Kuhn, M. R., & Stahl, S. A. (2003). Fluency: A review of developmental and remedial practices. *Journal of Educational Psychology, 95*(1), 3–21.

Leach, J. M., Scarborough, H. S., & Rescorla, L. (2003). Late-emerging reading disabilities. *Journal of Educational Psychology, 95*, 211–224.

Linnenbrink, E. A., & Pintrich, P. R. (2002). Motivation as an enabler for academic success. *School Psychology Review, 31*(3), 1–16.

Manzo, A. V., Manzo, U. C., & Thomas, M. M. (2006). Rationale for systemic vocabulary development: Antidote for state mandates. *Journal of Adolescent and Adult Literacy, 49*(7), 610–619.

Mastropieri, M. A., Scruggs, T., Mohler, L., Beranek, M., Spencer, V., Boon, R. T., et al. (2001). Can middle school students with serious reading difficulties help each other and learn anything? *Journal of Learning Disabilities, 16*, 18–27. (*)

Mastropieri, M. A., Scruggs, T. E., Levin, J. R., Gaffney, J., & McLoone, B. (1985). Mnemonic vocabulary instruction for learning disabled students. *Learning Disability Quarterly, 8*, 57–63. (*)

McCardle, P., & Chhabra, V. (2004). *The voice of evidence in reading research.* Baltimore: Brookes.

McLoone, B. B., Scruggs, T. E., Mastropieri, M. A., & Zucker, S. F. (1986). Memory strategy instruction and training with learning disabled adolescents. *Learning Disabilities Research*, 2(1), 45–52. (*)

Mercer, C. D., Campbell, K. U., Miller, M. D., Mercer, K. D., & Lane, H. B. (2000). Effects of a reading fluency intervention for middle schoolers with specific learning disabilities. *Learning Disabilities Research and Practice*, 15(4), 179–189.

Moore, P. J., & Scevak, J. J. (1995). The effects of strategy training on high school students' learning from science texts. *European Journal of Psychology of Education*, 10, 401–410. (*)

Morgan, P. L., & Sideridis, G. D. (2006). Contrasting the effectiveness of fluency interventions for students with or at risk for learning disabilities: A multilevel random coefficient modeling meta-analysis. *Learning Disabilities Research and Practice*, 21(4), 191–210.

Nagy, W., Berninger, V., & Abbott, R. D. (2006). Contributions of morphology beyond phonology to literacy outcomes of upper elementary and middle-school students. *Journal of Educational Psychology*, 98, 134–147.

Nagy, W. E., & Scott, J. A. (2000). Vocabulary processes. In M. L. Kamil, P. B. Mosenthal, P. D. Pearson, & R. Barr (Eds.), *Handbook of reading research* (Vol. III, pp. 269–284). Mahwah, NJ: Erlbaum.

National Institute of Child Health and Human Development. (2000). *Report of the National Reading Panel: Teaching children to read*. Washington, DC: U.S. Department of Health and Human Services.

National Joint Committee on Learning Disabilities. (2008). *Adolescent literacy and older students with learning disabilities*. Retrieved July 19, 2008, from *www.ldonline.org/article/25031*.

O'Shea, L. J., Sindelar, P., & O'Shea, D. J. (1987). Effects of repeated readings and attentional cues on the reading fluency and comprehension of learning disabled readers. *Learning Disabilities Research*, 2, 103–109. (*)

Paris, S. G., Lipson, M. Y., & Wixson, K. K. (1983). Becoming a strategic reader. *Contemporary Educational Psychology*, 8, 293–316.

Penney, C. G. (2002). Teaching decoding skills to poor readers in high school. *Journal of Literary Research*, 34, 99–118. (*)

Perfetti, C. A. (1985). *Reading ability*. New York: Oxford University Press.

RAND Reading Study Group. (2002). *Reading for understanding: Toward an R & D program in reading comprehension*. Santa Monica, CA: RAND Corporation.

Rasinski, T. V., Padak, N. D., McKeon, C. A., Wilfong, L. G., Friedauer, J. A., & Helm, P. (2005). Is reading fluency a key for successful high school reading? *Journal of Adolescent and Adult Literacy*, 49(1), 22–27.

Reed, D. K. (2008). A synthesis of morphology interventions and effects on reading outcomes for students in grades K–12. *Learning Disability Research and Practice*, 23(1), 36–49.

Reeve, J., & Jang, H. (2006). What teachers say and do to support students' autonomy during a learning activity. *Journal of Educational Psychology*, 98(1), 209–218.

Roberts, G., Torgesen, J. K., Boardman, A., & Scammacca, N. (2008). Evidence-based strategies for reading instruction of older students with learning disabilities. *Learning Disabilities Research and Practice*, 23(2), 63–69.

Rubin, H., Patterson, P. A. S., & Kantor, M. (1991). Morphological development and writing ability in children and adults. *Language, Speech, and Hearing Services in Schools, 2*, 228–235.

Rumelhart, D. E. (1975). Notes on a schema for stories. In D. Bobrow & A. Collins (Eds.), *Representation and understanding: Studies in cognitive science* (pp. 211–236). New York: Academic Press.

Saenz, L. M., & Fuchs, L. S. (2002). Examining the reading difficulty of secondary students with learning disabilities: Expository versus narrative text. *Remedial and Special Education, 23*(1), 31–41.

Scammacca, N., Roberts, G., Vaughn, S., Edmonds, M., Wexler, J., Reutebuch, C. K., et al. (2007). *Interventions for adolescent struggling readers: A meta-analysis with implications for practice.* Portsmouth, NH: RMC Research Corporation, Center on Instruction.

Scott, J. A., Jamieson-Noel, D., & Asselin, M. (2003). Vocabulary instruction throughout the day in twenty-three Canadian upper-elementary classrooms. *Elementary School Journal, 103*(3), 269–286.

Shaywitz, S. E. (2003). *Overcoming dyslexia: A new and complete science-based program for reading problems at any level.* New York: Knopf.

Snider, V. E. (1989). Reading comprehension performance of adolescents with learning disabilities. *Learning Disability Quarterly, 11*, 87–96. (*)

Snow, C. E., Burns, M. S., & Griffin, P. (Eds.). (1998). *Preventing reading difficulties in young children.* Washington, DC: National Academy Press.

Stahl, S. A., & Fairbanks, M. M. (1986). The effects of vocabulary instruction: A model-based meta-analysis. *Review of Educational Research, 56*(1), 72–110.

Swanborn, M. S. L., & de Glopper, K. (2002). Impact of reading purpose on incidental word learning from context. *Language Learning, 52*(1), 95–117.

Swanson, H. L., & Hoskyn, M. (2001). Instructing adolescents with learning disabilities: A component and composite analysis. *Learning Disabilities Research and Practice, 16*(2), 109–119.

Swanson, H. L., Hoskyn, M., & Lee, C. M. (1999). *Interventions for students with learning disabilities.* New York: Guilford Press.

Taylor, L. K., Alber, S. R., & Walker, D. W. (2002). The comparative effects of a modified self-questioning strategy and story mapping on the reading comprehension of elementary students with learning disabilities. *Journal of Behavioral Education, 11*(2), 69–87.

Texas Education Agency, University of Houston, and the University of Texas System. (2008). *Texas middle school fluency assessment teacher's guide.* Austin, TX: Author.

Thorndyke, P. W. (1977). Cognitive structures in comprehension and memory of narrative discourse. *Cognitive Psychology, 9*, 77–110.

Torgesen, J. K., Houston, D. D., Rissman, L. M., Decker, S. M., Roberts, G., Vaughn, S., et al. (2007). *Academic literacy instruction for adolescents: A guidance document from the Center on Instruction.* Portsmouth, NH: RMC Research Corporation, Center on Instruction.

Veit, D. T., Scruggs, T. E., & Mastropieri, M. A. (1986). Extended mnemonic instruction with learning disabled students. *Journal of Educational Psychology, 78*(4), 300–308. (*)

Vogel, S. (2001). A qualitative analysis of morphological ability in learning disabled and achieving children. *Journal of Learning Disabilities, 16*(7), 416–420.

Wanzek, J., & Vaughn, S. (2007). Research-based implications from extensive early reading interventions. *School Psychology Review, 36*(4), 541–561.

Wexler, J., Vaughn, S., Edmonds, M., & Reutebuch, C. K. (2008). A synthesis of fluency interventions for secondary struggling readers. *Reading and Writing, 21*(4), 317–347

Wexler, J., Vaughn, S., & Roberts, G. (in press). The relative effects of repeated reading, wide reading, and a typical instruction comparison group on the comprehension, fluency, and word reading of adolescents with reading disabilities. *Learning Disabilities Research and Practice.*

Wilder, A. A., & Williams, J. P. (2001). Students with severe learning disabilities can learn higher order comprehension skills. *Journal of Educational Psychology, 93*, 268–278. (*)

Williams, J. P., Brown, L. G., Silverstein, A. K., & deCani, J. S. (1994). An instructional program in comprehension of narrative themes for adolescents with learning disabilities. *Learning Disabilities Quarterly, 17*, 205–221. (*)

Wolfe, M. B. W., & Mienko, J. A. (2007). Learning and memory of factual content from narrative and expository text. *British Journal of Educational Psychology, 77*(3), 541–564.

Yair, G. (2000). Reforming motivation: How the structure of instruction affects students' learning experiences. *British Educational Research Journal, 26*(2), 191–210.

Yovanoff, P., Duesbery, L., Alonzo, J., & Tindal, G. (2005). Grade-level invariance of a theoretical causal structure predicting reading comprehension with vocabulary and oral reading fluency. *Educational Measurement: Issues and Practices, 24*, 4–12.

8

RTI in Mathematics
Beginnings of a Knowledge Base

Ben Clarke
Russell Gersten
Rebecca Newman-Gonchar

Writing a chapter on response to intervention (RTI) in mathematics is challenging. As several of the authors in this volume have pointed out, the term RTI means different things to different people. Is RTI a means to provide research-based instruction to all students in all schools through an elaborate cascade of tiered interventions and a dramatic increase in the quality of classroom mathematics instruction (i.e., Tier 1 math instruction)? Or is it a special education identification system whose primary goal is more valid identification of true mathematics learning disabilities?

Our difficulty is further compounded because mathematics lacks the research base found in the area of reading. A recent (Gersten, Clarke, & Mazzocco, 2007) analysis found a ratio of greater than 15:1 in the research studies in the area of reading compared with mathematics. A visit to any school or district would detail this discrepancy in practice. A visitor to a school might see a protected block of time for reading instruction, a reading coach or specialist providing support to teachers or instructing students, and multiple intervention and supplemental programs for students struggling in reading at each grade level. Although there is widespread acknowledgment of its importance, the same visitor would be unlikely to see the same level of built-in support and services in the area of mathematics.

However, a number of hopeful developments have occurred in the past few years. Trends in National Assessment of Educational Progress (NAEP) data show consistent increases in fourth-grade scores and student understanding of whole-number concepts (Lee, Grigg, & Dion, 2007). Although this trend has not yet been evidenced at the middle and high school levels, hope remains that by establishing a solid base of understanding at the earlier grades significant gains will be reaped in later years.

Although the quantity of research conducted in mathematics is limited, the quality is quite high. Furthermore, the number of new studies appearing in journals (both longitudinal and intervention oriented) continues to increase.

The business community has put a good deal of pressure on state and federal agencies to increase the quality of mathematics education. Meaningful linkages to work in the fields of mathematics education and developmental psychology contextualize much of the contemporary research in mathematics. Advances in these fields have informed the construction of intervention programs, and elegant research designs have moved beyond focusing on rather simple questions (e.g., carrying out mathematics procedures) to delving into more complex topics such as problem solving (Jitendra, Griffin, Deatline-Buchman, & Sczesniak, 2007), with a focus on building students' conceptual understanding of mathematics.

Interest in mathematics is growing among educators and the general public. The convening of a National Mathematics Advisory Panel (NMAP) similar to the National Reading Panel (2000) reflected increased recognition of the importance of mathematics. The recent release of their findings (2008) served to summarize the existing research base in mathematics and has the potential to drive the teaching of mathematics in our nation's schools.

Our first goal for this chapter is to shed light on the area of mathematics and provide encouragement to schools to approach mathematics instruction with the same degree of seriousness and intensity as they do reading instruction. To do so, our second goal for this chapter is to provide a working definition of RTI mathematics, including what we see as critical components of any RTI system, and link these components to the emerging research base in the instruction and assessment of mathematics. We are candid about the origins of recommendations, whether they are based on rigorous research or on expert professional opinion, as codified, for example, in the NMAP report and in *Adding It Up*, the National Research Council (2001) report.

WHAT IS RTI IN MATHEMATICS?

As part of the changes in the 2004 reauthorization of Individuals with Disabilities Education Act (IDEA), states were allowed to conceptualize and identify learning disabilities (in math and other areas) as a lack of learning progress, despite the presence of evidence-based instructional programs and practices. RTI is integrally linked to the concept of providing intensive early intervention to *prevent later academic failure.* The prevention component to RTI, although most developed in beginning reading, also has an empirical basis in the area of early mathematics. Studies conducted over 2 or 3 years (e.g., Hanich & Jordan, 2001) and recent analysis of the Early Childhood Longitudinal Study data set have documented that mathematics achievement trajectories are stable and established as early as kindergarten and first grade (Bodovski & Farkas, 2007; Morgan, Farkas, & Wu, 2009). The research of Griffin, Case, and Siegler (1994) and subsequent research by individuals such as Sarama and Clements (2004), Starkey, Klein, and Wakeley (2004), and others demonstrate the power and effectiveness of early intervention in mathematics, that is, as early as age 3 in preschool settings.

A FRAMEWORK FOR RTI IN MATHEMATICS

A strong multi-tier RTI model requires:

1. A focus on essential mathematics content and the use of evidence-based practices in regular classroom instruction so that a minimal number of students will struggle to learn grade-level mathematics content.
2. Regular screening of all students using valid and reliable measures to determine which students require additional support and the use of formative assessments to measure the response or growth of students identified as at risk and receiving a research-based intervention.
3. Use of research-based intervention programs or instructional strategies for the students requiring additional assistance.

In the next section, we detail the evidence supporting each of these components and offer practical advice for educators, schools, and districts to consider when beginning to develop an RTI system of service delivery in mathematics.

Component 1: Critical Content to Ensure That Mathematics Instruction Is Likely to Benefit Students in the Long Term

Recently released national reports, statements, and opinion papers from prominent research mathematicians (Milgram & Wu, 2002; NMAP, 2008;

Schmidt & Houang, 2007), as well as international comparisons of American texts with those from other nations, all characterize the mathematics content taught in U.S. schools as being "a mile wide and an inch deep" (NMAP, 2008; Schmidt & Houang, 2007). Curricula used in the United States cover numerous topics at each grade level. Typically, strands such as algebraic understanding, number sense, or statistics and probability return each year, without clear focus on student mastery of specific crucial topics.

In contrast, the curricula from high-achieving countries take the opposite approach, introducing only a handful of critical mathematical concepts each year. Curriculum materials and instruction focus on teaching those concepts with rigor to ensure a depth of understanding of the underlying mathematics. Once students develop mastery of the underlying principle or concept, the topic is not revisited but rather is used in a progressively more sophisticated manner.

Attempting to reverse this trend, the National Council of Teachers of Mathematics (NCTM; 2006), in its *Curriculum Focal Points*, made a powerful statement about reform of mathematics curriculum for all students by calling for the end of brief ventures into many topics over the course of a school year. The topics they suggest heavily emphasize whole number (i.e., properties, operations, problem solving) and, most especially, fractions and related topics involving rational number (i.e., proportion, ratio, decimals).

The report is equally clear that algorithmic proficiency is critical for understanding number properties and related concepts and that algorithmic proficiency, quick retrieval of mathematics facts, and in-depth knowledge of concepts, such as place value and properties of whole number, are all equally important instructional goals. This position was reinforced and further streamlined in the report of the NMAP (2008) 2 years later, which emphasized that students need to obtain proficiency in three key areas in order to succeed in algebra. These three areas—whole number, rational number, critical aspects of geometry and measurement—have profound implications for the content of intervention curricula, including "intervention classes" increasingly established in middle schools to prepare "at-risk" students for algebra.

To prepare for algebra, students should be proficient and fluent with whole numbers by the end of grades 5 or 6. Proficiency in whole number entails:

- A solid grasp of place value and the number line.
- The ability to compose and decompose whole numbers.
- An understanding of the meanings of division, multiplication, subtraction, and addition and how to apply these operations to problem solving,
- Facility with computations using standard algorithms.

- Fluent retrieval of basic arithmetic facts for all four operations.
- An understanding of the commutative, associative, and distributive properties of whole numbers.

These should be major goals of mathematics interventions, and research suggests that a focused intervention using what we know about effective instructional strategies can help students attain select objectives (Bryant, Bryant, Gersten, Scammacca, & Chavez, 2008; Fuchs, Fuchs, & Prentice, 2004; VanDerHeyden & Burns, 2005). (See Component 2: *Research-Based Interventions and Instructional Strategies* section later for further detail.)

The second major proficiency required for success in algebra involves fractions, decimals, ratio, and proportion (often called *rational number*). As data from the NAEP (Lee et al., 2007) and recent research by Hecht, Vagi, and Torgesen (2007) have demonstrated, this is an area in which American students often fail dramatically. These are critical objectives for students in grades 4 through 7 and essential for success in algebra, in part because work with proportions and fractions entails a level of abstraction not necessary for success with whole numbers. If anything, this needs to be critical content for intervention courses or intervention curricula for students in these grade levels, although, to date, we have few empirical demonstrations of efficacy. Students need to be able to:

- locate both positive and negative fractions on a number line and be able to compare the magnitude of fractions such as 8/11 and 2/3 or –1/3 and –2/5 and decimals such as .2 and .09 or .77777, .8, and .597;
- carry out operations involving fractions and decimals proficiently and effectively;
- understand how to use these operations for solving problems involving fractions, ratios, percents and decimals in the wide array of contexts in which they naturally arise;
- know how to translate decimals into fractions or fractions into decimals or percents and know the meanings of percent.

This type of in-depth knowledge sets the stage for further use of symbolic notation and generalizability of principles, which are cornerstones of algebra. In part because so many students struggle with fractions and related concepts, schools could deliver focused instruction in this area as a supplemental program to all students instead of just as an intervention program for at-risk students.

As the third area of proficiency, the NMAP panel targets select topics of geometry and measurement, viewing understanding of the concepts underlying similar fractions as the final cornerstone for algebra readiness. For example, students who understand similar triangles are well positioned to benefit from instruction that addresses concepts of proportion (see NMAP, 2008, p. 18, for an outline of specific geometry topics).

The insights gained by NMAP (2008) and NCTM *Curriculum Focal Points* (2006) can serve as a basis for ensuring that the content of intervention materials is relevant and appropriate. However, one barrier that will have to be overcome in providing quality interventions is the degree of comfort and knowledge teachers have in these areas, in particular topics such as fractions, formal definitions of inverse operations, even and odd numbers, and equivalence (Hill, Rowan, & Ball, 2005; Ma, 1999). It is common to hear educators in schools make statements like "I'm just not that good at mathematics." It would be shocking to hear a teacher lament being a poor reader. The contrast between how teachers view and speak about reading and mathematics drastically illustrates the lack of comfort many educators have about their own knowledge of mathematics and thus their ability to effectively instruct their students in the topic. Districts and schools will have to work to alleviate these fears and provide corresponding professional development to build teacher content and pedagogical knowledge of mathematics.

From an RTI perspective, the need for focused math instruction in general education for all students is vital. Good instruction in this setting should limit the number of students who require additional services. However, we do believe that once students are identified for RTI services, the emphasis on covering a small number of critical topics in much greater depth is of even greater importance. If students who are struggling are to catch up to their peers, intervention materials must cover the most critical content.

Across the grade spectrum, interventions should also include materials designed to build fluent retrieval of basic arithmetic facts. Although this statement seems self-apparent for the early elementary grades, students in grades 4 through 8 will also require additional work to build fluent retrieval of basic arithmetic facts, and some will require additional work involving basic whole number topics. Once students gain fluency with basic number facts and operations, they are able apply that knowledge to the execution of problems involving rational numbers. For example, when solving 7/8 divided by 5/6 the students must know the basic number combinations of 7 × 6 and 8 × 5 in order to solve a rational number problem. The need for focused instruction in the area of basic number combinations is especially true for students with the most serious mathematics difficulties (Geary & Brown, 1991).

We suggest that schools select intervention curricula materials that not only focus on critical content but also meet the following criteria: (1) the materials integrate computation with solving problems and pictorial representations rather than teaching computation in isolation from problem solving, (2) the materials stress the reasoning underlying calculation methods and focus students' attention on making sense of the mathematics, (3) the materials ensure that students build algorithmic proficiency, and (4) the materials include frequent review for both consolidating and understanding the linkages of the mathematical principles.

Component 2: Research-Based Intervention and Instructional Strategies

Fuchs and Deshler (2007) identified two types of interventions schools might use in an RTI framework: a standard protocol approach and a problem-solving approach. A standard protocol intervention is a supplemental program that is offered to all students identified as at risk. Because many of the standard protocol programs are scripted or orchestrated in a step-by-step fashion, it is easier for school personnel to ensure that the program is being implemented correctly. Therefore, when a student does not respond to Tier 2 or Tier 3 instruction, the school can more easily assume that this nonresponse is likely due to a mathematics disability rather than inadequacies in instruction.

In a problem-solving approach, educators design an intervention specifically for each individual student. They can tailor a supplemental program or use a variety of research-based instructional strategies to design an intervention specifically aimed at meeting the needs of the at-risk student. For examples, see VanDerHeyden, Witt, and Gilbertson (2007) and Burns, Griffiths, Parson, Tilly, and VanDerHeyden (2007).

The intervention, whether via a standard protocol or a problem-solving approach, should be research based, but the amount of research is often too sparse. Therefore, in most instances, districts will have to select programs or strategies that are not evidence based. Several meta-analyses (Baker, Gersten, & Lee, 2002; Gersten et al., in press; Kroesbergen & Van Luit, 2003) have identified key instructional strategies that should be considered when developing an intervention with a problem-solving approach or when selecting an intervention curriculum for use as a standard protocol. These strategies are described briefly next.

Models and Think-Alouds

Effective instruction should begin with a clear, unambiguous exposition of concepts, step-by-step models of how to perform operations, and reasons for the procedures (e.g., Darch, Carnine, & Gersten, 1984; Jitendra et al., 1998; Woodward, 2006). Teachers should think aloud, or make their thinking processes public, as they model each step of the process. Teachers need to not only tell students about the steps and procedures they are perform-ing but also allude to the reasoning behind them (i.e., link to the underly-ing mathematics). A common example is a teacher instructing students in adding the ones column in a two-digit by two-digit addition problem and carrying when the answer is greater than 9 (e.g., 8 + 5). The teacher might show the process of carrying the 1 but not reference or provide a think-aloud about the underlying concept of composing and decomposing within a base 10 system.

Instructional materials should provide sample think-alouds or possi-ble scenarios for explaining concepts and working through operations that teachers or interventionists can use during instruction. Ideally, instructional materials would assist teachers as they explain the reasoning behind the pro-cedures or problem-solving methods using mathematically correct explana-tions that students can understand.

Student Verbalization

As teachers talk through the explanations for the procedures they are using, students will learn why they are performing each problem-solving step. As students work on acquiring new math concepts, the teacher should ask stu-dents to think aloud and communicate the strategies they are using to com-plete each step of the process and provide reasons for their decisions (e.g., Schunk & Cox, 1986).

Students solving the problem "Add 1/2 to 1/3" might provide an answer of 1/5 (i.e., adding the 2 and 3 in the denominator). Rather than correcting the procedural answer, the teacher should ask the students to locate the three fractions (i.e., the two addends and the answer) on a number line and justify their thinking about how adding two fractions results in a smaller number. This type of interactive teaching allows students to focus on the underly-ing concepts rather than quickly correcting their work. Students need to be active learners by consistently thinking through mathematical decisions.

Scaffolded Practice

In order for students to become proficient in performing mathematical pro-cesses, they need scaffolded practice (Darch et al., 1984; Jitendra et al., 1998; Tournaki, 2003). Teachers should play an active role in problem solving at first and then gradually transfer the practice to the students over time. At the beginning, the teacher and the students should solve problems together. The students should gradually complete more steps of the problem with decreas-ing guidance from the teacher. Eventually, when the students are able to solve the problem with minimal or no teacher support, they should proceed to independent practice. It is critical that students are provided with sufficient opportunity to practice previously learned concepts and procedures to ensure that their mathematical knowledge is maintained over time.

Visual Representations

Another key component of effective instruction is the use of visual representations to represent mathematical ideas and concepts. Mathematical ideas such as fraction equivalence and the commutative property of addition and multiplication can, and often are, represented by a wide array of pictorial representations, including number lines, graphs, and drawings of concrete objects such as blocks, cups, and birds. A major problem for students who struggle with mathematics is that their understanding of the relationships between the abstract symbols of mathematics and the various visual and concrete representations is weak (Hecht et al., 2007). These students require a good deal of systematic instruction in the use of visual representations (and concrete objects when necessary).

Rather than providing quick exposure to visual representations, a major goal of interventions should be to systematically teach students how to develop visual representations and how to transition this representation to the standard symbolic representation used in problem solving. This type of instruction requires the long-term building of robust representations and allows students to have a consistent way to engage in complex mathematical thinking. One powerful example that has been extensively researched is teaching students to classify word problems according to certain schemas (e.g., change) and then using that schema and an associated visual representation to represent and solve the problem (Jitendra et al., 2007).

There may be intervention programs that do not incorporate a sufficient number of these instructional strategies to improve students' math performance. Schools or districts should work to adapt the curricula so that they contain these key features.

We see several benefits to the use of standard protocol interventions in Tier 2, at least as districts begin implementation of RTI in mathematics. First and foremost is feasibility. Interventionists (be they teachers, instructional assistants, or adjunct faculty) can receive professional development on the same curriculum and learn from each other. In addition, a school or a district can fairly easily develop a database on how students respond to the intervention and what are typical patterns in implementation or areas where the intervention curriculum is weak. Neither would be possible if each classroom used differing interventions for its struggling students. Districts could also obtain a sense of how their universal screening and progress monitoring measures are working and whether cut scores need to be adjusted. Finally, there is a small but important body of research on specific intervention curricula that have documented success (see Newman-Gonchar, Clarke, & Gersten, 2009, for a review).

Component 3: Screening and Progress Monitoring

Universal Screening

Universal screening serves as a first step in determining those students who are on track and those who might need the extra support provided by an RTI system. In contrast to typical assessment in schools that may target specific groups of students (e.g., at risk), screening in a multi-tiered system of support involves all students, which means that the process needs to be efficient to avoid prolonged disruption of regular instruction. Any students identified as possibly at risk can take more time-intensive diagnostic tests at another time and as needed.

The content covered in a screening measure should reflect the instructional objectives for the particular grade level, with an emphasis on the most critical content. In the lower elementary grades, the core focus of instruction is on building student understanding of whole number. As students establish an understanding of whole number, rational number becomes the focus of instruction in the upper elementary grades. Therefore, screening measures used in the lower and upper elementary grades should have items designed to assess students' understanding of whole and rational number concepts, respectively.

In much the same way that beginning reading assessment systems focus on discrete skills at kindergarten and first grade (e.g., naming letters, segmenting words in sounds), transitioning later in grade 1 and higher to measures that function as global indicators of reading proficiency (e.g., oral reading fluency), early mathematics assessments should focus on discreet skills in kindergarten and transition to measures of global indicators for subsequent grade levels. In kindergarten and first grade, assessments have focused on more discrete skills such as identifying geometric figures (e.g., squares, circles, triangles), identifying the number of objects, number identification, sequence counting, discriminating between quantities (using both number symbols and objects), and determining missing numbers in a sequence. Validation studies in kindergarten and first grade on these types of measures have been undertaken only in recent years and are still rare but consistently show quite promising technical characteristics (Clarke & Shinn, 2004; Fuchs et al., 2005; Lembke, Foegen, Whittaker, & Hampton, 2008; VanDerHeyden, Witt, Naquin, & Noell, 2001).

In contrast to many of the kindergarten and first-grade measures that focus on discrete proficiencies, measures for use from grade 2 and higher focus on a broader range of skills. In the upper elementary and middle school grades, measures available include those reflecting a proportional sampling of objectives for a grade level in the areas of operations and procedures, number combinations or basic facts, and concepts and applications (for examples, see the Research Institute on Progress Monitoring website, *www.progressmonitoring.net*, and the National Center on Student Progress Monitoring website, *www.studentprogress.org*). Foegen, Jiban, and Deno (2007) completed a summary of measures for use in screening in the elementary grades and found that measures were quick and efficient to administer, and showed moderate to strong validity and adequate reliability.

Progress Monitoring

Districts and schools can use a two-step process to identify at-risk students. In the first phase, students scoring below a certain threshold on the state test in the spring or fall would be considered at high risk and eligible for an intervention. Once students are identified and placed in an intervention program, a second phase of assessment begins. The key goal of this assessment is to see whether the intervention is working. In most cases, the same screening measures used to place students are then used to measure their progress, or their response to the intervention. Screening and progress monitoring measures can be used to gauge overall progress across a general period of time (e.g., 1 school year) or a specific time interval (e.g., 10 weeks of intervention instruction), because the measures are tied to a common metric and the proportional sampling used to construct the measures reflects key benchmarks established by the NCTM *Curriculum Focal Points* (2006), NMAP (2008), and state standards. Schools should administer progress monitoring measures at set intervals (e.g., every 2 weeks) and compare student results with expected rates of growth to gauge the effectiveness of an intervention.

There is a body of evidence detailing progress monitoring, including summary reviews of mathematics progress monitoring research (Foegen et al., 2007) and summary information provided by the Research Institute on Progress Monitoring (*www.progressmonitoring.net*) and the National Center on Progress Monitoring (*www.studentprogress.org*). The reviews provide information on the reliability and validity of the measures (similar to the evidence presented on screening measures) as well as data regarding average growth rates, which are critical for gauging the effectiveness of an intervention.

It is important to note, however, that very little research evidence exists that specifically addresses the use of mathematics progress monitoring data to make decisions (e.g., maintaining or ending an intervention program) within the context of RTI. In an annotated bibliography on RTI in mathematics (Newman-Gonchar et al., 2009), each identified RTI study included a progress monitoring component; however, educational decisions (e.g., exiting a student from the program) were not made using the data. Rather, each student completed the whole program and then was evaluated in a summative fashion to determine whether or not the intervention was effective.

Curriculum-Embedded Tests

Many Tier 2 and Tier 3 intervention programs include curriculum-embedded tests (sometimes called unit tests, mastery tests, or daily probes) that educators can use to guide instruction. The results of these tests can be used to determine which concepts need to be reviewed, which need to be retaught, and which have been mastered within the context of the program (Bryant et al., 2008; Jitendra, 2007). Curriculum-embedded tests often result in very useful information for interventionists because they directly assess the content that is the focus of the intervention. However, interventionists need to be cautious about assuming that mastery of individual skills and concepts will translate into improvements in overall proficiency. Because of the need to assess whether the intervention has generalized to overall performance, we recommend using curriculum-embedded tests in conjunction with the broader progress monitoring measures detailed previously. Schools should administer progress monitoring measures to determine whether an intervention is impacting students' performance in a broader domain.

CONCLUDING THOUGHTS AND NEXT STEPS

RTI is not something that can be done alone. It requires a commitment on the part of education professionals, from the head of the school district to the school principal, the classroom teacher, the school psychologist, and instructional assistants. In other words, for RTI to be successful, it truly has to be an effort across settings. Acting in isolation on any one component (e.g., implementing a screening system but not providing intervention services to children identified as at risk) is not likely to produce positive changes in mathematics achievement.

Many of the governing principles of an RTI mathematics system of support can be derived from previous work in reading. Schools that have structures in place and have spent the time thinking about how to make RTI in reading work will be able to transfer that knowledge to structuring RTI systems in mathematics. Although structurally RTI mathematics and RTI reading share much in common, there will be differences. Foremost among these is that schools need to be aware of and develop support systems for mathematics in the upper elementary and middle school grades as the content of mathematics in the general education setting becomes increasingly more complex and additional students begin to struggle with new concepts. The need for interventionists with relevant content knowledge is strong. Individuals will also need training in management and motivational strategies to use with at-risk learners and means for balancing the extended practice necessary to build proficiency while maintaining student engagement. This must be done based on a quite limited amount of research (Gersten et al., 2009).

Another real constraint that researchers have experienced in the area of mathematics is the difficulty in finding the time needed to provide mathematics support to students. A common scenario involves a student who struggles in reading and receives instruction in both a core and intervention program. If this student also struggles in mathematics, adding a mathematics intervention to this child's already full day will be challenging and require difficult choices and flexible thinking among all parties involved.

When schools, districts, or states speak of RTI or develop RTI initiatives, it is not uncommon for their definition and practice to be based on the use of some sort of universal screening system and to include small-group interventions (commonly from a commercially available supplementary curriculum). Often schools also use frequent assessments, such as tests based on district standards or other types of brief assessments, to monitor student progress. However, those same efforts are not often directly linked toward a formal identification process for special education. Hence, schools or districts will have individual practices that fit within an RTI framework but do not conceptualize RTI as intended in the 2004 reauthorization of IDEA.

Schools and districts need to have honest discussions regarding whether or not they are engaging in best practices and, if so, the extent that these individual elements meet a rigorous standard such that they could be included or developed into a formal procedure for making special education eligibility decisions. As a field, we have a good deal of work to do in establishing how to use progress monitoring information to systematically inform potential special education referrals and address issues of disproportionality.

There still are many gaping holes in the knowledge base on teaching and learning mathematics in general, and we have only a rudimentary understanding of how to translate this knowledge base into instructional strategies that succeed with students who struggle with the abstractions involved in mathematics. Yet the field has made significant progress in the past decade, and we do now know enough to set up programs and approaches and to then rigorously evaluate their effectiveness. As our knowledge of mathematics' instruction and assessments increases, schools will have greater access to research-based instructional practices and assessments. Translating this knowledge into feasible, effective interventions for struggling students is a major but critical task for the field.

REFERENCES

Baker, S., Gersten, R., & Lee, D. S. (2002). A synthesis of empirical research on teaching mathematics to low-achieving students. *Elementary School Journal, 10,* 51–73.

Bodovski, K., & Farkas, G. (2007). Mathematics growth in early elementary school: The roles of beginning knowledge, student engagement, and instruction. *Elementary School Journal, 108,* 115–130.

Bryant, D. P., Bryant, B. R., Gersten, R., Scammacca, N., & Chavez, M. (2008). Mathematics intervention for first and second grade students with mathematics difficulties: The effects of tier 2 intervention delivered as booster lessons. *Remedial and Special Education, 29*(1), 20–32.

Burns, M. K., Griffiths, A., Parson, L. B., Tilly, W. D., & VanDerHayden, A. (2007). *Response to intervention: Research for practice.* Alexandria, VA: National Association of State Directors of Special Education.

Clarke, B., & Shinn, M. (2004). A preliminary investigation into the identification and development of early mathematics curriculum-based measurement. *School Psychology Review, 33,* 234–248.

Darch, C., Carnine, D., & Gersten, R. (1984). Explicit instruction in mathematical problem solving. *Journal of Educational Research, 4,* 155–165.

Foegen, A., Jiban, C., & Deno, S. (2007). Progress monitoring measures in mathematics: A review of the literature. *Journal of Special Education, 41,* 121–139.

Fuchs, D., & Deshler, D. D. (2007). What we need to know about responsiveness to intervention (and shouldn't be afraid to ask). *Learning Disabilities Research and Practice, 22,* 129–136.

Fuchs, L. S., Compton, D. L., Fuchs, D., Paulsen, K., Bryant, J. D., & Hamlett, C. L. (2005). The prevention, identification, and cognitive determinants of math difficulty. *Journal of Educational Psychology, 97,* 493–513.

Fuchs, L. S., Fuchs, D., & Prentice, K. (2004). Responsiveness to mathematical problem-solving instruction: Comparing students at risk of mathematics disability with and without risk of reading disability. *Journal of Learning Disabilities, 37,* 293–306.

Geary, D. C. (2004). Mathematics and learning disabilities. *Journal of Learning Disabilities, 37,* 4–15.

Geary, D. C., & Brown, S. C. (1991). Cognitive addition: Strategy choice and speed-of-processing differences in gifted, normal, and mathematically disabled children. *Developmental Psychology, 27,* 787–797.

Gersten, R., Beckmann, S., Clarke, B., Foegen, A., Marsh, L., Star, J. R., et al. (2009).

*Assisting students struggling with mathematics: Effective response to interven-
tion (RtI) for elementary and middle schools* (NCEE 2009-05). Washington,
DC: National Center for Education Evaluation and Regional Assistance, Institute of Education Sciences, U.S. Department of Education. Retrieved from *ies.
ed.gov/ncee/wwc/publications/practiceguides.*

Gersten, R., Chard, D. J., Jayanthi, M., Baker, S. K., Morphy, P., & Flojo,
J. (in press). Mathematics instruction for students with learning disabili-
ties: A meta-analysis of instructional components. *Review of Educational
Research.*

Gersten, R., Clarke, B., & Mazzocco, M. M. M. (2007). Historical and contemporary perspectives on mathematical learning disabilities. In D. B. Berch & M.
M. M. Mazzocco (Eds.), *Why is math so hard for some children? The nature
and origins of mathematical learning difficulties and disabilities* (pp. 7–29).
Baltimore: Brookes.

Griffin, S. A., Case, R., & Siegler, R. S. (1994). Rightstart: Providing the central conceptual prerequisites for first formal learning of arithmetic to students at risk
for school failure. In K. McGilly (Ed.), *Classroom lessons: Integrating cognitive
theory and classroom practice* (pp. 24–49). Cambridge, MA: MIT Press.

Hanich, L., & Jordan, N. (2001). Performance across different areas of mathematical cognition in children with learning disabilities. *Journal of Educational Psychology, 93*, 615–626.

Hecht, S. A., Vagi, K. J., & Torgesen, J. K. (2007). Fraction skills and proportional
reasoning. In D. B. Berch & M. M. M. Mazzocco (Eds.), *Why is math so hard
for some children? The nature and origins of mathematical learning difficulties
and disabilities* (pp. 121–132). Baltimore: Brookes.

Hill, H. C., Rowan, B., & Ball, D. L. (2005). Effects of teachers' mathematical
knowledge for teaching on student achievement. *American Educational
Research Journal, 42*, 371–406.

Individuals with Disabilities Education Improvement Act of 2004, Public Law 108-
446 (2004).

Jitendra, A. K. (2007). *Solving math word problems: Teaching students with learning disabilities using schema-based instruction.* Austin, TX: Pro-Ed.

Jitendra, A. K., Griffin, C., Deatline-Buchman, A., & Sczesniak, E. (2007). Mathematical word problem solving in third grade classrooms. *Journal of Educational Research, 100*, 283–302.

Jitendra, A. K., Griffin, C. C., Deatline-Buchman, A., & Sczesniak, E. (2007). Mathematical word problem solving third-grade classrooms. *Journal of Educational
Research, 100*, 283–302.

Jitendra, A. K., Griffin, C. C., McGoey, K., Gardill, M. G., Bhat, P., & Riley, T.
(1998). Effects of mathematical word problem solving by students at risk or
with mild disabilities. *Journal of Educational Research, 91*, 345–355.

Kroesbergen, E. H., & Van Luit, J. E. H. (2003). Mathematics interventions for
children with special educational needs: A meta-analysis. *Remedial and Special
Education, 24*, 97–114.

Lee, J., Grigg, W., & Dion, G. (2007). *The nation's report card: Mathematics 2007*
(NCES 2007-494). Washington, DC: National Center for Education Statistics.

Lembke, E. S., Foegen, A., Whittaker, T. A., & Hampton, D. (2008). Establishing technically adequate measures of progress in early numeracy. *Assessment for Effective Intervention, 33,* 206–214.

Ma, L. (1999). *Knowing and teaching elementary mathematics.* Mahwah, NJ: Erlbaum.

Milgram, R. J., & Wu, H. (2002). *The key topics in a successful math curriculum.* Unpublished manuscript, University of California, Department of Mathematics. Retrieved November 26, 2008, from *math.berkeley. edu/~wu.*

Morgan, P. L., Farkas, G., & Wu, Q. (2009). Five-year growth trajectories of kindergarten children with learning difficulties in mathematics. *Journal of Learning Disabilities, 42,* 306–321.

National Council of Teachers of Mathematics. (2006). *Curriculum focal points for prekindergarten through grade 8 mathematics: A quest for coherence.* Reston, VA: Author.

National Mathematics Advisory Panel. (2008). *Foundations for success: The final report of the National Mathematics Advisory Panel.* Washington, DC: U.S. Department of Education.

National Reading Panel. (2000). *Teaching children to read: An evidence-based assessment of the scientific research literature on reading and its implications for reading instruction* (NIH Publication No. 00-4769). Washington, DC: National Institute of Child Health and Human Development.

National Research Council. (2001). *Adding it up: Helping children learn mathematics.* Washington, DC: National Academy Press.

Newman-Gonchar, R., Clarke, B., & Gersten, R. (2009). *A summary of nine key studies: Multi-tier intervention and response to interventions for students struggling in mathematics.* Portsmouth, NH: RMC Research Corporation, Center on Instruction.

Sarama, J., & Clements, D. H. (2004). Building blocks for early childhood mathematics. *Early Childhood Research Quarterly, 19,* 181–189.

Schmidt, W. H., & Houang, R. T. (2007). Lack of focus in mathematics: Symptom or cause? In T. Loveless (Ed.), *Lessons learned: What international assessments tell us about math achievement.* Washington, DC: Brookings.

Schunk, D. H., & Cox, P. D. (1986). Strategy training and attributional feedback with learning disabled students. *Journal of Educational Psychology, 78,* 201–209.

Starkey, P., Klein, A., & Wakeley, A. (2004). Enhancing young children's mathematical knowledge through a pre-kindergarten mathematics intervention. *Early Childhood Research Quarterly, 19*(1), 99–120.

Tournaki, N. (2003). The differential effects of teaching addition through strategy instruction versus drill and practice to students with and without disabilities. *Journal of Learning Disabilities, 36,* 449–458.

VanDerHeyden, A. M., & Burns, M. K. (2005). Using curriculum-based assessment and curriculum-based measurement to guide elementary mathematics instruction: Effect on individual and group accountability scores. *Assessment for Effective Intervention, 30*(3), 15–31.

VanDerHeyden, A. M., Witt, J. C., & Gilbertson, D. (2007). A multi-year evaluation of the effects of an RTI model on identification of children for special education. *Journal of School Psychology, 45,* 225–256.

VanDerHeyden, A. M., Witt, J. C., Naquin, G., & Noell, G. (2001). The reliability and validity of curriculum-based measurement readiness probes for kindergarten students. *School Psychology Review, 30,* 363–382.

Woodward, J. (2006). Developing automaticity in multiplication facts: Integrating strategy instruction with timed practice drills. *Learning Disability Quarterly, 29,* 269–289.

9

RTI in Writing Instruction

Implementing Evidence-Based Interventions and Evaluating the Effects for Individual Students

Susan De La Paz
Christine Espin
Kristen L. McMaster

Response to intervention (RTI) typically comprises a three-tiered approach to instruction in which increasing levels of support (or services) are provided to students who are not progressing adequately in the general education curriculum (Council for Exceptional Children, Division for Learning Disabilities, 2007). This approach posits that the focus of Tier 1 is on prevention, because worthwhile instruction is delivered to all students in general education classrooms. The goals of Tier 2 are early detection and support for students who are not progressing adequately, although instruction continues to be delivered in the general education classroom. If an individual does not sufficiently respond to this second level of support, then teachers respond by providing highly specialized, Tier 3 interventions designed to address the unique underlying reasons for why the student is not making adequate progress in the given domain. Two assumptions are implicit in this approach with respect to each tier: (1) that a scientific base, or empirical support, exists for recommended instructional approaches and (2) that teachers monitor each student's progress to determine the effectiveness of instruction. We begin the chapter with a review of the scientific base, or empirical support, for various instructional approaches in writing. In the second half of the chapter, we turn our attention to evaluating the effects of instruction for individual students.

SCIENTIFIC BASIS FOR WRITING INTERVENTIONS

Tier 1 Writing Approaches

Many of the most common general education writing programs are easy to describe, and in so doing, we note the level of empirical support for each approach. Much of the writing research in general education makes use of qualitative or descriptive approaches rather than experimental designs to address research questions (Pritchard & Honeycutt, 2006). Thus, we select a representative sample of general education practices based on their frequency of use and consider them as possible Tier 1 programs. We present research findings, when available, for these interventions and comment on the robustness of the results. Instructional approaches that are common in general education classrooms include (1) a process approach to instruction, or Writer's Workshop; (2) *Step Up to Writing*, a commercial program from Sopris West; (3) a writing program based on rubrics, *6+1 Traits*, from the Northwest Regional Educational Laboratory (NWREL); (4) *Write Source*, a basal program, from Great Source, a division of Houghton Mifflin; and (5) theoretically focused, domain-specific writing-to-learn and literature-based writing connections that are common in secondary settings. The first and last approaches are generic methods that can vary in substantial ways from teacher to teacher, whereas other methods are likely to appear more similar because they have been disseminated from a central source.

Process Approach

In the 1960s, a process approach to writing instruction emerged in American schools as researchers realized that professional writers compose in a series of stages, or processes (Pritchard & Honeycutt, 2006). This approach shifted teachers' attention away from an emphasis on students' finished products to what students think and do as they write (Tompkins, 2004). In an effort to impose organizational structure within the writing process, teachers began to provide mini-lessons on cognitive processes underlying each phase, such as planning or prewriting; developed mechanisms for monitoring what students did as they worked; and provided authentic opportunities for children to share their finished projects with wide-ranging audiences. The resulting block of instruction was called Writer's Workshop (Dean, 2006; Graves & Murray, 1980; Routman, 2000).

Writing research in subsequent decades broadened process writing along several lines of inquiry: Researchers considered the influences of transcription difficulties on novice writers (McCutchen et al., 2002), the influences of problem solving (Englert, Raphael, Anderson, Anthony, & Stevens, 1991), the need to include editing and revision as distinct phases (Graves & Murray, 1980), the roles of audience (Frank, 1992) and genre (Kamberelis, 1999), the recursive nature of writing phases (Flower & Hayes, 1980; Hayes & Flower, 1980), the role of long-term memory (Hayes, 1996), and so on. Graham and Perin's recent (2007a) meta-analysis of 21 experimental and quasi-experimental writing process approach studies provides a current view of the efficacy of this type of instruction. Their work revealed a small but positive average weighted effect size of 0.32. However, this overall effect size masked an important relation. In six of the studies, the teachers received training from the National Writing Project (NWP; teachers in these studies were mostly volunteers who would subsequently serve as trainers), whereas teachers in the remaining studies did not receive such training. The average weighted effect size for NWP-trained teachers was 0.46 compared with a nonsignificant .03 for nontrained teachers.

Step Up to Writing

A commercial program by Sopris West, *Step Up to Writing*, is used with students beginning in elementary school and includes multiple genres and instruction in skills such as transitions, writing outlines, using conjunctions, writing multiparagraph essays, and writing paragraphs that increase in length and complexity, making it relevant for secondary students. Students are taught to use the colors of a traffic signal corresponding to different parts of a composition as a heuristic for text structure. The color green initially signifies the topic sentence, which is written to correspond to each genre; yellow means "slow down" and is used to identify key ideas or concepts to the reader; and red signifies "stop and explain," which is the writer's opportunity to provide evidence, explanations, and examples. A final green indicator is used to restate the topic or position. Students learn to "add more red" to their writing as well as how to add other color parts, such as "blue sentences" (these come before the first green indicator and signal the background or hook for the reader).

Step Up to Writing incorporates the use of models, rubrics, and direct, explicit instruction; however, there have been no empirical studies other than those published by Sopris West, and these data were analyzed in terms of gain scores (improvement from fall to spring) rather than a comparison of results between conditions (students who used this program vs. those who used another approach to writing). Thus, claims regarding the efficacy of this approach should be viewed as tentative.

6 + 1 Trait Writing Assessment and Instructional Model

The *6+1 Trait* materials were developed by NWREL and are widely disseminated in workshops, in books, and via the Internet. This approach to teaching and assessment focuses on specific features of good writing: ideas, organization, voice, word choice, sentence fluency, and conventions (and, if teachers choose, presentation). Each of the traits is defined by an analytic rubric, or writing guide, typically on a scale ranging from 1 to 6 points,[1] with the intent that the rubric communicates to both teachers and students a means of establishing the goals for writing and providing feedback for student work (Culham, 2003; NWREL; 2005; Spandel, 2005). Teachers who use the *6+1 Trait* model apply the rubrics to writing examples that have been written by unknown, grade-equivalent students or their peers. Students then analyze these samples and discuss how to improve the examples to achieve the highest level of criteria that are in the rubrics. Teachers then provide specific mini-lessons on writing elements (e.g., using "words that sparkle") to influence key criteria such as word choice that they found to be important for many students. It is important to note that teachers who use the *6+1 Trait* model often incorporate it within a Writer's Workshop approach.

Research addressing the efficacy of this approach was undertaken by NWREL in 2003–2004 in a randomized field study at three grade levels (4–6) in which teachers in the treatment group received a 2-day workshop in the use of the *6+1 Trait* model. Although the results did not show a treatment effect for the *6+1 Trait* model, data did reveal that teachers were not implementing the targeted instruction at the levels expected by the researchers. Moreover, this was a rigorous evaluation, appropriately using teacher as the unit of analysis, a rarity in research conducted by the developers of an intervention. Finally, a key dimension of the *6+1 Trait* model is the use of specific product goals, in which students attempt goals for the writing they are to complete. The use of specific product goals in a writing program was found to have a weighted mean effect size of 0.70 in Graham and Perin's (2007a) meta-analysis.

Write Source

Teachers in many schools rely on textbooks such as Houghton Mifflin's *Write Source* series to form the basis of their writing program. This particular series incorporates the *6 Trait* model within a writing process approach and defines as well as presents age-appropriate samples featuring different

---

[1]Rubrics for younger writers are shorter and reworded to tell what each trait looks like ("Everything ties together") rather than technical ("Sequencing is logical and effective").

genres in each grade-level basal. One feature that is especially kid friendly is that key elements of each genre are labeled in the writing samples, thus serving as examples of text structure to students. Revisions, such as adding or moving text, are also described and clearly shown in sample text. Teachers receive typical supporting curricular materials, such as a teacher's edition and accompanying classroom resources, and a collection of writing prompts and student papers are available via the Internet that prior teachers have posted on the *Write Source* website (*www.thewritesource.com*).

Direct evidence supporting the use of the *Write Source* curriculum is based on a series of case studies with weak designs and no outside review; however, there appears to be value in one of its underlying tenets (as well as the *6+1 Traits* approach), because the study of models was found to have a weighted mean effect size of 0.25 in Graham and Perin's 2007a meta-analysis of instructional approaches in writing.

Theoretically Focused, Domain-Specific Approaches

The final Tier 1 writing approach that we mention is a collection of models for writing instruction, commonly seen in English, social studies, or science classrooms, where students engage in literature-based writing activities or domain-specific, writing-to-learn connections.[2] English teachers often use the writing process to engage students in a variety of genres (e.g., biographical, fictional) and writing forms (e.g., technical documents, reflective compositions, historical investigation). In addition, they ask students to write responses to literature to indicate their comprehension of significant ideas in the text, their awareness of an author's use of imagery, or their appreciation of ambiguities, nuances, complexities, or themes within a given piece of text (California Department of Education, 1999). High school science and social studies teachers also use writing as a means for students to demonstrate content understandings (Bangert-Drowns, Hurley, & Wilkinson, 2004), often in the form of writing lab reports or providing interpretations of historical accounts. In fact, many educators view instruction in reading comprehension and writing for secondary students as requiring disciplinary perspectives (Shanahan & Shanahan, 2008). Moreover, specific instruction that links writing to disciplinary ways that professionals reason in both science and social studies has been found to improve secondary students' thinking in these content areas as well as their writing abilities (De La Paz, 2005; Hand, Prain, & Yore, 2001).

---

[2]In their 2007b report to the Carnegie Corporation, *Writing Next*, Graham and Perin called this approach "writing for content learning" and noted an effect size of 0.23.

Moving Beyond Tier 1

When students do not make adequate writing progress within the general curriculum, based on district assessments or progress monitoring data, the student is moved to Tier 2 and possibly on to Tier 3. However, just as there is a weak research base for defining Tier 1 writing programs, we lack adequate information on what constitutes appropriate Tier 2 versus Tier 3 writing intervention. In contrast to the field of reading, writing has received little attention in research or policy: To wit, the What Works Clearinghouse has yet to release any reports on writing interventions. On the other hand, where the child receives instruction and the size of the group are features that will likely distinguish Tier 2 from Tier 3 instruction. More importantly, what ideally differentiates Tier 3 from Tier 2 is that instruction with the former is more intense and individualized than that which a child might receive in Tier 2. Increased intensity and individualization might be achieved by increasing the frequency and/or duration of the instruction or adding more individualized modeling and scaffolding, including more practice time, individualizing materials, and so on.

Thus, although there is some overlap between Tier 2 and Tier 3 writing recommendations, recent syntheses of this research provide several evidence-based suggestions that teachers can follow to help students who struggle with the writing process. Therefore, we now turn to what has emerged as evidence-based recommendations in writing, first for elementary students and then for secondary students. We assume, again, that teachers monitor students' progress when they implement these approaches, and describe how to do so later in this chapter.

Elementary-Age Students

Transcription Skills

Typically developing children vary in their overall writing development when they enter first grade, for various physiological and environmental reasons (Berninger, 2008). One of the greatest initial hurdles children have in learning to write is mastering the mechanical demands for producing text (i.e., transcription, or letter formation, spelling, and mechanics; Dyson, 1984). As children develop writing skills, they gradually transition from using a combination of drawings and letters to relying on graphemes alone to signal their intent.

Researchers have formally evaluated the impact of transcription demands on youngsters' composing capacities as they move into their elementary years. Graham, Berninger, Abott, Abbott, and Whitaker (1997) found that handwriting and spelling accounted for one-quarter of the variance of elementary students' composition quality and two-thirds of the variance for fluency. With respect to handwriting, Graham, Berninger, and Weintraub (2001) found that by the second half of first grade virtually all children were able to produce legible lowercase manuscript letter for 80% of the letters of the alphabet. By second grade, children were able to write 92% of the letters and a ceiling effect occurred in third grade. In addition to considering legibility, teachers may consider children's speed in copying and dictation tasks (Gregg & Mather, 2002).

When children in the elementary grades need explicit, systematic, and sustained handwriting and spelling instruction, they may benefit from interventions such as those designed by Graham, Harris, and Fink (2000). One program was developed for first- and second-grade children with poor spelling and poor handwriting skills. The handwriting instruction taught children how to write lowercase manuscript letters accurately and fluently. Children first learned to name and identify letters of the alphabet. Next, they were introduced to and practiced sets of letters that shared common formational characteristics (e.g., *l*, *i*, and *t*). Students then practiced tracing and writing the letters individually and in context. Finally, they copied a short sentence that contained multiple instances of the letters quickly and accurately for 3 minutes. Students evaluated their efforts (e.g., by circling the best formed letter), monitored their performance, and set goals to write faster. In comparison to children who received extra reading instruction, those who received handwriting instruction improved not only handwriting but also writing skills. They wrote better sentences and longer stories than children in the control group and maintained these gains 6 months later.

The spelling instruction was designed to teach children basic sound–letter combinations, spelling patterns involving long and short vowels, and common words that fit those patterns. In the first lesson of each unit, students sorted word cards into two or more patterns that were represented by keywords (e.g., m*a*de, m*ai*d, and m*ay* for the long-*a* sound) and discovered and learned rules for the patterns emphasized in each word sort. During the remaining four lessons, students examined eight new spelling words that matched one of the spelling patterns emphasized in that unit. Students practiced identifying sound–letter associations for consonants, blends, digraphs, and short vowels as well as building words by joining these combinations to rimes that fit the spelling patterns emphasized in the unit. The children demonstrated improved spelling on words they practiced, improved standardized tests scores, as well as improved word attack and sentence-writing skills. The results of this study are consistent with a recent synthesis on spelling methods with older elementary students with learning disability (primarily in third to sixth grade; Wanzek, Vaughn, Wexler, Swanson, Edmonds, & Kim, 2006) that confirmed findings from earlier reviews that explicit instruction, with multiple practice opportunities and immediate corrective feedback after a word was misspelled, consistently led to improved spelling outcomes.

In summary, some children in the elementary grades will need additional help from their teachers to master handwriting and spelling. Others may need direct instruction that focuses on a different aspect of mechanics (i.e., grammar) during elementary or secondary school. Unfortunately, common exercises (diagramming sentences, daily oral language exercises) do not have evidence demonstrating their effectiveness, most likely because most students do not apply what they learn from these activities to their own writing (Andrews et al., 2006); thus, we next discuss a more promising approach for teaching sentence construction skills.

Sentence Construction

Sentence combining appears to be an effective approach for teaching sentence construction skills when the goal is to increase students' syntactic complexity, regardless of students age (range = 5–16), writing genre (persuasive, narrative, or expository), or presence of a learning disability (as demonstrated with fourth-grade students; Saddler, 2007). In Graham and Perin's (2007a) meta-analysis, the effect size for sentence combining was 0.50, suggesting that it contributed positive effects to children's writing. Briefly, sentence combining refers to teaching students explicitly how to restructure sentences, for example, revising two simple sentences (referred to as "kernel sentences") to form a more interesting complex sentence (often by modifying nouns or by creating complex sentences with coordinate or subordinate phrases). Students then use standards such as clarity and directness of meaning to judge the adequacy of their new sentence combinations.

Composition

From the time they are in the mid- to late-elementary grades, students narrate, write persuasive essays, compose a variety of fictional accounts, and are asked to write friendly and business letters, describe familiar objects or places, as well as compose informational text (e.g., "how-to" essays). Thus, composing may be another area of need for Tier 2 and Tier 3 approaches to instruction. When composing, many subprocesses in writing must be coordinated, because children think about the writing task, think about how to generate (and organize) ideas for their specific work, consider expectations (such as how to entertain their audience), and attempt online revisions to correct errors in substance and mechanics. Children who struggle with one or more of these subprocesses beyond the level of their grade-equivalent peers should receive more intensive, targeted instruction. Importantly, evidence-based recommendations for composing have not been found to be grade specific, meaning they work well with both younger and older children who struggle to coordinate one or more aspects of the writing process. We describe methods for older students (grades 4 through high school) next, noting when researchers have specifically included younger participants in their investigations.

Evidence-Based Recommendations for Teaching Composing

So few meta-analyses of writing have been conducted that one can list them as they have appeared in the literature in a few citations: Hillocks, 1986; Bangert-Drowns, 1993; Gersten and Baker, 2001; Graham and Harris, 2003; Goldring, Russell, and Cook, 2003; Graham, 2006; and Graham and Perin, 2007a. The meta-analyses vary from inclusive reviews (e.g., Graham & Perin, 2007a; Hillocks, 1986) to studies with constrained topics (e.g., Bangert-Drowns, 1993, focused on the effects of word processing). Of these studies, Graham and Perin's recent findings provide the most useful information for practitioners, based in large part on their methodology in which they partitioned the effects (i.e., effect sizes) of moderating variables from the effect sizes of other variables. A summary of the evidence-based findings is presented in Table 9.1, which highlights key findings from their meta-analysis within a framework of a tiered approach to instruction.

Strategy Instruction

There now exists a large body of research, with students in both general and special education settings, supporting the efficacy of teaching writing strategies, which involves teaching students how to accomplish specific writing tasks, such as brainstorming or organizing ideas when planning or adding or modifying ideas when revising. Strategies are typically demonstrated in specific writing genres (e.g., compare–contrast) or writing forms (e.g., friendly letters). Teachers generally model problem-solving behaviors that writers use as they approach the writing task (Collins, 1998; Tompkins, 2004), demonstrating by thinking aloud the steps they engage in while composing. In addition, mnemonics may be used to remind students of text structure or to follow a series of steps when engaged in either planning or revising processes (e.g., Schumaker & Lyerla's, 1991, paragraph-writing strategy or a more general revising schema, "compare–diagnose–operate," by Scardamalia & Bereiter, 1985). According to Graham and Perin's 2007a study, strategy instruction is a highly effective approach for students from the fourth through the tenth grade (weighted effect size = 0.62 in 12 studies).

TABLE 9.1. Summary of Evidence-Based Composing Interventions

Evaluated at which grade level?	Type of intervention	Description of implementation	Suggested tier	Typical areas of outcomes
4–10	Writing strategies	Involves teaching the steps in the process of writing a quality essay or narrative as well as management of the overall writing and task environment. Overall effect size = 0.62.	2 or 3	Length, structure, and quality of the genre
2–8	Writing strategies with self-regulation	Students learn how to set goals, self-monitor, provide self-instructions, and/or reinforce themselves to regulate their use of the target strategies, the task, and their behaviors while learning the writing strategy. Effect size = 1.14.	3	Length, structure, and quality of the genre
5–12	Summarization	Implies teaching a specific process for writing summaries of texts that students read; however, specific methods vary considerably, ranging from explicit strategies to systematically fading good models of summaries. Effect size = 0.82.	2 or 3	Structure and quality of summaries
4–high school	Writing with peers	Refers to an instructional arrangement rather than a specific approach. Students work in pairs or small groups to talk about and help each other with one or more aspects of the writing task. Effect size = 0.75.	2 or 3	Improvement will correspond with the focus of the intervention

(continued)

213

TABLE 9.1. (continued)

Evaluated at which grade level?	Type of intervention	Description of implementation	Suggested tier	Typical areas of outcomes
4–12	Word processing	Refers to a mode of composing rather than a specific approach. An obvious advantage is that students can revise and edit their compositions more easily than for papers composed by hand. Effect size = 0.55.	2 or 3	Length and quality, especially if combined with instruction in revising
4–9	Prewriting	This includes group and individual planning before composing. Strategy instruction may be used to enhance prewriting activities, such as how to select and organize ideas that have been brainstormed on a given topic. Effect size = 0.32.	2	Improvement will correspond with the depth of the intervention
7–11	Inquiry activities	Specific activities (e.g., Hillock's shell game) engage students in targeted goals (e.g., using similes) to help them develop ideas and content for a particular writing task, such as narration. Effect size = 0.32.	2	Varies with the targeted element

214

Self-Regulated Strategy Instruction

A form of strategy instruction developed by Harris and Graham and referred to as self-regulated strategy development (SRSD) emphasizes students' strategic behaviors, self-regulation skills, and motivational dispositions (Santangelo, Harris, & Graham, 2008). In this approach, students learn procedures for regulating the writing process along with information how to accomplish specific writing tasks, such as planning expository or persuasive essays. Students learn how to set goals, self-monitor, provide self-instructions, and reinforce themselves to regulate their use of the target strategies, the task, and their behaviors, all to advance the important skill of self-regulation. Teachers scaffold instruction so that the responsibility for recruiting and using the writing strategies, accompanying knowledge and skills, and self-regulation procedures gradually shifts from the teacher to students. Importantly, the effect size reported in Graham and Perin's (2007a) meta-analysis (1.14 in eight studies) provides support for adding self-regulation to strategy instruction because it resulted in improved writing outcomes over strategy instruction in isolation. In addition, recent SRSD studies with children in second and third grades have shown strong outcomes (Graham, Harris, & Mason, 2005; Harris, Graham, & Mason, 2006).

Summarization

Teachers may assign students the task of writing summaries for a variety of reasons, ranging from the belief that it encourages active, purposeful reading (Kirkland & Saunders, 1991) to the notion that it facilitates students' understanding of the relationships among main and subordinate ideas (Armbruster, Anderson, & Ostertag, 1987). Writing summaries while reading may also help students acquire and organize information (Hammann & Stevens, 2003), which in turn may facilitate their ability to acquire knowledge that is needed for other expository writing tasks. In the research cited by Graham and Perin (2007a), only four studies met standards for inclusion in the meta-analysis. Therefore, we recommend that teachers incorporate basic principles of explicit instruction (i.e., the use of models or specific product goals) to ensure that summarization instruction is beneficial for their students.

Writing with Peers

Most teachers who follow a Writer's Workshop approach encourage students to work with each other for at least part of the writing process. Students may brainstorm together, seek reaction to ideas they might write about, and read each other's compositions either as an interested listener or as a reflective reader who uses a rubric to evaluate an essay to make suggestions on various ways to improve specific elements. Moreover, despite the limitation that peers typically are not as effective at conferencing as teachers (Dean, 2006), Graham and Perin found a large weighted mean effect size of 0.75 across seven studies for the use of peers when writing. Future research will be needed to differentiate the most effective roles for students to engage in when working together.

Word Processing

A fairly large body of research (18 studies from Graham and Perin's meta-analysis) has been conducted on the use of computers in composing, and the mean weighted effect size of 0.55 indicates that word processing does have an advantage over composing by hand. One must assume that students are also proficient in using word processing for this to be beneficial; moreover, students who struggle with typing are less likely to benefit from this modality (MacArthur, 2006).

Prewriting

In Graham and Perin's recent work, five studies focused on individual or group activities for planning in advance of composing, with a mean weighted effect size of 0.32. These activities may be done to help students brainstorm ideas as well as to prioritize which ideas may best serve rhetorical purposes for the given task and ways to organize ideas once selected. Strategy instruction and SRSD strategies may enhance prewriting.

Inquiry Activities

Hillocks described inquiry activities in his original meta-analysis in 1986. He also describes several in a recent text on narrative writing (2007), in which students are given specific lessons that focus on objectives such as learning how to create dialogue to represent the internal states of characters, which is begun in response to a series of age-appropriate scenarios for students to react to, through a series of scaffolds that the teacher provides across one or more lessons. The mean weighted effect size for inquiry activities was 0.32.

Summary

The suggestions for helping students improve their composing abilities are primarily based on the recent meta-analysis by Graham and Perin (2007a). One disadvantage in calling attention to these specific instructional methods is that other potentially promising approaches are omitted, such as the use of procedural facilitators (i.e., written reminders, or cues on handouts, to prompt students to follow routines that trigger subprocesses involved in composing) or the use of text structure (e.g., whole–whole or block pattern vs. a point-by-point comparison in compare/contrast essays), neither of which had an adequate number of methodologically strong research studies to be adequately critiqued in the recent meta-analysis. A second word of caution in interpreting this set of recommendations is that they are not mutually exclusive. Many strategy instruction studies, including those involving SRSD, have focused on sentence combining, prewriting, or using peers, and word processing has been used so frequently in investigations on writing that it seems ubiquitous for teachers, at least those with adequate instructional resources. Teachers may wish to combine several approaches that make sense in the context of their classroom demands and based on the needs of their students.

Regardless of the approach chosen and its associated effect size, teachers can never be certain that any given approach will be effective for any given student. It is important, therefore, especially within an RTI approach, that the effects of interventions be evaluated for individual students. We now turn our attention to evaluating the effects of interventions for individual students.

EVALUATING THE EFFECTS OF INTERVENTIONS FOR INDIVIDUAL STUDENTS

A cornerstone of special education is individualization of instruction, but how can individualization be coupled with evidenced-based instruction? If an intervention has empirical support, is it necessary to examine its effectiveness for an individual?

These questions, and their answers, reflect the difference between *nomothetic* and *idiographic* approaches to the study of human behavior (see Deno, 1990, for a description of these concepts within the context of special education). A nomothetic approach entails a search for rules or laws that govern the behavior of a specific group or population of persons. These laws or rules cannot be extended to any single individual in the group but can be said to describe the general behavior of the group. Via a nomothetic approach we seek to establish an evidence base. We search for evidence that an intervention works for a particular group of students (e.g., students with learning disabilities), but such evidence does not tell us whether the intervention works for any given student within that group. An idiographic approach entails a search for rules or laws that govern the behavior of a single individual. These rules or laws cannot be extended to a larger group but rather describe the general behavior of the individual. Via an idiographic approach we seek to individualize. We search for evidence that an intervention works for a particular student, but such evidence does not tell us whether the intervention works for students in general.

In an RTI instructional framework, nomothetic and idiographic approaches are combined. Interventions with an evidence base are the place for teachers to begin when designing instructional programs. The effectiveness of these interventions for the individual is measured by collecting data reflecting the individual's response to the instruction. The first part of this chapter focused on recommendations for Tier 1 through Tier 3 interventions in writing. In this section we turn our attention to the use of a progress monitoring system called curriculum-based measurement (CBM) to evaluate the individual's response to writing interventions.

Curriculum-Based Measurement

CBM is a method for monitoring the academic progress of students on an ongoing basis (Deno, 1985). In a CBM approach to progress monitoring, student performance is sampled on an ongoing and frequent basis (e.g., once per week for an entire school year). Scores from the samples are graphed to create a picture of student growth over time. The graphs are used to inform instructional decision making. If a student is progressing at a desired and predicted rate, the instruction continues as is. If a student is not progressing at a desired and expected rate, a change in instruction is made, such as moving from a Tier 1 to a Tier 2 approach to instruction. Such a change might involve modification of the current instructional program or implementing an entirely new instructional program. After instruction is modified or changed, data continue to be collected to examine the effects of the change on the student's rate of progress.

One unique characteristic of CBM is the emphasis placed on the development of measures that are technically adequate and practically feasible (Deno, 1985). CBM measures are designed to sample performance in a broad domain rather than to sample subsets of skills within that domain (Deno, 1985; Fuchs & Deno, 1991); thus, the measures must be valid and reliable indicators of performance in the domain. For example, CBM writing measures are designed to sample global writing performance rather than subsets of writing skills such as grammar, word choice, theme, or coherence. For the measures to be global indicators, evidence must exist that they consistently relate to other measures of writing performance, and that improvement on the measures represents improvement in the general domain. Yet CBM measures must also be practical; that is, they must be time efficient, inexpensive, easy to administer, and easy to score if teachers are to administer and score them weekly over an extended period of time (Deno, 1985).

In the 1980s, an initial set of CBM measures in reading, written expression, and spelling were developed by Deno and colleagues through the Institute for Research on Learning Disabilities (Deno, 1985). Since that time, a large body of research has addressed the development and use of CBM measures in reading, written expression, spelling, mathematics, and content learning. Much of this research has been summarized elsewhere (Espin & Tindal, 1998; Foegen, Jiban, & Deno, 2007; Marston, 1989; McMaster & Espin, 2007; Stecker, Fuchs, & Fuchs, 2005; Wayman, Wallace, Wiley, Ticha, & Espin, 2007). In this portion of the chapter, we briefly review the CBM research as it relates to writing. (For a more detailed review of the research on writing, see McMaster & Espin, 2007.) We organize our content on CBM according to the steps involved in its implementation: selecting measures, establishing a current level of performance, setting goals, collecting and graphing the data, and using the data to evaluate the effects of instruction. We end with a case study illustrating the use of CBM as part of an RTI approach in writing.

Selecting Measures

The first step in the implementation of CBM progress monitoring is the selection of a measure. The selection of an appropriate measure will depend on the age and skill level of the student and will involve decisions regarding (1) type of prompt, (2) sample duration, and (3) scoring procedures to be used. Recall that the measures used in CBM progress monitoring must be reliable and valid indicators of generalized writing performance and progress and at the same time must be time efficient for teachers.

In a recent review of the literature on CBM in writing (CBM-W), McMaster and Espin (2007) reported on the technical adequacy (e.g., reliability, criterion-related validity, and sensitivity to growth) of various measures. Among the conclusions from the review, three are relevant to this chapter. First, research to date suggests that longer writing samples and more complex scoring procedures are needed to produce reliable and valid scores for older and more skilled students. Second, the criterion validity—the relation between CBM-W measures and other measures of writing—across studies is moderate, although similar to or better than criterion validity for other writing measures. The moderate criterion validity of writing measures in general illustrates the problems associated with defining and measuring "good writing." Finally, few researchers have examined sensitivity of CBM-W measures to progress or growth in writing. Most validity studies have focused on the measures as indicators of performance at a specific time.

These conclusions translate into three cautionary notes as teachers select and implement CBM-W measures. First, selection of measures will depend on the characteristics of the students in the class. Second, to measure performance and progress in writing, teachers must think carefully about how they or their district define good writing. Finally, because little work has been done on the use of the measures as progress measures, some information (e.g., typical growth rates) may need to be determined locally. In sum, we encourage teachers to keep abreast of continued research on the development of CBM-W measures. We base the remainder of the chapter on what is known to date and highlight areas where caution is needed.

What Type of Prompt to Use?

In Table 9.2, we list types of prompts, writing durations, and scoring procedures that have yielded reasonable reliability and criterion validity coefficients for students at different grade levels. For lists of sample prompts, readers are referred to the following websites: Research Institute on Progress Monitoring (*www.progressmonitoring.org*), Write Source (*www.thewritesource.com*), and NWREL (*www.nwrel.org/assessment/pdfGeneral/Prompts_BlowingAway.pdf*).

The format used most often for CBM-W is to provide the students with a starter phrase or sentence, a short amount of time to think about what to write (30 seconds to 1 minute), and a set amount of time to write. Little research has been conducted on differences related to the format of the prompt, for example, whether it is better to provide 30 seconds or 1 minute to think, to provide a starter phrase ("It was a dark and stormy night and ... ") or a sentence ("It was a dark and stormy night when I went outside"), or what the optimal content for the prompt is. For purposes of progress monitoring, 30 seconds appears to be sufficient time for students to formulate ideas for writing in response to the prompt.[3] We have noted few differences related to the use of an open-ended phrase (i.e., a sentence starter) versus a sentence. Marston and Deno (1981) found high correlations between the words written and words spelled correctly in writing samples elicited by story starters, topic sentences, and picture stimuli. Few other studies have systematically investigated the format of the prompt.

With regard to the content of the prompts, common sense dictates that prompts be of a generic nature, not requiring specific background knowledge. For example, if one were to use the prompt "Yesterday we had a baseball game and ... ," scores on the writing sample might reflect not only writing performance but also background knowledge related to the game of baseball. The influence of background knowledge in this context would

---

[3]However, in nonassessment conditions, substantially more time is typically, and appropriately, devoted to planning.

TABLE 9.2. CBM Writing Tasks, Durations, and Scoring Procedures by Grade Level

Grade level	Type of prompt	Duration	Scoring procedures	References
1–2	Sentence copying	3–5 min	WW, WSC, CWS	Lembke, Deno, & Hall (2003); McMaster, Du, & Petursdottir (2009)
	Sentence dictation	3–5 min	WW, WSC, CWS	Lembke, Deno, & Hall (2003)
	picture–cord	3–5 min	WW, WSC, CWS	McMaster et al. (2009)
	Narrative	3–5 min	WW, WSC, CWS	Deno, Marston, & Mirkin (1982); Jewell & Malecki (2005); McMaster et al. (2009); Parker, Tindal, & Hasbrouk (1991); Videen, Deno, & Marston (1982)
3–4	Narrative	3–5 min	CWS, CIWS	Deno et al. (1982); Jewell & Malecki (2005); McMaster & Campbell (2008); Parker et al. (1991); Tindal & Parker (1991); Videen et al. (1982); Weissenburger & Espin (2005)
5–6	Narrative	3–5 min	CWS, CIWS	Deno et al. (1982); Jewell & Malecki (2005); McMaster & Campbell (2008); Parker et al. (1991); Tindal & Parker (1989, 1991); Videen et al. (1982)
	Expository	5 min	CWS, CIWS	McMaster & Campbell (2008)
7–8	Narrative	5–10 min	CWS, CIWS, %CWS	Espin et al. (2000); Jewell & Malecki (2005); McMaster & Campbell (2008); Parker et al. (1991); Tindal & Parker (1989); Weissenburger & Espin (2005)
	Expository	5–10 min	CWS, CIWS	Espin, De La Paz, Scierka, & Roelofs (2005); Espin et al. (2000); McMaster & Campbell (2008)
10–11	Narrative	7–10 min	CWS, CIWS	Espin et al. (1999); Espin et al. (2008); Parker et al. (1991); Weissenburger & Espin (2005)

Note. WW, words written; WSC, words spelled correctly; CWS, correct word sequences; CIWS, correct minus incorrectly word sequences.

introduce error into scores comparing groups of students, perhaps inflating scores for those with more knowledge and deflating scores for those with less knowledge of baseball. Similarly, background knowledge would introduce error into the repeated measurement scores for an individual student, with the baseball prompt score perhaps being higher or lower than the scores generated by other prompts. In general, it is best to reduce, to the extent possible, the need for specific background knowledge to respond to the writing prompt.

A small amount of research has been conducted on differences related to the genre of writing (e.g., narrative vs. persuasive vs. expository) elicited by the prompt. Although narrative prompts (i.e., also referred to as story starters) have been the most commonly used stimuli for CBM writing measures, several groups of researchers (e.g., Deno, Mirkin, & Marston, 1980; Espin, De La Paz, Scierka, & Roelofs, 2005; Espin et al., 2000; Marston & Deno, 1981; McMaster & Campbell, 2008) have examined the technical adequacy of other types of prompts. In general, the results of these studies reveal few differences in the validity and reliability of CBM-W measures related to genre of prompt. This is not to say that there are no differences in student writing under the two prompt conditions. For example, Espin et al. (2000) found that students tended to write less when given a prompt designed to elicit descriptive writing versus narrative writing; however, the reliability and validity of the writing samples produced under the two prompt conditions were similar. Anecdotally, we have noted that it is somewhat easier to produce multiple parallel prompts (i.e., those that do not require specific background knowledge) when the prompts are narrative than when they are expository. However, there are other factors to consider, including the face validity of the data produced by the measures. For older students, teachers and students may more easily accept essay prompts because they fit more closely with the curriculum or with state standards. For example, Espin et al. (2005) made use of persuasive essay prompts modeled after those required to pass the state's competency test in writing. In this study, prompts were designed to minimize the need for specific background knowledge, for example "Think about rules you think are not fair. In an essay, state what rules you think should be changed and why they should be changed."

In sum, more research is needed on the effects of different prompts and prompt formats on the technical adequacy of the writing samples produced by students and on the implementation of the measurement system by teachers. However, based on our experience and the studies referenced previously, we recommend that students be given either a phrase or sentence to elicit either narrative or expository writing, that the prompts be designed to reduce reliance on background knowledge, and that students be given 30 seconds to think before they begin writing, unless students have been explicitly taught to plan before writing, in which case 1 minute is appropriate. The amount of time students should be given to write varies with age, as is discussed in the following section.

Up to this point, we have discussed CBM-W prompts for students who have developed basic writing skills. Recently, researchers have begun to examine CBM-W measures for beginning writers. These measures have included word and sentence dictation (Lembke, Deno, & Hall, 2003), word and sentence copying (Lembke et al., 2003; McMaster, Du, & Petursdottir, 2009), and the use of picture prompts (McMaster et al., 2009). Thus far, sentence-copying prompts appear to consistently yield reliable and valid scores and show sensitivity to growth. Copying tasks were developed based on evidence that transcription skills involved in copying relate strongly to writing composition (e.g., Berninger, Abbott, Abbott, Graham, & Richards, 2002; Graham et al., 1997; Graham et al., 2000) and that copying tasks could discriminate among students across a wide age range (Graham, Berninger, Weintraub, & Schafer, 1998). However, because the face validity of copying tasks as a writing measure might seem suspect to some teachers, other measures might also be considered, including "picture–word" (students are given lists of words paired with pictures, and they write sentences using those words) and narrative prompts, which have also yielded sufficiently reliable and valid scores (McMaster et al., 2009).

What Duration?

Whereas few differences have been found related to type of prompt, sample duration *has* been found to influence the technical adequacy of CBM-W measures. In the early research on CBM-W, Deno et al. (1980) found that for students in grades 3 to 6, a 3-minute writing sample tended to produce larger validity coefficients than a 1-minute sample, but that there were few differences between 3-, 4-, and 5-minute samples. At the secondary level, studies have revealed stronger reliabilities associated with longer sample durations (Espin et al., 2008; McMaster & Campbell, 2008; Weissenburger & Espin, 2005). Generally, 5- to 7-minute durations have yielded more reliable scores than shorter durations. Espin et al. (2008) recommended that 5 minutes be used for ongoing progress monitoring and 7 minutes for screening purposes or for fall, winter, spring benchmark testing. In Table 9.2, we have listed durations of writing samples for students at each grade level.

What Scoring Procedures?

Researchers have examined a variety of procedures for scoring CBM-W samples. Among these, the most commonly used procedures have been counting the number of total words written (WW) or the number of words spelled correctly (WSC). These two scoring procedures were found to be reasonably good predictors of general writing performance for elementary school students in the original CBM writing research (Deno, Marston, & Mirkin, 1982). However, more recent research has suggested that more complex scoring procedures (correct word sequence [CWS] and correct minus incorrect word sequence [CIWS]) may yield more reliable and valid scores than WW or WSC for both younger and older students (Espin, Scierka, Skare, & Halverson, 1999; Espin et al., 2000, 2008; Jewell & Malecki, 2005; McMaster & Campbell, 2008). Table 9.2 lists scoring procedures that have yielded reasonable technical adequacy at each grade level in past research. Some investigators have found percentage measures (e.g., %WSC and %CWS) to yield stronger reliability and validity coefficients for elementary and secondary students than straight counts (Jewell & Malecki, 2005; Parker, Tindal, & Hasbrouck, 1991; Tindal & Parker, 1989); however, percentage measures may not be optimal for progress monitoring. For example, if a student produces 10 WSC of 20 WW in fall and 50 WSC of 100 WW in spring, %WSC would not reflect this growth. Thus, we do not recommend using percentage measures for monitoring students' writing progress.

We next provide definitions of scoring procedures that have been frequently examined in CBM-W research. These definitions have been gleaned from the studies cited previously. Note that slight differences in scoring have been used across studies.

1. *Words written.* The number of words written in the sample. A "word" is defined as a sequence of letters separated by a space from another sequence of letters. In some studies, single-letter words are counted only when they are actual words (e.g., "I"), and other times they are always counted as words. When scoring by computer, single letters would be counted as words written.

2. *Words spelled correctly.* The number of correctly spelled words written in the sample. In some studies, words correct are counted regardless of whether they are used correctly within the context of the sentence (e.g., "I saw a bare when I was camping.") and in others only when the words are used correctly within the context. If scoring by computer, words would be counted as correct regardless of context.

3. *Correct word sequences* (Videen, Deno, & Marston, 1982). The number of adjacent correctly spelled words that are syntactically and semantically correct within the context of the sample. In some studies, CWS is calculated without regard to beginning capitalization and ending punctuation. In other studies, capitalization and punctuation are taken into account. Typically, the simpler approach (no regard for beginning capitalization and end punctuation) has been used for elementary school students and the more

complex approach for secondary school students. Examples for the simple (Example 1) and more complex (Example 2) approaches are as follows:

Example 1: "The^ man^ saw^ a bare in^ the^ tree^ and begn to^ run." CWS = 7

Example 2: "^The^ man^ saw^ a bare in^ the^ tree^ and begn to^ run^." CWS = 9

4. *Correct minus incorrect word sequences* (Espin et al., 1999). The number of incorrect word sequences subtracted from the number of correct sequences. Variation across studies relates to the variation cited previously for CWS. The number of CIWS from the prior examples would be 3 (7-4) and 5 (9-4), respectively.

We provide these tentative guidelines for scoring, although they are open to change based on future research. For beginning writers (K–2), for whom grammar, spelling, and punctuation are still under development and the goal often is to just produce words, we recommend scoring WSC. For older elementary school students (grades 3–5), for whom grammar, spelling, and punctuation take on a more important role, we recommend scoring CWS. Finally, for students in middle and high school, for whom grammar, spelling, and punctuation are tools to be used to enhance writing, we recommend use of CIWS.

Establishing Current Levels of Performance

Once a measure has been selected, the teacher determines the current level or baseline performance for the student. Within an RTI framework, information on the current level of performance is gathered within Tier 1, often as a part of district- or schoolwide screening. If the district or school does not conduct screening, teachers might be asked to collect screening data within their own classrooms. The screening data are used to determine which students might be at risk for writing difficulties.

Few guidelines exist related to the number of samples needed to reliable determine the student's current level of performance in writing. It stands to reason that multiple samples are likely to yield a more reliable value than a single sample, but how many samples is not known. We suggest that at least two or three writing samples be collected to obtain a reasonable estimate of a student's current level of performance. A mean or median can be calculated and used as the baseline or beginning point for setting a goal for the student.

Setting Goals

Within an RTI approach, frequent monitoring of students sometimes takes place in Tier 1 (e.g., those identified as at risk are monitored once a month) but almost always in Tiers 2 and 3, where monitoring is usually done on a weekly basis. In all three tiers, an important decision to be made is what level of performance and rate of improvement constitute success in the instructional program. If a student is not successful in the instructional program, a change in instruction is considered, which might involve a modification within the existing instructional program or a move to a different tier of instruction, where a student can receive more intensive, more differentiated instruction.

The desired level of performance and rate of improvement are represented on the CBM graph as a goal line extending from the current level of performance to the desired level of performance some weeks in the future. Within an RTI approach, the goal might be set for 8 weeks following placement into a given tier of instruction. Once in special education, the goal is usually set for the academic year.

To set a goal, three pieces of information are needed: the student's current level of performance, a desired level of performance and rate of progress, and the amount of time the student will be monitored. For example, if the student's current level of performance is 20 CWS in 3 minutes, an end-of-year goal might be set at 50 CWS in 3 minutes, representing a desired rate of growth of 1 CWS per week if the academic year is 30 weeks (50 − 20 = 30 CWS; 30 CWS/30 weeks = 1 CWS increase per week).

Despite the importance of goal setting within an RTI approach, there are, as of yet, no clear guidelines as to how much growth to expect from students in writing CBM. As with any progress monitoring approach, it is critical that goals be reasonable but also ambitious, such that it is possible that students will attain their goal but expectations are high. However, there are no nationally normed standards to aid in the determination of what is reasonable but ambitious. Factors that teachers might want to consider in goal selection are discussed next.

Published Norms

The teacher might wish to refer to norms that are published by companies that provide CBM-W materials and graphing options, such as AIMSweb (*www.aimsweb.com*). These norms are based on national samples aggregated over several years. If such data are used, the teacher may wish to examine the extent to which the demographics of the sample are representative of the demographics of his or her own students. The use of published norms are most appropriate when the materials used for monitoring are the same as those used to determine norms (e.g., the teacher uses AIMSweb for monitoring and uses the norms established by AIMSweb). One disadvantage of published materials is that the measures or scoring procedures may lag a few years behind the latest research. An advantage of published materials, of course, is that everything is ready-made for immediate use, reducing teacher time and effort, and that a normative database is provided.

Local School or District Norms

Another source of information for goal setting is local school or district norms. If the school or district collects benchmark data (e.g., in fall, winter, and spring) as a part of RTI, the teacher can use the data to determine reasonable long-term goals. For example, if district third graders perform, on average, 15 CWS on narrative prompts in the fall and 45 CWS in spring, the teacher might divide the difference (45 – 15 = 30) by the number of weeks between benchmark data collection to obtain the average growth rate for third graders (1 CWS per week), and use that as the expected rate of growth for the student.

An alternative approach to using district data is to tie the CBM-W scores to performance on state standards tests. For example, Espin et al. (2008) created Tables of Probable Success, in which scores on CBM-W for students in eighth grade were associated with the probability of passing the state standards test in writing. Teachers could use such tables to select scores that would represent reasonable goals, bringing their students closer to a level of performance that would predict success on a state test.

Classroom Data

A final option—using classroom data—may be especially desirable if school and district norms are not available (but might also be used in conjunction with such data if they are available). The teacher might monitor progress of his or her entire class and determine each student's rate of growth as well as the class average. The teacher could then use this information to decide on a reasonable rate of growth for individual students. For example, if average-performing writers are making a gain of 0.50 CWS per week, the teacher might consider this a reasonable but ambitious goal to set for a struggling writer.

Collecting Weekly Data

Administering and Scoring CBM-W on a Weekly Basis

A critical feature of CBM administration is that it is standardized (Deno & Fuchs, 1987). Administering CBM-W in a standardized way increases the

228 THE PROMISE OF RESPONSE TO INTERVENTION

likelihood of producing reliable data that are useful for making instructional decisions. If administration conditions change each time the measures are given, student performance might vary as a function of different administration conditions rather than of writing skill. The following administration instructions are taken from work on writing within the Research Institute on Progress Monitoring (*www.progressmonitoring.org*; see also McMaster & Campbell, 2008). The instructions are derived from earlier work conducted as a part of the Institute for Research on Learning Disabilities at the University of Minnesota (e.g., Deno et al., 1980; Videen et al., 1982).

Narrative and Expository Prompt Administration Instructions

1. Provide the students with a pencil and paper, with the prompt listed at the top of the paper or on the board for older students. Make sure the students have enough paper to continue writing for the entire duration.

2. Say to the students: "Today you are going to write a [story/essay]. Before you write, I want you to think about the [story/essay]. First you will think, then you will write. You will have [30 seconds or 1 minute] to think and [X] minutes to write. Do your best work. If you do not know how to spell a word, you should guess. Keep your pencils down and listen. Your story/essay will begin with … (*read the prompt*). You have [30 seconds or 1 minute] to think of a [story/essay] to go with your [story/essay] starter."

3. After [30 seconds or 1 minute], say, "Now you have [X] minutes to write. Keep writing until I tell you to stop. Are there any questions? You may begin."

4. Start your stopwatch immediately. During the administration, if you see a student put their pencil down and stop writing, give the classwide prompt: "Please continue writing until I tell you to stop."

5. After [X] minutes, say: "Stop, thank you; put your pencils down."[4]

Graphing the Weekly Data

Progress monitoring data are most useful for instructional decision making when student scores are graphed on regular basis. The graph allows the teacher to view and evaluate the student's overall progress. Because student performance may vary on a weekly basis for a variety of reasons (e.g., the specific writing prompt used, the student's background knowledge, the

---

[4]If students are to continue writing for instructional purposes, they may create a clear mark on their paper (e.g., "/") for scoring purposes and then continue composing.

student's physical and emotional condition on a given day), it is best to consider the overall trend in the data rather than to consider only individual data points. The data can be graphed by hand or using a spreadsheet program like Microsoft Excel.

Using the Data to Make Instructional Decisions

After collecting weekly data for a set period of time, a trend or slope line is drawn through the data and compared with the goal that set for the student. The teacher examines the graph to answer the following questions: (1) Is my student making sufficient progress to reach his or her goal? (2) Is there a need for an instructional change? Does that change involve movement to a different tier of instruction? (3) Is the instructional change effective?

There has been little research on the number of data points needed to obtain a reliable slope of performance in writing. In reading, collection of seven to 10 data points is often recommended (see review by Wayman et al., 2007, and chapter by Fuchs, 1989). Until specific research is conducted in writing, we suggest that teachers use the reading data as a guideline and collect seven to 10 data points before calculating the slope. If using a computer-graphing program, the slope can be drawn via the computer. If drawn by hand, the teachers can draw the slope using the split-middle method (White & Haring, 1980).

Once a slope is drawn through the data, the teacher compares the slope to the goal line. If the slope is steeper than or parallel to and above the goal line, the teacher might continue the existing instructional program for the student or move the student to a different tier (e.g., from Tier 2 back to Tier 1). If the slope is less steep than or parallel to but below the goal set for the student, the teacher might change the instructional program or move the student to a more intensive tier of instruction (e.g., from Tier 1 to Tier 2). The student's progress would then continue to be monitored to assess the effectiveness of the instructional change.

In the following case study, we provide an illustration of how a teacher uses CBM-W to monitor the progress of a struggling writer, Jamie.

Case Study

Tier 1: Universal Screening, Classwide Instruction, and Progress Monitoring

Jamie's school administers benchmark writing prompts to all students three times per year (fall, winter, and spring) in grades 2 through 5 as part of Tier 1 universal screening. During the second week of September, teachers group-administer three writing prompts across 3 days, score them for CWS, and record the mean of the three scores as the fall score. Jamie's teacher, Mrs. Penn, examines her class data and sees that Jamie, her lowest performing writer, scored 10 CWS compared with the fifth-grade class mean of 40 CWS. Because Jamie is at risk for difficulty in learning to write, Mrs. Penn will monitor Jamie's weekly progress as a part of the RTI process used in the district.

Mrs. Penn first sets a goal for Jamie. Based on grade-level CBM-W data the school has been collecting for several years, Mrs. Penn expects fifth graders to write, on average, 60 CWS by the end of the school year. This means that, on average, the class needs to improve by 0.54 CWS per week. If Jamie improved by 0.54 CWS per week, he would be producing only about 30 CWS at the end of the year (37 weeks from now). Jamie's teacher decides to set a more ambitious goal (1 CWS per week). Mrs. Penn determines Jamie's goal to be 47 CWS (10 + [1 CWS × 37 weeks]). She plots this number on the graph and inserts a goal line from Jamie's baseline score to the goal (see Figure 9.1).

Mrs. Penn monitors Jamie's progress on a weekly basis for the first 8 weeks of Tier 1 writing instruction, which consists of a Writer's Workshop approach to instruction 30 to 45 minutes each day. At least twice a week, students work on their writing assignments in pairs. To determine whether Jamie is making sufficient progress, Mrs. Penn examines Jamie's slope of progress in relation to the goal line (see Figure 9.1, Tier 1). After 8 weeks, it is clear that Jamie is making very little, if any, progress. Mrs. Penn determines that if she doesn't make an instructional change, Jamie will not be able to meet his end-of-year goal. She consults with the special education teacher and literacy specialist, and they decide that Jamie will receive a Tier 2 writing intervention.

Tier 2: Small-Group, Targeted Instruction

Mrs. Penn examines samples of Jamie's writing (both from CBM writing prompts and class work). Mrs. Penn notes that Jamie's stories and essays are much shorter than his peers and that his samples contain more misspelled words than she would have predicted from his typically successful weekly spelling test results. Mrs. Penn asks Jamie to read some of his entries aloud to her and determines that Jamie is able to elaborate on several of his ideas with prompting. Mrs. Penn suspects that Jamie has an adequate fund of knowledge on most topics but is generally not able to independently retrieve and translate his ideas into his writing. Jamie's limited planning skills are posing significant barriers to the quantity and quality of his writing, and Jamie may benefit from more explicit instruction in planning. Mrs. Penn decides to try a more structured approach to planning, using a formal curriculum, and decides to deliver this instruction in a small group, including

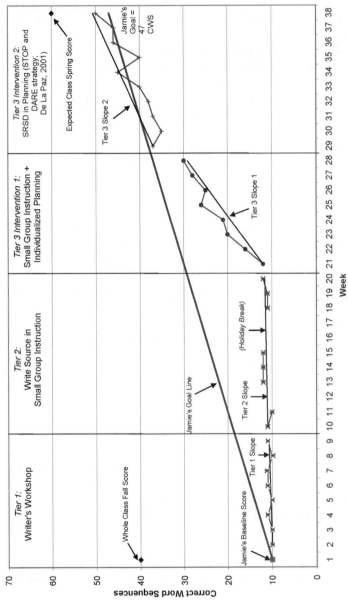

FIGURE 9.1. Jamie's writing progress (SRSD, self-regulated strategy development; CWS, correct word sequence).

Jamie and three other children who have also been struggling with generating ideas.

Jamie participates in small-group instruction for 30 minutes per day using the *Write Source* curriculum with its accompanying embedded 6 *Trait* model, and Mrs. Penn continues to monitor Jamie's progress. After an additional 8 weeks, Mrs. Penn, the special education teacher, and the literacy specialist again examine Jamie's slope of progress in relation to his goal line. Although Jamie appears to be making some progress, his current growth rate is far below what it needs to be to meet his end-of-year goal. Whereas Jamie's planning and elaboration of ideas have improved somewhat, this improvement is not translating to increased progress on the CBM-W measures (see Figure 9.1, Tier 2 intervention).

Tier 3

Mrs. Penn and her colleagues decide to refer Jamie for a special education evaluation. In the meantime, they agree that Jamie should receive more intensive, individualized instruction. For 30 minutes each day, Jamie works with the special education resource teacher, Mr. Marks, who also teaches Jamie specific mini-lessons such as webbing and several graphic organizers to help him elaborate his ideas before he writes, selecting and individualizing literature-based writing lessons from educators such as Tompkins (2004) and Routman (2000). During 8 weeks of this specialized instruction, Jamie begins to make substantial progress, although his performance level is still far below his goal (see Figure 9.1, Tier 3 Intervention 1).

Mr. Marks observes that Jamie has become somewhat better at planning but realizes that Jamie remains dependent upon his help to organize his ideas before writing. He teaches Jamie and another student an SRSD strategy to aid them in planning and composing persuasive essays (De La Paz, 2001) and implements this approach in a peer-mediated format for the last 8 weeks of school. Jamie not only becomes self-sufficient in planning, but his teachers observe a substantial jump in his performance level on the CBM-W measure (see Figure 9.1, Tier 3 Intervention 2). He continues receiving writing instruction in the special education resource room and is very close to his writing goal by the end of his fifth-grade year.

Summary

In summary, much work remains to be done in the area of writing with regard to an RTI approach. First, although we have a substantial knowledge base regarding some types of instruction (e.g., self-regulated strategies for composition), we have limited knowledge in many other key areas (transcription, grammar, summarization, working with peers) at several grade levels, including adolescence. Especially absent from the extant research base is information about various writing programs and models that can be used to differentiate Tier 2 from Tier 3 interventions. Future research that addresses this need will be useful in an RTI context for schooling.

Second, despite the research base available for CBM-W, there is still much to be learned, especially regarding its use within an RTI framework. Many of the gaps in knowledge have already been discussed in previous sections. However, we return to three important issues here. First, more work is needed with very young (K–2) and older (grades 10–12) students. Second, what constitutes good writing is a topic open to various interpretations. Finally, given the importance of rate of growth within RTI decision making, more work is needed related to the validity and reliability of the slopes generated by CBM-W data and on determination of reasonable but ambitious goals.

REFERENCES

Andrews, R., Torgerson, C., Beverton, S., Freeman, A., Locke, T., Low, G., et al. (2006). The effect of grammar teaching on writing development. *British Educational Research Journal, 32*, 39–55.

Armbruster, B. B., Anderson, T. H., & Ostertag, J. (1987). Does text structure/summarization instruction facilitate learning from expository text? *Reading Research Quarterly, 22*, 331–346.

Bangert-Drowns, R. L. (1993). The word processor as an instructional tool: A meta-analysis of word processing in writing instruction. *Review of Educational Research, 63*, 69–93.

Bangert-Drowns, R. L., Hurley, M. M., & Wilkinson, B. (2004). The effects of school-based writing-to-learn interventions on academic achievement: A meta-analysis. *Review of Educational Research, 74*, 29–58.

Berninger, V. (2008). Evidence-based written language instruction during early and middle childhood. In R. Morris & N. Mather (Eds.), *Evidence-based interventions for students with learning and behavioral challenges* (pp. 215–235). Mahwah, NJ: Erlbaum.

Berninger, V. W., Abbott, R. D., Abbott, S. P., Graham, S., & Richards, T. (2002). Writing and reading: Connections between language by hand and language by eye. *Journal of Learning Disabilities, 35*, 39–56.

California Department of Education. (1999). *Reading/language arts framework for California public schools*. Sacramento, CA: Author.

Collins, J. L. (1998). *Strategies for struggling writers*. New York: Guilford Press.

Council for Exceptional Children, Division for Learning Disabilities. (2007). *Thinking about response to intervention and learning disabilities: A teacher's guide*. Arlington, VA: Author.

Culham, R. (2003). *6+1 Traits of writing: The complete guide grades 3 and up*. Jefferson City, MO: Scholastic.

De La Paz, S. (2001). Stop and dare: A persuasive writing strategy. *Intervention in School and Clinic, 36,* 234–243.

De La Paz, S. (2005). Reasoning instruction and writing strategy mastery in culturally and academically diverse middle school classrooms. *Journal of Experimental Psychology, 91,* 310–311.

Dean, D. (2006). *Strategic writing: The writing process and beyond in the secondary English classroom.* Urbana, IL: National Council of Teachers of English.

Deno, S. L. (1985). Curriculum-Based Measurement: The emerging alternative. *Exceptional Children, 52,* 219–232.

Deno, S. L. (1990). Individual differences and individual difference: The essential difference of special education. *Journal of Special Education, 24,* 160–173.

Deno, S. L., & Fuchs, L. S. (1987). Developing curriculum-based measurement systems for data-based special education problem solving. *Focus on Exceptional Children, 19*(8), 1–15.

Deno, S. L., Marston, D., & Mirkin, P. (1982). Valid measurement procedures for continuous evaluation of written expression. *Exceptional Children, 48,* 368–371.

Deno, S. L., Mirkin, P., & Marston, D. (1980). *Relationships among simple measures of written expression and performance on standardized achievement tests* (Research Rep. No. 22). Minneapolis: University of Minnesota, Institute for Research on Learning Disabilities.

Dyson, A. (1984). Learning to write/learning to do school: Emergent writers' interprétations of school literacy tasks. *Research in the Teaching of English, 18,* 233–264.

Englert, C. S., Raphael, T. E., Anderson, L. M., Anthony, H. M., & Stevens, D. D. (1991). Making strategies and self-talk visible: Writing instruction in regular and special education classrooms. *American Educational Research Journal, 28,* 337–373.

Espin, C., Wallace, T., Campbell, H., Lembke, E. S., Long, J. D., & Ticha, R. (2008). Curriculum-based measurement in writing: Predicting the success of high-school students on state standards tests. *Exceptional Children, 74,* 174–193.

Espin, C. A., De La Paz, S., Scierka, B. J., & Roelofs, L. (2005). Relation between curriculum-based measures in written expression and quality and completeness of expository writing for middle-school students. *Journal of Special Education, 38,* 208–217.

Espin, C. A., Scierka, B. J., Skare, S., & Halverson, N. (1999). Criterion-related validity of curriculum-based measures in writing for secondary students. *Reading and Writing Quarterly, 15,* 5–27.

Espin, C. A., Skare, S., Shin, J., Deno, S. L., Robinson, S., & Brenner, B. (2000). Identifying indicators of growth in written expression for middle-school students. *Journal of Special Education, 34,* 140–153.

Espin, C. A., & Tindal, G. (1998). Curriculum-based measurement for secondary students. In M. R. Shinn (Ed.), *Advanced applications of curriculum-based measurement* (pp. 214–253). New York: Guilford Press.

Flower, L. S., & Hayes, J. R. (1980). The dynamics of composing: Making plans and juggling constraints. In L. W. Gregg & E. R. Steinberg (Eds.), *Cognitive processes in writing* (pp. 31–50). Hillsdale, NJ: Erlbaum.

Foegen, A., Jiban, C., & Deno, S. (2007). Progress monitoring measures in mathematics: A review of the literature. *Journal of Special Education, 41,* 121–139.

Frank, L. A. (1992). Writing to be read: Young writers' ability to demonstrate audience awareness when evaluated by their readers. *Research in the Teaching of English, 26,* 277–298.

Fuchs, L. S. (1989). Evaluating solutions: Monitoring progress and revising intervention plans. In M. Shinn (Ed.), *Curriculum-based measurement: Assessing special children* (pp. 153–181). New York: Guilford Press.

Fuchs, L. S., & Deno, S. L. (1991). Paradigmatic distinctions between instructionally relevant measurement models. *Exceptional Children, 57,* 488–499.

Gersten, R., & Baker, S. (2001). Teaching expressive writing to students with learning disabilities: A meta-analysis. *Elementary School Journal, 101,* 251–271.

Goldring, A., Russell, M., & Cook, A. (2003). The effects of computers on student writing: A meta-analysis of studies from 1992–2002. *Journal of Technology, Learning, and Assessment, 2,* 1–51.

Graham, S. (2006). Strategy instruction and the teaching of writing: A meta-analysis. In C. MacArthur, S. Graham, & J. Fitzgerald (Eds.), *Handbook of writing research* (pp. 187–207). New York: Guilford Press.

Graham, S., Berninger, V., & Weintraub, N. (2001, September). Which manuscript letters do primary grade children write legibly? *Journal of Educational Psychology, 93*(3), 488–497.

Graham, S., Berninger, V., Weintraub, N., & Schafer, W. (1998). Development of handwriting speed and legibility in grades 1–9. *Journal of Educational Research, 92,* 42–52.

Graham, S., Berninger, V. W., Abbott, R. D., Abbott, S., & Whitaker, D. (1997). The role of mechanics in composing of elementary school students: A new methodological approach. *Journal of Educational Psychology, 89,* 170–182.

Graham, S., & Harris, K. R. (2003). Students with learning disabilities and the process of writing: A meta-analysis of SRSD studies. In H. L. Swanson, K. R. Harris, & S. Graham (Eds.), *Handbook of learning disabilities* (pp. 323–344). New York: Guilford Press.

Graham, S., Harris, K. R., & Fink, B. (2000). Is handwriting causally related to learning to write? Treatment of handwriting problems in beginning writers. *Journal of Educational Psychology, 92,* 620–633.

Graham, S., Harris, K. R., & Mason, L. (2005). Improving the writing performance, knowledge, and self-efficacy of struggling young writers: The effects of self-regulated strategy development. *Contemporary Educational Psychology, 30,* 207–241.

Graham, S., & Perin, D. (2007a). A meta-analysis of writing instruction for adolescent students. *Journal of Educational Psychology, 99,* 445–476.

Graham, S., & Perin, D. (2007b). *Writing next: Effective strategies to improve writing of adolescents in middle and high schools—A report to Carnegie Corporation of New York.* Washington, DC: Alliance for Excellent Education.

Graves, D. H., & Murray, D. M. (1980). Revision: In the Writer's Workshop and in the classroom. *Journal of Education, 162,* 38–56.

Gregg, N., & Mather, N. (2002). School is fun at recess: Informal analyses of written language for students with learning disabilities. *Journal of Learning Disabilities, 35,* 7–22.

Hammann, L., & Stevens, R. J. (2003). Instructional approaches to improving students' writing of compare–contrast essays: An experimental study. *Journal of Literacy Research, 35,* 731–756.

Hand, B., Prain, V., & Yore, L. (2001). Sequential writing tasks' influence on science learning. In G. Rijlaarsdam (Series Ed.) & P. Tynjälä, L. Mason & K. Lonka (Volume Eds.), *Studies in writing: Volume 7. Writing as a learning tool: Integrating theory and practice* (pp. 105–129). Dordrecht, the Netherlands: Kluwer Academic.

Harris, K. R., Graham, S., & Mason, L. H. (2006). Improving the writing, knowledge, and motivation of young struggling writers: The effects of self-regulated strategy development. *American Educational Research Journal, 43,* 295–340.

Hayes, J. R. (1996). A new framework for understanding cognition and affect in writing. In C. M. Levy & S. Ransdell (Eds.), *The science of writing: Theories, methods, individual differences, and applications* (pp. 1–27). Mahwah, NJ: Erlbaum.

Hayes, J. R., & Flower, L. S. (1980). Identifying the organization of writing processes. In L. W. Gregg & E. R. Steinberg (Eds.), *Cognitive processes in writing* (pp. 3–30). Hillsdale, NJ: Erlbaum.

Hillocks, G. (1986). *Research on written composition: New directions for teaching.* Urbana, IL: National Council of Teachers of English.

Hillocks, G. (2007). *Narrative writing: Learning a new model for teaching.* Portsmouth, NH: Heinemann.

Jewell, J., & Malecki, C. S. (2005). The utility of CBM written language indices: An investigation of production-dependent, production-independent, and accurate-production scores. *School Psychology Review, 34,* 27–44.

Kamberelis, G. (1999). Genre development and learning: Children writing stories, science reports, and poems. *Research in the Teaching of English, 33,* 403–460.

Kirkland, M. R., & Saunders, M. A. P. (1991). Maximizing student performance in summary writing: Managing cognitive load. *TESOL Quarterly, 25,* 105–121.

Lembke, E., Deno, S., & Hall, K. (2003). Identifying an indicator of growth in early writing proficiency for elementary school students. *Assessment for Effective Intervention, 28,* 23–35.

MacArthur, C. A. (2006). The effects of new technologies on writing and writing processes. In C. A. MacArthur, S. Graham, & J. Fitzgerald (Eds.), *Handbook of writing research* (pp. 248–262). New York: Guilford Press.

Marston, D. (1989). A curriculum-based measurement approach to assessing academic performance: What it is and why do it. In M. Shinn (Ed.), *Curriculum-based measurement: Assessing special children* (pp. 18–78). New York: Guilford Press.

Marston, D., & Deno, S. (1981). *The reliability of simple, direct measures of written expression* (Research Rep. No. 50). Minneapolis: University of Minnesota Institute for Research on Learning Disabilities.

McCutchen, D., Abbott, R. D., Green, L. B., Beretvas, N., Cox, S., Potter, N. S., et al. (2002). Beginning literacy: Links among teacher knowledge, teacher practice, and student learning. *Journal of Learning Disabilities, 35,* 69–86.

McMaster, K., & Espin, C. A. (2007). Literature synthesis on curriculum-based measurement in writing. *Journal of Special Education, 41,* 68–84.

McMaster, K. L., & Campbell, H. (2008). New and existing curriculum-based writing measures: Technical features within and across grades. *School Psychology Review, 37,* 550–566.

McMaster, K. L., Du, X., & Petursdottir, A. (2009). Technical features of curriculum-based measures for beginning writers. *Journal of Learning Disabilities, 42,* 41–60.

Northwest Regional Educational Laboratory, Assessment Program. (2005). *Seeing with new eyes: A guidebook on teaching and assessing beginning writers using the 6+1 Trait writing model.* Portland, OR: Author.

Parker, R., Tindal, G., & Hasbrouck, J. (1991). Progress monitoring with objective measures of writing performance for students with mild disabilities. *Exceptional Children, 58,* 61–73.

Pritchard, R. J., & Honeycutt, J. (2006). Process writing. In C. MacArthur, S. Graham, & J. Fitzgerald (Eds.), *Handbook of writing research* (pp. 275–290). New York: Guilford Press.

Routman, R. (2000). *Conversations: Strategies for teaching, learning, and evaluating.* Portsmouth, NH: Heinemann.

Saddler, B. (2007). Improving sentence construction skills through sentence-combining practice. In S. Graham, C. A. MacArthur, & J. Fitzgerald (Eds.), *Best practices in writing instruction* (pp. 163–178). New York: Guilford Press.

Santangelo, T., Harris, K., & Graham, S. (2008). Using self-regulated strategy development to support students who have "trubol giting thangs into werds." *Remedial and Special Education, 29,* 78–89.

Scardamalia, M., & Bereiter, C. (1985). Development of dialectical processes in composition. In D. Olson, N. Torrance, & A. Hildyard (Eds.), *Literacy, language, and learning: The nature and consequences of reading and writing* (pp. 307–329). Cambridge, UK: Cambridge University Press.

Schumaker, J. B., & Lyerla, K. D. (1991). *The paragraph writing strategy.* Lawrence: University of Kansas Center for Research on Learning.

Shanahan, T., & Shanahan, C. (2008). Teaching disciplinary literacy to adolescents: Rethinking content area literacy. *Harvard Educational Review, 78,* 40–59.

Spandel, V. (2005). *Creating writers through 6-trait writing: Assessment and instruction* (4th ed.). Boston: Pearson.

Stecker, P., Fuchs, L. S., & Fuchs, D. (2005). Using curriculum-based measurement to improve student achievement: Review of research. *Psychology in the Schools, 42,* 795–819.

Tindal, G., & Parker, R. (1989). Assessment of written expression for students in compensatory and special education programs. *Journal of Special Education, 23,* 169–183.

Tindal, G., & Parker, R. (1991). Identifying measures for evaluating written expression. *Learning Disabilities Research and Practice, 6,* 211–218.

Tompkins, G. (2004). *Teaching writing: Balancing process and product* (4th ed.). Upper Saddle River, NJ: Pearson.

238   THE PROMISE OF RESPONSE TO INTERVENTION

Videen, J., Deno, S. L., & Marston, D. (1982). *Correct word sequences: A valid indicator of proficiency in written expression* (Research Rep. No. 84). Minneapolis: University of Minnesota Institute for Research on Learning Disabilities.

Wanzek, J., Vaughn, S., Wexler, J., Swanson, E. A., Edmonds, M., & Kim, A. H. (2006). A synthesis of spelling and reading interventions and their effects on the spelling outcomes of students with LD. *Journal of Learning Disabilities, 39*, 386–406.

Wayman, M., Wallace, T., Wiley, H. I., Ticha, R., & Espin, C. A. (2007). Literature synthesis on curriculum-based measurement in reading. *Journal of Special Education, 41*, 85–120.

Weissenburger, J. W., & Espin, C. A. (2005). Curriculum-based measures of writing across grade levels. *Journal of School Psychology, 43*, 153–169.

White, O. R., & Haring, N. G. (1980). *Exceptional teaching* (2nd ed.). Columbus, OH: Merrill.

10

Evidence-Based Interventions within a Multi-Tier Framework for Positive Behavioral Supports

Tanya Ihlo
Melissa Nantais

Today's schools are faced with the challenge of providing supports that efficiently and effectively meet students' needs. Given an increased awareness of the significant consequences associated with ongoing behavior challenges among school-age children, attention to student behavioral concerns is on the rise. Educators are beginning to respond to the steady increase over the past two decades in the number of students with antisocial, disruptive, and aggressive behaviors and in the number of students being identified with emotional and behavioral disorders (Office of Special Education Programs, 2003; Sugai & Horner, 1999). Unfortunately, the difficult life challenges associated with behavioral concerns are great. Students with behavioral difficulties perform more poorly in school, exhibit increased truancy, and participate more frequently in criminal activities than those without behavioral challenges (e.g., Kauffman, 1997; Shinn, Ramsey, Walker, Stieber, & O'Neill, 1987).

Historically, school personnel have implemented reactive, punitive approaches to remediating student discipline problems (Sugai & Horner, 2002). Zero-tolerance policies that require expulsion for specific behaviors are prevalent in U.S. schools despite research spanning 25 years that suggests this approach is not effective in preventing further behavior problems

239

(Farmer, 1996; Phay, 1975; Skiba & Knesting, 2002; Skiba, Peterson, & Williams, 1997; Tebo, 2000) and can often even lead to negative consequences (e.g., increased dropouts, lower academic achievement; Mayer & Sulzer-Azaroff, 1991).

In addition, current disciplinary practices that involve removing students from schools have resulted in a decrease in students' exposure to necessary academic content. Such practices continue to perpetuate further behavior concerns for students with co-occurring academic problems (a common scenario) as students attempt to avoid situations in which they are unable to experience academic success. While the students miss key instruction, their peers continue to gain skills, causing them to fall even further behind.

Behavior researchers and interventionists have called for a more proactive approach to discipline, in which schools provide an environment that is conducive to learning and is perceived as safe and secure (Walker & Shinn, 2002), and several federal initiatives (e.g., Individuals with Disabilities Education Improvement Act of 2004) have increased schools' awareness and interest in developing and implementing proactive, multi-tier systems of support. One proactive approach to discipline that fits within a multi-tier prevention framework is the Positive Behavior Supports (PBS) model. Although PBS has a long history in the research literature and in schools and other settings for individual supports, the application of PBS within a multi-tier service delivery model with all students has only more recently gained significant popularity in school settings. According to the Positive Behavior Interventions and Supports website (*www.pbis.org*), there are currently more than 9,000 schools in 44 states at various stages of adopting and implementing schoolwide PBS in the United States (Horner et al., 2009; Bradshaw, Mitchell, & Leaf, 2009).

The framework for a multi-tier PBS model for response to intervention (RTI) is often characterized by a triangle depicting a continuum of supports across three tiers. Within a multi-tier PBS approach, school or district teams typically design and implement primary/universal supports to address the needs of 80 to 90% of all students (the base of the triangle), secondary/targeted interventions to assist students exhibiting behavior concerns requiring additional support (the middle portion of the triangle), and more individualized tertiary/intensive interventions to support those students who do not respond to primary or secondary efforts or who require more immediate intensive attention (the tip of the triangle). As part of this process, teams collect data on implementation and student behavior to guide planning and decision making at a systems level and individual student level. Screening data are collected to identify students who may need additional support, and progress is monitored and used to make decisions about intervention effectiveness and the need for modifications for individual students receiving intervention.

Although the empirical literature on behavior interventions for remediating a variety of behavioral concerns (uncontrolled anger, violent behavior, bullying, social skills problems) is vast, research on supports and interventions provided within a PBS multi-tier model appropriate for RTI has only begun to emerge. The purpose of this chapter is to provide a synopsis and discussion of the research on behavior supports within the context of a multi-tier PBS model of prevention and intervention. We provide an overview of supports and interventions at each of three tiers (primary/universal, secondary/targeted, and tertiary/intensive supports), review the research on these supports and interventions, and discuss implications for practice and future research needs.

Several parameters were set for including research in our synopsis. First, the scope of the reviewed studies was limited to interventions implemented in elementary and middle school settings. Research conducted in preschool and high school settings, clinics, family home environments, therapeutic environments, or other settings has not been included in our discussion. Additionally, we focused on prevention and intervention efforts for students who were not already identified with an emotional/behavioral disorder. Finally, studies included in the accompanying tables had to report primary data on student behavioral outcomes from research employing experimental or quasi-experimental group designs or well-designed single-case studies that at least partially controlled for potential confounds impacting interpretations about study conclusions.

PRIMARY/UNIVERSAL SUPPORTS

At the universal level of a multi-tier PBS model, district or school teams examine schoolwide data on implementation of key features of effective behavioral supports as well as student behavior data to guide development of a system to support the behavioral needs of the majority of students. Implementation of key schoolwide behavior supports is designed to prevent problem behavior for about 80 to 90% of students in the school (Walker & Shinn, 2002).

Several measures commonly used to measure fidelity to a PBS model, including the Schoolwide Evaluation Tool (SET; Sugai, Lewis-Palmer, Todd, & Horner, 2001), Implementation Phases Inventory (IPI; Bradshaw, Barrett, & Bloom, 2004), and the Team Implementation Checklist (TIC; Sugai, Todd, et al., 2001), have been investigated in preliminary research (Cohen, Kincaid, & Childs, 2009; Horner et al., 2004; Bradshaw, Debnam, Koth, & Leaf, 2009). These instruments include direct observation of aspects of PBS within the school setting; examination of permanent products such as behavior policies; interviews with administrators, teachers, school staff, and students (SET); and team self-assessment of level of implementation of key features (IPI and TIC).

Typical measures used for screening student behavior and making decisions about the appropriateness of primary PBS supports include office discipline referrals (ODRs; Irvin et al., 2006) and various behavior and social skills rating scales (Severson, Walker, Hope-Doolittle, Kratochwill, & Gresham, 2007). Emerging research suggests that ODRs may be valid indicators for use in decision making within a PBS framework (Irvin, Tobin, Sprague, Sugai, & Vincent, 2004) and that the number of student ODRs may be predictive of later behavior concerns (McIntosh, Horner, Chard, Boland, & Good, 2006). Additional research is needed to determine the predictive utility of ODRs within an RTI model.

In discussing the empirical literature pertaining to primary-level PBS supports appropriate for RTI, we first focus on key support features of primary prevention supports. Next, we provide a synopsis of research relevant to two specific aspects of primary-level implementation: (1) the explicit teaching and reinforcement of behavioral expectations and (2) the implementation of a system of consequences and supports for addressing behavioral problems. We then summarize research on fully implemented primary supports and identify the need for future investigations.

Key Features of Primary Prevention Supports

Several principle components have been identified as essential to building a schoolwide system that promotes positive behavior in schools: (1) developing and operationally defining a small set of expectations for student behavior in all settings within the school, (2) explicitly teaching the behavioral expectations with opportunities for students to practice displaying behavior within the natural context, (3) providing positive reinforcement/acknowledgment for students displaying appropriate behavior, and (4) using a systematic continuum of consequences and supports for students displaying problem behaviors (Lewis & Sugai, 1999; Sugai et al., 2005).

These principle PBS components are founded on methods established in the 1960s from applied behavior analysis, and have a wealth of research support for their use at the individual level. Adaptation of these components for implementation to the whole-school population in efforts to provide a prevention-oriented positive environment has only emerged in the last two decades (Dunlap, 2006). Despite the increase in support for implementation of schoolwide models of PBS, very few experimental studies have been conducted to examine impact on student behavior (Bradshaw et al., 2009; Horner et al., 2009).

Unfortunately, although many school and district evaluations (Barrett, Bradshaw, & Lewis-Palmer, 2008; Colvin, Kame'enui, & Sugai, 1993; Eber,

2006; Gottfredson, Gottfredson, & Hybl, 1993; Kincaid, Childs, Blase, & Wallace, 2007; Muscott, Mann, & LeBrun, 2009) suggest that schools implementing universal PBS supports and their principal components are able to maintain implementation fidelity and experience decreases in ODRs, student suspension, and expulsion rates and increases in academic achievement and perceived school safety by students and staff, many existing evaluation efforts have not been conducted using rigorous research methods. They often lack adequate control/comparison conditions, sufficient fidelity measurement, and regular measurement of all dependent variables. A lack of experimental rigor prevents these reports from fitting within the parameters for inclusion in our review and summary tables for this chapter.

Explicitly Teaching and Reinforcing Behavioral Expectations

Just as research findings indicate that students benefit from the direct instruction of specific academic skills, they also suggest that students benefit from the use of explicit instructional methods to convey behavioral expectations (Colvin, Kame'enui, & Sugai, 1993; Engelmann & Carnine, 1991; Langland, Lewis-Palmer, & Sugai, 1998; Sugai & Lewis, 1996). Within the primary level of a multi-tier framework, schools develop a small set of expectations (e.g., "Be Respectful," "Be Responsible," "Be a Problem Solver"); define expectations across all settings (e.g., in the cafeteria, on the playground); provide explicit instruction in those settings (e.g., take students to the cafeteria and directly teach the behavior, providing examples of what does and does not look like); and provide reinforcement for students when they exhibit appropriate behaviors (e.g., implement a lottery system in which students earn tickets for appropriate behavior and enter those tickets in a schoolwide drawing; e.g., Project PREPARE; Colvin et al., 1993; Nelson, 1996; Nelson, Coloin, & Smith, 1996). Teaching and reinforcement of appropriate behaviors has been found to be an effective strategy in nonclassroom settings (Hirsch, Lewis-Palmer, Sugai, & Schnacker, 2004; Lewis, Powers, Kelk, & Newcomer, 2002; Putnam, Handler, Ramirez-Platt, & Luiselli, 2003; Warren et al., 2003) as well as within the classroom (De Pry & Sugai, 2002). Implementation of explicit rules and routines has been shown to be effective in decreasing student ODRs and increasing perceived school safety by students and school staff (Colvin et al., 1993; Nelson, 1996).

System of Consequences and Supports for Addressing Problem Behaviors

In addition to teaching students appropriate behaviors, school personnel implement systematic procedures for providing consequences for inappropriate behaviors. Nelson and colleagues (Nelson, 1996; Nelson, Martella, & Galand, 1998) expanded on the research examining processes for establishing, teaching, and reinforcing behavioral expectations by investigating a Think Time strategy used to address behavioral concerns in a systematic manner at the classroom level. Utilizing this strategy, teachers notice and respond to inappropriate behaviors immediately. Students exhibiting minor behaviors are first given a prompt of the appropriate behavior and then reinforcement if they comply. If a student does not comply, he or she is sent to another classroom for Think Time. When examining implementation of teaching and reinforcing behaviors compared to teaching and reinforcing behaviors combined with a system of consequences for misbehavior, Nelson et al. (1998) found that students had fewer rule violations when the combination approach was used. Nelson (1996) used a pre–post research design without a comparison group, and Nelson et al. (1998) utilized a phased time-series research design without any control mechanisms; therefore, these studies were not included in the accompanying tables.

Full Implementation of Primary/Universal Supports

Several studies, including two randomized controlled effectiveness trials (Bradshaw et al., 2009; Horner et al., 2009), have examined the impact of full implementation of primary supports (i.e., defining and explicitly teaching behavioral expectations and providing systematic acknowledgment of appropriate behaviors and consequences for inappropriate behaviors). Results from these studies indicate that (1) schools were able to implement primary supports with fidelity, (2) students and teachers perceived the schools as safer after implementation, and (3) there were reductions in student behaviors, as indicated by ODR and suspension/expulsion data (Colvin & Fernandez, 2000; Lewis et al., 1999; Luiselli, Putnam, Handler, & Feinberg, 2005; Nelson, 1996; Scott, 2001; Sprague et al., 2001; Sugai et al., 2000; Turnbull et al., 2002). Additionally, Horner et al. (2009) have found preliminary empirical support for the use of schoolwide PBS in bolstering students' academic achievement. Table 10.1 provides a summary of the randomized controlled effectiveness studies examining the full implementation of the primary prevention tier of PBS across the entire school setting.

Future Research Needs

In considering research on primary/universal-level behavior supports, additional investigations are needed to strengthen confidence in preliminary findings and to provide guidance for schools implementing multi-tier models of behavior support. First, although ODRs have been identified as a valid measure of impacts of PBS implementation (Putnam, Luiselli, Handler, &

TABLE 10.1. Primary Prevention: Full Implementation of Primary/Universal PBS Supports

Study procedures	Design	Participants/setting	Measures	Results
		Horner et al. (2009)		
T (SWPBS): School teams received training delivered in three to four training events of 1–2 days each per year over a 2-year period	Randomized wait-list controlled effectiveness trial with repeated measures	30 elementary (K–5) school teams from Hawaii, Illinois, Chicago	SET to examine fidelity to the SWPBS model SSS ODRs State standardized tests (Illinois, Hawaii)	School teams' fidelity to implementation of SWPBS components increased, as shown by a significant difference in SET scores between the T and C/D groups and pre–post scores for each group.
C/D (delayed SWPBS): School teams received SWPBS training 1 year later than the T schools		23 elementary school (K–5) teams from Hawaii, Illinois, Chicago	Data were collected at three points in time; T1, before implementation; T2, after approximately 1 year of training and before control/delay schools began training; T3, after all schools had initiated SWPBS training	School administrators and other staff members perceived their schools as safer environments, as shown by significant differences in SSS scores between T and C/D schools and a statistically significant decrease in risk immediately following initial training for both T and C/D schools.
				Although ODRs for T and C/D schools decreased over time and showed comparatively lower rates of ODRs per 100 students than 1,010 schools in the national SWIS sample, these results cannot be attributed to implementation of SWPBS because there were no predata available for either T or C/D schools and, therefore, no comparison data between T and C/D schools.

(continued)

TABLE 10.1. *(continued)*

Study procedures	Design	Participants/setting	Measures	Results
		Bradshaw, Mitchell, & Leaf (2009)		
T: School teams received training in PBIS (an initial 2-day summer training; ongoing technical assistance from local PBIS coaches and the state leadership team; 2-day summer booster sessions each year) over a 5-year period (*n* = 21)	Randomized controlled effectiveness trial	37 Maryland elementary schools from five rural and suburban districts volunteered for the study and agreed to be randomly assigned to T or C	SET	Schools implemented PBS with fidelity, as indicated by significant differences between T and C on the SET across all 4 years; significant differences were found on all subscales except Behavioral Violations.
			ODRs collected only from the T schools using SWIS, and no baseline data from the trained schools	The study suggests that student behavior improved, as indicated by ODRs being lower across all years than the 0.34 to 0.37 national range in the SWIS system, significant decreases in the percentage of students with a major or minor ODR, and significant decreases in the number of students with ODR events.
C: Teams did not receive training and refrained from implementing PBIS over 5-year period (*n* = 16)			Suspension rates from MD State Department of Education	
				Additionally, T schools had significant decreases in the number of students receiving suspensions over time, but the C schools did not.
			Achievement tests results (combined advanced/proficient scores) from third- and fifth-grade math and reading from the Maryland School Assessment System; no baseline data because the assessment was adopted after the 1st year of implementation	There was a slightly greater improvement in achievement scores for T schools than C schools; however, there were no significant differences in the percentage of students meeting proficiency standards between the T and C schools.

Note. PBS, positive behavioral supports; T, treatment; C/D, control/delayed; C, control; ODR, office discipline referral; SWPBS, schoolwide positive behavior supports; SET, Schoolwide Evaluation Tool; PBIS, positive behavior intervention supports; SSS, School Safety Survey; SWIS, schoolwide intervention system; T1, Time 1; T2, Time 2; T3, Time 3.

246

Jefferson, 2003; Sugai, Sprague, Horner, & Walker, 2000; Wright & Dusek, 1998), the experimental studies reviewed did not involve the collection or analysis of preintervention or control ODR data, likely because tools for collecting ODR data are considered to be a component of PBS implementation (Bradshaw et al., 2009; Horner et al., 2009). The inability to report significance of findings related to ODRs severely limits confidence in results regarding effectiveness of PBS in reducing behavior concerns. Future research is needed to examine the impact of PBS on behavior using a student measure that can be collected preintervention and for comparison students.

In addition, research is needed to evaluate measures screening for behavior difficulties within a PBS model. Although ODRs may be useful indicators to identify students' externalizing behaviors and may predict future behavior concerns (McIntosh, Campbell, Carter, & Dickey, 2006), additional research is needed to investigate screening assessments useful for identifying students with internalizing behaviors who may need social/emotional support.

Given school pressures to provide effective and efficient integrated student supports, expansion of current research to further examine the combination of academic and behavioral support systems at the schoolwide level will provide critical and valuable information to schools in their implementation efforts. Academic concerns may lead to problem behavior over time (Hinshaw, 1992; Maguin & Loeber, 1995). Students with academic skills deficits often exhibit problem behaviors to escape or avoid difficult academic tasks. In turn, they are unable to obtain the necessary instruction and practice and continue to fall farther behind their peers. Over time, problem behavior continues or worsens. A recent descriptive study of school implementation of PBS and a multi-tier model for academic supports found potentially promising results (McIntosh, Chard, Boland, & Horner, 2006). Behavioral primary supports included implementation of the key components of schoolwide PBS, as previously described. Academic primary supports included a focus on improved instruction in critical reading content (e.g., phonemic awareness, phonics, fluency, comprehension, vocabulary). Additionally, teams used academic and behavioral screening data to make decisions about student needs. Students demonstrated improved reading achievement, as indicated by increased numbers of students meeting benchmarks on reading measures, and improved behavior, as indicated by decreases in ODRs and in the number of students with ODRs. Although these findings may be promising, they are the result of a descriptive investigation conducted without comparison schools. Additional rigorous research is needed to investigate the impact of combined academic and behavioral supports at the school level.

Additional investigations are also needed to study the impact of individual model components and the expansion of primary-level PBS to other settings. Although rigorous experimental research has been conducted in elementary schools, research on the implementation of primary-level PBS in preschool, middle school, and high school settings has been less rigorous. Additional research is needed in these other settings. Manipulation studies evaluating individual components of primary prevention would also be useful for determining the relative contribution of various aspects of the intervention process and could provide important information to schools as they are planning for implementation.

SECONDARY/TARGETED INTERVENTIONS

Targeted behavioral interventions within a multi-tier PBS model are provided to the 10 to 15% of students whose behavioral needs are not sufficiently addressed by the schoolwide supports. They are an efficient, cost-effective part of the established school system and are a component of a data-based decision-making process (Hawken, 2006).

Although decision rules for selecting targeted-level behavioral supports vary, schools commonly use rates of ODRs as a guide for identifying students in need of targeted behavioral intervention. Schools also rely on teacher recommendations and/or more formalized screening measures (i.e., Social Skills Rating Systems; Gresham & Elliot, 1990) in identifying students eligible for targeted service delivery.

When considering targeted behavioral interventions, it is important to take into account the integration of behavioral and academic intervention needs. Although academic interventions are beyond the scope of this chapter, the reader is encouraged to refer to other chapters in this book for detailed information on academic interventions appropriate for multi-tier service delivery for RTI.

Three behavioral intervention approaches for secondary-level student support are discussed in this chapter: the Behavior Education Program (also known as Check-In/Check-Out), First Step to Success, and a social skills instructional approach. We provide a brief description of each intervention approach and its research support.

Behavior Education Program (Check-In/Check-Out)

The Behavior Education Program (BEP), also known as Check-In/Check-Out (CICO), is a targeted behavioral intervention (Crone, Horner, & Hawken, 2004) with demonstrated positive outcomes for students. The BEP consists of five components:

1. A student checks in with a designated adult before school each day and is given a daily progress report form to take to each class; the

adult reviews the behavioral expectations and the behavioral goal with the students.

2. The student gives the teacher the daily progress report form at the beginning of each class period. The teacher uses this form to provide feedback on behavior using a 3-point rating scale and offers immediate verbal praise for appropriate behavior during the class period.

3. At the end of the day, the student meets with the designated adult for check-out; which involves a quick review of students' performance for the day, calculation of points earned for the day, and praise and tangible rewards if the goal is met.

4. The student takes the daily progress report home to be reviewed and signed by his/her parent/guardian.

5. The student returns a signed daily progress report the next day at check-in (Hawken & Horner, 2003).

Unlike typical classroom behavior management interventions, the BEP is integrated into the school system, readily accessible to students, and all teachers and staff are trained and agree on its implementation (Crone et al., 2004).

Typically, students are selected to participate in the BEP based on teacher or parent recommendations or the frequency of ODRs. Because of the design of the intervention, students whose behavior is maintained by escape or avoidance of adult attention may not be ideal candidates for the BEP or the BEP may need to be modified to involve more self-monitoring and less adult–student interaction (March & Horner, 2002; McIntosh et al., 2009).

Although there currently are no randomized controlled studies in the research literature related to the BEP/CICO, multiple single-case design studies have investigated the impact of the BEP/CICO on problem behaviors in the classroom. Typically utilizing a multiple-baseline across-subjects design, these studies have examined the impact of BEP/CICO on behaviors in both middle school and elementary school students (Hawken & Horner, 2003; Hawken, MacLeod, & Rawlings 2007; Todd, Campbell, Meyer, & Horner, 2009). BEP/CICO implementation has typically been investigated in schools with established schoolwide PBS practices in place (i.e., with scores of 80% or higher on the SET; Horner et al., 2002). Results have indicated decreases in problem behaviors and ODRs for both middle school and elementary school students (Fairbanks, Sugai, Guardino, & Lathrop, 2007; Hawken, MacLeod, & Rawlings, 2007; March & Horner, 2002; Todd et al., 2009), changes in teacher ratings of behaviors (Fairbanks et al., 2007; McIntosh et al., 2009), and increases in academic engagement (Hawken & Horner, 2003). Data also suggest that the BEP is an acceptable intervention based on ratings from parents, teachers, and students on the BEP Acceptability Questionnaire (Hawken & Horner, 2003; Hawken, MacLeod, & Rawlings, 2007; Todd et al., 2009), and that the BEP/CICO can be implemented within schools with a high degree of fidelity (Hawken & Horner, 2003; McIntosh et al., 2009). However, most of the studies have taken place in the Pacific Northwest and with small numbers of students. Table 10.2 summarizes this research.

Future research is needed to address the implementation of the BEP with a larger number of students across a wider range of age groups, including elementary and middle schools, and a wider variety of geographical settings. Additional studies are required to further address the impact of the BEP/CICO on both academic engagement and academic achievement beyond engagement, using more direct measures of academic performance. Future research may also examine whether and how the BEP/CICO may be modified to support students who display behaviors that are not maintained by adult attention.

First Step to Success

First Step to Success, a secondary prevention intervention program designed to address antisocial behavior patterns in at-risk kindergarten to third-grade students (Walker, 1998), has demonstrated positive outcomes for young students. The program has three components: (1) a universal screening procedure to identify the students demonstrating early signs of antisocial behaviors; (2) a school-based intervention designed to teach students an adaptive behavior pattern for bolstering school success and making friends; and (3) a home-based component designed to include parents in helping to teach key skills that are factors in school success (Walker, 1998).

Table 10.3 summarizes research on First Step to Success. Initial research on the First Step to Success early intervention program used a randomized, experimental, wait-list control group design and found that kindergarten students across two cohorts (from two different school years) demonstrated substantial mean improvements on four of the five measures at postintervention compared with the preintervention scores and statistically significant differences in four of the five measures compared with the wait-list control participants (Walker et al., 1998). The four measures that demonstrated change were adaptive and maladaptive teacher rating scales and the academic engaged-time observational measure from the Early Screening Project (Walker, Severson, & Feil, 1994) and teacher ratings on the Aggression subscale of the Teacher Report form of the Childhood Behavior Checklist (Achenbach, 1991). Golly, Stiller, and Walker (1998) produced similar findings in a replication study.

Beard and Sugai (2004) also implemented First Step to Success with six kindergarten students to assess treatment conditions using only teacher-directed components and a combination of teacher-directed and parent-directed components. Decreases in rates of problem behaviors and increases

TABLE 10.2. Targeted Intervention: Behavior Education Program/Check-In/Check-Out

Study	Design	Participants/setting	Target behaviors	Measures	Results
Hawken and Horner (2003)	Multiple-baseline, across-students	Four middle school male students in a rural middle school in the Pacific Northwest; each student's problem behaviors were maintained by adult and/or peer attention	Problem behaviors: talking out, talking back, being out of seat, inappropriate language, threatening gestures, throwing objects, not following teacher directions within 10 seconds, physical aggression toward others	20-minute observations using 10-second partial interval coding system for problem behaviors and academic engagement with peer comparisons	Reductions in the mean level of problem behaviors were found for all four students with a reduction in the variability of performance across days during the implementation of the BEP.
				Social validity was assessed using the BEP Acceptability Questionnaire	The mean level of academic engagement increased.
			Academic engagement		
			Social validity		
Hawken, MacLeod, and Rawlings (2007)	Multiple-baseline, across-students	Urban elementary school with a SET score of 88% fidelity; 12 students (10 male & two female); eight participants qualified for free/reduced lunch; one student receiving special education services for a learning disability in reading	ODRs	Total number of ODRs per group of three students per month	Reductions in average total ODRs per month across all four groups were found with the implementation of BEP.
			Referrals to more intensive behavior supports and to special education	Number of students receiving more intensive behavior supports and number referred to special education for problem behaviors	75% of individual students demonstrated statistically significant reductions in their average ODR per month.
			Social validity (parents, students and teachers)	Social validity as assessed using the BEP Acceptability Questionnaire	Two students needed additional supports (one qualified for special education services under the category of emotional disturbance; one received more intensive behavior supports). Mean ratings from teachers, students, and parents demonstrated acceptability of the BEP intervention. High levels of BEP implementation were found in four of five critical elements; a form signed by parents was consistently low across all three checks.
			Fidelity of BEP implementation	Review of permanent products from BEP for five critical elements of BEP	

(continued)

251

TABLE 10.2. *(continued)*

Study	Design	Participants/setting	Target behaviors	Measures	Results
Todd, Campbell, Meyer, and Horner (2009)	Multiple-baseline, across-students	Four elementary school-age boys (K, first, second, and third grades); rural elementary school in the Pacific Northwest; seven teachers and three CICO staff	Problem behaviors: wrong location, talking out, noncompliance, talking to peers, disruptive, negative physical or verbal interactions ODRs Social validity Contextual fit	Functional Assessment Checklist for Teachers and Staff (FACTS) 20-minute partial-interval recording system with 10-second intervals; composite index of classroom behavior was also collected ODRs Teacher version of CICO Program Acceptability Questionnaire Self-Assessment of Contextual Fit in Schools	All participants demonstrated attention-maintained behaviors based on FACTS. Reductions in level and variability of problem behaviors were found for all participants. Average ODRs for all four students before CICO was 0.14 per day; after CICO, 0.04. CICO was demonstrated to be a socially valid intervention. Overall, CICO was demonstrated to be a contextual fit to the school in which it was implemented.

Note. ODR, office discipline referrals; BEP, Behavior Education Program; CICO, Check-In/Check-Out; SET, Schoolwide Evaluation Tool.

TABLE 10.3. Targeted Intervention: First Step to Success

Study	Design	Participants/ setting	Target behaviors	Measures	Results
Beard and Sugai (2004)	ABA and ABAB case studies across students and classrooms	Six kindergarten students (four boys and two girls) in two urban elementary schools in the Pacific Northwest	Problem behaviors: talking out, touching others and property, noncompliance, out of seat AET	24-minute observation sessions divided into eight 3-minute intervals Frequency count of problem behaviors converted into rate per minute Percentage of time spent academically engaged during observation periods	Rate of problem behavior for all students decreased to nearly 0 during intervention period and AET increased to a mean YY 90%; four of six students maintained outcomes over 5-month period after intervention was withdrawn; two needed to return to intervention phase but were able to subsequently decrease rates of problem behaviors and increase percentage of AET with the reintroduction of the intervention.
Walker et al. (1998)	Randomized, experimental, wait-list control group design	46 kindergartners and their families in the Pacific Northwest; two cohorts: Cohort 1 through grade 2 and Cohort 2 through grade 1	Adaptive behavior rating; maladaptive behavior rating; aggression rating; social withdrawal rating; AET	Data collected at four points: preintervention, postintervention, first-grade follow-up, and second-grade follow-up (for Cohort 1 only); adaptive and maladaptive teacher rating scales of the ESP), Aggression and Social Withdrawal subscales of the CBCL Teacher Report, and the AET observational methods of the ESP	Four of the five measures demonstrated significant gains from pre- to postintervention (no change in social withdrawal); statistically significant differences were found in four of the five measures when compared with wait-list control participants; reported effect sizes averaged 0.86; follow-up in grades 1 and 2 demonstrated long-lasting effects across time, settings, teachers, and peers for both cohorts

Note. CBCL, Child Behavior Checklist; AET, academic engaged time; ESP, Early Screening Project.

253

in academic engaged time for all students were found, with four of the six students maintaining behavioral changes for up to 5 months after the intervention components were removed (Beard & Sugai, 2004).

Future research is needed to examine the impact of First Step to Success on academic skills such as those measured by Dynamic Indicators of Basic Early Literacy Skills (Good & Kaminski, 2002). In addition, investigations are needed to explore the contribution of each component (home and school) as well as the impact or need for booster sessions to reteach desired behaviors throughout the school year (Beard & Sugai, 2004). Additional larger group experimental design studies conducted in a wider variety of school settings and with students from more diverse backgrounds and grade levels will be useful for determining the impact of First Steps to Success in various different contexts.

Social Skills Instruction

Much of the current literature on PBS identifies social skills instruction/ training as an option for targeted intervention for students who demonstrate a behavioral skill deficit (can't do it) rather than a performance deficit (won't do it). Although there is a wealth of literature in the area of social skills training, particularly for those students with or considered to be at risk for emotional or behavioral disorders (Lane, Gresham, & O'Shaughnessy, 2002) as well as students already identified as having educational disabilities (Gresham, Sugai, & Horner, 2001), we focus in this chapter on social skills instruction implemented in schools with primary-level schoolwide PBS supports in place.

Lane et al. (2003) examined the impact of social skills instruction on social, behavioral, and academic outcomes of elementary school students already receiving primary prevention addressing both behavioral and academic outcomes. The social skills instruction provided was based on lessons from the *Social Skills Intervention Guide: Practical Strategies for Social Skills Training* (Elliot & Gresham, 1991) and targeted specific skill deficits identified for participating students. Outcomes included decreases in disruptive behavior, increases in mean levels of academic engaged time, and decreases in negative social interactions for most students in the study. Table 10.4 summarizes procedures and findings from this research.

More research is needed on the provision of social skills instruction as a targeted intervention in schools implementing schoolwide PBS. Current findings are limited to single-case investigations of student behavior. Additional larger group experimental research is needed to understand whether findings from the specific cases studied can be generalized to other students. Future research should also investigate (1) the provision of social skills instruction within the general education setting by general education staff,

TABLE 10.4. Targeted Intervention: Social Skills Instruction

Study	Design	Participants/setting	Target behaviors	Measures	Results
Lane et al. (2003)	Multiple-baseline, across-intervention-groups design	Seven students (five boys, two girls) from grades 2–4; all students were part of schoolwide academic and behavior supports; students were identified based on teacher recommendation and SSRS scores; all students hand participated in schoolwide intervention for 3 months prior to social skills instruction Seven peer models also participated in the social skills instruction	Total disruptive behavior—class of behaviors that disturbs the classroom environment and interferes with instructional activities Academic engaged time—time spent actively engaged in instructional activities Negative social interactions—behaviors that impede ongoing play activities, including verbal and physical aggression	10-minute observations during morning literacy block for total disruptive behavior and academic engaged time using duration recording 10-minute observations during morning and afternoon recesses using duration recording	All seven students demonstrated decreases in total disruptive behavior with effect sizes from −5.87 to −0.38, with six of the seven students demonstrating decreases in variability in performance during the intervention phase. Six of seven students demonstrated increases in mean levels of academic engaged time between baseline and intervention phases. Six of seven students demonstrated decreases in negative social interactions during recesses.

Note. SSRS, Social Skills Rating Scale.

(2) the implementation of additional social skills instruction/lessons and/or programs, and (3) implementation efforts with a wider variety of student demographic groups (students varying in age, gender, grades, geographical locations). Future examinations with additional measures assessing academic skills are also needed.

TERTIARY/INTENSIVE INTERVENTIONS

Intensive interventions are designed for the 1 to 5% of students for whom the supports provided through primary-level schoolwide PBS and targeted interventions are not sufficient. Implementation of intensive intervention supports involves executing an individualized behavior intervention plan (BIP) based on the use of a functional behavioral assessment (FBA) to determine the functions of a student's behavior. A great deal of information outlining procedures for conducting FBAs and developing BIPs can be found in scholarly journals (i.e., *Journal of Positive Behavior Interventions*, *Journal of Applied Behavioral Analysis*), texts, and reference books (i.e., Crone & Horner, 2003; O'Neil, et al., 1997) and on various websites (i.e., *www.pbis.org*). Interested readers are encouraged to refer to these and other sources for additional information. We have focused in this chapter on the intensive intervention supports for students in elementary school and middle school settings using both primary-level schoolwide PBS and targeted behavioral interventions.

In a descriptive investigation, Medley, Little, and Akin-Little (2008) assessed the technical adequacy of individualized PBS plans in schools implementing schoolwide PBS versus those not implementing schoolwide PBS. Although they found preliminary support for the additional technical adequacy of individualized PBS plans in schools with school wide PBS, there was no indication whether these schools were actually implementing targeted behavioral intervention supports. Furthermore, although individualized plans in the schoolwide PBS settings were found to be stronger, there was still an observed need to strengthen their technical adequacy.

Limited published research is currently available that examines the implementation of intensive intervention supports for students in schools with full implementation of both primary-level schoolwide PBS and targeted intervention. Some of this research is limited to investigations of only a very small number of individual students, which do not permit generalizations about the efficacy or effectiveness of intensive intervention approaches. For example, Lane et al. (2007) investigated the use of function-based interventions with two students (one elementary and one middle school) within the context of a three-tier model. Although Lane et al. found a functional relationship between the implementation of intensive intervention supports and changes in the targeted behaviors (participation and compliance), they provided no indication about implementation efforts at the primary level of schoolwide PBS or targeted intervention. Further, given the research design, inferences about these findings should be restricted to the cases studied.

Brooks, Todd, Tofflemoyer, and Horner (2003) used a multiple-baseline across-setting design to address the academic engagement and work completion for a student with Down syndrome. Although the investigators indicated that primary-level schoolwide PBS was implemented, they did not report the level of implementation (i.e., provide a SET score), whether targeted interventions were in place within the school, or whether the student demonstrated a need for intensive intervention supports as a result of not responding to targeted intervention. The participating student's engagement across multiple settings (fourth-grade seatwork, resource room seatwork, and resource room group instruction) and work completion were examined. The intervention plan was developed based on the competing pathway model (O'Neil et al., 1997) and involved self-management as a key component. Increases in academic engagement during seatwork in both the general education fourth-grade classroom and the resource room were found. A decrease in academic engagement was found during fourth-grade seatwork when the self-management intervention was removed (return to baseline conditions). Increases in academic engagement were not found during group instruction in the resource room. In addition, cumulative work completion increased during the implementation of the intervention plan. Given this investigation's focus on a single student, inferences about these findings should be restricted to this single case.

Two studies among those reviewed (Fairbanks et al., 2007; March & Horner, 2002) examined the implementation of intensive interventions in addition to the use of primary-level schoolwide PBS and CICO/BEP implemented with documented intervention fidelity. Students participating in these studies were identified as needing intensive intervention supports based on nonresponsiveness to targeted intervention supports. Each study utilized a multiple-baseline across-subjects design. FBAs were conducted and individualized behavioral support plans were developed for each student. All student intervention plans included components to address identified setting events, antecedents and consequences, and specific skill instruction. Each plan was developed based on the hypothesized function of the behaviors targeted. The intervention plans resulted in decreases in identified problem behaviors (e.g., out of seat, calling out, noncompliance, physical aggression, inappropriate language; Fairbanks et al., 2007; March & Horner, 2002) and, in one study, increases in academic engagement (March & Horner, 2002). Table 10.5 summarizes the research design, participants, intervention development/components, and results from these studies.

Although emerging research provides promising support for the impact

TABLE 10.5. Intensive Intervention

Study	Design	Participants/setting	Target behaviors	Measures	Intervention development and components	Results
Fairbanks, Sugai, Guardino, and Lathrop (2007)	Multiple-baseline, across-subjects design across five or six phases	Four second-grade students (three boys, one girl) who were unresponsive to CICO intervention	Problem behaviors: inappropriate physical contact, inappropriate placement, talking out, noncompliant, nondisruptive off-task behavior Academic Engagement	30-minute observations three to four times per week using 10-second partial-interval recording system	Teacher and school counselor completed the FACTS for each student; identified function of behavior and alternative behaviors to develop behavior support plans Plans included instructional and intervention strategies to address setting events, antecedents, consequences; plans also outlined tasks for implementation, data collection, goals, and decision rules	All four students demonstrated decreases in problem behaviors with the function-based phase compared with baseline and CICO phases, and all four students' mean percentage of intervals with problem behaviors were lower than peer comparisons during the function-based phase.
March and Horner (2002)	Multiple-Baseline, across-subjects design	Three students (two boys, one girl); grades 6, 7; students who had not demonstrated decreases in ODRs despite involvement in BEP	Problem behaviors: yelling and talking out, being out of seat during instruction, inappropriate languag, verbal harrassment, noncompliance, and physical aggression Academic engagement	15-minute observations three to five times per week using 10-second intervals; problem behaviors were coded if they occurred anytime during the 10-second intervals; academic engagement was scored if the student is looking at or attending to the teacher or materials for an entire 10-second interval; included peer comparisons	Intervention plans were developed using a four-step process: development of FBA hypotheses, confirmation of hypotheses, designing plan, implementing plan All intervention plans included components to address setting events, antecedents, teaching new skills, and consequences.	Reductions in levels and variability of problem behaviors were found across all three students; increases in levels and trend of academic engagement were also found for all three.

Note. FACTS, Functional Assessment Checklist for Teachers and Staff; DCICO, Check-In, Check-Out; FBA, functional behavioral assessment; ODR, office discipline referral; BEP, Behavior Education Program.

258

of intensive, tertiary-level behavioral supports, additional investigations are needed to verify the validity and generalizability of extant findings. This research should focus both on the relative contributions of various aspects of intensive interventions and general intervention effects evaluated using rigorous randomized experimental methods that permit strong inferences about study conclusions.

SUMMARY

Today's schools are faced with myriad expectations for supporting students' academic and social competences. With these increasing demands, there are often limited supports available to schools. Those working within a multi-tier service delivery model for RTI may be better positioning themselves to respond to the academic and behavioral needs of students today and in the future. Emerging research on the implementation of schoolwide PBS to meet the needs all students within a multi-tier model has produced encouraging results, but, as discussed throughout this chapter, there are many areas in which further research is needed. In particular, there are no published reports of rigorous randomized experimental studies evaluating the impact of a full multi-tier PBS model that includes primary, secondary, and tertiary behavioral prevention and intervention supports. Additional rigorous investigations are also needed to study the relative contributions of various intervention components. Future research examining the impact of the full continuum of behavioral supports will be useful.

REFERENCES

Achenbach, T. (1991). *The Child Behavior Checklist: Manual for the Teacher's Report Form.* Burlington: University of Vermont, Department of Psychiatry.

Barrett, S., Bradshaw, C., & Lewis-Palmer, T. (2008). Maryland statewide PBIS initiative: Systems, evaluation, and next steps. *Journal of Positive Behavior Interventions, 10*, 1005–114.

Beard, K., & Sugai, G. (2004). First step to success: An early intervention for elementary children at risk for antisocial behavior. *Behavioral Disorders, 29*(4), 396–409.

Bradshaw, C. P., Barrett, S., & Bloom, J. (2004). The Implementation Phases Inventory (IPI). Baltimore: PBIS Maryland. Available from *www.pbismaryland.org/forms.htm.*

Bradshaw, C. P., Debnam, K., Koth, C. W., & Leaf, P. (2009). Preliminary validation of the Implementation Phases Inventory for assessing fidelity of schoolwide positive behavior supports. *Journal of Positive Behavior Interventions, 11*(3), 145–160.

Bradshaw, C. P., Mitchell, M. M., & Leaf, P. J. (2009). Examining the effects of schoolwide positive behavioral interventions and supports on student outcomes: Results from a randomized controlled effectiveness trial in elementary schools. *Journal of Positive Behavior Interventions.*

Brooks, A., Todd, A. W., Tofflemoyer, S., & Horner, R. H. (2003). Use of functional assessment and self-management system to increase academic engagement and work completion. *Journal of Positive Behavior Intervention, 5*(3), 144–152.

Cohen, R., Kincaid, D., & Childs, K. (2009). Measuring school-wide positive behavior support implementation: Development and validation of the "Benchmarks of Quality." *Journal of Positive Behavior Interventions.*

Colvin, G., & Fernandez, E. (2000). Sustaining effective behavior support systems in an elementary school. *Journal of Positive Behavior Interventions, 2*(4), 251–253.

Colvin, G., Kame'enui, E. J., & Sugai, G. (1993). Reconceptualzing behavior management and school-wide discipline in general education. *Education and Treatment of Children, 16*, 361–381.

Colvin, G., & Sugai, G. (1988). Proactive strategies for managing social behavior problems: An instructional approach. *Education and Treatment of Children, 11*, 341–348.

Colvin, G., Sugai, G., Good, R. H., III, & Lee, Y. (1997). Using active supervision and precorrection to improve transition behaviors in an elementary school. *School Psychology Quarterly, 12*, 344–363.

Crone, D. A., & Horner, R. H. (2003). *Building positive behavior support systems in schools: Functional behavioral assessment.* New York: Guilford Press.

Crone, D. A., Horner, R. H., & Hawken, L. S. (2004). *Responding to problem behavior in schools: The behavior education program.* New York: Guilford Press.

De Pry, R. L., & Sugai, G. (2002). The effect of active supervision and precorrection on minor behavioral incidents in a sixth grade general education classroom. *Journal of Behavioral Education, 11*, 255–267.

Dunlap, G. (2006). The applied behavior analytic heritage of PBS: A dynamic model of action-oriented research. *Journal of Positive Behavior Interventions, 8*, 58–60.

Eber, L. (2006). *Illinois PBIS evaluation report.* LaGrange Park, IL: Illinois State Board of Education, PBIS/EBD Network.

Elliott, S. N., & Gresham, F. M. (1991). *Social skills intervention guide: Practical strategies for social skills training.* Circle Pines, MN: AGS.

Engelmann, S., & Carnine, D. (1991). *Theory of instruction: Principles and application* (rev. ed.). Eugene, OR: ADI Press.

Fairbanks, S., Sugai, G., Guardino, D., & Lathrop, M. (2007). Response to intervention: Examining classroom behavior support in second grade. *Exceptional Children, 73*(3), 288–310.

Fanning, P., Theodos, J., Benner, C., & Bohanon-Edmonson, H. (2004). Integrating proactive discipline practices into codes of conduct. *Journal of School Violence, 3*(1), 45–61.

Farmer, C. D. (1996). Proactive alternatives to school suspension: Reclaiming children and youth. *Journal of Emotional and Behavioral Problems, 5*(1), 47–51.

Golly, A. M., Stiller, B., & Walker, H. M. (1998). First steps to success: Replication and social validation of an early intervention program. *Journal of Emotional and Behavioral Disorders, 6*(4), 243–250.

Good, R. H., & Kaminski, R. A. (Eds.). (2002). *Dynamic indicators of basic early literacy skills* (6th ed.). Eugene, OR: Institute for Development of Educational Achievement.

Gottfredson, D. C., Gottfredson, G. D., & Hybl, L. G. (1993). Managing adolescent behavior: A multiyear, multischool experiment. *American Educational Research Journal, 30,* 179–216.

Gresham, F. M., & Elliot, S. N. (1990). *Social skills rating system.* Circle Pines, MN: American Guidance Service.

Gresham, F. M., Sugai, G., & Horner, R. H. (2001). Interpreting outcomes of social skills training for students with high-incidence disabilities. *Exceptional Children, 67*(1), 331–344.

Hawken, L. S., & Horner, R. H. (2003). Evaluation of a targeted group intervention within a school-wide system of behavior support. *Journal of Behavioral Education, 12,* 225–240.

Hawken, L. S., MacLeod, K. S., & Rawlings, L. (2007). Effects of the Behavior Education Program (BEP) on problem behavior with elementary school students. *Journal of Positive Behavior Interventions, 9,* 94–101.

Hinshaw, S. P. (1992). Academic underachievement, attention deficits, and aggression: Comorbidity and implications for intervention. *Journal of Consulting and Clinical Psychology, 60,* 893–903.

Hirsch, E. J., Lewis-Palmer, T., Sugai, G., & Schnacker, L. (2004). Using school bus discipline referral data in decision making: Two case studies. *Preventing School Failure, 48*(4), 4–9.

Horner, R. H., Sugai, G., Lewis-Palmer, T., & Todd, A. W. (2001). Teaching school-wide behavioral expectations. *Report on Emotional and Behavioral Disorders in Youth, 1*(4), 77–79.

Horner, R. H., Sugai, G., Smolkowski, K., Eber, L., Todd, A. W., Nakasato, A. W., et al. (2009). A randomized, wait-list controlled effectiveness trial of assessing school-wide positive behavior support in elementary schools. *Journal of Positive Behavior Interventions, 11,* 133–144.

Horner, R. H., Sugai, G., Todd, A. W., & Lewis-Palmer, T. (2005). School-wide positive behavior support. In L. Bambara & L. Kern (Eds.), *Individualized supports for students with problem behaviors: Designing positive behavior plans* (pp. 359–390). New York: Guilford Press.

Horner, R. H., Todd, A., Lewis-Palmer, T., Irvin, L., Sugai, G., & Boland, J. B. (2004). The school-wide evaluation tool (SET): A research instrument for assessing school-wide positive behavior support. *Journal of Positive Behavior Interventions, 6*(1), 3–12.

Horner, R. H., Todd, A. W., Lewis-Palmer, T., Irvin, L. K., Sugai, G., & Boland, J. B. (2002). The school-wide evaluation tool (SET): A research instrument for assessing school-wide positive behavior support. *Journal of Positive Behavior Interventions, 6*, 3–12.

Individuals with Disabilities Education Improvement Act of 2004. 20 U.S.C.§ 1400 *et seq.* (2004).

Irvin, L. K., Horner, R. H., Ingram, K., Todd, A. W., Sugai, G., Sampson, N., et al. (2006). Using office discipline referral data for decision-making about student behavior in elementary and middle schools: An empirical investigation of validity. *Journal of Positive Behavior Interventions, 8*(1), 10–23.

Irvin, L. K., Tobin, T., Sprague, J., Sugai, G., & Vincent, C. (2004). Validity of office discipline referral measures as indices of school-wide behavioral status and effects of school-wide behavioral interventions. *Journal of Positive Behavioral Interventions, 6*, 131–147.

Kaufman, J. M. (1997). *Characteristics of emotional and behavioural disorders of children and youth.* Columbus, OH: Merill/Prentice Hall.

Kincaid, D., Childs, K., Blase, K. A., & Wallace, F. (2007). *Journal of Positive Behavior Interventions, 9*(3), 174–184.

Lane, K. L., Gresham, F. M., & O'Shaughnessy, T. E. (Eds.). (2002). *Interventions for children with or at risk for emotional and behavioral disorders.* Needham, MA: Allyn & Bacon.

Lane, K. L., Rogers, L. A., Parks, R. J., Weisenback, J. L., Mau, A. C., Merwin, M. T., et al. (2007). Function-based interventions for students who are nonresponsive to primary and secondary efforts: Illustrations at the elementary and middle school levels. *Journal of Emotional and Behavioral Disorders, 15*(3), 169–183.

Lane, K. L., Wehby, J., Menzies, H. M., Doukas, G. L., Munton, S. M., & Gregg, R. M. (2003). Social skills instruction for students at risk for antisocial behavior: The effects of small-group instruction. *Behavioral Disorders, 28*(3), 229–248.

Langland, S., Lewis-Palmer, T., & Sugai, G. (1998). Teaching respect in the classroom: An instructional approach. *Journal of Behavioral Education, 8*, 245–262.

Lassen, S., Steele, M., & Sailor, W. (2006). The relationship of school-wide positive behavior support to academic achievement in an urban middle school. *Psychology in Schools, 43*(6), 701–712.

Lewis, T., Hudson, S., Richter, M., & Johnson, N. (2004). Scientifically supported practices in EBS: A proposed approach and brief review of current practices. *Behavior Disorders, 29*, 247–259.

Lewis, T., & Sugai, G. (1999). Effective behavior support: A systems approach to proactive schoolwide management. *Focus on Exceptional Children, 31*(6), 1–24.

Lewis, T. J., Colvin, G., & Sugai, G. (2000). The effects of precorrection and active supervision on the recess behavior of elementary school students. *Education and Treatment of Children, 23*, 109–121.

Lewis, T. J., Powers, L. J., Kelk, M. J., & Newcomer, L. (2002). Reducing problem behaviors on the playground: An investigation of the application of school-wide positive behavior supports. *Psychology in the Schools, 39*, 181–190.

Lohrmann-O'Rourke, S., Knoster, T., Sabatine, K., Smith, D., Horvath, G., & Llewellyn, G. (2000). School-wide application of PBS in the Bangor Area School District. *Journal of Positive Behavior Interventions, 2*(4), 238–240.

Luiselli, J., Putnam, R., & Sunderland, M. (2002). Longitudinal evaluation of behavior support interventions in public middle school. *Journal of Positive Behavior Interventions, 4*(3), 182–188.

Luiselli, J. K., Putnam, R. F., Handler, M. W., & Feinberg, A. B. (2005). Whole-school positive behaviour support: Effects on student discipline problems and academic performance. *Educational Psychology, 25*(2–3), 183–198.

Maguin, E., & Loeber, R. (1996). Academic performance and delinquency. *Crime and Justice: A Review of Research, 20*, 145–264.

March, R. E., & Horner, R. H. (2002). Feasibility and contributions of functional assessment in schools. *Journal of Emotional and Behavioral Disorders, 10*(3), 158–170.

March, R. E., Horner, R. H., Lewis-Palmer, T., Brown, D., Crown, D., Todd, A. W., et al. (2000). *Functional Assessment Checklist for Teachers and Staff (FACTS).* Eugene, OR: Educational and Community Supports. Available from *www.pbis.org/tools.htm.*

Mayer, G. R., & Sulzer-Azaroff, B. (1991). Interventions for vandalism. In G. Stoner, M. K. Shinn, & H. M. Walker (Eds.), *Interventions for achievement and behavior problems* (pp. 559–580). Washington, DC: National Association of School Psychologists Monograph.

McIntosh, K., Chard, D., Boland, J., & Horner, R. (2006). A demonstration of combined efforts in school-wide academic and behavioral systems and incidence of reading and behavior challenges in early elementary grades. *Journal of Positive Behavior Interventions, 8*(3), 146–154.

Metzler, C. W., Biglan, A., Rusby, J. C., & Sprague, J. R. (2001). Evaluation of a comprehensive behavior management program to improve school-wide positive behavior support. *Education and Treatment of Children, 24*, 448–479.

McIntosh, K., Campbell, A. L., Carter, D. R., & Dickey, C. R. (2009). Differential effects of a tier two behavior intervention based on function of problem behavior. *Journal of Positive Behavior Interventions, 11*(2), 82–93.

McIntosh, K., Horner, R. H., Chard, D., Boland, J., & Good, R. (2006). The use of reading and behavior screening measures to predict non-response to school-wide positive behavior support: A longitudinal analysis. *School Psychology Review, 35*, 275–291.

Medley, N. S., Little, S. G., & Akin-Little, A. (2008). Comparing individual behavior plans from schools with and without schoolwide positive behavior support: A preliminary study. *Journal of Behavior Education, 17*, 93–110.

Muscott, H., Mann, E., & LeBrun, M. R. (2008). Positive behavioral interventions and supports in New Hampshire: Effects of large-scale implementation of schoolwide positive behavior support on student discipline and academic achievement. *Journal of Positive Behavior Interventions, 10*, 190–205.

Nakasato, J. (2000). Data-based decision-making in Hawaii's behavior support effort. *Journal of Positive Behavior Interventions, 2*(4), 247–250.

National Center for Education Statistics. (2009). *Indicators of school crime and safety: 2008* (NCES 2009–022). Washington, DC: Author.

Nelson, J. R. (1996). Designing schools to meet the needs of students who exhibit disruptive behavior. *Journal of Emotional and Behavioral Disorders, 4,* 147–161.

Nelson, J. R., Colvin, G., & Smith, D. J. (1996). The effects of setting clear standards on students' social behavior in common areas of the school. *Journal of At-Risk Issues, 3,* 10–18.

Nelson, J. R., Martella, R., & Galand, B. (1998). The effects of teaching school expectations and establishing a consistent consequence on formal office disciplinary actions. *Journal of Emotional and Behavioral Disorders, 6,* 153–161.

Nersesian, M., Todd, A., Lehmann, J., & Watson, J. (2000). School-wide behavior support through district-level system change. *Journal of Positive Behavior Interventions, 2*(4), 244–246.

Office of Special Education Programs. (2003). *Twenty-fourth annual report to Congress on the implementation of the Individuals with Disabilities Act.* Washington, DC: Author.

O'Neil, R. E., Horner, R. H., Albin, R. W., Spague, J. R., Storey, K., & Newton, J. S. (1997). *Functional assessment for problem behavior: A practical handbook* (2nd ed.). Pacific Grove, CA: Books/Cole.

Putnam, R. F., Handler, M. W., Ramirez-Platt, C. M., & Luiselli, J. K. (2003). Improving student bus-riding behavior through a whole-school intervention. *Journal of Applied Behavior Analysis, 36,* 583–590.

Putnam, R. F., Luiselli, J. K., Handler, M. W., & Jefferson, G. L. (2003). Evaluating student discipline practices in a public school through behavioral assessment of office referrals. *Behavior Modification, 27,* 505–523.

Putnam, R. F., Luiselli, J. K., & Sunderland, M. (2002). Longitudinal evaluation of behavior support intervention in a public middle school. *Journal of Positive Behavior Interventions, 4,* 182–188.

Reynolds, C. R., & Kamphaus, R. W. (2004). *Behavior Assessment Scale for Children* (2nd ed.). Circle Pines, MN: American Guidance Service.

Sadler, C. (2000). Effective behavior support implementation at the district level: Tigard-Tualatin School District. *Journal of Positive Behavior Interventions, 2*(4), 241–243.

Safran, S. P., & Oswald, K. (2003). Positive behavior supports: Can schools reshape disciplinary practices? *Exceptional Children, 69,* 361–373.

Severson, H. H., Walker, H. M., Hope-Doolittle, J., Kratochwill, T. R., & Gresham, F. M. (2007). Proactive, early screening to detect behaviorally at-risk students: Issues, approaches, emerging innovations, and professional practices. *Journal of School Psychology, 45,* 193–223.

Shinn, M. R., Ramsey, E., Walker, H. M., Stieber, S., & O'Neill, R. E. (1987). Antisocial behavior in school settings: Initial differences in at risk and normal population. *Journal of Special Education, 21,* 69–84.

Skiba, R. J., & Knesting, K. (2002). Zero tolerance, zero evidence: An analysis of school disciplinary practice. In R. J. Skiba & G. G. Noam (Eds.), *New directions for youth development (no. 92: Zero tolerance: Can suspension and expulsion keep schools safe?).* San Francisco: Jossey-Bass.

Skiba, R. J., Peterson, R. L., & Williams, T. (1997). Office referrals and suspensions:

Disciplinary intervention in middle schools. *Education and Treatment of Children*, 20, 295–315.

Stewart, R. M., Benner, G. J., Martella, R. C., & Marchand-Martella, N. E. (2007). Three-tier models of reading and behavior: A research review. *Journal of Positive Behavior Interventions*, 9, 239–253.

Sugai, G., & Horner, R. H. (1999). Discipline and behavioral support: Preferred processes and practices. *Effective School Practices*, 17(4), 10–22.

Sugai, G., & Horner, R. H. (2002). The evolution of discipline practices: School-wide positive behavior supports. *Child and Family Behavior Therapy*, 24, 23–50.

Sugai, G., Horner, R. H., Dunlap, G., Hieneman, M., Lewis, T., Nelson, C. M., et al. (2000). Applying positive behavior support and functional behavioral assessment in schools. *Journal of Positive Behavior Interventions*, 2, 131–143.

Sugai, G., Horner, R. H., Sailor, W., Dunlap, G., Eber, L., Lewis, T., et al. (2005). *School-wide positive behavior support: Implementers' blueprint and self-assessment.* Eugene, OR: University of Oregon.

Sugai, G., & Lewis, T. J. (1996). Preferred and promising practices for social skills instruction. *Focus on Exceptional Children*, 29(4), 1–16.

Sugai, G., Lewis-Palmer, T., Todd, A., & Horner, R. H. (2001). *School-wide Evaluation Tool.* Eugene, OR: University of Oregon.

Sugai, G., Sprague, J. R., Horner, R. H., & Walker, H. M. (2000). Preventing school violence: The use of office discipline referrals to assess and monitor school-wide discipline interventions. *Journal of Emotional and Behavioral Disorders*, 8, 94–101.

Sugai, G., Todd, A. W., & Horner, R. (2001). *Team Implementation Checklists (Version 2.2).* Eugene, OR: University of Oregon, OSEP Center for Positive Behavioral Supports.

Taylor-Greene, S., Brown, D., Nelson, L., Longton, J., Gassman, Cohen, J., et al. (1997). School-wide behavioral support: Starting the year off right. *Journal of Behavioral Education*, 7, 99–112.

Taylor-Greene, S. J., & Kartub, D. (2000). Durable implementation of school-wide behavior support: The High Five Program. *Journal of Positive Behavioral Interventions*, 2(4), 233–235.

Todd, A. W., Campbell, A. L., Meyer, G. G., & Horner, R. H. (2009). The effects of a targeted intervention to reduce problem behaviors: Elementary school implementation of check in–check out. *Journal of Positive Behavior Intervention*, 10(1), 46–55.

Turnbull, A., Edmonson, H., Griggs, P., Wickham, D., Sailor, W., Freeman, R., et al. (2002). A blueprint for schoolwide positive behavior support: Implementation of three components [Electronic version]. *Exceptional Children*, 68, 377–402.

Walker, H. M. (1998). First steps to prevent antisocial behavior. *Teaching Exceptional Children*, 30, 16–19.

Walker, H. M., Kavanagh, K., Stiller, B., Golly, A., Severson, H. H., & Feil, H. H. (1998). First steps to success: An early intervention approach for preventing school antisocial behavior. *Journal of Emotional and Behavioral Disorders*, 6(2), 66–80.

Walker, H. M., Severson, H., & Feil, E. (1994). *The Early Screening Project: A proven child-find process.* Longmont, CO: Sopris West.

Walker, H. M., & Shinn, M. R. (2002). Structuring school-based interventions to achieve integrated primary, secondary, and tertiary prevention goals for safe and effective schools. In M. R. Shinn, H. M. Walker, & G. Stoner (Eds.), *Interventions for academic and behavior problems II: Prevention and remedial approaches* (pp. 681–701). Bethesda, MD: National Association of School Psychologists.

Warren, J. S., Edmonson, H. M., Griggs, P., Lassen, S. R., McCart, A., Turnbull, A., et al. (2003). Urban applications of school-wide positive behavior support: Critical issues and lessons learned. *Journal of Positive Behavior Interventions, 5,* 80–91.

Wright, J. A., & Dusek, J. B. (1998). Compiling school base rates for disruptive behaviors from student disciplinary referral data. *School Psychology Review, 27,* 138–148.

11

Special Education in an RTI Model

Addressing Unique Learning Needs

Matthew K. Burns
Theodore J. Christ
Christina H. Boice
Isadora Szadokierski

Special education is defined as "specialized instruction, provided at no cost to the parents or guardians, to meet the unique needs of a child with a disability" (Public Law 108-446, Part A, Sec. 602 [29]). The definition of special education has remained virtually unchanged in the revisions of the federal mandate and clearly emphasizes the unique learning needs of students and individually designed instruction to provide educational benefit to individual students (*Hendrick Hudson School Board of Education v. Rowley*, 1982).

The emphasis on unique learning needs is consistent with the response-to-intervention (RTI) approach to service delivery. RTI is best conceptualized as a resource allocation model that enhances learning for all students by matching school resources to student need (Tilly, 2008). Thus, RTI is designed to address the needs of all students and should also incorporate students with identified disabilities. Previous research found that implementing an RTI model reduced the number of students identified with a special education disability, and those identified with a learning disability

(LD) represented less than 2% of the student population (Burns, Appleton, & Stehouwer, 2005). Moreover, special education services in schools with a fully implemented RTI model generally (1) involve more services, of greater intensity, for individual students (Ikeda & Gustafson, 2002; Reschly & Starkweather, 1997); (2) occur at earlier grades (Reschly & Starkweather, 1997); (3) are more cost effective (Sornson, Frost, & Burns, 2005); and (4) more directly link resources to student needs (Tilly, 2003).

Despite the promising findings just described, the field has yet to establish a dominant model to define how special education fits with an RTI framework. The juxtaposition of RTI and special education is interesting, because both are essentially extensions of the same construct. Although special education is only part of a continuum of services that are needed within an RTI framework, both RTI and special education use data to address unique learning needs of students. Thus, the research on special education could enhance intervention practices within RTI, and the intervention design research could inform instructional practices within special education. In this chapter we describe how special education personnel and services could be conceptualized and used within an RTI model and discuss the basic premises of effective specialized instruction contextualized within RTI. Special education addresses a wide range of disabilities, but we limit our discussion to students with LDs because that is the disability category for which educational professionals are allowed to use RTI data to make eligibility decisions.

SPECIAL EDUCATION WITHIN RTI

Most Intensive Intervention

Most RTI models incorporate a three-tier service delivery model that matches intervention intensity and required resources with the intensity of student needs and problems (see Kovaleski & Black, Chapter 3, for more information). Perhaps one of the most well-known RTI implementation models is the Heartland Area Education Agency (2002), which has a long history of RTI implementation. Figure 11.1 is based on the Heartland RTI model but was modified to suggest how special education could fit within RTI, with Tier 3 being the level at which student needs are most severe and the most resources are used to address those needs. We also attempted to show that all students in Tier 2 and almost all in Tier 3 and special education also participate in Tier 1 services. Students are identified for special education in an RTI model through one of two ways: (1) Research-based interventions are implemented with fidelity, sometimes through multiple intervention phases, but the student does not make sufficient progress after an acceptable period of time and is referred for a multidisciplinary evaluation or (2) research-

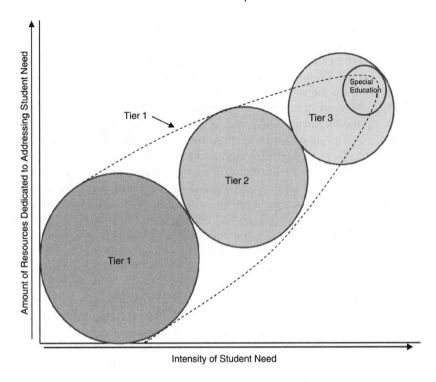

FIGURE 11.1. Special education in an RTI model.

based interventions are implemented with fidelity and the student makes sufficient progress has yet to reach the desired level of performance and the resources needed to continue the intervention exceed the resources available within general education. The latter is often the case when the problem severity is extreme or the problem will require substantial resources for an extended period of time and also results in the student being referred for a multidisciplinary evaluation.

The latter example suggests that special education is simply a mechanism to provide the most resource-intensive interventions to assist struggling learners. As stated, student response to the intervention is used to determine the necessary resources and is often evaluated with dual-discrepancy (DD) criteria that consider both the level and rate of student achievement (Fuchs, 2003). Interventions that result in a postintervention level and rate of growth that are below acceptable criteria, which represents a DD, are judged as ineffective and a more intensive intervention is attempted. Thus, a DD pattern among students receiving a Tier 2 intervention suggests that a

Tier 3 intervention may be needed, and a DD pattern among Tier 3 students may indicate a need for special education services. DD is consistent with the special education eligibility scenario described previously in which the interventions do not substantially alter the trajectory of growth and a student is referred for a multidisciplinary evaluation.

Pre- and postintervention skill levels are often assessed with curriculum-based measurement (CBM), but achievement tests may also inform this decision. Rate of growth is most often measured with CBM. Postintervention level has been evaluated by comparing performance with a normative standard such as the 25th percentile on norm-referenced measures (Torgesen et al., 2001) or with a criterion-referenced standard such as the benchmark proficiency levels associated with low risk utilized by the Dynamic Indicators of Beginning Early Literacy Skills (Good & Kaminski, 2002). For example, a CBM oral reading fluency score of fewer than 40 words read correctly per minute (WRCM) in the spring of first grade suggests that the student either demonstrates some risk for reading failure or is at risk for reading failure depending on the actual score.

Similar methods are used to define the discrepancies in the rate of academic growth. Published criterion-referenced standards for typical growth with CBM oral reading fluency are within the range of 1 to 2 WRCM/week (Deno, Fuchs, Marston, & Shin, 2001; Fuchs, Fuchs, Hamlett, Walz, & Germann, 1993; Fuchs, Fuchs, & Speece, 2002). Others have referenced local normative data to derive percentile cutoffs for CBM data (Fuchs, Fuchs, McMaster, & Al Otaiba, 2003) and group medians (Vellutino et al., 1996) to identify students with low rates of growth.

Previous research found that a DD approach led to better decision making than a single-discrepancy approach, which relied on either a low level or rate of achievement (Fuchs, 2003). The results of some studies provide evidence that DD criteria for identification and diagnosis converge with the outcomes of norm-referenced reading tests (Burns & Senesac, 2005; McMaster, Fuchs, Fuchs, & Compton, 2005; Speece & Case, 2001; Speece, Case, & Molloy, 2003). In fact, several DD models consistently differentiated reading scores on norm-referenced measures between students who are responding and students who are not responding adequately to their current instructional environment, which was something that other approaches to LD diagnosis did not do (Burns & Senesac, 2005).

Early Intervention

The 2004 reauthorization of the Individuals with Disabilities Education Act allows school districts to use up to 15% of their annual federal special education funds to implement coordinated early intervention and prevention services. These services are for students in all grades who require additional academic and behavior support to be successful in general education but who have not been identified as needing special education and related services (Public Law No. 108-446, § 613 [f]). Thus, special education personnel can deliver interventions within general education as part of an RTI model. This is consistent with the conceptualization of RTI as a resource allocation model for service delivery because RTI finds, prevents, and remediates academic and behavior problems before they disable learning.

Rather than delay services from highly qualified personal, effective RTI implementation will allow educational diagnosticians, school psychologists, and special education personnel to join the problem-solving process. They might consult or deliver services to students with deficit achievement as part of Tier 2 and Tier 3 early intervention and prevention services. Special education personnel are often well trained in many of the basic concepts of RTI and intervention delivery, among them data-based decision making, goal setting, and individualizing instruction (Lerner, 2002), and including them in efforts to address student difficulties in general education improves outcomes for students (Burns, 1999).

Future Research Regarding the Use of Special Education Services within RTI

The use of special education services to prevent and remediate academic and behavior problems for students who are at risk for disability classification is a relatively recent development; thus, there is limited research investigating how best to do so. Additional research is needed to determine how best to identify students in need of special education resources within RTI. Specifically, empirical inquiry should investigate how best to define a DD and how to determine whether an effective intervention exceeds general education resources. DD models generally involve either criterion- or norm-referenced decisions for postintervention level of skill and slope of growth. That is, DD criteria usually involve either (1) criterion-referenced level (e.g., reading rate that predicts passing the state test) and norm-referenced criterion for slope (e.g., 1 SD below the grade-level mean); (2) norm-referenced level (e.g., at or below the seventh percentile for oral reading fluency) and criterion-referenced slopes (e.g., rate of growth among grade-level peers that predicts passage of the state test; Silberglitt & Gibbons, 2005); or (3) criterion-referenced level and criterion-referenced slopes. Research that compares these definitions is ongoing and generally uses performance on a group-administered reading test and prevalence of students being identified with each (Burns & Senesac, 2005; Burns, Silberglitt, Christ, & Gibbons, 2009). Moreover, the effects of using RTI data to identify children with a special education disability and for using special education services for early intervention should be examined. Implications for student and systemic outcomes (Burns et al., 2005) and cost-effectiveness (Hartman & Fay, 1996) should be considered.

SPECIALIZED INSTRUCTION

The basic tenet of special education is specialized instruction to address unique learning needs. As stated, special education is quite consistent with an RTI model and fits well within the framework. Next, we describe how the basic tenets of specialized instruction to meet the unique learning needs of students with disabilities are best implemented and demonstrate how they are consistent with an RTI framework.

Effective Interventions

There is an extensive literature regarding effective interventions for students diagnosed with LDs. Thus, there are potential interventions from which special education teachers can choose when working with students with disabilities. Large mean adjusted effect sizes (ESs) were found for many academic areas, including word recognition (ES = 0.82), reading comprehension (ES = 0.95), word skills (ES = 0.87), general reading (ES = 0.90), mathematics (ES = 0.91), writing (ES = 0.82), and spelling (ES = 0.77; Swanson & Sachse-Lee, 2000).

Forness (2001) summarized meta-analytic research among students with disabilities by identifying practices with large (mnemonic strategies, ES = 1.62, and direct instruction, ES = 0.84) and moderate (ES = 0.70 for formative evaluation) mean effect sizes. Teachers of students with disabilities would be wise to select interventions that are consistent with these highly effective approaches. However, some instructional methodologies persist among special education teachers despite data that convincingly demonstrate ineffectiveness. For example, a mean effect size of 0.14 was reported for modality instruction, which could be classified as a small effect (Cohen, 1989). A recent survey of special education teachers found that modality instruction was the second most commonly used intervention, and it was used more frequently than formative evaluation and mnemonic strategies (Burns & Ysseldyke, 2009), which had moderate to large effects (Forness, 2001).

The use of ineffective interventions among teachers of children with disabilities is somewhat baffling given that we have a solid research base from which to work and can confidently identify effective interventions. Modality instruction, which had an average effect size close to zero (Kavale & Forness, 2000), was reportedly used on a daily basis by 30% of special education teachers who responded to the survey (Burns & Ysseldyke, 2009). Although 30% is a low number, given the apparent and well-documented lack of effect, any use of modality instruction as an intervention is questionable. Perhaps modality instruction continues because it is based in the learning styles concept, which is commonly used and valued in teacher training programs (Honigsfeld & Schiering, 2004) or because it is seen as easy to implement, but simply matching an instructional approach to a child's preferred modality will not be the intervention that teaches a struggling learner how to read. It should be noted that direct instruction was reportedly used on a daily basis by 83.3% of special education teachers who responded to the survey (Burns & Ysseldyke, 2009), and the research base for direct instruction is well established (Ellis, 2001).

Selecting an effective intervention is an important step in educating students with disabilities, but special education teachers must also determine how best to implement the intervention. Much of the effectiveness of an intervention is related to the components of the intervention; those that include the following instructional components have the largest effects: (1) high amounts of repetition with feedback, (2) segmenting information into small learning units, (3) controlling task difficulty, (4) modeling problem-solving steps, (5) using cues to prompt use of strategies, and (6) directed response/questioning of students (Swanson, 1999). Thus, the components of effective interventions within special education should be considered when addressing the unique learning needs of students with disabilities, as should the method with which they are delivered.

Frequency, Duration, and Intensity

Students who receive a Tier 3 intervention may require greater frequency, higher intensity, or longer duration of instruction than can be provided within general education in order for the intervention to be effective. Students are then found eligible for special education under an RTI model if the frequency, intensity, or duration of the well-matched and properly implemented intervention exceeds the available resources of general education, and the necessary elements of the intervention are spelled out in the individual educational plan.

Frequency is the number of times each week an intervention is provided, and *duration* is the time period over which a specified intervention is presented (Warren, Fey, & Yoder, 2007). Previous research found that the greater the number of minutes per day engaged in a research-based intervention, the higher the likelihood for success (Torgesen et al., 2001), which is why many researchers use frequency and duration as definitions of intensity, but those may not be the most important aspects of the intervention.

A recent meta-analysis among students with LDs found that interventions implemented for fewer than 11 days, between 12 and 30 days, and at least 30 days had similar adjusted mean effect sizes that exceeded 0.80 (Swanson & Sachse-Lee, 2000). However, the adjusted mean effect size for interventions with more than three steps was 0.89, compared with an adjusted mean effect size of 0.67 for those with fewer steps (Swanson & Sachse-Lee, 2000). Thus, it seems that the number of intervention components had a stronger effect on student outcomes than the length of the intervention.

Intervention intensity and resource allocation are parallel constructs because different interventions may require the same level of resources, but more intense interventions require more resources than less intensive interventions. Intervention intensity is best conceptualized as the interaction of dose, dose frequency, and intervention duration, with dose being defined as the number of "properly administered teaching episodes during a single intervention session" (Warren et al., 2007, p. 71). More teaching episodes or longer lasting episodes require additional time from school personnel than fewer or shorter ones, which equates to additional resources.

Future Research Regarding Specialized Instruction and RTI

There is a robust research base to guide the use of effective interventions for students with LDs, but there is also a long history of research suggesting that special education teachers do not always use research-based interventions (Burns & Ysseldyke, 2009; Espin & Deno, 2000; Witt, 1986). Noell and colleagues (Noell, Witt, Gilbertson, Ranier, & Freeland, 1997; Noell et al., 2000, 2005) have demonstrated the positive effects of performance feedback in enhancing implementation integrity, which is an important step in closing the research-to-practice gap, but performance feedback does not affect intervention selection. Thus, future researchers could examine how best to close the research-to-practice gap by further studying variables that impact special education teacher selection of interventions.

In addition to intervention selection, intervention intensity in special education is an area in need of additional research. The difference between Tier 2 and Tier 3 interventions and special education is individualization of type and amount (Tilly, 2008). There is an emerging body of evidence regarding some aspects of RTI including the importance of Tier 2 interventions (Burns, Hall-Lande, Lyman, Rogers, & Tan, 2006; Vaughn, Wanzek, Linan-Thompson, & Murray, 2007) and the need for those interventions to be explicit and more intensive than instruction in preceding tiers (Torgesen, 2004). However, the frequency, duration, and dose requirements for each tier need to be identified and differentiated from instruction delivered by special education.

ADDRESSING UNIQUE NEEDS

It is impossible to address unique learning needs for individual students without first identifying what those needs are. Thus, assessment is a critically important part of special education. Matching instruction to student characteristics in order to improve learning is a long-standing concept within education that has been applied in many ways. One example is the use of aptitude × treatment interactions (ATIs), in which a student's inherent abilities (e.g., learning style, cognitive strengths) are used to select the intervention that is presumed to be the most likely to help. Because evidence has accumulated that such methods are ineffective (Cronbach & Snow, 1977; Kavale & Forness, 1987; Ysseldyke, 1973), the focus has shifted away from underlying aptitudes to considering the student's level of performance on classroom relevant tasks to determine how to best intervene.

The dynamic process of assessment to inform intervention could be conceptualized as problem analysis (Christ, 2008), which is "the collection, summary and use of information to systematically test, reject, or verify relevant hypotheses to establish a problem solution" (p. 159). The likelihood of successful problem analysis is substantially influenced by the type of measurement used and questions addressed. The potential to establish efficient and effective problem solutions is enhanced when school psychologists and educators work with direct measures to examine the low inference and relevant questions/hypotheses. In his conceptualization, Christ puts forth that effective problem solvers rely on a skills by treatment interaction rather than an ATI approach to instill greater and more immediate potential for success.

The skills by treatment approach is direct and low inference. The ATI approach is indirect and high inference. Rather than evaluating indirect and high-inference hypotheses associated with sometimes ambiguous and difficult-to-measure constructs (e.g., executive functioning), a skills by treatment approach identifies the most relevant skill deficits to target for intervention (e.g., sound identification, decoding, word identification), evaluates the effect of targeted treatments, and can be used to identify unique learning needs. Next we describe a framework for identifying learning needs for reading based on a skill by treatment paradigm.

The areas examined by the National Reading Panel (NRP; 2000) could be conceived as a developmental framework for a reading intervention selection model. One of the first acts of the NRP was to divide reading into major topic areas, including alphabetics (phonemic awareness and phonics instruction), reading fluency, and comprehension (including vocabulary instruction and text comprehension instruction). These areas are similar to those presented by Chall (1983) and others (Adams, 1990; Snow, Burns, & Griffin, 1998) and represent a general progression of reading skill development (Berninger, Abbott, Vermeulen, & Fulton, 2006). Reading interventions can be targeted to students' needs within such a framework because each skill relies on at least basic-level proficiency of preceding skills before it can develop.

Once the appropriate target area is developed, then learning theory can be used to focus intervention efforts more clearly. Learning theory suggests that skills generally progress from a laborious process filled with errors to accurate but slow execution and eventually to efficient application of skills. This process can be described by a dynamic model of skill development, called the learning hierarchy (LH; Haring & Eaton, 1978). This model proposes that students progress through four phases when learning a new skill: acquisition, proficiency, generalization, and adaptation. As discussed next, each phase is defined by a characteristic type of skill development, which can directly translate into intervention methods.

During the acquisition phase, when first learning a skill, students are slow and have a high rate of errors. For example, in the development of reading fluency, students in this stage read very slowly and make several errors in decoding individual words. Entering the proficiency phase, students can perform the skill accurately but remain slow in execution; thus, the aim of this phase is to increase the rate of accurate skill production. In the case of reading fluency, students may be able to accurately decode words but still read at a very slow word-by-word rate. During the generalization phase, students can quickly and accurately apply the skill within the context in which it was learned and begin to apply the skill to a variety of material and contexts. Students in the generalization phase of reading fluency may apply the skill to reading a variety of different types of text such as letters, poems, and even science texts. Finally, in the adaptation phase, students learn to extract and apply the abstract meaning or goal of the skill to new situations without direction; the learned skill may also be used to further future development of new skills. In the case of reading fluency, the abstract goal of fluent reading is to decode the text in a reasonable amount of time so that its meaning can be efficiently extracted.

The LH is closely aligned with the commonly used intervention heuristic called the instructional hierarchy (IH; Ardoin & Daly, 2007; Haring & Eaton, 1978), which could provide the basis for effective analyses of academic problems (Christ, 2008). The IH provides guidance on the types of instructional strategies that match students' learning needs at each stage of the LH. Interventions for children in the acquisition phase focus on building response accuracy and could include demonstration, modeling, guided practice, frequent feedback, and routine drill. Once children reach the proficiency stage, they benefit most from instruction designed to increase the rate of skill performance such as novel practice opportunities, which includes frequent opportunities to respond and reinforcement for fluent performance.

The goal of the later stages of learning (i.e., generalization and adaptation) is to use the mastered skill effectively in a variety of materials and contexts. Students at these stages may require different instructional strategies such as problem solving, discrimination/differentiation training, and practice to apply mastered skills under novel conditions and more complex tasks (Haring & Eaton, 1978). Research has consistently demonstrated that the LH is an effective intervention heuristic (Ardoin & Daly, 2007).

Although an RTI framework can be used to identify LD in any of the areas for which LD can be diagnosed (e.g., basic reading skills, math computation, math reasoning, written expression), most implementation efforts address reading. Thus, we provide an example of how to match interventions with student needs based on the work of the NRP with the LH for reading. To identify an intervention with a high likelihood of success, special education teachers and Tier 3 interventionists could determine which instructional area is most appropriate for an individual student using the areas of the NRP and then determine which instructional activities from which phase of the LH are most appropriate for an individual student. Once the appropriate reading target is paired with the phase of instruction, then the appropriate intervention can be identified. As shown in Table 11.1, a repeated-reading intervention has a well-established research base (Therrien, 2004), but it may be appropriate only for someone for whom reading fluency is the best intervention target and who reads slowly but accurately (i.e., more than 93% of the words read correctly).

The appropriate phase of the LH is identified by collecting data regarding the accuracy and fluency with which the skill is completed. How fluently a skill is completed is commonly accepted as an indicator of proficiency and frequently assessed with CBMs such as words read correctly per minute, digits correct per minute, and correct letter sequences per minute. However, accuracy is less commonly examined despite the importance of these data. Betts (1946) first noted the importance of assessing how accurately a skill is performed by reporting that a student must be able to automatically recognize about 95% of the words while reading in order for comprehension to occur. Subsequent research found that when students can effortlessly read between 93 and 97% of the words, they not only comprehend well but also spend more time on task and complete a greater percentage of the activity compared with material that is too difficult (less than 93% known) or too easy (more than 97% known; Gickling & Armstrong, 1978; Treptow, Burns, & McComas, 2007). For other nonreading tasks, sometimes called drill tasks (e.g., spelling, phonics, sight word recognition; Gickling & Thompson, 1985), a different set of instructional-level criteria has been indicated suggesting that 90% of known items be included in the learning stimulus set (Burns, 2004). Thus, students who complete a reading task with less than 90 to 93% accuracy require explicit instruction in the task,

TABLE 11.1. Interventions Based on National Reading Panel and Learning Hierarchy

Learning hierarchy phases	Instructional strategies	Example interventions		
		Phonemic awareness	Phonics	Fluency
Acquisition	1. Demonstration 2. Models 3. Cues 4. Routine drill	• Explicit instruction (Blackman, Ball, Black, & Tangel, 2001) • Language and listening games (Adams, Foorman, Lundberg, & Beeler, 1998)	• Incremental rehearsal with letter sounds (Tucker, 1989) • Explicit instruction (Carnine, Silbert, Kame'enui, & Tarver, 2004) • Word sorts (Joseph, 2000)	• Incremental rehearsal (Tucker, 1989) • Listening passage preview (Rose & Sherry, 1984) • Phrase drill (O'Shea, Munson, & O'Shea, 1984) • Repeated reading with incentives (Moyer, 1982) • Read Naturally Inc. (2004)
Proficiency	1. Repeated novel drills 2. Reinforcement			
Generalization	1. Discrimination training 2. Differentiation training			
Adaptability	1. Problem solving 2. Simulations			

modeling, and immediate error correction. Those who still work slowly but complete more than 90% of the items (e.g., 93% of the words read correctly or 90% of the correct letter sounds given) require additional practice with the items followed by immediate feedback.

Future Research Regarding Unique Learning Needs and RTI

Unlike most topics in education, research has clearly informed practice in how we assess the unique learning needs of individual students. The movement away from the search for an ATI was fueled by a lack of research supporting it, but research has yet to identify what should replace the ATI approach for intervention design. The model presented previously is based on a well-confirmed research base, but the specifics need to be better developed. For example, there are few instructionally relevant measures of phonetic skills for students above the second grade, which is often the appropriate instructional target for older students with disabilities. Moreover, a better understanding of how to measure skills is only a part of establishing an alternative to the ATI model, and additional research is needed regarding the interventions that could be developed based on assessment data.

In addition to informing intervention design, additional research is needed to determine how best to assess whether the intervention is effective for each individual student with whom it is attempted. We know that well-constructed single-subject research designs to test intervention effectiveness can lead to valid decisions, and Christ (2006) demonstrates that slopes of student growth based on CBM data are not sufficiently reliable for decision making until at least six to eight data points are collected. However, the criteria with which student growth can be compared have yet to be definitively determined.

CONCLUSION

Torgesen (2004) recommended that supplemental instruction be explicit and more intensive than core instruction, and that the intensity of instruction be increased for students for whom supplemental instruction is not sufficient. As stated, intensity can be defined as the number of teaching episodes during a single intervention session (Warren et al., 2007, p. 71) and the number of components to the intervention, the level of curriculum modification that the intervention involves, or the amount of adult supervision required to implement the intervention (Barnett, Daly, Jones, & Lentz, 2004). However, that is not to say that time is not important. There is a direct relationship between amount of time engaged in instruction and student success (Torgesen et al., 2001), but simply individualizing the amount of instruction alone will not ensure success unless the type of instruction is also individualized, which is part of the fundamental definition and purpose of special education.

As schools continue to implement RTI, the role of special education will likely evolve. The model presented in Figure 11.1 represents special education in a fully functioning RTI model. It is somewhat of an ideal, an ideal that some schools have reached after years of implementation (Ikeda, Tilly, Stumme, Volmer, & Allison, 1996). Special education in most schools may look more like Figure 11.2 in which students with disabilities are served in various tiers. However, as special education becomes a mechanism with which to increase individualization of instructional type and amount, and as student response data are used to make eligibility decisions, the situation depicted in Figure 11.1 will slowly become a reality. In this model, special education would truly be individualized instruction to meet the unique learning needs of children with disabilities, and students with severe difficulties would receive individualized instruction to meet their needs regardless of an LD label or not. In other words, in a fully implemented RTI model, all education is special.

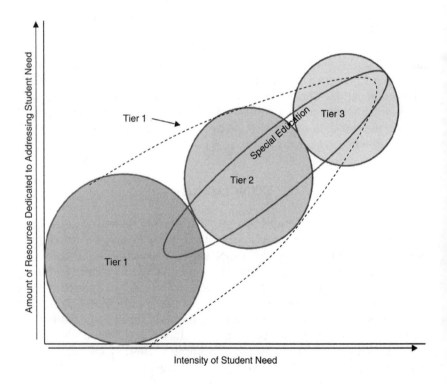

FIGURE 11.2. Special education in an RTI model in most schools.

REFERENCES

Adams, M. J. (1990). *Beginning to read: Thinking and learning about print.* Cambridge, MA: MIT Press.

Adams, M. J., Foorman, B. R., Lundberg, I., & Beeler, T. (1998). *Phonemic awareness in young children.* Baltimore: Brookes.

Ardoin, S. P., & Daly, E. J., III. (2007). Introduction to the special series: Close encounters of the instructional kind—How the instructional hierarchy is shaping instructional research 30 years later. *Journal of Behavioral Education, 16,* 1–6.

Barnett, D. W., Daly, E. J., III, Jones, K. M., & Lenz, F. E., Jr. (2004). Empirically based special service decisions from single-case designs of increasing and decreasing intensity. *The Journal of Special Education, 38,* 66–79.

Berninger, V. W., Abbott, R. D., Vermeulen, K., & Fulton, C. M. (2006). Paths to reading comprehension in at-risk second-grade readers. *Journal of Learning Disabilities, 39,* 334–351.

Betts, E. A. (1946). *Foundations of reading instructions with emphasis on differentiated guidance.* New York: American Book Company.

Blackman, B., Ball, E., Black, S., & Tangel, D. (1994). Kindergarten teachers develop phoneme awareness in low-income, inner-city classrooms: Does it make a difference? *Reading and Writing, 6,* 1–17.

Blackman, B., Ball, E., Black, S., & Tangel, D. (2001). *Road to the code.* Baltimore: Brookes.

Burns, M. K. (1999). Effectiveness of special education personnel in the intervention assistance team model. *Journal of Educational Research, 92,* 354–356.

Burns, M. K. (2004). Empirical analysis of drill ratio research: Refining the instructional level for drill tasks. *Remedial and Special Education, 25,* 167–175.

Burns, M. K., Appleton, J. J., & Stehouwer, J. D. (2005). Meta-analytic review of response-to-intervention research: Examining field-based and research-implemented models. *Journal of Psychoeducational Assessment, 23,* 381–394.

Burns, M. K., Hall-Lande, J., Lyman, W., Rogers, C., & Tan, C. S. (2006). Tier II interventions within response-to-intervention: Components of an effective approach. *Communiqué, 35*(4), 38–40.

Burns, M. K., & Senesac, B. K. (2005). Comparison of dual discrepancy criteria for diagnosis of unresponsiveness to intervention. *Journal of School Psychology, 43,* 393–406.

Burns, M. K., Silberglitt, B., Christ, T. J., & Gibbons, K. A. (2009). *Comparing norm- and criterion-referenced criteria for dual discrepancy within RtI.* Manuscript submitted for publication.

Burns, M. K., & Ysseldyke, J. E. (2009). Reported prevalence of evidence-based instructional practices in special education. *Journal of Special Education, 43,* 3–11.

Carnine, D. W., Silbert, J., Kame'enui, E. J., & Tarver, S. G. (2004). *Direct instruction reading* (4th ed.). Upper Saddle River, NJ: Prentice Hall.

Chall, J. S. (1983). *Stages of reading development.* New York: McGraw-Hill.

Christ, T. J. (2006). Short term estimates of growth using curriculum-based measurement of oral reading fluency: Estimates of standard error of the slope to construct confidence intervals. *School Psychology Review, 35,* 128–133.

Christ, T. J. (2008). Best practices in problem analysis. In A. Thomas & J. Grimes (Eds.), *Best practices in school psychology* (5th ed., pp. 159–176). Bethesda, MD: National Association of School Psychologists.

Cohen, J. (1989). *Statistical power analysis for the behavioral sciences* (2nd ed.). Hillsdale, NJ: Erlbaum.

Cronbach, L., & Snow, R. (1977). *Aptitudes and instructional methods: A handbook for research on interactions.* New York: Irvington.

Deno, S. L., Fuchs, L. S., Marston, D., & Shin, J. (2001). Using curriculum-based measurement to establish growth standards for students with learning disabilities. *School Psychology Review, 30,* 507–524.

Ellis, A. K. (2001). *Research on educational innovations* (3rd ed.). Larchmont, NY: Eye on Education.

Espin, C. A., & Deno, S. L. (2000). Research to practice: Views from researchers and practitioners. *Learning Disabilities Research and Practice, 15,* 67–68.

Forness, S. R. (2001). Special education and related services: What have we learned from meta-analysis? *Exceptionality, 9,* 185–197.

Fuchs, D., Fuchs, L. S., McMaster, K. N., & Al Otaiba, S. (2003). Identifying children at risk for reading failure: Curriculum-based measurement and dual-discrepancy approach. In H. L. Swanson & K. R. Harris (Eds.), *Handbook of learning disabilities* (pp. 431–449). New York: Guilford Press.

Fuchs, L. S. (2003). Assessing intervention responsiveness: Conceptual and technical issues. *Learning Disabilities Research and Practice, 18,* 172–186.

Fuchs, L. S., Fuchs, D., Hamlett, C. L., Walz, L., & Germann, G. (1993). Formative evaluation of academic progress: How much growth can we expect? *School Psychology Review, 22,* 27–48.

Fuchs, L. S., Fuchs, D., & Speece, D. L. (2002). Treatment validity as a unifying construct for identifying learning disabilities. *Learning Disability Quarterly, 25,* 33–46.

Gickling, E. E., & Armstrong, D. L. (1978). Levels of instructional difficulty as related to on-task behavior, task completion, and comprehension. *Journal of Learning Disability, 11,* 559–566.

Gickling, E. E., & Thompson, V. (1985). A personal view of curriculum-based assessment. *Exceptional Children, 52,* 205–218.

Good, R. H., & Kaminski, R. A. (2002). *Dynamic indicators of basic early literacy skills.* Eugene, OR: Institute for the Development of Educational Achievement.

Haring, N. G., & Eaton, M. D. (1978). Systematic instructional technology: An instructional hierarchy. In N. G. Haring, T. C. Lovitt, M. D. Eaton, & C. L. Hansen (Eds.), *The fourth R: Research in the classroom* (pp. 23–40). Columbus, OH: Merrill.

Hartman, W. T., & Fay, T. A. (1996). Cost-effectiveness of instructional support teams in Pennsylvania. *Journal of Educational Finance, 21,* 555–580.

Heartland Area Education Agency. (2002). *Improving children's educational results through data-based decision making.* Johnston, IA: Author.

Honigsfeld, A., & Schiering, M. (2004). Diverse approaches to the diversity of learning styles in teacher education. *Educational Psychology, 24,* 487–507.

Ikeda, M. J., & Gustafson, J. K. (2002). *Heartland AEA 11's problem solving process: Impact on issues related to special education* (Research Rep. No. 2002-01). Johnston, IA: Heartland Area Education Agency 11.

Ikeda, M. J., Tilly, D. W., Stumme, J., Volmer, L., & Allison, R. (1996). Agency-wide implementation of problem-solving consultation: Foundations, current implementation, and future directions. *School Psychology Quarterly, 11,* 228–243.

Joseph, L. M. (2000). Developing first graders' phonemic awareness, word identification, and spelling: A comparison of two contemporary phonic instructional approaches. *Reading Research and Instruction, 39,* 160–169.

Kavale, K. A., & Forness, S. R. (1987). Substance over style: Assessing the efficacy of modality testing and teaching. *Exceptional Children, 54,* 228–234.

Kavale, K. A., & Forness, S. R. (2000). Policy decisions in special education: The role of meta-analysis. In R. Gersten, E. P. Schiller, & S. Vaughn (Eds.), *Contemporary special education research: Synthesis of the knowledge base on critical instructional issues* (p. 281–326). Mahwah, NJ: Erlbaum.

Lerner, J. W. (2002). *Learning disabilities: Theories, diagnosis, and teaching strategies* (8th ed.). Boston: Houghton Mifflin.

McMaster, K. L., Fuchs, D., Fuchs, L. S., & Compton, D. L. (2005). Responding to nonresponders: An experimental field trial of identification and intervention methods. *Exceptional Children, 71,* 445–463.

Moyer, S. B. (1982). Repeated reading. *Journal of Learning Disabilities, 15,* 619–623.

National Reading Panel. (2000). *Teaching children to read: An evidence-based assessment of the scientific research literature on reading and its implications for reading instruction: Reports of the subgroups.* Bethesda, MD: National Institute for Literacy.

Noell, G. H., Witt, J. C., Gilbertson, D. N., Ranier, D. D., & Freeland, J. T. (1997). Increasing teacher intervention implementation in general education settings through consultation and performance feedback. *School Psychology Quarterly, 12,* 77–88.

Noell, G. H., Witt, J. C., LaFleur, L. H., Mortenson, B. P., Ranier, D. D., & LeVelle, J. (2000). A comparison of two follow-up strategies to increase teacher intervention implementation in general education following consultation. *Journal of Applied Behavior Analysis, 33,* 271–284.

Noell, G. H., Witt, J. C., Slider, N. J., Connell, J. E., Gatti, S. L., Williams, K. L., et al. (2005). Treatment implementation following behavioral consultation in schools: A comparison of three follow-up strategies. *School Psychology Review, 34,* 87–106.

O'Shea, L. J., Munson, S. M., & O'Shea, D. J. (1984). Error correction in oral reading: Evaluating the effectiveness of three procedures. *Education and Treatment of Children, 7,* 203–214.

Read Naturally Inc. (2004). *Read naturally masters edition.* St. Paul, MN: Author.

Reschly, D. J., & Starkweather, A. R. (1997). *Evaluation of an alternative special education assessment and classification program in the Minneapolis public schools.* Minneapolis, MN: Minneapolis Public Schools.

Rose, T. L., & Sherry, L. (1984). Relative effects of two previewing procedures on

LD adolescents' oral reading performance. *Learning Disabilities Quarterly, 7,* 39–44.

Silberglitt, B., & Gibbons, K. A. (2005). *Establishing slope targets for use in a response to intervention model (technical manual).* Rush City, MN: St. Croix River Education District.

Snow, C. E., Burns, M. S., & Griffin, P. (1998). *Preventing reading difficulties in young children.* Washington, DC: National Research Council.

Sornson, R., Frost, F., & Burns, M. K. (2005). Instructional support teams in Michigan: Data from Northville public schools. *Communiqué, 33*(5), 28–30.

Speece, D. L., & Case, L. P. (2001). Classification in context: An alternative approach to identifying early reading disability. *Journal of Educational Psychology, 93,* 735–749.

Speece, D. L., Case, L. P., & Molloy, D. E. (2003). Responsiveness to general education instruction as the first gate to learning disabilities identification. *Learning Disabilities Research and Practice, 18,* 147–156.

Swanson, H. L. (1999). Reading research for students with LD: A meta-analysis in intervention outcomes. *Journal of Learning Disabilities, 32,* 504–532.

Swanson, H. L., & Sachse-Lee, C. A. (2000). A meta-analysis of single-subject intervention research for students with LD. *Journal of Learning Disabilities, 33,* 114–136.

Therrien, W. J. (2004). Fluency and comprehension gains as a result of repeated reading: A meta-analysis. *Remedial and Special Education, 25,* 252–261.

Tilly, W. D. (2003, December). *How many tiers are needed for successful prevention and early intervention? Heartland Area Education Agency's evolution from four to three tiers.* Paper presented at the National Research Center on Learning Disabilities Responsiveness-to-Intervention Symposium, Kansas City, MO.

Tilly, W. D., III. (2008). The evolution of school psychology to science-based practice. In A. Thomas & J. Grimes (Eds.), *Best practices in school psychology V* (pp. 18–32). Washington, DC: National Association of School Psychologists.

Torgesen, J. K. (2004). Lessons learned from research on interventions for students who have difficulty learning to read. In P. McCardle & V. Chhabra (Eds.), *The voice of evidence in reading research* (pp. 355–382). Baltimore: Brookes.

Torgesen, J. K., Alexander, A. W., Wagner, R. K., Rashotte, C. A., Voeller, K. K. S., & Conway, T. (2001). Intensive remedial instruction for children with severe reading disabilities: Immediate and long-term outcomes for two instructional approaches. *Journal of Learning Disabilities, 34,* 33–58.

Treptow, M. A., Burns, M. K., & McComas, J. J. (2007). Reading at the frustration, instructional, and independent levels: The effects on students' reading comprehension and time on task. *School Psychology Review, 36,* 159–166.

Tucker, J. A. (1989). *Basic flashcard technique when vocabulary is the goal.* Unpublished teaching materials, University of Tennessee at Chattanooga.

Vaughn, S., Wanzek, J., Linan-Thompson, S., & Murray, C. (2007). Monitoring response to intervention for students at-risk for reading difficulties: High and low responders. In S. R. Jimerson, M. K. Burns, & A. M. VanDerHeyden (Eds.), *Handbook of response to intervention: The science and practice of assessment and intervention* (pp. 234–243). New York: Springer Science.

Vellutino, F. R., Scanlon, D. M., Sipay, E. R., Small, S., Chen, R., Pratt, A., et al. (1996). Cognitive profiles of difficulty-to-remediate and readily remediated poor readers: Early intervention as a vehicle for distinguishing between cognitive and experimental deficits as basic causes of specific reading disability. *Journal of Educational Psychology, 88,* 601–638.

Warren, S. F., Fey, M. E., & Yoder, P. J. (2007). Differential treatment intensity research: A missing link to creating optimally effective communication interventions. *Mental Retardation and Developmental Disabilities, 13,* 70–77.

Witt, J. C. (1986). Teachers' resistance to the use of school-based interventions. *Journal of School Psychology, 24,* 37–44.

Ysseldyke, J. E. (1973). Diagnostic-prescriptive teaching: The search for aptitude-treatment interactions. In L. Mann & D. A. Sabatino (Eds.), *The first review of special education* (pp. 5–32). Philadelphia: JSE Press.

12

Developing Systems-Level Capacity for RTI Implementation

Current Efforts and Future Directions

George Sugai
Robert H. Horner
Dean Fixsen
Karen Blase

Response to intervention (RTI) provides a reasonable and considered approach to using assessment information to improve the effectiveness, efficiency, and relevance of the implementation of evidence-based academic and behavioral practices for all students (Kame'enui, 2007; Sugai & Horner, 2009). RTI represents an integration of a number of recommended component practices into a package in which the "whole is better than the sum of the parts." An underlying necessity to RTI implementation is defining the systems-level support and capacity that are needed to ensure sustainable and accurate implementation and durable outcomes.

RTI is more than a set of discrete practices. Rather, it is an approach to school improvement that begins with high-quality foundation instruction/support and uses data-based decision making to add graduated levels of assistance where needed to ensure academic and/or behavioral success for students. RTI incorporates evidence-based practices but within a structure emphasizing a "systems" logic. This emphasis on the systems is needed to implement and sustain effective practices that guides the content of this chapter. Specifically, we provide (1) a rationale and background for adopting a systems capacity perspective, (2) a description of the elements and processes of this perspective, and (3) an overview of current implementation practice. To contextualize this discussion, we use our combined empirical and applied experiences with the implementation of schoolwide positive behavior supports (SWPBS; *www.pbis.org*) and the National Implementation Research Network (NIRN; *www.fpg.unc.edu/~nirn*).

RATIONALE AND BACKGROUND[1]

Maximizing the academic achievement and social behavior competence of all students in school is one of our nation's most important education priorities (Kauffman & Landrum, 2009; Kutash, Duchnowski, & Lynn, 2006; Walker et al., 1996). However, reaching this goal is not just about adopting another new initiative; it is also about requiring schools to

1. increase instructional accountability and justification;
2. improve the alignment between assessment information and intervention development;
3. enhance the use of limited resources and time;
4. make decisions with accurate and relevant information;
5. initiate important instructional decisions earlier and in a more timely manner;
6. engage in regular and comprehensive screening for successful and at-risk learners;
7. provide effective and relevant support for students who do not respond to core curricula; and
8. enhance fidelity of instructional implementation (Sugai, 2008, p. 1).

To achieve the priorities and to address these requirements, RTI has evolved as a policy statement in the Individuals with Disabilities Education Improvement Act of 2004 (IDEA) for improving teaching and learning environments for all students (Sugai & Horner, 2009). The developmental history of RTI includes significant contributions from applied behavior analysis, curriculum-based measurement, precision teaching, prereferral intervention, teacher assistance teaming, diagnostic prescriptive teaching, data-based decision making, early universal screening and intervention, behavioral and instructional consultations, and team-based problem solving

---

[1]RTI background content for this section is based on Sugai, G. (2008). *School-wide positive behavior support and response to intervention*. Washington, DC: RTI Action Network.

(Sugai, 2007). It should be noted that the term *RTI* never appears in IDEA or the No Child Left Behind Act of 2001; however, RTI is linked to references to "scientifically-based research" (Sugai & Horner, in press-a).

As described in previous chapters, variations exist in how RTI is defined and operationalized; however, it is generally described as a systemic problem-solving or decision-making framework that is composed of (1) universal screening procedures, (2) team- and data-based decision making, (3) continuous progress monitoring, (4) direct measurement and monitoring of student performance as indicators of intervention effectiveness, (5) a continuum of integrated evidence-based practices, and (6) accountability for high levels of intervention implementation fidelity (Sugai, 2008; Sugai & Horner, 2009). As a complete "package," RTI operates within the context of data-based decision rules that enable formative evaluation of student performance and inform adjustments in instruction. That is, students' responsiveness and nonresponsiveness to intervention are used to judge the appropriateness of that intervention and to guide decisions about intervention improvements. As a general rule, the greater the degree of student nonresponsiveness, the greater the need for instructional modifications and often the more specialized and intensive the intervention. This logic is based on the assumption and requirement that students receive the interventions or instruction needed to achieve educational success. The root philosophy of RTI is guided by pragmatic use of resources to assist children to meet academic and social expectations.

Fidelity generally refers to the extent to which (1) implementation occurs with high enough accuracy or integrity that full impact of implementation is realized and (2) statements about observed outcomes can be attributed to the implementation. Implementation fidelity is considered at multiple levels (e.g., state, district, school, classroom, student), each affecting the interpretation of the next level. For example, in efforts to improve the social culture of schools, a state might adopt a system change process (independent variable) that would affect district functioning (dependent variable). In turn, district functioning (independent variable) is expected to affect school operations (dependent variable). School operations (independent variable) are designed to enhance classroom routines (dependent variable). Finally, enhanced classroom routines (independent variable) will be linked to enhancements in student achievement (dependent variables). In this example, each independent variable becomes the dependent variable for the previous level. In addition, the implementation accuracy of each independent variable is examined to maximize what can be said about the dependent variable. Depending on the degree of accuracy required, implementation fidelity can be assessed through outside or internal evaluators using checklists, observations, content audits, and so on.

RTI is good policy; however, its multicomponent nature and requirement for generalized application across academic and social behavior curriculum areas (e.g., literacy, numeracy, language arts, science, fine arts, history, social skills, character education) require thoughtful and prioritized pre- and inservice professional development. In this case, good intent (policy) does not guarantee widespread adoption and accurate and sustained implementation (practice). Dean Fixsen of NIRN has described policies like RTI as "the allocation of limited resources for unlimited needs" (Fixsen et al., 2005). Further, he suggests that training efforts are generally inadequate at translating policy into meaningful action. Fortunately, guidance and experience are available to enable a more systemic and organizational sound approach to the adoption, accurate and sustained implementation, and controlled scaling of RTI as a framework. In addition, a promising research base is developing (Bradley, Danielson, & Doolittle, 2007; Sugai & Horner, 2009). The challenge is ensuring an effective and long-lasting transfer of what we know (research) into policy and practice (Carnine, 1997; Detrich, Keyworth, & States, 2004; Glasgow, Lichtenstein, & Marcus, 2003; Peters & Heron, 1993).

In summary, RTI is generally considered good policy that unifies a number of evidence-based practices into a promising framework to improve instructional decision making for enhanced academic and behavioral outcomes for all students. RTI is a policy framework that is composed of a number of validated practices (e.g., data-based decision making, universal screening). This framework of practices is used to guide implementation of specific academic and/or social behavior intervention programs or approaches (e.g., early literacy, schoolwide positive behavior support). The current challenge is less "identification of what do to" than building a better understanding of how to "implement what is known" on a scale and with a level of fidelity that produces socially important changes in education.

SYSTEMS CAPACITY ELEMENTS AND PROCESSES

RTI implementation must be carefully anticipated and systemically operationalized when put in place. In this section, we describe general system-level elements and processes within the context of establishing capacity for successful RTI implementation. In particular, we describe the general phases of a systems-level implementation and the processes that facilitate movement through those phases.

Implementation Phases

Most system-level change agents agree that implementation does not occur in a linear, stepwise manner (Elmore, 1996; Fixsen, Naoom, Blase, Friedman, & Wallace, 2005). Ever-changing combinations of factors must be considered at any point in time (e.g., change in personnel, new policy priority from a superintendent, increase/decrease in enrollments and resources, demographic shifts). Thus, a process of continuous regeneration is required to identify and adapt to change in personnel, policy, outcomes, and so on (McIntosh, Horner, & Sugai, 2009; Sugai, Horner, & McIntosh, 2008). We conceptualize implementation as a series of phases to assist in understanding the process and to enhance fidelity and outcomes. Generally, the implementation process is characterized in six phases.

Determination of Need and Desired Alternative

The implementation process begins when an individual or group of individuals identifies the need to do something differently because results are not being achieved at an acceptable level or rate or because a new problem arises that cannot be addressed by existing programs or practices. This phase is characterized by data and information gathering to confirm that the need exists and is sufficient to warrant attention and resources. In addition, data collected during this phase serve as the baseline for evaluating outcomes or student responsiveness when interventions are put in place. Determination of the need should result in clear responses to the following types of questions:

1. What does the need look like?
2. Is the need data based, outcome driven, and socially valid?
3. When and under what conditions is the need most and least likely to be observed?
4. How often is the need observed or how long has it existed?
5. Who is involved and/or affected by the need?
6. What response, solution, or alternative is desired to address the need?

For example, a school determines that waiting until the end of the semester is too late for identifying students who are not responding to the reading program; however, the current reading curriculum does not have early and regularly scheduled opportunities and personnel to screen for non-responders. The *need*, rationale, or justification for adopting or adapting an intervention, practice, or program should be data based, outcome driven, and socially valid.

Equally important to defining the need is describing what alternative is desired, that is, what an adequate solution would look like. Each of the descriptors used to define the need would be used with the alternative. Using the previous example, the need would be addressed by scheduling a grade-level administration of a 1-minute probe for each student at the beginning of the grading period and once every 2 weeks thereafter. A team of two paraprofessionals would rotate across grade-level classrooms to assist teachers in conducting assessments and summarizing results.

Determination of need is often reactive in that attention is redirected when a problem begins to affect current functioning or quality of desired outcomes. For example, the number of disciplinary referrals to the office reached a level at which the school administrator was not able to conduct daily morning and afternoon walk-throughs of the school building. In contrast, determination of need also could be more preventive in that regular screening or self-assessments are conducted to determine whether problems or needs are "emerging," and practices can be identified and put in place before the need becomes problematic. In this example, every 2 weeks, teachers review their class enrollments to see which students have made little or no progress on current reading lessons. Rather than waiting for failure at the end of the grading period to trigger the provision of supports, literacy intervention is implemented early in the instructional schedule.

The challenge for teachers and administrators is reducing the number of needs to be addressed and prioritizing them from most to least important. Priority should be given to those needs and alternatives that are measurable, achievable, directly related to student outcomes and performance, and validated by everyone involved.

Exploration and Adoption

Once the need and alternative are confirmed, identified, and given priority, the implementation process shifts to searching for a practice or intervention to achieve the desired alternative. The goal is to identify possible practices or interventions that are first and foremost evidence based, that is, they are:

1. *Effective.* Do empirical demonstrations exist of a functional relationship between desired outcomes and manipulation of the practice? How much confidence and support exist to suggest that a given practice can be responsible for producing the desired effects or outcomes?
2. *Efficient.* Is the practice doable with local implementers and resources?
3. *Relevant.* Can the practice be adapted to fit within the parameters of the local context or culture?
4. *Sustainable.* Can the practice be implemented with fidelity over time with local resources and capacities?
5. *Scalable.* Can the practice be transported or extended to other similar settings, units, and staff for implementation with fidelity and within the organization?

After one or more strategies or practices are identified, the process shifts to adoption, with an emphasis on adapting the practice to the unique features of the local implementation context and culture and evaluating it using the previous five characteristics: effective, efficient, relevant, sustainable, and scalable. The bottom line is that real implementers must be able to make adaptations and implement with fidelity and sustainability in real contexts. Using the previous example, the school literacy team found an evidence-based, phonics-based screening tool (curriculum-based measurement) that had multiple and equivalent variations of adaptable reading probes. Online training materials for training assessors were available to all teachers. The literacy team prepared a 15-minute presentation for school staff to secure agreement for program adoption and implementation.

Initial Implementation and Demonstration

Once a suitable practice or intervention has been adopted by a majority of faculty, the process shifts to initial implementation in a small number of sites, classrooms, schools, and so on to demonstrate what it looks like and learn about the effort, adaptations, and costs of implementation. The process begins with introduction of the practice to the implementers, securing agreements from those who will be affected by implementation, and development of implementation capacity with local resources.

The goals during this phase are to address the following questions:

1. What does the intervention implementation look like?
2. What resources are required to support accurate and sustainable implementation?
3. What adjustments are needed for this specific implementation context?
4. What levels of change and outcome can be expected?

A critical requirement during this phase is the careful and systematic collection of data related to fidelity of implementation and impact on desired student outcomes. If an intervention is not implemented with fidelity and in a contextually and culturally appropriate manner, intervention effectiveness and student performance responsiveness are impossible to demonstrate. In addition, enhancements and adjustments are difficult to make because decisions are not informed.

Full Implementation with Fidelity

If the requirements of initial implementation can be demonstrated in a convincing manner over time, plans and resources for broader implementation can be considered. Lessons learned from initial implementation are used to maximize the effectiveness, efficiency, and relevance of full implementation. The objective during this phase is to establish sustainable and accurate implementation with local and sustainable resources. Supplementary supports (e.g., consultants, full professional development days, training coaches) used during initial implementation are faded and eliminated. For example, a district pilots an eighth- to ninth-grade peer-mentoring intervention in one of three regional high schools. After 3 months of intensive training from an external consultant and 6 months of external coach-supported implementation, the district leadership team determines that (1) the mentoring program has been implemented with 90% accuracy and (2) 80% of students have improved their attendance and discipline referrals by more than 55%, well exceeding their goal of 25%. The goal for full implementation is to continue the same level of peer mentoring but with support from the counseling department instead of external coaching.

During this phase, data collection continues to enable intervention adjustments, fine-tuning, and maximized student outcomes. In addition, emphasis is directed toward establishing systemic supports and capacity for sustaining implementation with high fidelity (i.e., coaching, training, coordination, policy, evaluation; see implementation blueprint presented later). In the previous example, the district leadership team took over the coaching functions and focused its attention on increasing the counseling department's capacity to coordinate and evaluate the program.

Another feature of the full implementation phase is replicating the implementation and outcomes of an intervention in comparable units (e.g., classrooms, schools, districts). If additional implementation examples can be replicated, future investments in sustainable resources and in scaling implementation across the administrative unit or organization can be more easily justified. For example, because of concern about the growing number of behavior incidents related to teasing and harassment behavior, a district implements a character education program in one of six middle schools. After a successful year of implementation in one school, the district team selects a second school for implementation of the same curricula. The district school psychologists were trained by the developers of the character education curricula to coach, train, and evaluate implementation fidelity and student outcomes and independently prepared and coached a second school through the adoption and implementation process. One year later, both schools were implementing fully with high fidelity and experiencing improved schoolwide social behavior.

Sustainability with Continuous Regeneration

The real indicator of successful adoption and implementation of an intervention is the sustained use of that intervention with (1) high fidelity over a full implementation cycle (e.g., academic school year); (2) durable and acceptable levels of student outcome performance; (3) systems coordination, coaching, and training without external supports (i.e., grants, paid consultants); and (4) evaluation processes that permit ongoing data-based decision making for adjustments that improve implementation and outcomes and summative consideration of the overall program effectiveness and impact. The goal is to ensure that implementation is sustained through continuous regeneration of practices and processes in response to ever-changing context factors. Continuous regeneration is "the process of (a) iterative monitoring of both fidelity and outcomes, (b) adaptation and readaptation of a practice over time while keeping its critical features intact, and (c) ongoing investment in implementation and reimplementation" (McIntosh et al., 2009, p. 336). This function is usually the responsibility of the leadership or management team.

In the previous example, after the two initial schools fully implemented the character education curricula, the remaining four middle schools initiated the implementation process and after 24 months documented full implementation with fidelity and acceptable outcome data. The implementation process was coordinated by the district leadership team, whose members provided school team training, external facilitation support, and regular evaluation reports on the quality of implementation and impact on discipline climate, classroom behavioral incident reports, and school–community relations (e.g., local crime, number of school/community events). Implementation was adjusted over the 24-month period in response to increases in the number of supported schools and organizational changes that occurred at the district level. For instance, because the number of district coaches remained unchanged as middle schools were added, internal (school-based) coaches or facilitators were identified to share in coaching functions. These internal coaches were school counselors, special educators, and social workers. During that same time, the district adopted a new science curriculum that reduced the number of professional development days available for faculty members from science departments to also participate in character education preparation. The solution was to invite a paraprofessional from science departments to be their representative on the school character education leadership team.

Thus, one of the most important characteristics of the sustainability phase is the capacity to continually self-assess the status of implementation fidelity and outcomes and to use these analyses to adapt or regenerate structures and processes, enabling implementation to continue in an effective, efficient, and relevant manner, that is, continuous regeneration. Resource management focuses on sustained implementation of existing investments while leaving open opportunities to address new or different implementation needs.

Scaling with Continuous Regeneration

The final and definitive implementation outcome is the controlled and sustainable distribution of an intervention or practice across other similar organizational units. For example, if a state management team successfully implements an intervention fully in one district, can the state organize its resources and capacities to implement the same intervention in multiple districts? If a regional implementation team in a large school district successfully implements a program in five of its 45 elementary schools, can it accomplish the same level of implementation in its remaining 40 elementary schools and 15 middle schools? If a countywide regional implementation team successfully implements an effective safe schools initiative in 14 districts, can it retool to support adoption of a new health curriculum while simultaneously and efficiently maintaining implementation of the safe schools initiative?

As in the sustainability phase, the emphasis during scaling is on establishing an efficient and effective organizational structure that can sustain its current implementation investments with high fidelity *and* simultaneously expand implementation across new sites with a relatively unchanged level of resources or retool for rollout of a new initiative implementation. For example, in the first year, a state management team initiates an intervention implementation in five schools in each of three school districts. The team consists of one full-time coordinator, two half-time program-level supervisors, and the program leaders from four other state-level initiatives or programs. This team provides training, coaching, and evaluation supports directly to each of the three districts through their local district implementation teams. Given the success of this implementation, the state superintendent approves a 5-year plan to double the number of new districts in each year. As can be seen in Table 12.1, although state capacity, in terms of full-time equivalence (FTE) and external coaching support, remains relatively constant, the total number of new and trained schools and districts increases exponentially.

The hypothetical state implementation data in Figures 12.1 and 12.2 illustrate the challenge of large-scale intervention expansion across schools and districts. In Figure 12.1, as the number of new districts doubles each year, the number of new schools needing implementation support increases at an even faster rate (slope). Given the additional number of schools that have been trained but need to be supported for sustainable implementation of the intervention, the increase in slope in total number of schools over the 5 years is even steeper. The likelihood that state resources would be increased at the same rate as the number of schools is extremely low.

In Figure 12.2, the number of external coaches and state FTE is relatively constant. However, to compensate for the exponential increase in

TABLE 12.1. Hypothetical State Intervention Scaling by District, School, and Year

	Year				
	1	2	3	4	5
Schools and Districts					
New districts	3	6	12	24	48
Total districts	3	9	21	45	53
New schools in new districts	9	18	36	72	144
Total schools	9	27	63	135	279
Total internal coaches	3	6	12	24	48
State capacity					
State FTE	2	2	3	3	3.5
Total external state coaches	1	2	3	3	5

Note. FTE, full-time equivalence.

schools, the number of district-level internal coaches is increased. Internal coaches are identified at the school and district levels to share the facilitation responsibilities initially assumed by the state coaches only. This example illustrates the anticipatory planning and continuous regeneration required at the coordination level to establish sufficient supports for sustaining implementing schools and districts and preparing new schools and districts.

To summarize, although the number of phases and the organization and sequencing of the implementation activities or functions will vary by

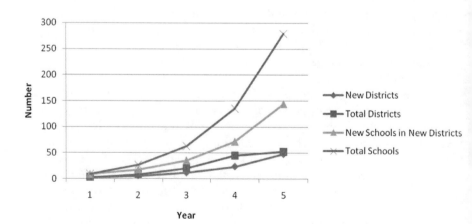

FIGURE 12.1. Hypothetical state 5-year school and district scaling.

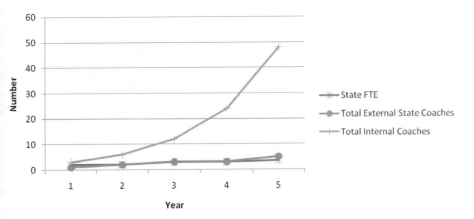

FIGURE 12.2. Hypothetical state 5-year implementation scaling support (FTE, full-time equivalence).

organizational model and context, the implementation sequence or process must (1) use data for decision making, (2) have clearly defined outcome objectives, (3) give priority to evidence-based practices, and (4) be systems oriented (Figure 12.3; Sugai et al., 2000). Each of these elements is described in Table 12.2.

Implementation Structures and Processes

Given these generic implementation phases, a number of structures and processes facilitate the process. In this section, we focus on (1) leadership

FIGURE 12.3. Main elements of implementation phases.

TABLE 12.2. Questions and Descriptions for Implementation Elements

Implementation elements	Questions	Description
Data	What do we currently see and know?	Data-based decision-making guides, selection and modification of curricula and practices, evaluation of progress, and enhancement of systems
Outcomes	What do we want to see?	Clearly specified outcomes that are related to academic achievement and social competence
Practices	What practice could effectively, efficiently, and relevantly achieve what we want to see?	Evidence-based practices with a high probability of outcome achievement for students
Systems	What needs to be in place to support (1) practice adoption that is informed and (2) full implementation that is contextualized, accurate, and sustainable?	Systems support of adult adoption, high-fidelity implementation, and sustained use of effective practices

teaming structures and functions and (2) operational features of continuous regeneration and capacity building.

Leadership Teaming

The use of outside experts and consultants can be important for introducing new ideas, stimulating new operating routines, justifying recommendations, providing overviews of intervention features and possible outcomes, and securing staff agreements. However, if the objective is to establish long-lasting and accurate intervention implementation, external expert approaches tend not to be effective. The emphasis must shift to and emphasize the establishment of local expert and leadership capacity for accurate, sustained, and scalable intervention or program implementation, that is, reduce dependence on outside expertise and resources.

Thus, a common recommendation of most organizational change approaches is the establishment of local leadership teams to lead, coordinate, and evaluate large-scale implementation efforts (e.g., Kaiser, Hogan, & Craig, 2008; Sugai et al., 2005). Development of a teaming structure is linked to the size and complexity of the implementation context (Fixsen et al., 2005). For example, in a school of 450 students, a single leadership team may be sufficient to guide the implementation effort. If the student enrollment is greater than 1,500, a single leadership team may be needed to establish policy and coordinate activities of a second layer of grade-level or learning community teams whose members have responsibility for actual intervention implementation. The same logic would apply to small versus large school districts or state departments of education. For example, a state leadership or management team might consist of policymakers (e.g., chancellor, superintendent, board of trustee), policy implementers (e.g., section, department, or division heads; initiative or program directors; field supervisors), and community or cross-organizational representatives (e.g., child and family services, juvenile justice, public health).

In general, team membership should represent major stakeholders whose target audience, client base, or end user would experience direct benefits from practice implementation. These stakeholders would share and be responsible for a variety of roles related to (1) policymaking and adaptation; (2) data-based decision making, progress monitoring and fidelity of implementation, and evaluation; (3) operationalizing of policy-based practices; (4) personnel and professional development; (5) funding and political support; and (6) implementation coordination and management.

Because state departments and districts generally operate on a 12-month calendar and schools build their activities around a 9-month academic year, establishing coherent time lines and deadline expectations can be difficult. Although specific implementation time lines are not well documented in the literature, we expect initial adoption and implementation to take 1 to 2 years, sustained implementation and durable outcomes to be realized in 3 to 5 years, and sufficient capacity for scaling and continuous regeneration to occur after 4 to 5 years. A variety of factors affect our ability to predict implementation time lines, for example, organizational size, resource access, consistency of agreement and commitment, and professional and personnel development capacity.

Operational Features of Continuous Regeneration and Capacity Building

Regardless of the size or organization of teams, attention is focused on the minimum operational functions and capacity to enable sustained and accurate intervention implementation: (1) policy, (2) administrative, (3) coordination, (4) training, (5) coaching, (6) evaluation, (7) visibility, (8) political support, and (9) funding (Sugai et al., 2005). Each of these capacity functions is described in Table 12.3.

An Example

The State Implementation and Scaling-up of Evidence-based Practices (SISEP) Center was funded by the Office of Special Education Programs, U.S. Department of Education "to promote students' academic achievement and behavioral health by supporting implementation and scaling-up of evidence-based practices in education settings" (SISEP, 2008). SISEP provides

TABLE 12.3. Description of Capacity Functions for Continuous Regeneration

Capacity functions	Description
Policy	Governance processes and procedures, rules, guiding principles, procedural requirements, documentation, etc., and routines for development, enforcement, and enhancement of practice adoption and implementation
Administrative	Recurring and adequate organizational structures and activities for policy enactment, funding, political support, organizational visibility, reporting, personnel
Coordination	Procedures, personnel, routines, and structures for organizing and implementing resources, interventions, professional development, and so on
Training	Curriculum, expert local trainers, and procedures for establishing accurate, fluent, and sustained implementation of evidence-based intervention or program
Coaching	Structures, routines, individuals, etc., that collectively facilitate accurate transfer, use, and adaptation of practice implementation
Evaluation	Questions, measures, procedures, schedules, and reporting formats for determining whether training outcomes are achieved, practices are implemented with fidelity, adaptations are made to maximize efficiency and effectiveness, and end outcomes are achieved
Visibility	Frequent and regular dissemination of activities, outcomes, etc., associated with implementation of a practice to stakeholders
Political Support	Formal relationships with individuals and/or organizations that have decision-making authority with respect to policy, resources, funding, personnel, etc., and that can experience directly from the outcomes of the practice implementation
Funding	Local, recurring, and sufficient fiscal support for ensuring accurate, sustained, and scaled implementation; continuous regeneration; and high-level achievement of end-outcomes

states with technical assistance to establish "large-scale, sustainable, high-fidelity implementation of effective educational practices" (SISEP, 2008) and provides an excellent example of an approach for systems level capacity building and RTI implementation.

Although the SISEP approach has many more defining characteristics than can be described in this chapter (e.g., implementation drivers, implementation stages; Fixsen, Blase, Horner, & Sugai, 2009), implementation teaming and systems transformation are particularly important and relevant to establishing systems-level implementation capacity. In Figure 12.4, a generic three-team organizational framework is presented as means of scaling up evidence-based practice, such as RTI, early literacy, or SWPBS. First, the state management team group provides the leadership, commitment, funding guidelines and sources, visibility, policy, and so on for establishing the operational and content priority (Figure 12.5). For example, a state management team might develop a blueprint for RTI implementation in which guiding principles, definitions, procedural descriptions, and evaluation instruments are delineated through policy. Second, the state transformation team operationalizes the vision of the state management team, incorporating features into the plan that ensure the establishment of imple-

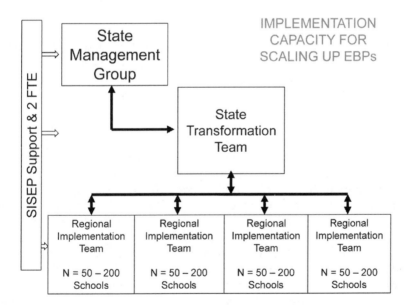

FIGURE 12.4. SISEP teaming structure for implementation capacity and scaling up of evidence-based practices (EBPs; FTE, full-time equivalence).

STATE MANAGEMENT GROUP ELEMENTS	
Purpose of this team is to provide leadership and policy support for sustained accurate implementation and controlled scaling of an evidence-based practice.	
Membership	**Functions and Capacities**
• Commissioner, superintendent, chancellor, deputy, assistant, associate commissioner, superintendent, chancellor • Department, division, section heads, directors (e.g., general and special education, curriculum and instruction) • Fiscal officers, chief executive officers, budget managers • Policymakers and implementers (e.g., union leadership, school board members) • Community representatives (e.g., mental health, families)	• Meet monthly (1 hour) to establish policy, review implementation outcomes, reinforce accomplishments, guide reform, and so on • Develop, change, redesign, and endorse policy and practice-informed policy guidelines • Develop data collection policy, evaluation questions, and procedures • Guide and endorse selection and prioritization of evidence-based practices • Review, align, integrate, and prioritize all related practice implementation efforts to improve opportunities for successful sustainability and scaling of evidence-based practices • Develop and redesign organizational structures and operations to enable successful sustainability and scaling of evidence-based practices

FIGURE 12.5. State management team example.

mentation capacity for coaching, training, evaluation, and so on is possible at the regional levels of practice adoption and implementation (Figure 12.6). For example, the state transformation team might develop working documents that convert relatively general policy into instruments and practices that guide local or regional implementation efforts at the district and school levels. Finally, a collection of local or regional implementation teams contextualize the implementation capacity and guidance from the state transformation team to reflect the unique demographic, social, and cultural characteristics of school implementers (Figure 12.7). The regional implementation team for RTI would be trained by the state transformation team to establish their capacity to implement RTI policies and procedures in a way that is understandable, doable, and effective within the contingencies (e.g., language, regional norms) of the local context.

The three-team SISEP framework comes to life through an assessment and transformation of how the system is structured and operates. Figure 12.8 illustrates the relationships between audience and functions of the implementation team (Fixsen et al., 2005). In particular, the two-way interaction between audience and team is mediated by emphasis on creating readiness for change and implementation and ensuring implementation confidence by acknowledging meaningful and measurable consumer benefits.

STATE TRANSFORMATION TEAM ELEMENTS	
The purpose of this team is to work with state management team to develop and implement an action plan that would establish regional implementation teams (RITs) across state.	
Membership	**Functions and Capacities**
• Program heads (e.g., dropout prevention, character education, early and adolescent literacy) • Professional development providers	• Select and train RIT staff • Establish RIT • Systematically replicate RIT across state • Develop and implement a plan for evaluation and monitoring of RIT implementation: fidelity of implementation and impact on student outcomes • Review and improve effectiveness, efficiency, fidelity, and relevance of RIT implementation • Adapt RIT design to local context and features • Guide identification and use of resources for RIT formation and implementation • Report monthly to the state management team • Provide an annual performance report to state management team

FIGURE 12.6. State transformation team example.

REGIONAL IMPLEMENTATION TEAM ELEMENTS	
The purpose of this team is to work with individual districts, schools, and staff members so that evidence-based practices are implemented with fidelity, durability, effectiveness, efficiency, and relevance.	
Membership	**Functions and Capacities**
• Local leadership (e.g., district supervisors, regional providers) • Professional developers (e.g., higher education, service districts) • Community providers (e.g., mental health, child and family services)	• Establish local (school and district) implementation teams • Provide implementation teams with effective training on the effective and sustained implementation of the evidence-based practice • Develop local coaching, coordination, training, and evaluation capacity to support the implementation of the evidence-based practice • Develop and implement a plan for monitoring and evaluating the fidelity and impact of local implementation of the evidence practice and supporting systems • Report monthly to the state transformation team • Provide an annual performance report to state transformation team and state management team

FIGURE 12.7. Regional implementation team example.

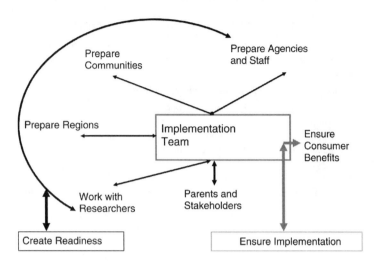

FIGURE 12.8. Implementation team functions.

A core feature of the three-team SISEP framework is the careful attention to the operational feedback loop between policy and practice (Figure 12.9). Dean Fixsen, Karen Blase, and colleagues have distilled the relationships among policy, structure, procedure, and practice into a formative process of planning, studying, acting, and doing. The objective is to establish internal capacity to use (1) outcomes and experiences from practice implementation to inform policy decisions (practice-informed policy, or PIP) and policy decisions and expectations to guide practice implementation (policy-enabled practices, or PEP). The key is the temporary use of external technical assistance to establish internal capacity to sustain the operations of the feedback loop. Initially, this capacity building may involve actual teaching and modeling of the PEP–PIP feedback loop, but the end goal is to give the state management team, state transformation team, and regional implementation teams the capacity for accurate and fluent implementation and continuous regeneration of the informed interaction between policy and practice.

To summarize, sustainable and effective operation of a systemic implementation process requires formal and prioritized organization of need, resources, and knowledge to ensure that continuous regeneration and local capacity building are achieved. We highlighted the importance of leadership teaming and described the main capacity functions (e.g., coordination, coaching, training, evaluation, funding, political support) that are required. Although initial implementation has a top-down organizational teaming structure (state to regional to school), functionally these teams interact in a

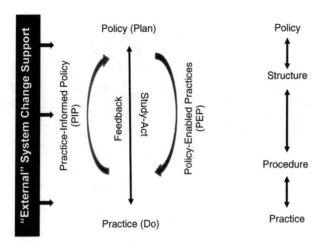

FIGURE 12.9. Policy–practice feedback loop.

close relationship in which policy enables practice and practice informs policy (e.g., PEP–PIP). The NIRN/SISEP implementation approach was used to illustrate how efficient teaming structures can be operationalized and how informed decision making and implementation can be supported.

CONCLUSIONS AND RECOMMENDATIONS

The purpose of this chapter was to describe systems-level considerations for the sustained and scaled implementation of evidence-based practices and large-scale initiatives, like RTI. Specifically, we provided a rationale and background for adopting a systems capacity perspective and described the elements and processes that characterize this perspective. We also gave an overview of current implementation practice using our combined empirical and applied experiences with the implementation of SWPBS and NIRN/SISEP.

In Figure 12.10, we provide a summary picture of the main concepts and elements highlighted in this chapter (Sugai, Horner, & McIntosh, 2008). Our focus was on establishing sustainable local implementation capacity, but we acknowledge the importance of (1) being clear about what we want to achieve (valued outcomes), (2) selecting effective practices that have promise to achieve these outcomes, (3) giving priority to supporting accurate and fluent implementation of these practices, and (4) having systems in place that enable continuous regeneration in response to ever-changing con-

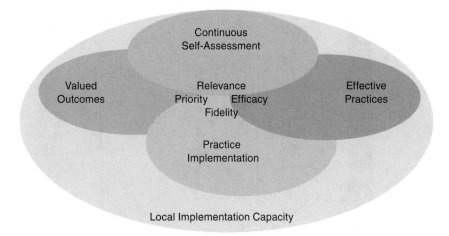

FIGURE 12.10. Maximizing implementation integrity through capacity building.

texts. In the end, systems implementation of practices and initiatives, like RTI, could be sustainable and scalable because they are relevant, prioritized, effective, and accurate.

It is important to acknowledge that a research base for a comprehensive approach to sustained and scaled implementation of evidence-based practices and large-scale initiatives, like RTI, is not well established (Fixsen et al., 2005). Although an implementation science in education is emerging, a number of research questions still need to be examined, for example,

1. What are the necessary readiness requirements (e.g., knowledge, knowledge fluency, leadership commitments, recurring funding) for a given organization (i.e., school, district, regional service agency, state department) to engage in a scaling effort of an evidence-based practice?
2. What are the necessary implementation phases and activities that predict accurate, sustained, and scalable implementation?
3. How much implementation fidelity (e.g., 95%, 90%, 80%) is required to ensure sustained and scalable implementation of an evidence-based practice?
4. What are the necessary practices that define RTI and produce maximum student outcomes?
5. What team-based organizational structures and functions are minimally required to maximize outcomes and ensure efficient and sustainable implementation?

6. What resources (e.g., FTE, funding) are minimally required as an organization moves through the implementation phases, and how do they shift or adapt to scaled implementation and continuous regeneration?

7. Does the implementation process operate similarly across implementation of different evidence-based practices (e.g., SWPBS, early literacy, numeracy, biology, art, music)?

8. What types of data are needed at the implementation and organizational level to inform, sustain, enhance, etc. operational efficiency and functioning?

9. What activities must an organizational unit (e.g., SEA, LEA) engage in to gain sufficient structural efficiencies and operational functions that occasion initial implementation enhancements and later sustained and independent continuous regeneration?

Clearly, we have much to learn from future research efforts. On the basis of on current demonstration and research findings, practitioners can improve their implementation outcomes by considering the following guidelines:

1. Use local data to define the implementation need and the desired outcome.

2. Specify long- and short-term outcomes in measurable terms that consider local context and culture and are based on local data.

3. Select evidence-based practices that have trustworthy documentation of efficacy and effectiveness in producing desired outcomes.

4. Select evidence-based practice that accommodates or is adaptable to the norms of the local context or culture.

5. Invest early in the establishment and capacity building of leadership and implementation teams that can lead the implementation process.

6. Establish implementation structures and supports that enable effective leadership and coordination (i.e., funding, policy, visibility, coaching/facilitation, training, evaluation).

7. Establish information loops and working structures that promote continuous regeneration within which policy enables practice and practice informs policy.

8. Formally plan for and regularly assess implementation of an evidence-based practice.

9. Formally plan for and regularly assess supports for sustained and scaled implementation of an evidence-based practice.

ACKNOWLEDGMENTS

The development of this chapter was supported in part by grants from the Office of Special Education Programs, U.S. Department of Education (H029D40055 and H326070002). Opinions expressed herein are the authors and do not reflect necessarily the position of the U.S. Department of Education, and such endorsements should not be inferred.

REFERENCES

Bradley, R., Danielson, L., & Doolittle, J. (2007). Responsiveness to intervention: 1997 to 2007. *Teaching Exceptional Children, 39*(5), 8–12.

Carnine, D. (1997). Bridging the research-to-practice gap. *Exceptional Children, 63,* 513–521.

Detrich, R., Keyworth, R., & States, J. (2004). A roadmap to evidence-based education: Building an evidence-based culture. *Journal of Evidence-Based Practices for Schools, 8,* 26–44.

Elmore, R. F. (1996). Getting to scale with good educational practice. *Harvard Educational Review, 66,* 1–26.

Fixsen, D. L., Blase, K. A., Horner, R. H., & Sugai, G. (2009). *Developing the capacity for scaling up the effective use of evidence-based programs in state departments of education.* Unpublished manuscript.

Fixsen, D. L., Naoom, S. F., Blase, K. A., Friedman, R. M., & Wallace, F. (2005). *Implementation research: A synthesis of the literature.* (FMHI Publication No. 231). Tampa, FL: University of South Florida, Louis de la Parte Florida Mental Health Institute, the National Implementation Research Network.

Glasgow, R. E., Lichtenstein, E., & Marcus, A. C. (2003). Why don't we see more translation of health promotion research to practice: Rethinking the efficacy-to-effectiveness transition. *American Journal of Public Health, 93,* 1261–1267.

Kaiser, R. B., Hogan, R., & Craig, S. B. (2008). Leadership and the fate of organizations. *American Psychologist, 63,* 96–110.

Kame'enui, E. J. (2007). A new paradigm: Responsiveness to intervention. *Teaching Exceptional Children, 39*(5), 6–7.

Kauffman, J. M., & Landrum, T. J. (2009). *Characteristics of emotional and behavioral disorders of children and youth* (9th ed.). Upper Saddle River, NJ: Pearson.

Kutash, K., Duchnowski, A. J., & Lynn, N. (2006). *School-based mental health: An empirical guide for decision-makers.* Tampa, FL: University of South Florida, Louis de la Parte Florida Mental Health Institute, Department of Child and Family Studies. Research and Training Center for Mental Health.

McIntosh, K., Horner, R. H., & Sugai, G. (2009). Sustainability of systems-level evidence-based practices in schools: Current knowledge and future directions. In W. Sailor, G. Dunlap, R. Horner, & G. Sugai (Eds.), *Handbook of positive behavior support* (pp. 327–352). New York: Springer.

Peters, M. T., & Heron, T. E. (1993). When the best is not good enough: An examination of best practice. *Journal of Special Education, 26,* 371–385.

State Implementation & Scaling-up of Evidence-based practice. (2008). Retrieved February 20, 2009, from *www.scalingup.org.*

Sugai, G. (2007, December 6). *Responsiveness to intervention: Lessons being learned* (invited keynote). Washington, DC: U.S. Department of Education RtI Summit.

Sugai, G. (2008). *School-wide positive behavior support and response to intervention.* Washington, DC: RTI Action Network.

Sugai, G., & Horner, R. H. (2009). Responsiveness-to-intervention and school-wide positive behavior supports: Integration of multi-tiered approaches. *Exceptionality, 17,* 223–237.

Sugai, G., Horner, R. H., Dunlap, G., Hieneman, M., Lewis, T. J., Nelson, C. M., et al. (2000). Applying positive behavioral support and functional behavioral assessment in schools. *Journal of Positive Behavioral Interventions, 2,* 131–143.

Sugai, G., Horner, R. H., & McIntosh, K. (2008). Best practices in developing a broad-scale system of support for school-wide positive behavior support. In A. Thomas & J. P. Grimes (Eds.), *Best practices in school psychology V* (Vol. 3, pp. 765–780). Bethesda, MD: National Association of School Psychologists.

Sugai, G., Horner, R. H., Sailor, W. Dunlap, G., Eber, L., Lewis, T., et al. (2005). *School-wide positive behavior support: Implementers' blueprint and self-assessment.* Eugene, OR: University of Oregon.

Walker, H. M., Horner, R. H., Sugai, G., Bullis, M., Sprague, J. R., Bricker, D., & Kaufman, M. J. (1996). Integrated approaches to preventing antisocial behavior patterns among school-age children and youth. *Journal of Emotional and Behavioral Disorders, 4,* 194–209.

Index